The Quest for Drug Control

The Quest for Drug Control

Politics and Federal Policy in a Period of Increasing Substance Abuse, 1963–1981

David F. Musto, M.D., and Pamela Korsmeyer

Yale University Press

New Haven and London

Set in Adobe Garamond and Stone Sans types by
The Composing Room of Michigan, Inc.
Printed in the United States of America by Edwards Brothers, Inc.

Library of Congress Cataloging-in-Publication Data

Musto, David F., 1936–
The quest for drug control : politics and federal policy in a period of increasing substance abuse, 1963–1981 / David F. Musto and Pamela Korsmeyer.
p. cm.
Includes bibliographical references and index.
ISBN 0-300-09036-6 (alk. paper)
1. Narcotics, Control of—United States—History—20th century.
2. Drug abuse—United States—History—20th century. I. Korsmeyer, Pamela, 1945– II. Title.
HV5825 .M845 2002
362.29′156′097309045—dc21

2002016702

A catalogue record for this book is available from the British Library.

The paper in this book meets the guidelines for permanence and durability of the Committee on Production Guidelines for Book Longevity of the Council on Library Resources.

10 9 8 7 6 5 4 3 2 1

To the memory of
Donald J. Cohen
1940–2001

Contents

Preface

Since the beginning of the twentieth century the government of the United States has struggled to impose legal controls on the distribution and consumption of psychoactive substances. The best-known example of this endeavor is the Eighteenth Amendment to the Constitution, adopted in 1919, and its accompanying legislation, the Volstead Act, which prohibited commerce in beverage alcohol throughout the nation. Federal control over other drugs, such as opium, heroin, morphine, and cocaine, emerged and solidified nearly simultaneously with alcohol prohibition, with the difference that legislation restricting the sale and use of these substances has, since its inception, enjoyed the support of a majority of American citizens and is still with us today. David Musto examined in depth the earlier periods of the campaign for national and international drug regulation in his book *The American Disease: A History of Narcotic Control* (3d rev. ed., New York: Oxford University Press, 1999). The present work, *The Quest for Drug Control,* picks up the story in the early 1960s, when the character of the anti-drug effort at the federal level, particularly from the point of view of the executive branch, began a process of fundamental change from what it had been since the passage of the Harrison Narcotic Act of 1914.

During the administration of Theodore Roosevelt (1901–1909), the United States experienced an era of militant reform agitation known as the Progressive Movement that profoundly affected both domestic life and foreign policy. At home, public unease with food-processing practices and addictive ingredients in popular patent medicines culminated in the passage of the federal Pure Food and Drug Act of 1906. Abroad, the nation, having acquired Cuba, Puerto Rico, and the Philippine Islands as a result of the Spanish American War, suddenly found itself in the unaccustomed role of an imperial power. In the Philippines the difficulties attendant upon administering new territories with alien languages and customs were particularly acute. For a start, Filipino nationalists, who had been waging guerilla war against Spain, shifted their enmity to their new governors. But another problem, common in the Philippines, loomed large in the minds of Americans—opium smoking. It simply would not do for so insidious and exotic a vice to be tolerated in a U.S. territory. In 1905 Congress banned the nonmedical use of opium by Filipinos and gave non-Filipino residents of the islands three years to abandon their habits.

The attempt at control was expanded to the international area in 1909, when the United States convened an international meeting known as the Shanghai Opium Commission, attended by thirteen nations, which adopted resolutions addressing opium smuggling and supporting China in its campaign against its own opium problem. Next, in 1912, the Hague Opium Convention, drafted under U.S. sponsorship, was signed by twelve nations agreeing to a series of controls on manufacture and export of opium and cocaine. It was in part to comply with the terms of that treaty that the U.S. Congress passed the Harrison Narcotic Act, which, after a number of Supreme Court rulings, came to form the basis for pervasive federal control over the manufacture, distribution, and consumption of a list of substances, principally opium and its derivatives and cocaine. Much to the distress of some in the medical profession, this control extended to the use of drugs in the practice of medicine and particularly curtailed the treatment of addicts by means of opiate maintenance.

From that time through the early 1960s, where this book begins, federal policy as developed, implemented, and interpreted by all three branches of government was essentially a police matter enforced by first the Narcotic Field Force (1920–1930) of the Prohibition Bureau and later the Federal Bureau of Narcotics (1930–1968). Addicts who came into the criminal justice system did, at various times and in various ways, receive some treatment and rehabilitation, but punishment was the principal motive of the system. And it seemed to work. Particularly after 1924, when all production of heroin was completely outlawed, addiction was reduced to the significance of a scary anecdote that might be relied upon to shock and titillate moviegoers and readers of dime novels but that did not affect the social or political environment of the nation in any important way. The same might be said of marijuana use, which was effectively criminalized at the federal level in 1937.

As much in eras of low consumption as in eras of widespread drug use, the unerring capacity of the mere specter of drug addiction, particularly heroin addiction, to evoke public fear and revulsion has made it a perennial subject of concern for policy makers. The records of the policy-making apparatus of the White House during the four presidential administrations between 1964 and 1980 provide a rich and colorful—though incomplete—picture of the federal government's response to public fear of the drug problem over the twenty-year period during which use of illicit substances was pervasive, as was, to the consternation of many, acceptance and even militant advocacy of the pleasures of drug consumption.

We the authors believe that policy analysts, elected officials, and the public at large will be better prepared to judge current drug policy and to choose more wisely among alternatives for the future if they understand the judgments and choices of the past and the circumstances under which these were made. In an effort to respond to our belief, we have surveyed the holdings of the National Archives in College Park, Maryland, the presidential libraries of Presidents Johnson through Carter, the National Library of Medicine, the Library of Congress, and some private collections of former government officials and have chosen documents that illuminate the policy process. These are reproduced on the CD that accompanies our book in full text-searchable form. In the book we have put these documents into a social and historical context. We have also discussed the significance of many of the reports, memoranda, and letters to the overall shape of drug policy as it developed in concert with the ever-expanding problem. The interpretations of the documents in the study are the responsibility of David Musto. We have reproduced direct quotations in the text without corrections.

As valuable as the documents are to understanding the federal response to the drug issue, the collection is not a complete record. Not every document produced by every administration finds its way to the National Archives or the presidential libraries; bureaucrats may take some files when they leave the government or may make decisions to withhold material on grounds that may seem to the historian to be ill advised. We would welcome additional government documents that illustrate the theme of federal drug policy and invite anyone holding such material to share it with us. We hope to continue this work into the Reagan, Bush, and Clinton years and to refresh or revise our analysis of prior administrations as we learn more.

Acknowledgments

The initial research on this book was made possible by a grant from the Robert Wood Johnson Foundation. Without the interest and support of Senior Vice President Ruby P. Hearn and Vice President Paul S. Jellinek we would never have been able to undertake such a task. Continuing support was provided by the National Institute on Drug Abuse (NIDA), which granted research funding as well as a Senior Scientist Award (no. K05DA00219-08) to David F. Musto. The Office of National Drug Control Policy provided a supplement to the NIDA research grant, which funded production of the CD.

We would like to express special gratitude to Dr. Jerome H. Jaffe for granting us unlimited access to his papers and for generously allowing many of his documents to be reproduced in the CD collection. Dr. Peter G. Bourne also donated a large number of important documents to David Musto.

In addition, many former officials of the administrations we studied willingly shared their recollections of their service in the U.S. government. They are Vernon Acree, Myles Ambrose, John Bartels, Karst Besteman, Lee Dogoloff, Jeffrey Donfeld, Robert DuPont, Henry

Giordano, John Ingersoll, Egil Krogh, Walter Minnick, Senator Daniel Patrick Moynihan, Eugene Rossides, Donald Santorelli, and Michael Sonnenreich.

Richard McGeary, Bob Farrington, Greg Casey, and Raisa Yakobson of McGeary and Associates brought their expertise, energy, and patience to the task of producing the document collection on CD-ROM.

The archivists and librarians at the National Archives, the presidential libraries, the National Library of Medicine, and the Library of Congress were unfailingly helpful and cheerful over several years of constant and sometimes repetitive requests.

Jean E. Thompson Black, our editor at Yale University Press, never flagged in her enthusiasm for our work, even in the face of daunting technical difficulties and what seemed like a very long time of being "almost finished."

Our thanks as well to two Ph.D. candidates in the History of Medicine, Gretchen Krueger and Mary Hague-Yearl, for their good-natured assumption of many of the mundane tasks associated with this lengthy project.

Introduction

The history of drug use in the United States between the early 1960s and 1980 is a tangled narrative of this country's attempts to deal with a rising tide of illicit substances that washed over social boundaries and ultimately overwhelmed determined attempts to dry it up or even simply to contain its destructive force. This is a story of bitter conflicts involving competing interpretations of criminal law and our traditional civil liberties as well as the role and efficacy of medicine and public health where questions of behavior and personal choice are concerned. As is true of most difficult public issues, political imperatives, social realities, the nature of bureaucracy, and the personal inclinations of influential individuals all coexisted in a sort of unstable amalgam from which policies had to be formed. The policies themselves then became subject to myriad influences that affected outcomes in uncertain and unexpected ways.

The spread of casual drug use beyond a small core of marginal social groups was quite outside the experience of those who tried to deal with it. In a conversation with David F. Musto, former Narcotics Commissioner Harry J. Anslinger described his astonishment at the explosion of drug use in the 1960s. He believed the Federal Bureau of Narcotics had reduced the level of addiction to a minimum, and the rise of heroin and marijuana usage in the later 1960s was a phenomenon he had never seen before nor expected.[1] No one had any real knowledge of previous widespread drug use such as had occurred at the end of the nineteenth century, when opiate abuse was rampant, and in the first decades of the twentieth, when cocaine was popular. While stereotypes like the crazed heroin addict or the reefer-smoking jazz musician were the stuff of popular legend, no one was prepared for the emergence of a drug-using, politicized counterculture centered on youthful rebellion that chose cannabis and LSD as the symbols and sacraments of a new faith in personal actualization and rejection of established norms of behavior. The majority of Americans reacted quite negatively to the whole phenomenon, and both the legislative and executive branches of the federal government struggled to respond in an effective or at least politically satisfying way. At the same time, a small number of intellectuals and professionals who had been questioning the traditionally punitive approach to the problem of illegal drug use began to attract greater attention. This group advocated recognition of the medical consequences of substance use, consideration of its possible validity as a personal choice, and investigation of appropriate treatments. No one anticipated that the problem would not only still be a burning issue twenty years later but would also continue to grow over that entire period. The drug of fashion would change and the image of the typical user would evolve according to what was supposed to be the "worst" substance at a given point in time. The inner-city criminal addict was joined in the popular imagination by the stoned flower child, then the speedfreak, the disco queen on downers, and the cocaine-powered Yuppie. (The crack-addicted prostitute with AIDS and the heroin-snorting rocker would come along in due time.)

Two principal elements of the social and political environment of the early sixties both defined the way drug use was perceived and contributed to its spread, particularly among middle-class youth. One was the fact that rates of violent crime, including homicide, and property crime began to rise in the 1960s after having fallen to very low points (for the United States) the previous decade. A popular explanation for the increase, which had been trotted out with regularity at least since the 1920s, was that drug users, particularly heroin users, stole such huge amounts of money and property to pay for their habits that this alone could account for the crime wave. A second factor was the escalating conflict in Southeast Asia. As more and more young men were drafted to fight in a war whose justification was widely debated, the generation that was

Name: Blair, Kathryn

Board Bill

Item:	Cost	Description
Food	$915.13	Includes meals, open-kitchen food, cost of supplies, kitchen capital, and chef's salary.
Social	$121.05	Includes social events such as ski trip, parties, house gatherings, and special dinner.
Social Other	$43.86	Optional. Includes alcohol and is not compulsory.

Total $1,080.04

Existing Balance: $33.33 One quarter deposit.

Total Due: $1,113.37

Due Date: 1/30/2004

For questions or concerns regarding your board bill or additional balance items, please see Emil in room 312.

3 0 8 7 4 4 5 5 4 0 3 0 3 0 8 3 0 2 7 4 5 0 0 10 9 6 8 0 7 0 0 4 5 0 0 7 3 5 0 1 5 3

4 0 5 0 2 0 0 3 9 0 1 10 7 4 8 8 3 10 8 5 0 0

3 2 2 1

10

most affected by military service—and which incidentally was the largest generation in history—erupted in rebellion. Rejection of the war became rejection of the entire value system and lifestyle choices of the majority. Given that most people associated all illicit drugs with crime and degeneration and reacted to drug users with horror, using any drug was a perfect in-your-face statement of a rebellious young person's politics and philosophy of life. The rebels of the young generation found some sympathy among those more or less "establishment" politicians and academics who had been questioning the punitive basis of narcotics control since the late 1950s. Some of these older sympathizers even predicted a fundamental change in the nature of human society. Charles Reich foresaw that, with the help of marijuana and other mood-altering substances, we would enter an entirely new culture, drastically changing our lives and relations with one another.[2] He called this new utopian condition "consciousness III" and described it as an extreme autonomy that would dispense with hierarchy, property rights, and even rational thought.

JOHNSON (1963–1969)

Lyndon Johnson, who became president in November 1963 after the assassination of John F. Kennedy, had the dubious fortune of presiding over the escalation of an unpopular war and of confronting both increasing crime and massive civil disobedience on several fronts: the struggle for the civil rights of African-Americans, demonstrations for peace in Vietnam, and increasing consumption of illicit substances, principally marijuana. His administration's response to this last was guided by the report of a presidential commission on drug abuse established by Kennedy and known as the Prettyman Commission after its chair, Judge E. Barrett Prettyman. The Johnson-era drug control initiatives were of a piece with all that followed them. At the outset it was not entirely clear how the federal government could legitimately intervene in a phenomenon that seemed to be the province of local police and social service agencies. But once it became clear that the threat posed by substance abuse had to be faced on a national scale, the fact that most illicit drugs were produced in foreign countries and the fact that their manufacture and distribution were controlled by international and interstate criminal commerce provided the constitutional justification for a large-scale federal intervention in drug control. On that basis, Johnson's policy staff began a three-part approach to the drug problem that was the skeleton later fleshed out by LBJ's Republican successor, Richard Nixon. The initiative included domestic legislative reform that attempted to address the peculiar nature of the drug problem as both a criminal justice and a public health problem, diplomatic overtures to foreign countries that sought to persuade them to reduce or eliminate drug source crops, and bureaucratic reorganization designed to rationalize drug policy development and implementation. All of these efforts took place in a context of extreme social turmoil and intense debate among professional bureaucrats, politicians, and medical and legal experts over the nature of drug use, the size of the problem, its moral symbolism, and the political perils of various attempts to solve it.

NIXON (1969–1974)

Richard Nixon seized upon the issue of increasing use of illicit drugs in the United States as an opportunity to discredit "Great Society" liberalism—particularly as represented by Johnson's attorney general, Ramsey Clark—and to make good on a promise to lead an attack on crime. The people in charge of implementing his directives tended to accept at face value the proposition that a relationship existed between drug use and criminal behavior—and additionally between drug use and counterculture lifestyles and political opinions. Even those White House planners who were skeptical about such links were aware of the political potential of the issue—the logic of the relationship between drugs and crime was easily communicated to the public, and the desirability of eliminating such a pernicious habit seemed self-evident. Furthermore, the fledgling policies put in place by the departing Johnson team were theirs to appropriate regardless of the "liberal" origins of those policies.

Nixon's war on drugs was big and bold. It reached into the activities of more than a dozen federal agencies in an attempt to mount offensives against both the criminal and the public health aspects of drug abuse with a view toward reducing crime and reassuring middle-class voters that both their possessions and their cultural values were being looked after by a concerned and competent federal government. Relations with Turkey and Mexico and the conduct of the war in Vietnam were all affected in one way or another by drug control. Local law enforcement was drawn into the orbit of the federal fight against drugs through the Office of Drug Abuse Law Enforcement; and under the aegis of the Special Action Office on Drug Abuse Prevention (SAODAP) opiate addicts could obtain a maintenance narcotic from government-sponsored clinics for the first time since the early 1920s.

None of these initiatives was an unequivocal success: internal management problems, conflicts over priorities, and the competing political agendas of

Congress and the White House bedeviled them all. Within the administration, there were personality clashes and turf battles between officials in the Treasury and Justice Departments and between the leaders of SAODAP and the Department of Health, Education, and Welfare. In the attempt to identify goals and evaluate results, there were persistent difficulties in arriving at an acceptable estimate of the size of the addict population or even consensus on the meaning of the word "addict." In Congress and the general public, minority opposition to criminal penalties for some drug use was ever stronger and more vocal, while the majority clamored for forceful measures to deal with the disconcerting spectacle of what appeared to be large-scale flouting of the law. This situation colored the choices made by Nixon's planners as they quite naturally attempted to turn the policy-making process to their political advantage. Nevertheless, a number of the entities established under President Nixon to address drug abuse survived more than twenty years of shifting political winds and exist today under somewhat different organizational identities. The Nixon administration can be fairly credited with a persistent and massive federal response to an ever-changing, ever more confusing social problem.

FORD (1974–1977)

During the summer of 1974, as the Watergate affair came to its shattering denouement, awareness was growing among presidential advisors that no new, dramatic declines in drug use were in the offing and that interdiction of foreign supplies was proving frustrating. Among the citizenry, toleration toward the so-called recreational use of some drugs was becoming more common, and more than a few Americans actively and openly advocated drug use. This was particularly true of marijuana, which not so very long before had inspired fear and revulsion. With no suspicion that the trend would ever wane, it appeared to many policy makers and opinion leaders that adjustment to the new reality had become a political necessity. The assumption that drug use was a crisis that could be effectively met and resolved with an overwhelming commitment of federal money and expertise[3] gave way to a rueful awareness that the road would be long and progress slow.

Gerald Ford's personal style and political priorities were very different from those of Richard Nixon and more compatible with newly reduced expectations about what the federal government could do in an environment of tight budgets, increasing drug use, and diminishing public concern about it. He called his approach to governance the "new realism" and sought to keep his words and deeds in line with the philosophy of restraint the phrase implied. Meanwhile Congress kept up the pressure on the administration to clarify its drug policy and to reestablish a White House office to oversee that policy. Congressional leaders were particularly upset by the fact that the newly formed Drug Enforcement Administration (DEA) had gotten off to a rocky start; it was torn by internal strife and suffering from weak leadership. But Ford stuck to his conviction that neither pouring money into federal drug programs nor resurrecting a White House–based policy office would stem the tide of drug use when it was painfully obvious that the gains registered by the same measures as undertaken by his predecessor had not been sustained over the longer term.

The White Paper on Drug Abuse, the Ford administration's most important statement on narcotics policy, moved away from the goal of complete eradication of the drug problem and returned to such words as "minimize" that had been banished from Nixon-era documents. The White Paper was well received by a public that was tired of being harangued on the evils of pot smoking and the imminence of "victory" in the war on drugs. At the time, the report seemed to indicate a new appreciation on the part of the federal government of the long and difficult struggle that would be necessary to make a dent in the consumption of illegal substances.

CARTER (1977–1981)

Jimmy Carter took office near the peak of the trend toward at least grudging toleration of some drug use among sectors of the population that had overwhelmingly rejected it until about fifteen years earlier. The most salient aspect of the electoral campaign between Carter and Ford with respect to the drug issue was that neither candidate addressed the problem in any depth. What attention was devoted to drugs took the form of a competition between the candidates as to who would be more understanding of his children's experimentation with marijuana.

A key player in Carter's victory was a psychiatrist, Peter Bourne, who was also an expert in the contemporary drug problem. Dr. Bourne quickly became Carter's chief advisor on drugs and was appointed assistant to the president. Bourne shared a number of convictions held by the more sophisticated professionals in the drug field, whose way of thinking was evolving in concert with the sector of public opinion that was inclined to accept as inevitable some degree of recreational drug use. He and many others thought that the new attitude toward substance use would eventually establish itself as a permanent fixture of American society. It was not widely understood that the level of drug use, along with the public's relative willingness to live with it, had risen and fallen in the past and was likely to continue to do so in the future.

Even as it appeared that marijuana would finally be decriminalized and that cocaine would become as acceptable and available as champagne, the ground shifted beneath the feet of Bourne and his colleagues. Their fundamental miscalculation lay in their estimate of how deep and lasting the apparent public mood of accommodation to drug use really was. They did not see that a grassroots counterrebellion was brewing among parents who did not want their children growing up in a society that could apply the word "recreational" to any drugs. In July 1978, Peter Bourne was accused of having used cocaine at a party given by the National Organization for the Reform of Marijuana Laws (NORML). That was just too much—Peter Bourne had to resign.

Between 1978 and 1980 the forces of this counterrevolt, frequently referred to as the Parents' Movement, gained the ascendancy, and the American public's willingness to tolerate any drug use at all began to decline. As if further awkwardness were needed to discredit the accommodationist approach to the drug issue, the heroin situation began to unravel. Southwest Asia—chiefly Iran, Afghanistan, and Pakistan—was producing increasing amounts of opium, which was finding its way to the West as heroin. As the Carter presidency came to an end, it was not clear how increased heroin production, confusion over marijuana and cocaine policy, and congressional resistance to funding new treatment capacity could be overcome.

DRUG CONTROL OVER TWENTY YEARS OF INCREASING USE

Looking back over the first twenty years of the modern "epidemic" of substance abuse, two of the most significant characteristics of federal efforts to control the traffic in, and consumption of, illicit substances appear to be, first, the extreme complexity of the task, which may at first seem simple and straightforward, and, second, the difficulty of judging public attitudes toward drugs and drug users, especially trends into the future. Public policy planners can rarely, if ever, grasp the issue in all of its dimensions—political, emotional, epidemiological, medical, and legal—and the lack of a long-term perspective of this country's experience with psychoactive substances has consistently hindered a balanced estimate of what can be expected of a given policy alternative. If we look closely at the past, it should be obvious that drug use floods and subsides over decades, not in the course of a presidential term or two. The first epidemic of drug abuse saw opiate and cocaine consumption rise from the post–Civil War period until around the turn of the century, then decline slowly and unevenly until the early 1930s, not to rise again until the 1960s.

The present work is meant to be just such a close look at the federal politics and bureaucracy of drug control policy and implementation during a period in American history in which our nation confronted a phenomenon that most people regarded as unprecedented. The book follows the 1999 publication of the revised and expanded edition of David F. Musto's *The American Disease: Origins of Narcotic Control,* which in its later chapters covers some of the same events and actors but from the broad perspective of the entire history of drug use and control in the United States. In this new study and in the electronic document collection that accompanies it we have relied on the material deposited in the various presidential libraries and in the National Archives as well as some from private collections, principally those of Jerome H. Jaffe and Peter G. Bourne, to draw a picture of the federal political and bureaucratic response to the perceived drug crisis. We also have included information on the social environment of the time to provide some feeling for the context in which policy makers worked. Although the White House documents are only a fraction of the mountain of material produced on the drug issue, they have the virtue of being of a manageable size and representing a discrete but fundamental aspect of the American Way with drugs. Perhaps, in some small way, this enterprise will reduce the likelihood that future drug control policy will be made in a historical vacuum.

Acronyms and Abbreviations

ABA American Bar Association

ADAMHA Alcohol, Drug Abuse, and Mental Health Administration

AMA American Medical Association

BDAC Bureau of Drug Abuse Control

BNDD Bureau of Narcotics and Dangerous Drugs

BOB Bureau of the Budget

CCINC Cabinet Committee on International Narcotics Control

CDC Centers for Disease Control

CIA Central Intelligence Agency

CRP Committee to Re-elect the President

DATERA Drug Abuse Treatment, Education, and Rehabilitation Administration

DEA Drug Enforcement Administration

DNADA Division of Narcotic Addiction and Drug Abuse

DOD Department of Defense

DOJ Department of Justice

EOP Executive Office of the President

FBN Federal Bureau of Narcotics
FDA Food and Drug Administration
FY Fiscal Year
HEW Health, Education and Welfare
HHS Health and Human Services
H.R. House of Representatives
INM International Narcotics Matters (State Department)
IRS Internal Revenue Service
JFK John Fitzgerald Kennedy
LBJ Lyndon Baines Johnson
LEAA Law Enforcement Assistance Administration
LSD lysergic acid diethylamide
NARA National Addict Rehabilitation Act
NATO North Atlantic Treaty Organization
NIDA National Institute on Drug Abuse
NIEHS National Institute of Environmental Health Sciences
NIMH National Institute of Mental Health
NORML National Organization for the Reform of Marijuana Laws
ODALE Office of Drug Abuse Law Enforcement
ODAP Office of Drug Abuse Policy
OE Office of Education
OEO Office of Economic Opportunity
OMB Office of Management and Budget
ONNI Office of National Narcotics Intelligence
PACEO President's Advisory Council on Executive Organization
PCLEAJ Presidential Commission on Law Enforcement and the Administration of Justice
PCP phencyclidine
P.L. Public Law
PRIDE Parent Resources Institute on Drug Education
S. Senate (bill)
SAODAP Special Action Office for Drug Abuse Prevention
TASC Treatment Alternatives to Street Crime
THC tetrahydrocannabinol
TLC thin-layer chromatography
VA Veterans Administration
WHCF White House Central File
WHSF White House Special File

Chapter 1 The Johnson Administration: Drug Abuse as a Policy Issue

Between 1920 and the early 1960s, illicit drug use in the United States declined significantly from the levels it had reached early in the century, although few appreciated it at the time. Americans had feared psychoactive drugs for a long time—opiates and cocaine in the early part of the century, then nearly exclusively heroin, especially after World War II—and that fear persisted even though, by the 1950s, use was minuscule compared both to the historical high point and to the surge in substance abuse that lay in the future. Still, the drugs were a minor problem, dealt with to the satisfaction of most Americans, and the debate that began to develop late in the 1950s among medical and legal professionals over how best to deal with what was mostly a problem of inner-city heroin addiction was at first a fairly low-key affair. The controversy, then as now, pitted advocates of law enforcement, who believed that the decline in drug use was directly attributable to the application of stringent legislation, against critics of this approach, who pointed out that the problem had not gone away in spite of vigorous prohibitory enforcement. The debate grew more heated and its participants more numerous as drug use levels rose; by the early

1970s drug abuse would emerge as one of the top concerns of the nation (though usually outranked by fears of war, racial unrest, or economic troubles).

Even the most superficial memories of the period we now refer to as the Sixties include the controversy over the Vietnam War, assassinations, violence, and the breakdown of traditional norms of behavior, both private and public, including norms about deference to established authority, sexual activity, and the use of mind-altering chemicals. No precise date can be assigned to the origin of the era in spite of its name, but the emergence of drug abuse as a policy issue into national life was certainly evident by early 1965. President Lyndon Johnson had been inaugurated after decisively defeating Barry Goldwater the previous November. In his State of the Union address Johnson proclaimed the advent of the "Great Society." A few days later, the Viet Cong attacked the American barracks at Pleiku. Malcolm X was assassinated in February. U.S. and South Vietnamese troops attacked North Vietnam in March. The same month, civil rights demonstrators marched from Selma to Montgomery, Alabama, and in August the Watts section of Los Angeles exploded in violence. Somewhat like Dorothy realizing that she was not in Kansas anymore, Americans began to realize that they weren't in the Fifties anymore. Some also began to notice another trend: people they knew, or people who seemed just like people they knew, were using illegal drugs. Awareness of the phenomenon developed slowly, and reactions to it varied widely.

In the late 1950s and early 1960s, drug use in the United States was thought to be largely confined to the urban poor, criminal elements, and such small nonconformist groups as jazz musicians and "beatnik" artists and intellectuals. The *National Survey on Drug Abuse* for 1977 summarizes the retrospective data: "Prior to 1962 lifetime experience with any illicit drug was limited to 2% or less of the population in most areas of the country and among most large population subgroups. At that time, the prevalence of marihuana use was slightly above average (about 5%) among males and racial minorities and people living in the Western region of the country."[1] Even as late as 1968, heroin use was confined to the major port cities of the Northeast corridor, as well as Miami, New Orleans, San Diego, Los Angeles, and San Francisco.[2]

The larger picture of the personal hopes and fears of the American people also indicates that drug use was not a primary concern just before and during the early years of the Johnson presidency. From 1959 through 1964 Americans' most important personal hopes were for good health, a better standard of living, and achievement of their aspirations for their children. In 1959 their three greatest fears were of ill health (both their own and that of their families) and a loss of living standard. By 1964 war had become America's worst fear, followed by ill health.[3] That year, when asked by the Gallup organization to name the most important problem facing the nation, 41 percent of respondents cited the "racial problem," tied with "international problems (Russia, threat of war)." When asked "What do you, yourself, think is the cause of the lack of respect for law and the increase in crime in the United States today?" 41 percent blamed "parents, home life." Far down the list, with a 2 percent response rate, was "drinking, dope addiction."

Even so, there was a growing sense that the character and extent of the phenomenon were changing, and the media began to take notice (Table 1-1). Increased marijuana use by middle-class youth had begun to appear in the early 1960s, grew dramatically in 1966, and seemed to explode in 1967. Heroin addiction, while still perceived as an affliction of the urban poor, seemed an ever-increasing threat to public order and public health.[4] In fact, deaths related to narcotics abuse in New York City had been rising fairly steadily since 1950, although they stayed below 400 per year until 1967, when they nearly doubled.[5]

In the mid-fifties some academics (notably Alfred Lindesmith),[6] medical professionals, and lawyers had begun to be critical of the federal government's almost exclusive reliance on law enforcement to control drug abuse. The American Bar Association (ABA) and the American Medical Association (AMA) established a committee to study drug policy reform, which published its *Interim*

Table 1-1 Number of Articles Indexed Under Each Category in the *Readers Guide to Periodical Literature* and the *New York Times* by Year

Year	Drugs* (*NYT*)	LSD (*RGPL*)	Marijuana (*RGPL*)	Narcotics (*RGPL*)
1959	138	1	0	16
1960	98	1	0	15
1961	76	1	0	10
1962	160	4	0	26
1963	56	10	1	4
1964	109	4	0	12
1965	200	6	2	37
1966	358	49	1	41
1967	430	40	27	40
1968	368	24	31	42
1969	558	11	41	68

*Index headings vary. Only articles relevant to illicit drugs were counted.

Report in 1958, followed in early 1959 by a very brief *Final Report*. The reports recommended such seemingly radical approaches as outpatient treatment of opiate addicts, legal reform, and extensive research into relapse, education, and prevention. The chair of the committee, Judge Morris Ploscowe, wrote a detailed appendix to the *Interim Report* that is likely to seem dishearteningly familiar to the present-day reader. Judge Ploscowe cited information that indicated that not all drug users were necessarily drug addicts, that data on the real extent of drug addiction were very difficult to obtain, and that public—and even "expert"—opinion on the drug problem was fraught with misconceptions and mythology. As examples of new and forward-looking research, he cited studies at New York University and the University of Chicago that showed that the people "most likely to become extreme delinquents or drug users are those who by virtue of their personal histories are least responsive to the expectations of conventional society. Thus, the problem of differences between those who do and those who do not become drug addicts in the world of the street boy may be regarded as a problem of the difference in life history among individuals, with each life history constituting a unique equation of forces."[7]

In addressing the question of the relationship between drug addiction and crime, Judge Ploscowe quoted from various sources to the effect that opiate users were far more likely to become passive than violent under the influence of their drug, although many drug users were also violent sociopaths who would be so with or without drugs. He went on to ask, "Since opiate drugs do not act as a stimulant for the commission of violent crime, should not confirmed addicts have a means of obtaining such drugs legally, so that they will not have to engage in crime in order to raise the money necessary for their needs? This basic question goes to the heart of our present policy in dealing with drug addiction."[8]

The *Interim Report* of the ABA/AMA committee provoked an energetic and thoroughly negative response from the Federal Bureau of Narcotics (FBN), then under the direction of Commissioner Harry J. Anslinger. The rebuttal published and disseminated by the FBN took the form of a collection of comments on the ABA/AMA report from fourteen law enforcement officers, judges, former federal agents, and physicians, along with a number of excerpts from congressional documents, United Nations reports, and the like. It is prefaced by reproductions of Judge Ploscowe's letter to Anslinger conveying a copy of the ABA/AMA report to the commissioner and requesting a meeting in order to discuss it, and Anslinger's reply to the judge. The commissioner declared that he found it "incredible that so many glaring inaccuracies, manifest inconsistencies, apparent ambiguities, important omissions, and even false state-

Harry Anslinger in his heyday as commissioner of the Federal Bureau of Narcotics. To his left is a hollowed-out book used to smuggle drugs. (Library of Congress.)

ments could be found in one report on the narcotic problem."[9] The language used in the commentaries that follow is remarkable for its vitriolic tone and for its total rejection of the legitimacy of even broaching the subjects addressed by the committee. Open discussion of such questions as providing maintenance supplies of opiates to addicts was evidently intolerable to people who had spent their careers in harmony with the national consensus that drug use was a horrifying menace to society. For Anslinger and his colleagues, the only response possible was uncompromising application of the most severe prohibitive measures. But the intransigence of the FBN became untenable over the next few years. The determination of both Commissioner Anslinger and his successor, Henry Giordano, to resist emerging interpretations of, and solutions to, the rising use of illegal substances in all segments of society, as well as their commitment to methods of policing and public information that were regarded as antiquated and benighted, eventually spelled the end of the bureau. The bureau had not changed, but Americans' attitudes were shifting, and so were the viewpoints of the more-liberal policy makers. An intense debate between traditionalists and innovators, between advocates of police action against drug users and those who favored a new emphasis on public health measures, developed over the next few years.

Order and respect for authority were extremely important to most Americans, but at the same time, both ordinary citizens and professional people in health and law, such as those who served on the ABA/AMA committee, were asking some basic questions about the nature of drugs and the measures used to control their use. The debate between old and new centered mainly on three substances: marijuana, LSD, and heroin (cocaine would not return as an issue until much later). Was marijuana really harmful? If so, how harmful? Should LSD be controlled as a menace to health and sanity or celebrated as a "door of perception"? Was addiction to heroin and other opiates a crime or a disease, moral turpitude or misfortune? How one answered these questions determined what solutions one favored. Why one answer was chosen above another depended upon one's personal experience, political and moral convictions, and, not least, vested interests.

Policy makers in the Johnson administration struggled to find some sort of equilibrium among the disparate forces of political necessity and programmatic efficacy and, in the process, established the outline for narcotics control policy for years to come. They sought to turn the controversy over drugs to their political advantage through real progress against both the crime and the misery and disease thought to be related to drug use. They focused their efforts on (l) gaining control of the bureaucracy of the executive branch by ridding it of uncooperative agencies through reorganization; (2) establishing federal public health and education measures aimed at treating abusers and controlling use (demand); and (3) reforming drug control legislation to achieve a better balance between punishment of drug-related crime and care for victims of drug abuse. They and their successors were to discover that the complexity of the problem, its poorly understood social and individual causes, its emotional resonance among voters, and its susceptibility to political manipulation made results of attempts to solve it unpredictable at best.

THE PRETTYMAN COMMISSION

FBN Commissioner Anslinger announced his retirement in the spring of 1962, and the way was opened for reconsideration of drug policy. In 1960 then-candidate John Kennedy had promised to convene a White House Conference on Drug Abuse in a telegram to California's attorney general.

> I am aware of House Resolution 431 which was adopted in April of this year suggesting a White House conference. In addition Resolution 20 adopted by the National Conference of Attorneys General in July called for a similar conference on this problem. I believe such a conference can serve a valuable purpose. It should seek a method for securing uniform state-federal enforcement. It should recommend a method for implementing machinery for consultation between the United States, Mexico and Canada and it should consider a federal-state program for the addict as well as such other appropriate matters that will hold alert the nation and contribute to the solution of the narcotics problem. In answer to the question in your telegram, I assure you that if I am elected president I will convene the White House Conference on narcotics as soon as it is reasonably practicable.[10]

The White House Conference was convened in September of 1962 and was the first concrete indication that the federal government was beginning to acknowledge the sort of public-health-oriented thinking about drug use that had informed the ABA/AMA investigation, and that it might take some small steps toward abandonment of the punitive-deterrent philosophy. As a result of the conference, the president issued an executive order on 15 January 1963 appointing a presidential Advisory Commission on Narcotic and Drug Abuse under the leadership of Judge E. Barrett Prettyman. The executive director of the commission was Dean F. Markham, and assistant secretaries from the Departments of State, Treasury, Defense, Justice, and Health, Education, and Welfare (HEW) served as liaisons.

The commission's report was completed just weeks before President Kennedy was assassinated. Although the published version is dated 1 November 1963, the report was not released by Kennedy before his death, and it remained in confidential draft form until 24 January 1964, when it was officially accepted by Lyndon Johnson and released to the press.

The commission summed up its guiding principles as follows:

1. The illegal traffic in drugs should be attacked with the full power of the federal government. The price for participation in this traffic should be prohibitive. It should be made too dangerous to be attractive.
2. The individual abuser should be rehabilitated. Every possible effort should be exerted by all governments—federal, state, and local—and by every community toward this end. Where necessary to protect society, this may have to be done at times against the abuser's will. Pertinent to all, the causes of drug abuse must be found and eradicated.
3. Drug users who violate the law by small purchases or sales should be made to recognize what society demands of them. In these instances, penalties should be applied according to the principles of our present code of justice. When the penalties involve imprisonment, however, the rehabilitation of the individual, rather than retributive punishment, should be the major objective.[11]

Twenty-five recommendations followed from these principles. The commission made no fewer than seven recommendations for reorganization of bureaucratic entities, the main thrust of which was that all enforcement activities could be more effective if located in the Justice Department. They also emphasized the need for effective interagency coordination, new scientific research, and information gathering and dissemination. They offered a total of seven suggestions for rehabilitation of drug abusers, leaving no doubt of the importance they placed on treatment—even of incarcerated drug offenders. Three recommendations for international diplomatic measures were made, and two dealt with the reform of federal legislation.

The importance of the Prettyman report lies in the fact that it articulated the general outline of a coherent approach to the narcotics problem that acknowledged emerging thinking on the subject while avoiding radical proposals that would conflict with widely held, extremely negative opinion with respect to drug use. W. B. Eldridge, author of *Narcotics and the Law* and director of narcotic study for the American Bar Foundation, criticized the report in a postscript to his book, saying that "without examination, without explanation, the commission has, for most purposes, equated drug use and drug abuse. The goal has been set at termination of drug use rather than at a satisfactory social adaptation of those persons presently considered to be abusing drugs."[12] As material to be discussed in later chapters will also indicate, the goal that Eldridge criticizes has been fundamental to drug control in the United States since the early twentieth century. No policy goal other than "termination of drug use" has ever achieved the necessary political support to see it through to implementation. The American public has been more or less tolerant of drug use at various periods of history, but even in times of relative acceptance of such behavior, tolerance is characteristic only of a large minority of citizens.[13] Eldridge himself observes that "no matter how cogent the arguments analogizing the use of narcotics to the use of alcohol, or even to tobacco and coffee, the use of narcotics, by and large, exceeds social tolerance. Whatever the reasons—social, scientific, emotional, religious—the public is strongly united in its opposition to drug use and in its demand for prevention and control."[14] The staying power of the concepts articulated by the Prettyman Commission is illustrated in the Appendix. Nearly all its recommendations found expression in one form or another in federal policy over the next four administrations and were adapted under later presidents; many are discernible today.

PRETTYMAN AND THE FBN: BUREAUCRACY AND POLICY INNOVATION

The Prettyman report was deeply disturbing to those imbued with the FBN's institutional culture and tradition. During the deliberations of the commission, Henry Giordano's office had put together a paper that was meant to rebut the notion that a reconsideration of drug policy was necessary at all. According to the FBN,

> During recent years, an extremely vocal effort has been made by a few members of the medical and legal professions to convince the public that the current laws and policies relating to narcotic drugs have resulted in complete failure; that addiction everywhere is on the increase and that we should abandon present methods in favor of a "more enlightened" approach.[15]
>
> Since 1953, The Bureau of Narcotics has been recording and compiling records on active addicts and to date their figures total 46,697. Recognizing that no system of reporting addicts can be absolutely foolproof, the actual count of addicts may be higher. In any event, the Bureau of Narcotics is convinced that the top figure would not exceed 60,000. It should be remembered, however, that the population of the country is now well over 180,000,000.[16]

Assistant Secretary of the Treasury James A. Reed, writing to Judge Prettyman, expressed an opinion held by most in his department that apparent declines in the prevalence of dramatic withdrawal symptoms among addicts in treatment

Narcotics agents pose with packages of marijuana in suitcases, 1963. (New York World Telegram and Sun Newspaper Photograph Collection, Library of Congress. Staff photo by Ed Ford.)

were attributable to effective law enforcement. "The decline in classic withdrawal symptoms is due in my opinion to the heavy adulteration of heroin. This is due, again in my opinion, to the 1956 Narcotics Control Act, the nine treaties and protocols in the international field, and the effort of the Bureaus of Narcotics and Customs, both abroad and in the United States, directed towards reducing the traffic. The phenomenon itself is a measure of the success of that effort. While I am sure that there are other factors, I am equally convinced that further research and study will prove that effective enforcement has been the most important."[17]

Treasury Department officials feared that the recommendations being considered by the commission, particularly those bearing on reorganization of the law enforcement bureaucracy, would threaten the accustomed independence and operational latitude that the bureau enjoyed, and might subject its activities to a scrutiny that it did not welcome. With the cooperation of Reed, Commissioner Henry Giordano and other FBN officials began a campaign of obstruction and resistance that delayed reorganization of narcotics law enforcement but, as the balance of power moved slowly away from the bureau and its traditionalist approach, was unable to stave it off indefinitely.

In December 1963 Dean F. Markham, executive director of the Prettyman Commission, composed a memorandum for the record in which he described the activities of Reed and Arnold Sagalyn, Treasury's law enforcement coordinator. They were following a pattern of behavior that would be repeated by other disgruntled law enforcement bureaucrats (particularly the Customs Bureau under Vernon Acree in the 1970s). Markham's memorandum asserted that Treasury staffers were involved in disseminating inaccurate information on the background of the recommendations and on the efficacy of narcotics enforcement operations by both the FBN and the Bureau of Customs (also a Treasury agency), as well as lobbying members of the commission in an effort to persuade them to change the committee's recommendations.[18] Markham noted, "It appears that when the courtesy was extended to Arnold Sagalyn and Henry Giordano to have a preview reading in my office of the report, although we could not send them a copy, they copied down verbatim certain passages which have since been read off to members of the Senate or the Congress."[19] Treasury officials also attempted to convince President Johnson's staff to avoid any unqualified public endorsement of the report. Reed was particularly concerned that the FBN's responsibility for the apparently significant decline in narcotic addiction over the previous thirty years not be questioned.[20] In late January 1964, parts of the report began to leak to the press, probably from Giordano's office. It was apparent that all Markham's attempts to keep the affected federal agencies calm until the White House had had a chance to evaluate the report were being ignored by the Treasury Department, and he was now in the position of having to recommend release of the report before he would have liked to. Even so, Giordano's campaign was fruitless. When the report was released on 24 January, the public response was extremely favorable, and the report became the touchstone of narcotics policy as it developed during the rest of the Johnson presidency.

FIRST STEPS TOWARD REFORM

By 1 April, Markham was able to report to Lee White of the White House staff that there had been considerable commentary in all the major media and that public expectation of significant federal action had been raised both by the president's message accepting the report and by his attention to the subject in a speech to Congress on health issues. Markham told White:

> No other social or public health problem gets so much disproportionate attention in the press, television and radio. There is almost a public hysteria regarding the dope situation that even reaches into the areas of the country that have no real problem. Mayor Wagner estimates that it costs New York City alone a billion dollars a year. It has also been estimated that narcotic and drug abuse costs the United States five million dollars a day, plus the human and social costs that deprive the country of a segment of our citizenry who could be contributing to society rather than having a parasitic effect. In view of the above points, this can be considered a national problem although it does not even approach alcoholism in scope as to the number of people affected. There is no comparable national problem where so much can be accomplished with such a small expenditure of money and interest.[21]

Markham's analysis of the political importance of the drug issue was quite similar to those of policy makers who followed him, particularly in the Nixon administration.[22] In view of the public attitudes toward the drug issue reflected in survey data, his reference to "public hysteria" requires an explanation. As discussed earlier, public opinion polls did not register great concern about the drug problem, but only because pollsters asked about it in the context of the overwhelming salience of issues such as war and civil rights. The reflexive fear of drugs was always there and ready to be inflamed. Press attention to drug use and abuse continued to impress and influence Markham's successors in later administrations in much the same way. Only his estimate that a "small expenditure of money and interest" would be necessary to obtain the desired political and social ends would prove to be dramatically off the mark.

As a first step in taking advantage of the political opportunity offered by the Prettyman report, Markham suggested that the first five recommendations be acted upon right away. These included a suggestion that the president direct all agencies with any involvement in narcotics control to initiate "more aggressive action in the national interest"; that he name a White House special assistant to coordinate the campaign; that a citizens' advisory committee be formed; that HEW establish a core of informational and educational materials; and that a comprehensive research plan be developed. Recommendation 25, for legislation offering the possibility of civil commitment instead of prison to convicted drug offenders, could also be taken up immediately. Markham referred to a civil commitment bill that Senator Kenneth Keating (R., NY) had introduced in the spring of 1961, and expressed the opinion that Keating's bill would not be effective because it was limited to addicts who were not guilty of other criminal offenses—an insignificant number, according to Markham.

The reorganization recommendations contained in the Prettyman report could be expected to generate controversy and resistance in the affected agencies, and they did. Justice and Treasury submitted their reactions to Markham between February and April, and neither was enthusiastic. Herbert J. Miller, Jr., assistant attorney general in charge of the Criminal Division, who had served as Justice Department liaison with the commission, felt that the commission had erred in judging law enforcement to be an inappropriate activity for the Treasury Department.[23] He was particularly concerned about the problem of coordination with the Customs Bureau should narcotics enforcement be moved out of Treasury. The commission's suggestion that mandatory minimum sentences be done away with in favor of a system that classified drug offenses as large-scale trafficking, small-scale trafficking, and simple possession seemed to Miller to be confusing and arbitrary. He also took issue with the commission's finding that narcotics and dangerous drugs could be more appropriately regulated under the federal government's interstate commerce powers than under its taxation authority—an idea that had first come up in 1909 at the dawn of federal efforts to control narcotics.[24] Although he felt that the change would eventually be held to be constitutional, he thought that any new law would be subjected to expensive and time-consuming litigation before it could be definitively implemented. Markham and his staff were upset by the lack of enthusiasm at Justice for the suggestions of the Prettyman Commission and felt that Miller had seriously misinterpreted the commission's report. They provided Lee White with a point-by-point clarification of the report and refutation of Justice's objections.[25]

The Treasury Department, in its official comments on the Prettyman report, completely rejected recommendations 7, 8, 9, 10, 20, and 23 and attached conditions to acceptance of 2, 4, 11, 13, 15, 16, and 17, but this reaction was to be expected given the resistance that Treasury had shown to the commission's work. Treasury's objections were based on its contention that "the facts prove that the Bureau of Narcotics has achieved an outstanding record of success both in administering its regulatory controls of the legitimate narcotic trade and in suppressing the illicit narcotics traffic and securing the arrest and imprisonment of the major criminal traffickers."[26] Unfortunately for Treasury's case, widespread skepticism with respect to just this sort of assertion was one of the motivating forces behind formation of the commission in the first place.[27]

President Johnson acted on the least problematic of the commission's recommendations on 15 July. He issued a statement in which he directed all federal units with any responsibility for antinarcotics activities to devote their best efforts to three objectives: "(1) the destruction of the illegal traffic in drugs, (2) the prevention of drug abuse, and (3) the cure and rehabilitation of victims of this traffic."[28] Significantly, and contrary to the beliefs expressed earlier by both Treasury and Justice officials, he cited the federal government's responsibility for the regulation of interstate commerce, rather than its taxation powers, as the authority for his directive, thereby weakening the case for keeping drug law enforcement in the Treasury Department. In the same directive, the president appointed Lee White of the White House staff to coordinate the efforts of the affected departments and bureaus and to see to the implementation of the directive. At the same time, Congress also took steps to improve control of narcotics and dangerous drugs.

THE DRUG ABUSE CONTROL AMENDMENTS OF 1965

The drive to revise federal drug abuse control legislation had begun in March 1965 with Johnson's "Special Message to Congress on Law Enforcement and the Administration of Justice." The president announced two major initiatives in the message. One dealt with addiction treatment—a proposal for a federal civil commitment statute that responded to Prettyman recommendation 25. The other, which addressed recommendation 10 and dealt with law enforcement, was an attempt at a new organizational response to the problem of so-called dangerous drugs (principally amphetamines and barbiturates, although "hallucinogenic effect" was written into the definition of "depressant and stimulant drugs" so that the law applied to LSD). The fact that these substances did not fall under the aegis of the FBN offered the opportunity to set up a new entity with police powers outside the traditional structure. The legislation, which became the Drug Abuse Control Amendments of 1965, established the Bureau of Drug Abuse Control (BDAC) within the Food and Drug Administration (FDA). The amendments further reduced the hegemony of the FBN by delegating to the new agency responsibility for regulating a whole category of abusable substances that were thought to enter the illegal market through diversion from legitimate channels of distribution. The interstate commerce clause was thus brought into the service of federal drug control. It also extended federal control to traffic in this type of goods within states on the theory that this was necessary to effectively control interstate commerce.

As is so often the case with legislation, the BDAC amendments solved some problems but created others. The 1965 amendments did not allow for the fact that the black market is not neatly divided among various types of drugs for the benefit of government agents. Thus BDAC agents would soon find themselves tangling with FBN agents, who were tangling with Customs agents—all were investigating and "busting" traffickers who were handling marijuana and heroin in addition to amphetamines, barbiturates, and LSD. Furthermore, the presence of a police operation in the Food and Drug Administration was no less an anomaly than that of the FBN in Treasury. In any event, BDAC lasted only a little over a year: it was finally operational in early 1966 and was reorganized out of the FDA in 1968.

NARCOTIC ADDICT REHABILITATION ACT OF 1966

The concept of civil commitment as a way of forcing drug addicts into treatment and out of circulation, supported by the Prettyman Commission, had been under consideration in Congress since the introduction of Senator Keating's bill in 1961.[29] The administration's version of the civil commitment legislation and related bills were considered by the Judiciary Committees of both houses between July 1965 and July 1966. During the hearings held by these committees a wide spectrum of opinion was expressed on the subject of treatment and civil commitment of drug abusers as well as on drug use in general.

Attorney General Katzenbach's testimony illustrates the dilemma that he and his colleagues faced as they tried to adjust to new concepts of drug abuse as a nuanced and poorly understood phenomenon that had health consequences but seemed to be related to crime as well. To make matters even more complex, drug use was charged with moral symbolism. They had to recognize the declining legitimacy of harsh legal sanctions for narcotics offenses while simultaneously maintaining a politically convincing anti-crime posture. For example, in his responses to a skeptical Representative Robert Ashmore (D.,SC), the attorney general tried to thread his way among the intricacies of whether marijuana was addicting (if not, would marijuana offenders need to be eligible for rehabilitation?); whether it led to heroin use; whether making marijuana offenders eligible for parole had anything to do with established mandatory minimum sentences; and whether the legislation would eventually lead to abrogation of mandatory sentences. Presidential advisors did not judge the moment to be right for outright abolition of mandatory minimum sentences for drug offenses, but politicians and bureaucrats who began to suspect that policy was moving in that direction were essentially correct.

> MR. ASHMORE. . . . You stated, and I have heard before, that marihuana is not a habit-forming drug, Is that correct?
>
> MR. KATZENBACH. That is right. Many marihuana users end up subsequently leading up to heroin, so it had the effect of leading one into addiction, but it is not addictive in itself.
>
> MR. ASHMORE. How about those who use it? The effect of it is unknown, is it not? It can cause one to commit murder, another sex violence, another something else?
>
> MR. KATZENBACH. That is right.
>
> MR. ASHMORE. In many ways it is as bad as heroin, morphine, and what have you?
>
> MR. KATZENBACH. From that point of view it is.
>
> MR. ASHMORE. Is there any difference in your bill with reference to a person who is using or dealing in, buying or selling and smuggling marihuana and heroin and other narcotics?
>
> MR. KATZENBACH. Not so far as people pushing marihuana as against heroin. The only difference we have is that we would permit parole procedures for marihuana violators.
>
> MR. ASHMORE. You would?
>
> MR. KATZENBACH. We would permit parole where there is presently a minimum sentence required on marihuana. We would permit parole on marihuana only.
>
> MR. ASHMORE. You would change the penalty in the present law?

MR. KATZENBACH. To the extent of permitting parole, yes, sir.

MR. ASHMORE. They are barred from parole at the moment?

MR. KATZENBACH. That is true. They are not eligible under the civil commitment section of the statute because they are not addicts.

MR. ASHMORE. Your bill would make them eligible for parole and for commitment?

MR. KATZENBACH. No, because there is no addiction. They don't need it.

MR. ASHMORE. No psychological treatment you know of?

MR. KATZENBACH. Most of the marihuana users, if they are not also users of other drugs, have not gotten to that stage, are mostly youthful offenders and sort of doing it for kicks, I guess.

They just started down the road.[30]

President Johnson signed the Narcotic Addict Rehabilitation Act (NARA) into law on 8 November 1966. As enacted, its first two titles conformed in essence to the measure sponsored by the administration. Title I offered the option of civil commitment to the custody of the surgeon general, in lieu of prosecution, of a narcotic addict charged with a nonviolent criminal offense. In an important variation from the original administration-sponsored bill, the version that emerged from the conference of the Senate and the House made ineligible for commitment in lieu of trial those addicts charged with selling narcotics. This item turned out to be a defect similar to the one that Dean Markham had identified in the Keating bill—it severely limited eligibility for treatment and greatly reduced the efficacy of the measure. It also is a measure of the tenacity of "old" views of the crime-abuse nexus—punishments seemed to creep into everything. Title II dealt with commitment in lieu of a prison sentence of those prosecuted and convicted of federal offenses. These addicts, whose conviction might be as a result of selling drugs as long as it could be demonstrated that they did so only to support their own habit, would fall under the jurisdiction of the attorney general. The third title had not formed part of the administration's proposal. It was designed to offer treatment to the noncriminal addict through a civil commitment proceeding initiated at the request either of the addict or of a relative. Acting Attorney General Ramsey Clark expressed some reservation about this section: he doubted the constitutionality of the provision that persons committed for treatment could be retained in a program against their will. Title IV, another addition to the administration's proposed bill, provided for grants totaling $15 million over two years to fund various research activities and local treatment facilities. This section would turn up later in attempts by the Department of Health, Education, and Welfare to fold narcotics treatment into the Community Mental Health Centers Act. In spite of these fairly significant changes to the administration's proposal, Clark recommended presidential approval of the bill and declared that "by and large this is an excellent measure which should be of considerable assistance in coping with criminal activity and drug addiction."[31]

The secretary of health, education, and welfare, whose department would share responsibility with the attorney general for implementing the act, also commented favorably on the measure, although he expressed some serious reservations. With the caution that has often characterized the federal health bureaucracy with respect to questions of authority over, and funding for, federal drug-addiction programs, the secretary stated that his department, while pleased with the opportunity to better serve voluntary patients, would have preferred that civil commitment legislation be limited to these patients until more was known about the medical characteristics of addiction. He was also worried about the "procedural complexity" of the bill, especially Title III; in this at least his concern proved to be well founded. Other sources of worry for HEW included the possible strain on federal facilities that would be created if states and localities succeeded in abdicating any responsibilities for addict treatment in favor of reliance on federal programs and the question of whether the "assistance" that HEW was authorized to provide to the states and municipalities would include money.[32]

NARA seemed to take a long step toward legitimizing a more public-health-oriented approach to drug addiction, and it did contribute to tilting federal policy ever so slightly away from the traditional police approach, but it was a mixed bag. In the original proposal, the administration had attempted to go even further toward reformation of the mandatory minimum sentences established by the Narcotics Control Acts of 1951 and 1956. That version had provided that young adult narcotic and marijuana offenders be eligible for indeterminate sentences as an inducement to rehabilitation. But the president and his advisors were under considerable political pressure not to appear to give ground on law enforcement issues, which severely limited their ability to maneuver, regardless of what their convictions were with respect to treatment and punishment of narcotics offenders. As Joseph Califano relates in his biography of Johnson, a tough and popular anti-crime bill was awaiting the president's signature at the same time as was NARA. Johnson vetoed that legislation owing to worries about the constitutionality of some of its provisions, but not without objection from Nicholas Katzenbach (who had left the Justice Department in September to become undersecretary of state) and from FBI director J.

Edgar Hoover.[33] The NARA bill as passed only went so far as to allow parole for marijuana offenders, rather than offer a real alternative to mandatory minimums, which was as much as the administration could have expected to achieve under the circumstances.

Unfortunately—as would often prove to be the case with federally sponsored public health measures and with law enforcement measures to deal with narcotics abuse—implementation of NARA proved to be extremely difficult, and its effects were nearly impossible to measure. The complexity of the problems it tried to address and its mixed-bag character probably made it unworkable. After the passage of the Comprehensive Drug Abuse and Control Act in October 1970 it would fall into disuse. Richard Lindblad, who served as a regional supervisor for implementation of NARA, identified the principal factors contributing to its fall from favor as (1) difficulties in quantifying the benefits of the program, which led to the perception that costs were excessive; (2) extremely high rejection rates of applicants to the program and exclusion of many addicts who had too many previous felony convictions or commitments; (3) misinterpretation of, and lack of enthusiasm for, the law at the state and local levels (Clark's observation that its constitutionality was suspect was never tested in court, but the question was widely discussed); and (4) the federal decision to adopt methadone maintenance as the principal treatment modality, especially after 1971, the year the most patients (4,245) were treated under NARA programs.[34]

LSD

According to Senator Thomas J. Dodd (D., CT), the Special Subcommittee on Narcotics of the Committee on the Judiciary decided to include testimony on LSD in its NARA hearings in order to "determine whether [LSD users] should be covered by the administration's narcotic addict rehabilitation bill."[35]

Lysergic acid diethylamide-25 had been developed by a Swiss chemist at the Sandoz laboratories in 1938. This same chemist, Albert Hofmann, accidentally ingested some of the substance in 1943 and thus discovered its hallucinogenic properties. At the time of the NARA hearings, the drug had experimental status in the United States, and its shipment in interstate commerce, except for approved clinical research, was prohibited. Nonmedical use of LSD had begun to attract attention in the press as early as the mid-1950s; nevertheless, its medical value as a therapeutic tool in the treatment of a number of psychiatric disorders was defended by some mental health professionals.[36] In the early 1960s, experiments in behavior change using LSD were conducted on criminal sex offenders in California, and a team of Harvard researchers under the direction of Dr. Timothy Leary attempted to demonstrate that recidivism rates among convicts paroled from the Concord Prison could be reduced through controlled use of psilocybin, a chemical with psychedelic properties found in a type of mushroom.[37] This history of early medical use of LSD and similar substances resembles that of cocaine and heroin, both of which had initially been received with great enthusiasm by the medical community only to be strictly controlled later as the drugs' potential for abuse and limited therapeutic value became apparent. By the early 1960s the rising popularity of LSD among mostly middle-class young people and open advocacy of its use as a key to spiritual awareness by adults with credible scientific and scholarly résumés—particularly Drs. Timothy Leary and Richard Alpert of Harvard—began to cause some alarm. Ironically, LSD use gained its first adherents in the academic community courtesy of the Central Intelligence Agency. Through the CIA's fervent search for a mind-control drug and its sponsorship of human experiments at a number of universities, scientists and the students and researchers who served as their subjects discovered the acid trip.[38] In 1965 manufacture and distribution of LSD were subjected to some controls by the Drug Abuse Control Amendments, and several states, beginning with New York and California, enacted criminal penalties for LSD production, trafficking, and possession.

By the time of the NARA hearings, members of Congress were wondering if there was a crisis that required more federal legislation. They listened to the testimony of Dr. Donald B. Louria, who represented Governor Nelson A. Rockefeller of New York and who described "uncontrolled aggression and violence" among some patients admitted to Bellevue Hospital suffering from adverse reactions to LSD. Dr. Louria also expressed skepticism that LSD had any well-documented psychotherapeutic benefit. He termed the phenomenon of recreational use among young people a "very substantial threat" but not a "crisis."[39] With respect to appropriate penalties for transgressions involving LSD, his opinion exemplified the "new" enlightened attitude that was increasingly common among both medical and legal professionals when faced with the prospect of severe criminal sanctions being applied to middle-class youth. Dr. Louria felt that LSD-using youths were being "nonsensical, and they may harm themselves and may harm others. But I don't think that we should ruin their lives with severe penalties. However, I think those who sell or manufacture it should be treated very harshly."[40]

Advocates of LSD use who testified before the committee included Dr.

Leary, by then the recognized prophet of psychedelic experience; Arthur Kleps, director of the Neo-American Church, who championed the use of LSD as a sacrament; and the beat poet Allen Ginsberg. One can only guess at what the senators felt upon being told by Dr. Leary that "the so-called peril of LSD resides precisely in its eerie power to release ancient, wise and, I would even say, at times holy sources of energy, which reside inside the human brain."[41] Arthur Kleps went further: "It is our belief that the sacred biochemicals [*sic*] such as peyote, mescaline, LSD, and cannabis are the true host of God and not drugs at all as that term is commonly understood. We do not feel that the Government has the right to interfere in our religious practice, and that the present persecution of our coreligionists is not only constitutionally illegal but a crude and savage repression of our basic and inalienable rights as human beings."[42] He made unfavorable comparisons between the governments of the United States and Nazi Germany and alluded to the possibility of violent resistance among his followers to attempts to control the use of LSD.

Dr. James L. Goddard, commissioner of the Food and Drug Administration, provided the senators with countervailing testimony. "As other witnesses have testified, [a drug can] become sometimes glamorous and attractive, and its use is spread through friends and through misinformed individuals. That is one of the dangers of a compound like LSD, where there are people who go around talking of its mind-expanding properties. Well, that is pure bunk. It does not have those properties."[43] Dr. Goddard also assured the senators that the powers of the new Bureau of Drug Abuse Control were being effectively used to clamp down on illegal manufacture and distribution of LSD.

In the end, LSD users were not addressed in the Narcotic Addict Rehabilitation Act of 1966, but the drug continued to cause concern, and controls were strengthened first in October 1968 and then again in 1970, when all the nation's drug laws were revamped.

PRESIDENT'S COMMISSION ON LAW ENFORCEMENT AND ADMINISTRATION OF JUSTICE

Just as the NARA legislation was nearing passage, presidential assistant Joseph Califano sent a memo to Attorney General Nicholas Katzenbach directing him to establish a President's Commission on Law Enforcement and Administration of Justice. (Katzenbach moved to the State Department just weeks later, and Ramsey Clark became acting attorney general.) Califano told Katzenbach that "this special Task Force effort reflects our deep concern with the many problems in the field of law enforcement and the administration of justice. We hope to develop, with your help, a vigorous and imaginative program for consideration by the first session of the 90th Congress."[44]

In late November, just after the passage of NARA and Johnson's veto of the crime bill, the new commission's Task Force on Narcotic Drugs submitted its recommendations to the Bureau of the Budget for review. The study was published in early 1967 as chapter 8 of the commission's full report, *The Challenge of Crime in a Free Society*.[45] The commission reviewed the conclusions of the 1963 President's Advisory Commission on Drug Abuse (the Prettyman Commission) as well as the changes to narcotics laws that had been enacted in the 1950s, when heroin was seen as the greatest social threat. (The 1951 law stipulated mandatory minimum sentences for all narcotic and marijuana offenses and prohibition of parole for second offenders, and the 1956 measure increased minimum sentences and provided the possibility of the death penalty for sales of heroin to minors.) The task force recommended that sentencing discretion be restored to judges and corrections officers; that all aspects of marijuana use be carefully studied in order to provide an information base for reconsideration of "present marijuana laws and the propositions on which they are based";[46] and that the enforcement staffs of both the Bureau of Customs and the Bureau of Narcotics be increased. The group did not make any specific recommendations regarding treatment or rehabilitation of drug abusers but observed, in language similar to that used today in describing addiction as a "chronic relapsing disease,"[47] that "careful and continuing evaluation of these programs, which has often been absent in the past, is imperative. There is great need for better standards for measuring the outcome of treatment. To think only in terms of 'cure' is not very meaningful in the case of a chronic illness such as addiction. There is little knowledge about why a good outcome is achieved for one addict but not another, by one method but not another. More trained personnel are desperately needed."[48]

The commission did specifically recommend that a concerted effort in the area of public education "be given continuing and central direction by a single agency."[49] The task force acknowledged its debt to the Prettyman Commission (see the Appendix), and expressed the belief that effective implementation of existing measures, such as NARA and the BDAC amendments, was the first order of priority. The Budget Bureau staff's analysis of the task force report grouped recommendations under seven headings, and in a meeting with Califano and the task force members, five of the recommendations were approved.

Rejected was a proposal for a national case register of addicts, perhaps because of questions regarding the constitutionality of such a list; and once again the suggestion that mandatory minimum sentences for drug offenses should be abandoned was tabled. The Budget Bureau staff, in its review of the task force's work, had bowed to the political reality of the moment while fully aware that the balance of opinion and emotion was in flux. The BOB staff observed:

> Because existing mandatory minimum sentences for drug offenses are inconsistent with the philosophy embodied in the new Narcotic Addict Rehabilitation Act (that addiction is a disease), they should be abolished. Such sentences are also inconsistent with modern penological theory, which holds that the purpose of criminal laws should be to enable those responsible for the correctional system to rehabilitate the offender rather than punish him. The mandatory minimum sentences and prohibition of parole provide a disincentive to the addict to work toward rehabilitation and the termination of his addiction. The Narcotic Addict Rehabilitation Act provides the first breach in the requirement for mandatory minimum sentences by authorizing indeterminate confinement for treatment for narcotic addicts who sell the drugs to finance their own addiction.
>
> In spite of the impressive arguments that can be made for abolishing these laws, they have a strong emotional appeal. A proposal that they should be abolished cannot be expected to have popular appeal.[50]

The White House staff then went about preparing a presidential statement that would delineate the policy that emerged from these deliberations. It is significant that, in the context of an activist Democratic administration, the statement made a point of the fact that the federal government was quite limited in what it could do to control crime, normally the responsibility of local law enforcement. This was an issue that the subsequent Republican administration was to confront and deal with in a way that would establish a lasting federal presence in local law enforcement. Johnson described the federal role as "to help, but not to dictate, the efforts of each community to mount its own enforcement program and develop its own plan to treat and rehabilitate the addicts."[51]

1967—YEAR OF GRASS

More or less simultaneously with the appearance of LSD and its attendant psychedelic movement, marijuana use began to spread out from its base among urban minorities and artistic communities. The marijuana controversy played itself out both in the federal bureaucracy and in the society at large as a kind of reduction of the larger drug issue. Traditionalists defended the notion that pot was both a menace in itself and a "stepping stone" to heroin. Others, generally younger and more skeptical of authority, lost faith in the extreme depiction of marijuana that had been repeated since the 1930s. They looked to scientific research to prove marijuana's harmlessness, at least when compared to "hard drugs," like heroin, or even legal drugs, like alcohol.

The social resonance of cannabis use was complicated and mostly negative. The drug had been legally proscribed by the federal government since 1937, and provoked in the public mind the same sort of unpleasant associations as did the opiates. Most responsible authorities and most citizens believed that cannabis impaired mental functions, incited its users to antisocial and even violent behavior, and frequently, if not inevitably, led to opiate addiction. But, as R.J. Bonnie and C.H. Whitebread ably describe, the "marihuana consensus" began to unravel as more and more people discovered that the effects of the drug were different from what they had been led to believe.

> Beginning in the mid-sixties, the marihuana consensus evaporated, as each of its essential supports wobbled and fell away. The drug's sudden attraction to the nation's university population was of primary importance. Although marihuana arrests and seizures had hit their all-time low point in 1960, by 1967 use of the drug was associated in the public mind with life on the campus. This new class of users, regardless of its size, had direct access to the public opinion process because it was drawn from the middle and upper socioeconomic brackets. As a result, this new use pattern incited a broad social awareness of the drug and awakened in the scientific and medical communities a new interest in research.[52]

An example of the new research was the isolation in 1966 of cannabis's active ingredient, tetrahydrocannabinol, or THC; its effects on humans were demonstrated in 1967.[53]

In the context of a general questioning of all sorts of received wisdom—from the "proper place" of African-Americans to the justification for an American military presence in Southeast Asia—the supposedly dire consequences of marijuana use were one more object of skepticism and one more target for the iconoclastic energies of the moment. Paradoxically, the welter of social and political rebellion (often lumped under the name "counterculture," one of the main targets of which was policies of the federal government) coexisted with faith in the ability of government to address social problems on a grand scale (the Great Society). In an odd nexus of the two forces, the increasing willingness of many "establishment" health professionals and legislators to reexamine the whole narcotics issue was key to a new consideration of what marijuana actually was and what penalties, if any, were appropriate to control its use.

Throughout 1967 public drug use and media coverage thereof continued to rise. In January, Timothy Leary appeared at a "happening" in San Francisco, and as the weather warmed in other parts of the country, gatherings of hippies and hippie wannabes where marijuana smoke hung in the air took place in New York and other cities. Between 1966 and 1967 there was an increase in state marijuana arrests of nearly 100 percent.[54] This type of arrest rose 1,000 percent between 1965 and 1970.[55] At the same time, data on the disposition of marijuana violations at the federal level indicate a change in how such violations were viewed by the judicial system: 87 percent of federal cases resulted in con-

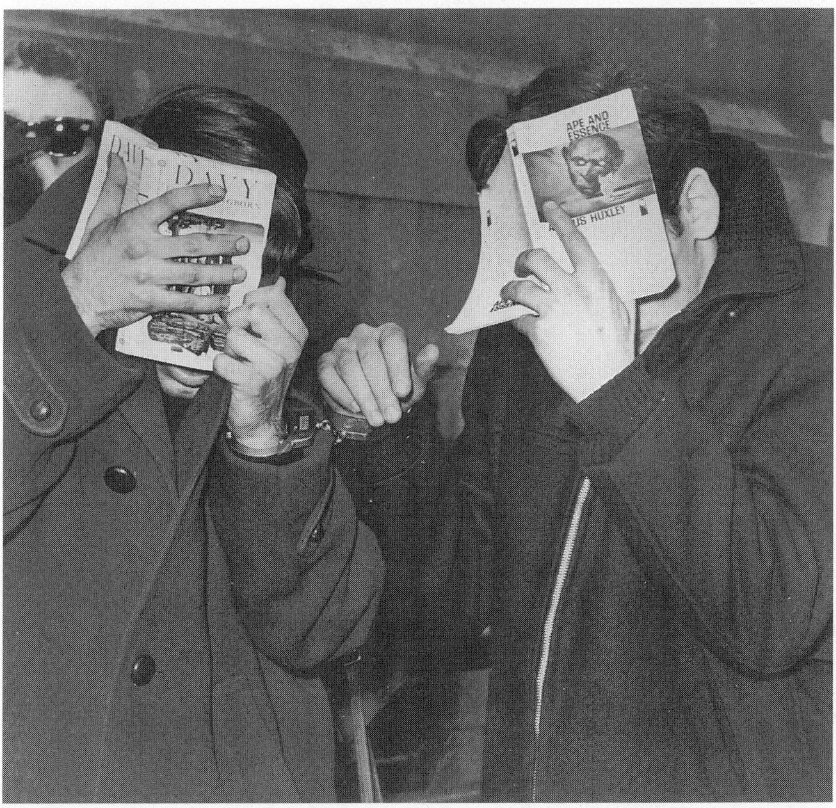

Two Hunter College students covering their faces with books at police headquarters after they were picked up on narcotics charges, 1968. (New York World Telegram and Sun Newspaper Photograph Collection, Library of Congress. Staff photo by Herman Hiller.)

victions in 1966; 80 percent did in 1967; the rate had fallen to 60 percent by 1971.[56] *Life* magazine ran an article on 7 July 1967 under the title "Marijuana: Millions of Turned-On Users," which began with the statement "Almost overnight the U.S. was embarked on the greatest mass flouting of the law since Prohibition."[57] The article contained a startling validation of Bonnie and Whitebread's contention with respect to the "collapse of the marihuana consensus." "Despite the stringent laws, Federal Food and Drug Administration Director James Goddard admits that narcotics agents are unable to control the situation, and even so dedicated a drug foe as former Federal Narcotics Commissioner Harry Anslinger concedes that present penalties are unrealistically severe for youthful offenders."[58] If Harry Anslinger could back away, even a little, from an uncompromising position in favor of severe penalties for pot offenses, the times were truly changing.

Treasury Department officials were quite aware of the pot controversy and its implications for law enforcement, social stability, and existing bureaucratic divisions of power should the legal status of cannabis be changed. A July 1967 memo from Assistant Secretary James P. Hendrick to Secretary Henry Fowler took note of press attention to questions of cannabis legalization, penalty structure, and organizational authority and provided the secretary with a concise overview of facts and opinions associated with these issues. Hendrick pointed out to the secretary that although questions of the real dangers of marijuana consumption had not been settled, the combination of lack of hard data supporting its safety and strong indications of its prejudicial effects on health and behavior tended to justify the status quo. He also opposed any reconsideration of which agency should be responsible for cannabis enforcement, the FBN or the newly formed BDAC in HEW. If any reorganization were to be contemplated, he favored moving all drug-related enforcement, including BDAC, to Treasury.[59] Herein are visible the mutual suspicion and rivalry between the law enforcement and health bureaucracies and the struggle among law enforcement entities (the Customs Bureau, the Narcotics Bureau, the Justice Department, and the Treasury Department) for control of the narcotics agenda that had existed in some form in the Treasury Department since 1919, with the foundation of the Narcotic Field Force of the Bureau of Internal Revenue, and that would continue over the next decades.

To add to the tension between Treasury and HEW, a number of officials from various agencies of the latter department made public statements during the fall of 1967 to the effect that marijuana was not as dangerous as it was thought and that it should be controlled as a "dangerous drug" rather than as a narcotic. (One result of such a change would be to subject violators of cannabis control measures to less severe penalties.) Dr. Goddard himself was widely quoted in the press as critical of marijuana penalties and as believing that marijuana was no more dangerous than alcohol. United Press International later apologized for quoting him out of context,[60] but the reports had already angered many in the administration and on Capitol Hill, where there were calls for his resignation. President Johnson himself was concerned and asked Harry C. McPherson, Jr., assistant White House counsel, to brief him about the situation.[61] Particularly worrisome was the possible political advantage to Republicans of the apparent disagreement within the administration; partisan conflict is a recurrent, sometimes major factor in the drug policy debate. McPherson informed Johnson that Goddard's comments had been misrepresented and that the FDA commissioner was concerned about the severity of marijuana penalties. He explained:

> What Goddard was trying to say was, there is something wrong about placing hundreds of thousands of young Americans under a potential felony indictment for behavior about which scientists, physicians, and police authorities have serious debates.
>
> The Narcotics Division of Justice takes the INTERPOL view, that harsh penalties are necessary to control the use of marihuana, because marihuana can and often does induce addiction to stronger drugs.
>
> This is an old Justice–medical community argument, brought into the open by the misleading *Post* story.
>
> This afternoon Justice and Treasury are meeting with Goddard to help him prepare his testimony for the coming week.[62]

THE CONFLICT BETWEEN PUBLIC HEALTH AND LAW ENFORCEMENT

The health bureaucracy and the law enforcement professionals were profoundly at odds. Their struggle over the right to define the drug abuse problem and implement policies to solve it was at least as old as the struggle to interpret the Harrison Act of 1914, which led to the closure of local morphine maintenance clinics in the mid 1920s and established law enforcement entities as arbiters of narcotics control. Now, as the disease concept of addiction continued to gain currency, government health professionals sought new legitimacy for their claims that treatment and prevention should be the principal basis of any new approach to addiction control. The National Institute of Mental Health (NIMH) already had a formidable institutional base for a full-scale public health initiative against drug use—the community mental health centers. President Kennedy had signed the Community Mental Health Centers Act in October 1963, which authorized funding for 145 such facilities, and President Johnson had expanded on the initiative in 1965 with amendments to the act giving $73.5 million for staffing grants.[63]

Two documents produced during the second half of 1967 within the health establishment illustrate the gulf between the health and law-enforcement mind-sets. The first, dated August, was entitled "Five-Year Program Plan for the Prevention and Treatment of Narcotic and Drug Abuse" and was produced by NIMH. The goal of the plan was "to radically reduce the human suffering, disability, death, and social disruption resulting from narcotic and other drug abuse." Five ways to reach the goal were articulated. The first three of these dealt with research. The last two were "4. Rapid expansion of versatile, comprehensive treatment and rehabilitation programs through use of existing Public Health Service programs, and through assistance to States and communities; 5. Development of new and innovative techniques directed toward primary prevention of narcotic and other drug abuse."[64] The report went on to state categorically that "the widespread acceptance of the primary role of prevention and treatment rather than reliance on enforcement in solving this problem is critical to the achievement of the stated objectives."[65]

The second document, a report of the Presidential Health Task Force, contained a section entitled "Controlling Drug Abuse, Narcotic Addiction, and Alcoholism," which reprised the recommendations of the Prettyman Commission and the Narcotics Task Force of the previous autumn and contained some elements of the August NIMH plan as well, but did not agree completely with any of its predecessors. For example, while the NIMH plan expressed the opinion that the decision to vest responsibility for control of psychedelics, stimulants, and depressants in the Food and Drug Administration "marked a significant step in shifting the Federal stance regarding these drugs from predominant emphasis on enforcement and punishment to one of prevention and treatment within a health context,"[66] the task force report advocated transfer of BDAC to the Justice Department. In spite of this disagreement, the task force suggestion was supported by a logic they shared—namely the need for addict rehabilitation services in local communities and the negative implications of associating such services with police action. The task force stated:

> Although there is growing recognition that narcotic addiction is basically a health problem, effective prevention, rehabilitation, and other control efforts are hampered by the excessive attention focused on the relationship between addiction and crime. . . .
>
> The lack of community-based services has also had a negative effect on the development of desperately needed skilled manpower. Professionals are reluctant to associate themselves with addict treatment programs which are isolated geographically or closely identified with enforcement agencies and procedures.[67]

The task force report proposed that these services be made available to localities by transferring to the Community Mental Health Centers Program the surgeon general's authority to make staff development, training, and program evaluation grants provided under section 402 of NARA. The effect of this would be that "needed community facilities for the treatment and rehabilitation of narcotic addicts [would] be developed and related to the activities of the Community Mental Health Center. Highest priority within this program should be given to intensive education and prevention efforts aimed at and involving key community workers, parents and children."[68]

Referring to recommendations 7 and 8 of the Prettyman Commission, the task force advocated locating all police activities in the Department of Justice and pointed out that such a move would require that the president submit a reorganization plan to Congress.[69]

Meanwhile, Joseph Califano had asked the Treasury Department to report on the actions that the Narcotics Bureau had taken in response to the recommendations of the Katzenbach Commission.[70] One of the commission's suggestions, which would have consequences for planners in the Nixon administration and which was also associated with constitutional limitations on federal police powers, was that the Bureau of Narcotics concentrate its efforts on the "upper echelons" of drug trafficking, thus leaving street-level enforcement to local agencies. Secretary of the Treasury Henry Fowler advised Califano in November that the FBN had already taken significant strides in that direction.[71] He went on to indicate that the department was developing draft legislation that would do away with mandatory minimum sentences in cases of marijuana possession. This was a new direction indeed for the FBN and may have reflected the pressure to loosen its grip on those aspects of the drug problem that were coming to be seen as questions of personal liberty (marijuana use) or public health (treatment of opiate addiction). An enormous change in traditional policy came with the approval of methadone, a long-acting, synthetic opiate for the maintenance of addicted heroin users.

METHADONE

Methadone had been used as an aid in dealing with opiate withdrawal in hospital settings since the early 1950s. Official acceptance of maintenance as a legitimate approach to opiate addiction represented a gradual abandonment of the federal campaign against the medical model of addiction management that began with the closure of opiate maintenance clinics in the early 1920s. Former FBN commissioner Giordano today recalls his own opposition to initial methadone research done by Drs. Vincent Dole and Marie Nyswander and attributes later rises in drug abuse to the ultimate failure of law enforcement to curtail this treatment method. Giordano's version of contacts between Assistant Secretary of the Treasury David Acheson and Dole and Nyswander also betrays his difference of opinion with Acheson, a conflict that put Giordano at odds not only with Acheson but also with Secretary Fowler.

> We were having some problems with Dole and Nyswander up in New York who were running this methadone maintenance. In fact, they weren't keeping records and I insisted they keep records. So they ran to see this Dave Acheson, who was the special assistant [to the secretary of the treasury for enforcement]. So he calls me over and says, "You know, these people are doing a great job up there, and what's all this?" And I said, "It's in the law! They're violating the law!" The law required that when they dispensed narcotics, they're supposed to keep a record of it. [Acheson said,] "Oh, okay." So as I say, methadone maintenance clinics got all over the country. So, during that period of five years is when it started down hill. That's when you can see the increase in drug abuse.[72]

Acheson and Fowler were both more inclined than was Giordano to consider the possible advantages of emerging "scientific" and therapeutic techniques in drug control. Fowler advised Joseph Califano of Acheson's contacts with Dole and Nyswander and of preparations in the Treasury Department for new regulations that would permit methadone maintenance.

> One of the supporting studies in the Task Force Report on Narcotics and Drug Abuse suggests the desirability of altering Treasury Regulations which now prohibit prescription of a narcotic substance to maintain an addict's narcotic habit. A principal source for this change is the development of an experimental treatment of heroin addicts with Methadone, a somewhat more benign narcotic. Members of the office of Special Assistant (for Enforcement [David Acheson]) have conferred with officials of the National Institute of Mental Health and with Drs. Dole and Nyswander (directors of New York's experiment in Methadone maintenance now under way with Treasury approval). Revised regulations are in preparation. These would permit li-

> censing by the Bureau, after consultation with an appropriate medical advisory group, of approved Methadone maintenance experiments.[73]

Giordano did his best to hold on to his bureau and the methods that had served it well since 1930, but his position on the methadone issue did not help him. His attitude appeared to indicate inability or unwillingness to adapt to the newer thinking that was gaining the advantage in drug policy assessment, and provided additional impetus for reorganization. By December, Califano was involved in plans to merge BDAC and FBN and to move the narcotics enforcement operation to the Justice Department.[74]

President Johnson receives the International Narcotics Enforcement Officers Association Award from Patrick O'Carroll as (*left to right*) Henry Giordano, John Finlator, and Arthur Kassell look on. (LBJ Library Collection. Photo by Yoichi R. Okamoto.)

REORGANIZATION PLAN 1 OF 1968

A notion that the nation's narcotics enforcement should be located in the Justice Department had been discussed in one form or another since the Hoover Commission on government organization had made the proposal in 1949. In late 1967 forces converged to make the reorganization politically and practically desirable. Public attention to the drug issue had increased exponentially that year: the concern was driven by marijuana and LSD use among young people but extended to preoccupation with the possible relationship between opiate addiction and crime. Violent rioting had broken out over the summer in largely black areas of Newark and Detroit, leading citizens to fear a general breakdown of public order. Lyndon Johnson's job approval rating, as gauged by the Gallup poll, was at 28 percent, and there were 485,000 American troops fighting an increasingly unpopular war in Southeast Asia. Johnson's stunning announcement that he would not run for reelection would not come until March of 1968, and decisive action against crime and disorderly conduct at home could do nothing but good for his political fortunes.

While the White House tried to carefully balance drug policy among changing attitudes toward drugs, the image enhancement of anti-crime initiatives, and bureaucratic rivalries, it had a lurking fear of what the frontline troops in the war on drugs might do to this carefully constructed system. Dean Markham quoted a Justice Department official who had put his finger on a problem that had plagued narcotics law enforcement from its inception and would continue to do so in the future:[75] "The Bureau of Narcotics agents are real 'bomb throwers' and their rough-neck ways are going to cause some serious embarrassment to the Treasury Department and the Administration someday."[76]

Important considerations of operational efficiency and integrity also had a large bearing on the reorganization discussion. The long and jealously guarded independence of the FBN in its little corner of the Treasury Department had isolated the bureau and imprisoned it in its increasingly outmoded institutional culture. Not only had a large segment of both lay and professional opinion come to question the bureau's approach and the assumptions upon which it was based, but there were many within the administration who felt that both law enforcement and public health would be better served by locating all police operations in the Justice Department, where a more up-to-date and professionally skilled atmosphere might prevail. This thought was even shared by some in Treasury. Califano indicated to President Johnson that Secretary Fowler was not personally against reorganization,[77] and according to Vernon Acree, retired commissioner of the Customs Bureau and at the time an inspector for the Internal Revenue Service, David Acheson (the same assistant secretary who had asked Henry Giordano for an explanation of his attitude toward Drs. Dole and Nyswander) asked Acree to conduct a secret investigation of the FBN's operations in New York.[78] Acree claims to have turned up evidence of corruption that led to criminal indictments of more than twenty agents. A background memorandum that was circulated among White House policy staff listed several partial rationales for reorganization, including the corruption mentioned by Acree:

> • Because of the upsurge in criminal activity in this area, this is the time to take action.
> • Both [FBN and BDAC] are now in departments that do not really concern themselves with this type of enforcement.
> • There is great overlap in the activities of the two bureaus.
> For example, in over 90% of all BDAC seizures of LSD, they have also found marihuana—yet they have no jurisdiction over marihuana.
> Both bureaus are involved in training programs and education work—which could be consolidated.
> The fragmentation is particularly a problem in the field—where in a medium sized city each agency might have 3 men—the cost of operating separate offices, maintaining separate files, etc.
> • Both bureaus need substantial upgrading in personnel. (Fred Vinson very strongly urges you not use this argument and this information—especially with people close to the Bureau of Narcotics.)
> In the Miami investigation last year the chief of the Bureau of Narcotics office was convicted, as well as a former agent.
> The current New York scandal has involved indictments not only against New York City and Nassau County narcotics agents, but a Bureau agent and 3 former agents. Also about 7 agents resigned in the course of the investigation. A special Task Force is now investigating this affair for the Treasury.
> Several BDAC agents are under criminal investigation.[79]

Most Treasury and FBN staffers, however, saw the implications of the move quite differently. "Since its creation under Commissioner Anslinger in 1930, the Bureau, with Treasury's support, has maintained a reputation for hard-line enforcement. (The Bureau is, in fact, changing very rapidly in its attitude towards experiment, treatment of addiction and penalties, but the reputation persists.) In a year in which crime in the streets is going to be one of the two most publicized campaign issues, it would seem highly desirable for the Administration to perpetuate or enlarge upon the Anslinger heritage."[80] The Treasury people were correct in their assessment of the political utility to the administration of appearing to take a strong stand against drug abuse and trafficking, but they were very wide of the mark with respect to the appeal of the Anslinger heritage to White House decision makers. Califano clarified the situation to the president in the following terms: "The Justice Department—and this now includes FBI Director Hoover—would like to bring both the HEW Bureau of Drug Abuse Control and the Treasury Bureau of Narcotics into the Justice Department under a new Special Assistant . . . , clean them up and bring their personnel up to the same kind of standards now required by the FBI and perhaps a few years down the road fold them into the FBI."[81]

By early February the decision to reorganize had been made. Attorney General Ramsey Clark forwarded to the president the plan and a draft presidential message to accompany it to Congress. Changes to Clark's draft that appeared in the final message, delivered to Congress on 7 February, are generally only cosmetic, with the exception of the addition of (1) "research" to the enumeration of the new bureau's tasks and (2) the obligation to "maintain worldwide operations, working closely with other nations, to suppress the trade in illicit narcotics and marihuana." These additions to the text were not a departure from the historical activities of the old FBN, but they do indicate that federal planners attached some importance to them. They continued to be sources of controversy. What exactly the "research" activities of the new bureau should be became a bone of contention in the Nixon administration when HEW officials clashed with the Justice Department over who should have the authority to decide what substances should be controlled. A lawyer for the Food and Drug Administration put his finger on the incipient conflict in a memo to DeVier Pierson, counsel to the president.

> The reorganization plan . . . transfers to the Attorney General all of "the functions of the Secretary of Health, Education, and Welfare under the Drug Abuse and Control Amendments of 1965. . . ." The effect of this language is to vest in the Attorney General rule-making functions given by statute to the Secretary of HEW and delegated by him to the Commissioner of Food and Drugs. These functions are essentially medical and scientific in nature, are totally unrelated to investigation or enforce-

ment, and have not been discharged by the Bureau of Drug Abuse Control. These functions should be retained in the department and agency having scientific, rather than law enforcement, competence.[82]

The struggle between science and law, between "cops and docs," over what really needs to be done to control drug abuse and deal with its effects on public health and social order is a theme that runs through the entire history of narcotics policy in the United States. The debate within these disciplines is no less intense. Medical professionals disagreed, and continue to disagree, over what the properties of various mood-altering substances are and how and whether they can or should be withheld from those who desire them. The internecine battles in law enforcement spring from the near impossibility of establishing meaningful distinctions among the responsibilities of agencies with similar missions—the FBN and the Customs Bureau, the FBN and the BDAC, then the new Bureau of Narcotics and Dangerous Drugs (BNDD) and Customs, and so forth. With respect to foreign operations, the activities of the BNDD, Customs, and later the Drug Enforcement Administration (DEA), have remained controversial, involving as they do questions of sovereignty, political and bureaucratic turf, and the efficacy—or lack of it—of drug interdiction and crop eradication. Coloring all of this is the emotional power of the drug issue as a focal point of national soul-searching, a convenient explanation for every conceivable social ill, and not least, an exciting, surefire path to prominence for ambitious bureaucrats and politicians.

The plan for the new agency was approved in March, and the reorganization became effective on 8 April. Henry Giordano, ex-chief of the FBN, and John Finlator, who had led BDAC, became interim codirectors of the new BNDD until a permanent director could be named. Giordano felt that he was the logical choice to head the new agency, and he had significant support in Congress.[83] But Attorney General Ramsey Clark had other ideas. He chose thirty-eight-year-old John Ingersoll, who had been a police chief, an executive with the International Association of Chiefs of Police, and assistant director of the Office of Law Enforcement Assistance in the Justice Department. Henry Giordano and his supporters were bitterly disappointed, and Giordano continued to hope that, after the presidential elections in the fall of 1968, Clark's appointments and policies would be discredited and he would have another chance.[84] But it was not to be. Giordano was too closely associated with attitudes and methods that had fallen from favor—to say nothing of his history of less than enthusiastic cooperation with administration initiatives.

CONCLUSION

As Lyndon Johnson's presidency came to an end, the broad outlines of what would develop into a massive response to the bewildering growth of drug use in the United States were in place. Although none of Johnson's advisors espoused radical notions of blanket legalization of drugs, most supported a search for innovative solutions to a problem that seemed both new (which it was not) and growing (which it was). Pressure on the policy agenda from the society at large sprang from public confusion and concern over the issue. The atmosphere was one in which fear and suspicion of drugs and drug users seemed mixed in equal measures with doubts about the real dangers of some of these substances. The "marihuana consensus" that had supported the view that cannabis was the "assassin of youth" had broken down, and methadone maintenance for opiate addicts was gaining adherents as a humane response to addiction disease. Respect for authority needed to be maintained, but many of the laws seemed arbitrary and archaic, and in the Great Society, sick people could not be left to languish in jail or to succumb to poverty and disease. What to do?

Deciding that the answers lay in the recommendations of the Prettyman Commission, Johnson's staffers undertook initiatives in three areas: bureaucratic reorganization designed to invigorate and modernize narcotics law enforcement, producing first the Bureau of Drug Abuse Control and then the Bureau of Narcotics and Dangerous Drugs in the Justice Department; improved access to treatment for both criminal and noncriminal drug users through the Narcotics Addict Rehabilitation Act; and, last, reform and rationalization of the whole corpus of existing drug law. The administration's one attempt to control heroin at its foreign source involved persuading Turkey to eliminate poppy cultivation. This effort began in 1966 and gained momentum after the Senate ratified the Single Convention on Narcotic Drugs in May of 1967. As Johnson was preparing to leave office in September 1968 a $3 million loan was extended to the Turkish government "for the purpose of improving control procedures and developing substitute crops."[85] President Nixon would build on this effort, and the notion of drug source control through foreign intervention would become a recurrent theme in discussions of drug control policy.

The task of studying existing drug legislation and recommending ways in which it could be changed and rationalized had originally been assigned to the National Commission on the Reform of the Federal Criminal Laws in accordance with President Johnson's crime message of February 1968. The commission delegated the job to the new BNDD, where it became the principal activity of Deputy General Counsel Michael Sonnenreich and a young lawyer on the staff of the commission named John W. Dean III. They drafted legislation that undertook a sweeping reform and consolidation of all narcotics legislation then on the books. Their proposal was on the table when Richard Nixon took office as president in January 1969, and it evolved into the Comprehensive Drug Abuse Prevention and Control Act of 1970.

Chapter 2 The First Nixon Administration: Early Approaches to Drug Policy

In January 1969, when Richard M. Nixon took office as president of the United States, drug use among Americans had been increasing for a decade. That year, according to survey data reported by the National Commission on Marijuana and Drug Abuse, 5.14 percent of college students reported having tried heroin at some time in their lives, up from 3.2 percent the previous year. Among high school students, the figure was 3.3 percent, compared to 0.4 percent in 1967.[1] In New York City (recognized by most sources as having by far the most opiate users in the country), deaths from drug overdoses as well as from drug-related diseases such as hepatitis had been rising dramatically since 1965.[2] Between 1960 and 1966 lifetime use of marijuana among young people aged eighteen to twenty-four had increased approximately threefold.[3] Lifetime experience with marijuana among high school students was estimated at 23 percent in 1969 and that of college students had reached 32 percent. Fourteen percent of high school students reported having used stimulants; only 4 percent had so reported in 1967. College students showed increased experience in this category, from 17 percent in 1968 to 22 percent in 1969. Hallucinogen use was still relatively low in both groups compared to the levels it would reach in 1972.[4]

In spite of the availability of statistics such as these (which may have been low because they necessarily excluded marginalized populations and suffered from the difficulty of eliciting truthful answers to questions regarding proscribed behavior), there was great disagreement among scholars and experts as to the true extent of the drug problem, particularly with respect to opiate use.[5] Few students of the subject put much faith in the figures supplied by the Federal Bureau of Narcotics, which reported in 1968 that the total number of active narcotic addicts was 62,045.[6] Using new statistical techniques, the Bureau of Narcotics and Dangerous Drugs, successor to the FBN, later estimated that the number of addicts in 1968 had been closer to 250,000.[7] L.G. Hunt and C.D. Chambers, writing in 1976, reanalyzed the BNDD estimates in an effort to account for hidden populations and produced the most extreme estimate of "several million rather than only several hundred thousand."[8]

PERCEPTIONS OF DRUG USE AS A PROBLEM

Whatever the actual extent of drug use was at the time Richard Nixon was elected (and it should be noted that among the population at large, *frequent* and *heavy* use of any drug is and always has been uncommon, and opiate addiction even rarer), it does appear undeniable that the rate of increase was dramatic and that the belief that drug use was threatening the social health of the nation was increasingly common among Nixon's constituents. Even so, concern about drugs was still relatively low when compared to other large issues of the day. In May 1969, when asked in a White House survey, "Aside from the Vietnam War and foreign affairs, what are some of the most important problems facing people here in the United States," only 3 percent of the respondents included drugs and alcohol on the list. The issues listed as most important were the "racial problem" (39 percent), "inflation/cost of living/taxes" and "student unrest" (34 percent each), and "crime/lack of law and order" (15 percent).[9] The Gallup poll on "national hopes and fears" did not include "solution of drug problem" under national hopes nor "drugs" under national fears until 1971. That year "solution to the drug problem" ranked eleventh among national hopes, and "drugs" ranked seventh among national fears, after war, national disunity/political instability, economic instability/inflation, communism, lack of law and order, and pollution. In December of that year, in answer to the question "What do you think is the most important problem facing this country today?" 8 percent of the respondents cited drugs, placing this issue a distant third after the economy, with 41 percent, and international problems, with 23 percent, and followed by racial problems and crime/lawlessness with 6 percent each.[10]

CHAOS AND POLICY: THE EVOLUTION OF AN ISSUE IN ITS ENVIRONMENT

When Nixon took office, the trend accelerated toward public consensus that the laws against marijuana possession and use that had prevailed since the Boggs Act of 1951 did not correspond to the damage that the drug might inflict on the individual and on society. However, the legislative process is slow to adjust to changing attitudes and customs, and both state and federal lawmakers and enforcement bureaucracies resisted attempts to moderate marijuana control statutes. (Nixon's policy staff did not abandon its punitive posture with respect to marijuana until October 1970, having initially supported the legal status quo and having implemented, then abandoned, an ill-advised attempt to completely curtail transborder marijuana traffic from Mexico.)[11] Writing in the proceedings of the Rutgers Symposium on Drug Abuse in 1968, Richard C. Allen, at the time director of the Institute of Law, Psychiatry, and Criminology of the George Washington University, described the dissonance between the emerging public opinion on the issue and government response.

> The . . . recommendations [of the President's Advisory Commission on Narcotics and Drug Abuse] that mandatory minimum sentences and denial of the hope of parole be done away with, that lesser penalties be substituted for possession for use as opposed to possession for sale, and for marijuana violation as opposed to transactions in the opiates, and for greater judicial discretion in sentencing offenders, have been largely ignored by Congress and the state legislatures, although to an increasing extent shared by the general public. (In a 1967 Harris poll 94 per cent would give a long prison sentence to an adult who sold narcotics to a minor, while 85 per cent said that hospital rather than jail was the place of an addict arrested for drug use.)[12]

This disconcertingly fractured political environment is what Nixon's advisors and staff were confronted with during his campaign and after his election. Significant numbers of citizens might favor reduced penalties for marijuana possession and at the same time believe that heroin use was an unmitigated evil; addicts might be seen as victims in need of treatment or as predatory criminals; some might extol the virtues of hallucinogens as gateways to a paradise of the imagination, while others condemned them as the surest road to a living hell. Again, the papers submitted to the Rutgers symposium offer a glimpse of the social environment of that moment.

> Try suggesting to some school superintendents that students should be given all the facts rather than biased ones or outright lies as part of drug education, and find out how that one sits with the conservative district. Or try suggesting to a group of liberal college teachers that narcotic officers are not only human but even know some rather important things about at least one large class of drug users, and see how your information is received. And finally, should you not be convinced that there will be opposition to almost any proposal which the originator in the best of intentions conceives as being aimed at the greater good, get ten people in this room together each representing a different profession, require that at least some be conservatives and some liberals politically, that some have tried illicit drugs and others have not, that some be young and some be old, and see what happens to any proposal about marijuana policy which any one of them sets forth in detail clear enough to allow its assumptions to become evident.[13]

Given the deep divisions in the electorate and that the Nixon constituency was drawn predominantly from the more conservative elements of that electorate, the issue of drug use and abuse had significant appeal as a focus of both political discourse and public policy. Even if drug use as a discrete concept elicited extreme concern from only a relatively small portion of the population, social unrest and lawlessness did inspire widespread anxiety.[14] (Presidential Assistant for Urban Affairs Daniel Patrick Moynihan was somewhat amused to report that even the "leading white liberals of Washington," including *Washington Post* publisher Katherine Graham, "had asked if the administration would not permanently station troops on the streets of Washington. *Vraiment.*")[15] Drug use and trafficking could be linked to crime and disorder, and concerted action against the former would be seen as government attention to the latter. The campaign staff and White House advisors charged with securing Nixon's political future must have seen narcotic control policies as an irresistible opportunity to reduce crime, to codify disapproval of disruptive behavior by a substantial minority of the youthful population, and to deflect some attention from problems of the economy and of international conflict that consistently resisted any sort of politically satisfactory solution.[16] This is not to say that such policies were utterly cynical attempts to manipulate the citizenry. Many, if not most, Nixon-era policy makers were quite sincere in their belief that crime, unrest, and drug abuse were, in fact, social ills that had to be dealt with, and to the extent that the federal government could contribute to the amelioration of those ills, the quality of American life would be improved, as would the political fortunes of the party responsible. Interaction and conflict, however, among individuals in positions of responsibility in government, entrenched bureaucratic interests, political and social groups and hierarchies, and the ebb and flow of "weather patterns" in the social climate create a degree of complexity in the policy system that, more often than not, ensures that the system as a whole will escape the control of both the best-intentioned and the worst-intentioned public actors.

NIXON BEGINS

In September 1968, Republican presidential candidate Nixon said, "Narcotics are the modern curse of American youth."[17] He promised five measures that his administration would take to remedy the situation. First, building on Johnson's Turkish initiative, he promised to seek cooperation with drug-producing nations to "stem the flow of drugs along our common borders and at other points of entry into the United States." He recommended that the number of Customs agents be increased from 331 to 1,000; he promised the development of new anti-smuggling technology; he declared that the Narcotics Rehabilitation Act of 1966 would be the object of renewed emphasis on treatment for drug abuse; and he announced that a conference of state and local law-enforcement officials would be convened by his new attorney general. So, at this early juncture, Nixon's vision for narcotics control consisted mainly of foreign initiatives and border interdiction to control drug supply; treatment; and some sort of cooperation with law enforcement entities below the federal level. Large-scale federal involvement in domestic drug-law enforcement began to develop quite soon after Nixon took office as he realized that it offered an opportunity to make good on campaign promises to control crime. Thus emerged a three-layered approach to narcotics control: foreign policy, law enforcement, and treatment. Each layer was added as policy makers perceived the complexity of the problem they sought to solve and adjusted their course according to what seemed like a constantly moving objective.

DRUG CONTROL AS FOREIGN POLICY

In a memo to the secretary of state (William Rogers) dated 7 April 1969, presidential advisor John Ehrlichman wrote, "Much of the discussion and deliberation here on the subject of law enforcement, crime control and the alleviation of urban problems comes back to the subject of narcotics as a root problem."[18] This memo, written as a cover note for a paper prepared by Daniel Patrick Moynihan for the attorney general, not only confirms that the possibility of addressing the crime problem through narcotics control had been seen early on in the newly formed Nixon administration[19] but also that at least one way for the federal government to become involved in the control of street crime (not generally within its constitutional powers) had been discovered in foreign policy (well within the mandate of the federal government). But Dr. Moynihan's paper shows that he at least was well aware that the complexity of the drug abuse phenomenon might well confound attempts to deal with it in this way. Although he suggested that the supply of heroin on the streets of American cities might be affected by some bold foreign-policy effort, he did not hold out much hope that such an approach would have a dramatic long-term effect.

> With a former Attorney General as Secretary of State, and the Washington crime situation being what it is, it may also be possible to do something never before, so far as I know, seriously attempted. Academic lore has it that most of the heroin brought into the East Coast is grown in Turkey and Syria, and processed in France. I know nothing of this: your people will. But it is grown somewhere, and it would seem to me possible to make clear to the governments involved that in our view to acquiesce in the traffic is to be an accomplice to it, and henceforth we will regard this as a hostile act.
>
> Even so, I fear we will never get very far until we dry up the slum population that is so manifestly "at risk" with respect to heroin addiction. Sorry to seem to be trying to talk you into becoming a social worker: but there is no escaping that you have on your hands a problem that is fundamentally social and probably not responsive to interdiction techniques.[20]

About ten weeks later, Elliot Richardson, then undersecretary of state, submitted comments on the Moynihan paper to Ehrlichman on behalf of his department. He recalled the $3 million loan that had been made to Turkey with a view toward helping that nation phase out opium production. These funds were to be used for both enforcement and crop substitution efforts. Richardson also mentioned that the BNDD was in the process of increasing interdiction and foreign operations. He discussed problems emerging in other countries with respect to heroin (Iran) and cocaine (Peru), and cooperation with France and Italy in efforts to eliminate processing and transshipment. He concluded:

> With respect to Dr. Moynihan's specific proposal, I believe that at present the best approach is to strengthen existing cooperative arrangements, and to continue the

> efforts to persuade other countries to cease opium production and restrict the cultivation and processing of these drugs. To accomplish this we will continue to work closely with the Bureau of Narcotics and Dangerous Drugs, the Agency for International Development and other Government organizations concerned. We will also continue to work to strengthen the procedures of the various international organizations involved. I think that in the long run this would be more effective than a "get tough" policy.[21]

While the policy that emerged was not as "tough" as Moynihan had suggested, it did go well beyond the status quo approach recommended by Undersecretary Richardson. Moynihan's caveat appears to have been lost during the enthusiastic pursuit of a policy initiated by Nixon on 22 September 1969. The president stated, "I feel very strongly that we have to tackle the heroin problem regardless of the foreign policy consequences. I understand that the major problem is with Turkey and to a lesser extent with France and Italy."[22] It should be noted that this directive coincided with Operation Intercept, an attempt to interdict marijuana shipments from Mexico that seriously jeopardized U.S.-Mexican relations.

In January 1970 an agreement was reached with France under which that country would cooperate with the BNDD, increase its police presence in the Marseilles area (locus of major heroin processing and transshipment operations), and send some of its agents to the United States for training. Optimistic White House sources reported that an understanding with Turkey to end the cultivation of opium poppies was nearly complete and that Mexico had agreed to curtail both poppy cultivation and heroin processing. The sources spoke of "drying up a very large part of the heroin traffic into the United States in the next one to three years."[23] More cautious opinions, in addition to those of Moynihan,[24] were aired within the White House but did not ultimately change the course on which the administration had embarked nor moderate the enthusiasm with which the policy was communicated to the public. Except for vague (and posterior) notes on the conversation, there does not appear to be any good indication that this occurred because of a cynical belief that whatever looked good was good or, to the contrary, that administration officials remained genuinely convinced that the policy had merit after careful review of the evidence. It seems likely that the drive to suppress heroin supplies—already begun before Nixon took office, then discovered by the new administration and seen by its members as an opportunity to address domestic concerns through a highly visible foreign policy initiative—had taken on a complex and unruly life of its own.

THE TURKISH POPPY MORATORIUM

Turkish opium poppy cultivation was the most obvious and perhaps the easiest target of the supply reduction policy: it was said that Turkey was responsible for between two thirds and 80 percent of the heroin reaching the United States; as noted, an effort to reduce Turkish poppy cultivation had already been undertaken by the Johnson administration; and the United States, because of its military and economic assistance, was in a position to exercise considerable diplomatic pressure on Turkey, whereas other countries (such as Burma), with which the United States had problematic or nonexistent relations, presented greater difficulties. But a major obstacle to convincing Turkey to halt cultivation of the opium poppy was that of appropriate compensation. The $3 million loan extended in 1968 to help with gradual eradication was too paltry a sum to inspire Turkey to undertake a major overhaul of its agricultural policy to the detriment of a large number of its farmers, so more tempting offers had to be funded. In early 1970 overtures were made to representatives of the only three drug companies licensed to import opium for medicinal use in an effort to persuade them to buy up the entire production of Turkish opium poppies,[25] but this effort was ultimately abandoned.

A new government had come to power in Turkey in March of 1971 amid leftist unrest and the threat of a military takeover. The new prime minister, Nihat Erim, proved to be more receptive to American concerns than his predecessor had been. In April foreign policy advisor Henry Kissinger informed John Ehrlichman that negotiations with Turkey were moving ahead and that the U.S. ambassador to Turkey, William Handley, and Secretary of State William P. Rogers would do their best to persuade the Turkish prime minister to announce that a total ban on poppy cultivation would go into effect by 1972. The only dissension Kissinger reported within the administration was between Treasury and State. (Secretary of the Treasury John Connally wanted all aid to Turkey conditioned on complete poppy eradication; Secretary Rogers naturally maintained that "too many other interests—especially the NATO relationship—are at stake to threaten cutting off all aid on this one issue, crucial as it is.")[26] By June $35 million dollars had been earmarked for a three-year program to aid Turkish farmers, and the agreement to end cultivation of opium poppies within a year was announced with great fanfare on 30 June. A draft of Nixon's announcement included the pledge of $35 million in assistance, but that detail did not appear in the final release.[27] The *New York Times* reported that "the President praised Premier Erim for 'courageous, statesmanlike action' and said the United States would provide money and technical assistance in helping Turkish farmers shift to other crops. Officials would not say how much American money would be involved, but the United States has made a $3-million commitment to Turkey on the heroin problem." (This figure is probably the same $3 million committed in 1968.)[28]

It is difficult to determine what the results of this first negotiated official ban on the cultivation of a drug source crop may have been. It was controversial from the outset, earning mixed reviews in the United States and outright opposition in Turkey. Senator William Proxmire (D.,WI) called the agreement a "pantywaist approach to the heroin problem."[29] When Republican Congressman Seymour Halpern of New York disclosed the $35 million price tag on the deal in November of 1971 he also expressed skepticism that the agreement, which involved voluntary registration on the part of poppy growers, would be enforceable.[30] A Turkish Cabinet minister was quoted as saying that $35 million was "absurdly inadequate" and that ten times as much would be necessary.[31]

It is doubtful that the poppy ban made any significant contribution to the shortage of heroin supplies that was reported in the fall of 1972. An American official quoted in the *New York Times* felt that it would take at least one year, possibly three, to judge the effects of the ban.[32] Delaying factors include the fact that the last legal opium crop had only just been harvested and, presumably, bought up by the Turkish government. There would have been sufficient morphine base in the manufacturing and distribution pipeline to maintain supplies for some time, and that is to say nothing of supplies of raw opium that surely were hidden away by farmers unwilling to observe the ban.

The shortage, as documented in a BNDD report published in October of 1972, had been developing in the eastern half of the United States "over the past several months." The agency's conclusion was based on:

a. Limited availability of heroin in wholesale quantities.
b. A general decrease in both weight and purity coupled with an increase in price at the wholesale as well as retail level.
c. A notable increase in the number of addicts seeking treatment.
d. A decrease in the number of reported heroin overdoses, reflecting restricted availability and reduced purity.
e. An increase in frequency of thefts of heroin substitutes from legitimate drug distributors.
f. The establishment of an increasing pattern showing East Coast traffickers at-

> tempting to establish new sources of supply in Western cities for Mexican and Asian heroin to replace the diminishing supply of European heroin.[33]

The BNDD report itself does not refer to the opium ban at all but rather attributes the shortage it documents to effective law enforcement and dates the onset of the scarcity to October of 1971. There were some within the administration who were openly skeptical of the Turkish move and still others who doubted that there was a heroin shortage. Myles Ambrose, who was commissioner of Customs until January of 1972, when he became director of the Office of Drug Abuse Law Enforcement, commented in February of that year that the attempt to check poppy cultivation was "one of those magic-wand statements born in ignorance."[34] Later, testifying before the Senate Committee on Government Operations, he attributed the scarcity of heroin to more effective law enforcement, as had the BNDD. The committee however, reported, "Both [former BNDD deputy director John] Finlator and *Newsday* senior editor [Robert W.] Greene challenged Mr. Ambrose's claim that the Federal crackdown on heroin had resulted in a heroin shortage, or 'panic' on the East Coast, resulting in a higher-priced, lower-quality drug. Messrs. Finlator and Greene agreed that the cost of heroin was up and purity was down generally. But they gave market manipulation, not tougher enforcement, as the reason. They also asserted that some district attorneys and agents in the field find no scarcity of heroin."[35] The *New York Times* also reported in October of 1972 that "no shortages have appeared in the illicit channels so far, according to all but a few of the Turkish and American officials and farmers questioned in 10 days of interviews."[36]

In March of 1974, bowing to internal pressure, Turkey lifted the ban, although instituting a harvesting method that did not depend on recovering opium gum in the field, thus reducing the likelihood of diversion to the black market. American and international law enforcement officials expressed their dismay, insisting that results were just beginning to be seen, and the U.S. ambassador to Turkey was recalled. By that time, most of the original architects of the plan had left the government, and the narcotics issue was no longer as high a priority as it had been for those policy makers who remained. Nevertheless, commentators have continued, even to the present, to refer to the Turkish opium ban as a great success.

In theory, negotiating a ban on the cultivation of opium poppies in Turkey had made perfect sense, even allowing for the fact that other sources of raw opium existed. In the first place, it was a way to use the foreign policy powers of the federal government to influence a domestic social problem. Even if heroin continued to enter the United States from other sources, if the approach to Turkey worked, it might serve as a model for similar approaches to other countries. The plan also made sense from the point of view of electoral politics: the Nixon administration had to be seen to be doing something about the narcotics problem, to which it had taken special pains to draw national attention as a kind of model for the crime problem in general; this was especially true in 1972, a presidential election year. But even at the outset, the complexity of the environment in which this particular initiative was attempted was not sufficiently appreciated. As noted before, Moynihan's essential insight was apparently ignored, and it seems likely that the political "sex appeal" of appearing to take vigorous action against a foreign source of domestic distress overwhelmed those who might have called for a more modest appraisal of what could actually be expected. Administration officials put as positive a spin on events as they could. A letter to the *New York Times* of 7 October 1972 signed by Jerome Jaffe and Myles Ambrose (who seemed to have changed his mind since the previous February) declared, "Few of us had 'illusions' that the agreement with Turkey to end production of opium would 'solve' the problem. But the cooperation of Turkey in answer to the President's initiatives is a significant step toward suppressing a primary source of opium and, in our judgment, will cause a serious disruption in the long-established operations of criminal syndicates responsible for manufacturing and smuggling heroin into the United States."[37] It does seem that rates of new heroin addiction declined slightly in 1972 and 1973, for whatever reason, although figures published by the administration were subject to the expected criticism from the opposition,[38] and use of other drugs appears to have continued to increase. The Drug Abuse Council claimed that "there actually was a decrease in the availability of heroin in the United States in 1973 and 1974," but cited the cause as enforcement successes in France and Turkey rather than the ban itself.[39] Even before the Turkish moratorium came into effect, the production of heroin in Southeast Asia and addiction among U.S. troops stationed there began to cause real alarm.

DRUGS AND WAR AND THE WAR ON DRUGS

Drug use among U.S. enlisted personnel increased during the 1960s along with similar increases among the general population. Given that the typical drug users have been young males, at least since the 1920s, it is reasonable to assume that subpopulations consisting largely of this group will show high levels of that behavior to begin with, but the rate of increase shown in a Department of

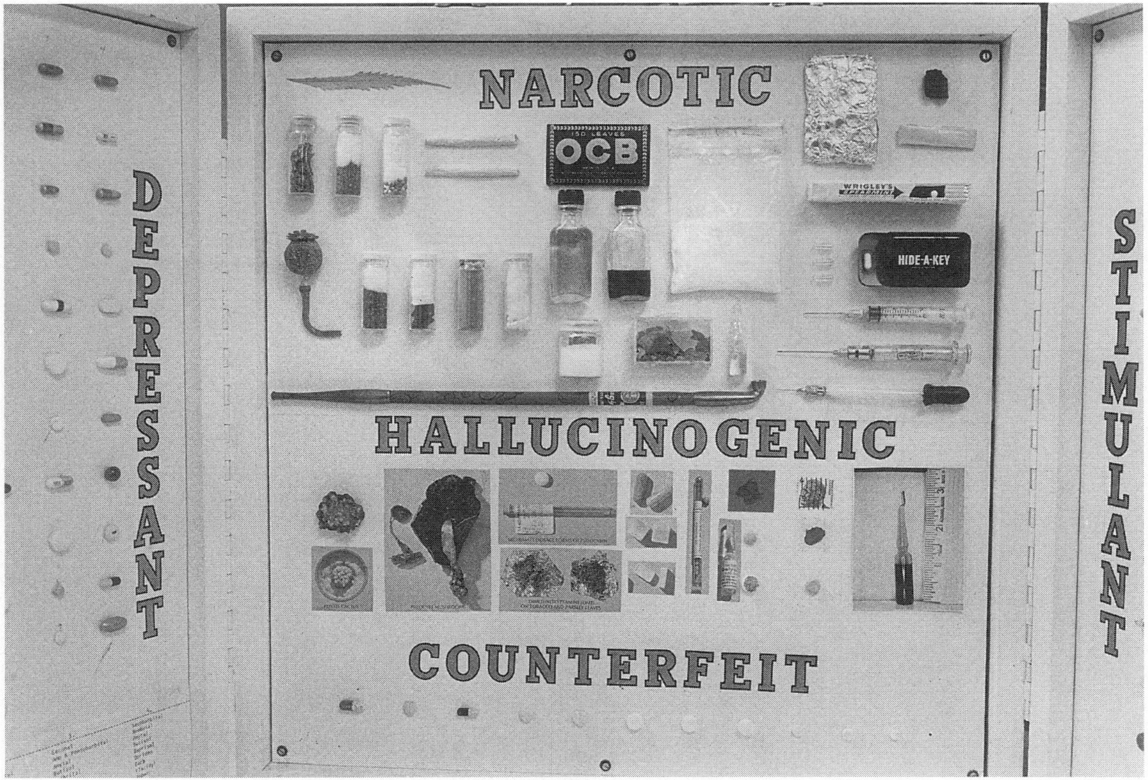

An informational display of the Bureau of Narcotics and Dangerous Drugs, 27 April 1970. (U.S. News and World Report Collection, Library of Congress.)

Defense study is remarkable. In 1967 DOD investigated 573 cases of "hard narcotics" use worldwide and 89 cases in Vietnam. In 1969 those numbers were 1,871 and 243, respectively. It was estimated, based on data from investigations, that use rates of hard narcotics per thousand personnel increased from 0.17 in 1967 to 0.67 in 1969 world wide. The figures for Vietnam were 0.19 and 0.59.[40] Obviously, these numbers are not very large. Their significance for both the public and for the administration lay in the rate of increase they represented. The increase in marijuana use among military personnel was far greater than was the increase in the use of heroin, but practically and conceptually little distinction was ever made between them. The Department of Defense reported that 19,139 cases of cannabis use had been investigated in 1969 (6,490 in Vietnam) and that the use rate had gone from 1.63 in 1967 to 7.6 in 1969 (from 2.69 to 14.77 in Vietnam).[41] The impact of drug use on combat readiness and the conduct of the war in Southeast Asia began to be a matter of great concern to both the executive and the legislative branches of government and to the public. In the Senate, testimony before the Subcommittee on Juvenile Delinquency in 1970 addressed the possibility that the soldiers involved in the incident that later became known as the My Lai Massacre were under the influence of cannabis at the time.[42] A psychiatrist who had commanded an army neuropsychiatric team at Nhatrang until the previous year estimated that 70 percent of his unit's patients had been heavy users of drugs and that between 50 and 80 percent of army personnel in Vietnam had tried marijuana.[43]

Reports of servicemen using drugs, smuggling drugs, and pushing drugs appeared at regular intervals in the press throughout 1970. In October, the U.S. command revealed that twenty-five soldiers had died from drug-related causes during the year; sixteen such deaths had occurred the previous year. The belief was expressed that the availability of cheap, high-quality heroin was at fault.[44] Egil Krogh, deputy assistant to the president for domestic affairs, wrote in January of 1971, "The newspapers, magazines and television have all elaborated the current drug conditions, so I don't think we need to point out that there is a problem. The public is beginning to become convinced of it."[45] On 27 May 1971, Congressmen Morgan F. Murphy (R., IL) and Robert H. Steele (R., CT) submitted a report to the House Committee on Foreign Affairs entitled *The World Heroin Problem.*[46] The congressmen enthusiastically endorsed the theory that the only practical way to control heroin use was at the source, and supported diplomatic pressure on Turkey as a starting point. They pointed out that a large proportion of the world's opium supply originated in Southeast Asia, but felt that once Turkey was under control, efforts could be more easily concentrated on Asia. Their assessment of the extent of heroin addiction among American servicemen in South Vietnam was so high (30,000 to 40,000 addicts among a total of U.S. troops at that time of approximately 300,000, or about 10 percent) that the report infuriated Jeffrey Donfeld, staff assistant in charge of treatment programs with the Cabinet Committee on International Narcotics Control, and he went so far as to call Congressman Steele a liar.[47] But the figure of 10 percent did find its way into official discussions of the problem and was used in initial planning for the drug-testing program begun in July of 1971.[48, 49]

As occurred nearly simultaneously with respect to attempts to reduce opium production at its foreign sources, administration officials saw a connection between drug use among American service personnel overseas and the domestic crime problem. Jeffrey Donfeld recalls the administration's view as follows: "There was great fear that people who were trained in the military would come back to the U.S. addicted and would use the skills they learned in the military to wreak havoc in the United States."[50] President Nixon defined the issue in a memorandum to Melvin R. Laird, secretary of defense: "The purpose of [identification of drug dependent persons] is to maintain military readiness by removing from the field, if necessary, incapacitated servicemen in order to provide rehabilitation. Veterans who are identified as addicted to opiates should undergo treatment and not simply be released into our cities."[51]

Three weeks before the announcement of the agreement with Turkey, an analysis of opium production in Southeast Asia done by the Central Intelligence Agency was made public. According to the CIA, the area where the borders of Burma, Laos, and Thailand intersect was regularly producing about 700 tons of opium annually. Production was reported to be rising, possibly to reach 1,000 tons by the end of 1971;[52] this compared to somewhere around 116 tons of illegal opium produced by Turkey, which was said to be responsible for 80 percent of the heroin sold on the streets of U.S. cities. The CIA analysis went on: "The reported increasing incidence of heroin addiction among U.S. servicemen in Vietnam and recent intelligence indicating that heroin traffic between Southeast Asia and the United States may also be increasing suggest that Southeast Asia is growing in importance as a producer of heroin."[53]

In spite of the manifest concern of the Nixon administration about drug use in the military and escalating heroin smuggling into the United States from Southeast Asia, the first and foremost objective of American foreign policy in the area was obviously *not* suppression of the opium trade. There is certainly much evidence to suggest that the loyalty and military assistance of various tribes and insurgent forces based in Laos, Burma, and Thailand were bought at the cost of, at the very least, turning a blind eye to their poppy cultivation and opium marketing activities. That the role of U.S. intelligence was more than this is a thorny issue at best and one that is beyond the scope of the present research. Even Alfred W. McCoy, much of whose work has focused on the CIA's putative role in worldwide drug trafficking, has had to deal with the extreme ambiguity of the evidence. He summarizes his findings thus:

> In the opium highlands of Southeast Asia, there are certain structural givens of land, economy, and politics that have inclined the CIA toward complicity in the opium trade. In most cases, the CIA's role involved various forms of complicity, tolerance, or studied ignorance about the trade, not any direct culpability in the actual trafficking. With its vast budget, the CIA had no reason to handle heroin. Instead, it was the agency's tactics of indirect intervention through local allies, some of them drug lords, that led to a similarly indirect involvement in drug trafficking. The CIA did not handle heroin, but it did provide its drug-lord allies with transport, arms, and political protection. In sum, the CIA's role in the Southeast Asian heroin trade involved indirect complicity rather than direct culpability.[54]

That U.S.-supported government officials and military personnel in several Southeast Asian countries, including South Vietnam, were involved in heroin marketing was widely reported. This, along with the fact that American G.I.s were important consumers of the drugs supplied by at least some of the supposed allies of the United States, must surely have been seen within the administration as jeopardizing "Vietnamization" of the war effort and complicating the war on drugs at home.[55, 56]

A program had to be devised that would not require compromising intelligence contacts among friendly elements in the immediate area of Vietnam and that would not depend on efficient cooperation on the part of the government of South Vietnam. The ideal program would not release drug-addicted former fighting men into the streets of American cities and would clearly demonstrate to the public that the Nixon administration was committed to helping unfortunate victims of drug addiction, especially war veterans; to fighting the crime that untreated addicts were thought to cause; and to cutting off the flow of drugs into the United States from whatever source. Still another element to be considered was the president's determination that drug abuse not be seen as one more disastrous consequence of U.S. involvement in Vietnam but rather as simply an aspect of generalized drug use among American youth.[57]

The solution to this equation, as calculated by the Nixon administration, was to establish an organization within the White House that eventually consisted of (1) an overall authority to develop and manage drug policy; (2) two secondary entities (ODALE and SAODAP; see Chapters 3 and 4), both with limited life spans, to mount immediate, high-profile rehabilitation and law enforcement initiatives; and (3) a committee to plan strategies to assist countries in which drugs were produced, refined, or transshipped in controlling or eliminating those activities. In addition to the considerations outlined above, a primary rationale for the organization's ultimate shape and location (within the White House) was the conviction of President Nixon and his associates that the existing bureaucracy of the executive branch, namely, BNDD, HEW, and to a lesser extent the Department of State, were unpredictable and unresponsive to the president's political priorities and personal convictions vis-à-vis the drug problem.[58] This structure did not come into existence all at once but rather piecemeal over the period between June 1971 and January 1972 in response to recommendations presented to the president in a memorandum prepared by Egil Krogh as background for a meeting on 27 May 1971.[59]

The Cabinet Committee on International Narcotics Control, formally established in September 1971, was the entity charged with responsibility for international drug policy. Its executive director, Egil Krogh, was also responsible for domestic drug policy. In August of 1971, Nelson Gross was appointed senior advisor to the secretary of state and coordinator for international narcotics affairs, but his position carried little practical authority. The unit charged with direct oversight of foreign narcotics control efforts was the Coordinating Subcommittee under the direction of Walter Minnick.

NARCOTICS CONTROL ACTION PLANS

According to Walter Minnick, the primary responsibility of the cabinet committee was to "put together a control plan for every country that had a material role to play in the heroin or cocaine problem."[60] The focus of his office was "to try to . . . give [drug control] a proper place in the list of U.S. governmental priorities with respect to a country and proper allocation of resources."[61] To do this, U.S. diplomatic missions in fifty-seven countries deemed to play a role in the "production, processing, consumption, or transmitting of illicit hard drugs"[62] were to develop action plans appropriate to the situations in their countries, and a procedure was established for approval of each action plan by the Department of State.

But in spite of whatever good intentions might have existed to tailor the action plans to the specific needs of each of the subject countries and to pursue

The Cabinet Committee on International Narcotics Control, 20 March 1972. (Nixon Project, National Archives.)

the goal of eradicating drug source crop cultivation, those considerations were eventually forced into the background by the complexities of geopolitical reality and competing policy objectives. Egil Krogh, writing to Robert G. Neumann, U.S. ambassador to Afghanistan, in January of 1972, clearly stated the major purpose of these plans. "[A] decision of the Cabinet Committee was to give highest priority to intelligence and law enforcement in our international narcotics control program. Relatively lesser emphasis will be placed on other facets of the overseas drug effort. Because of this decision, your comprehensive crop substitution proposal may be reduced in scope. This should not be taken as a lack of Washington interest in drug control in Afghanistan. It only reflects the Cabinet Committee's decision on relative priorities."[63]

In spite of earlier statements by administration officials, and indeed by President Nixon himself, to the effect that the elimination of drug crop cultivation represented the best hope for narcotics control, and even that drug control should override all other foreign policy considerations, it seems clear that, by the date of Krogh's letter, basing narcotic control action plans on the Turkish model had been found to be unrealistic—although the approaching ban still had political value for the 1972 presidential campaign. Afghanistan, in fact, had already banned opium production, but the medieval political structure in that remote kingdom made enforcement impossible. In the case of Burma, diplomatic relations were extremely difficult owing to that country's determined isolationism and refusal to cooperate with international narcotics control efforts; U.S. priorities in the rest of Southeast Asia have already been noted.

Yet another example of the complex nature of narcotics control policy implementation is the case of Panama. In the light of the U.S. invasion of Panama and arrest of its president, Manuel Noriega, on drug-trafficking charges in the mid-1980s, it is important to note that there were allegations that the leadership of that country was deeply involved in the narcotics traffic well before those events. In March 1972 Representative John M. Murphy (D., NY) claimed that heroin smuggling reached into the "highest levels" of the Panamanian government.[64] The foreign minister, Juan Tack; the ambassador to Spain, Moisés Torrijos (also the president's brother); and the president himself were suspect. But the State Department was anxious not to jeopardize delicate negotiations regarding the Panama Canal Treaty that had been under way since the previous June. Congressman Murphy's subcommittee on the Panama Canal had submitted a report that cited testimony from BNDD agents implicating the foreign minister and the ambassador in the narcotics trade. As the *New York Times* reported, "The State Department said that the bureau had denied 'in writing' that its agents had implicated Mr. Tack or Mr. Torrijos in its briefings of the House subcommittee. A bureau spokesman, who confirmed this, was unable to explain the conflict with the subcommittee's report, which said that bureau agents had 'confirmed' information about the 'involvement['] of the Panamanian officials."[65]

The policies that had begun in 1969 and had seemed logical and effective methods to reduce the flow of heroin into the United States through diplomatic pressure on the countries where opium originated had become, by 1972, a far more complex and confusing collection of initiatives the real results of which were difficult to identify. Whatever credence policy makers gave at first to Nixon's statement that drug control should be given priority over other foreign policy considerations[66] had dissipated in the face of the imperatives of the war in Southeast Asia, interagency conflict, and the inherent complexity of the drug phenomenon.

LAW AND ORDER THROUGH NARCOTICS CONTROL: THE COMPREHENSIVE DRUG ABUSE PREVENTION AND CONTROL ACT OF 1970

Along with foreign policy initiatives aimed at controlling supplies of opiates at their sources, Richard Nixon's planners and staff began to add a second level to emerging anti-drug policy—domestic law enforcement. The effort to enact effective legislation against drug trafficking and use had its origins both in the political circumstances of the Nixon campaign and in basic beliefs about the relationship between crime and drugs that had had at least some currency among bureaucrats and policy makers since before the Harrison Act of 1914. Richard Nixon may have felt some pressure to emphasize the crime issue by the threat to his conservative base of support posed by the candidacy of George Wallace; and the belief Nixon shared with many of his advisors that a strong relationship existed between crime and drug use fit neatly into the efforts to reform narcotics laws that had begun in the Johnson administration. During 1967 and 1968 the staff of the National Commission on Reform of Federal Criminal Laws had worked on a new federal criminal code that built on the work of the Katzenbach Commission and laid the groundwork for the penalty structure for drug offenses that would emerge over the coming year.

At the outset of Nixon's first term, in January 1969, the White House and the Justice Department, principally Michael R. Sonnenreich, deputy chief counsel of the Bureau of Narcotics and Dangerous Drugs, and John W. Dean III, then deputy assistant attorney general, undertook to recast the Johnson-era initiative into what would become a sweeping consolidation and rationalization of the drug control laws that had been accumulating since 1909. The measure they drafted opened various possibilities for controversy and political difficulty that were not lost on its supporters.[67] The early drafts of the bill provided for generally lower penalties for narcotics offenses: mandatory minimum terms for first offenses relating to traffic in narcotics and marijuana were eliminated; all penalties relating to marijuana were reduced; simple possession offenses were classified as misdemeanors; and the death penalty was eliminated.

Another important component of the proposed new measure was that it established four classifications, or schedules, for narcotics, dangerous drugs, and cannabis according to abuse potential and usefulness in legitimate medical practice. The ultimate responsibility for assigning a substance to one category or another was to lie with the attorney general. This provision, at least theoretically, created the possibility that the attorney general could, in effect, legalize a given substance by simply reclassifying it—however difficult it might be to imagine John Mitchell doing such a thing—and was eventually modified to require congressional approval for reclassification of a Schedule I substance or removal of a substance from the list. Initially, the only counterbalance to the possibility that the bill would be regarded as "soft" was a section that allowed the court "to double the penalty otherwise authorized on a finding that the person convicted was involved in a continuing criminal enterprise."[68] Soft or not, the bill was clearly designed to deal with the drug abuse problem through criminal justice.

Opposition to the emerging legislation among the health professionals at the Department of Health, Education, and Welfare was fierce. In early May, the department submitted a report to the Budget Bureau registering its opposition to the direction that the legislation was taking and suggesting a number of changes that would make the bill more compatible with its view of the drug problem as a scientific and public health matter.[69] HEW objected to empowering the attorney general to license manufacturers, researchers, and health practitioners and to classify dangerous substances according to the new schedules. Qualified approval for the more lenient penalty structure was expressed in the document, but suggestions for further relief for recidivists and addicts prosecuted for simple possession were favored. The HEW document also reopened an old debate about the advisability of Reorganization Plan 1 of 1968, which had moved the regulatory and enforcement functions of the Bureau of Drug Abuse Control from HEW to the new Bureau of Narcotics and Dangerous Drugs in Justice.

From the point of view of the Justice Department, a fundamental difference in perspective between Justice and HEW was that "it is a *policy* determination as to whether nor not a drug should be controlled. At that point in time, since the control of the drug will require enforcement, it is necessary to evaluate that recommendation, *along with practical problems of enforcement,* to determine whether the drug should be placed under control. This is not something that the Secretary of Health, Education and Welfare is as qualified to perform as is the Attorney General [emphasis original]."[70]

While HEW supported the most lenient possible sanctions, there was opposition from other quarters. Congressman Richard H. Poff (R., VA) warned Attorney General Mitchell that "Congress is in no temper to buy this penalty structure. An attempt to make the sale might poison the rest of the reform package. Yes, the present penalty structure is disjointed. However, I would recommend that Congress be asked to use its own judgment in correcting present penalty conflicts, inconsistencies and inequities. In other words, you could leave the penalty definitions in Title V blank and in the message invite Congress to make its own decisions."[71]

Michael Sonnenreich defended the Justice Department draft penalty structure. "From the point of view of halting illicit drug traffic, simple possession is the least meaningful enforcement tool in terms of agent time, court time, and the Bureau's overall mission. . . . As to [people caught in possession of dangerous drugs], maximum flexibility in sentencing should be maintained."[72] Sonnenreich did offer the possibility of amending the section on continuing criminal enterprise to prohibit suspension of sentence and probation for such offenses.

Pressure to complete the bill and get it to Congress was intense. In addition to anticipation among the public and the legislative branch of government generated by speculation and commentary in the press, the Supreme Court had handed down a decision in the case of *Leary v. U.S.* (395 US 6) that endangered the legal basis of marijuana prohibition in taxation law. If the federal government was to retain control over this drug and perhaps others, new legislation based on interstate commerce law had to be promulgated. A decision to finalize the measure at a leadership meeting to be held on 8 July was made at the urging of John Dean.[73] Notes on the meeting prepared for the President's Meeting File record that

> the only area of controversy in the discussion [of the narcotics bill] was over penalties. It appeared that in some areas Justice Department felt it was most feasible to reduce penalties for drugs like marijuana for the simple reason that it was almost impossible to get convictions for the stronger penalties. However, the President argued on the political basis that it would be unwise for the Administration to appear to be reducing in any way the penalties for drug users or especially dope peddlers. It was generally agreed that any change in the sentences regarding penalties would be left up to the wisdom of the Congress. The Administration would not take responsibility for this by including it in any message or legislation.[74]

Meanwhile, various senators and congressmen were busy introducing bills that took every conceivable approach to the problem of drug abuse. It is curious that members of Congress of both parties agreed with the administration that controlling the use and abuse of narcotics and dangerous drugs was a pressing necessity. At the time, the Gallup Organization was reporting that a mere 1 percent of the population considered drugs to be the "most important problem facing the country today" (39 percent cited Vietnam, 15 percent student unrest, 12 percent race relations).[75] The fact that the Vietnam War was cited as the most important problem by a wide margin probably had a depressing effect on other percentages, but the White House was relying on a survey that excluded Vietnam as an issue, and even so, drugs (in this case including alcohol) were named by only 3 percent of the respondents.[76] In the face of this apparently low public alarm about drug abuse, the enthusiasm for narcotics legislation on the part of elected officials may be a bit hard to understand. Again, as pointed out with respect to Johnson's anti-drug initiatives and the observations of such Nixon advisors as Moynihan and Ehrlichman, the explanation probably lies in the fact that such legislation did respond to a broad but low-intensity public unease. Drug control bills offered the opportunity for politicians to express concern for the poor and the wretched (narcotics addicts) *and* for middle-class youth, whose misguided but understandable attempts at rebellion required both compassion and correction, while *simultaneously* lowering the boom on criminals. Differences among competing measures were differences of emphasis—in some cases more power was accorded to law enforcement agencies, in others, to reliance on the health bureaucracy.

Probably the most significant of the drug measures introduced prior to the administration's bill was that sponsored by Senator Thomas Dodd (D., CT), on 18 April (S. 1895). Dodd's proposal appears to have been based on the Justice Department drafts but was intended to establish a joint committee drawn from the National Institute of Mental Health and the attorney general's office to study alternative marijuana laws and would increase the staff of both the BNDD and the Bureau of Customs, two measures also suggested by the Katzenbach Commission. There were other technical differences between the two documents, particularly having to do with classification of drugs, that made Dodd's version unacceptable to the administration.[77]

Another proposal, introduced by Senator Frank Moss (D., UT), called for the establishment of a presidential commission to study marijuana use and abuse and to render a report within two years (S. 2590). Later, in August, the Justice Department in consultation with Senator Dodd's staff would develop an amendment to the administration's bill that would establish such a commission through a combination of some of the features of Dodd's bill with some from Senator Moss's version. This amendment turned out to be a thorn in the side of the administration. Nixon's staff was ultimately unable to control the activities and conclusions of the commission, and a considerable effort at political damage control had to be mounted.

THE CONTROLLED DANGEROUS SUBSTANCES ACT OF 1969: INITIAL CONGRESSIONAL ACTION

On 14 July 1969 President Nixon announced a national "war on drugs." His "Special Message to the Congress on Control of Narcotics and Dangerous Drugs" was a prelude to introducing the new legislation that would be the first battle plan of the war. (The bill was formally introduced in the Senate on 16 July by Everett Dirksen [R., IL] as S. 2637.) And so began a sixteen-month process of legislative give-and-take, political maneuvering, and bureaucratic jockeying.

The president seemed to acknowledge the less-than-complete public agreement with respect to the size and importance of the drug problem in saying, "A national awareness of the gravity of the situation is needed: a new urgency and concerted national policy are needed at the Federal level to begin to cope with this growing menace to the general welfare of the United States." He went on to draw the parallel between narcotics use and crime in no uncertain terms, saying, "Narcotics have been cited as a primary cause of the enormous increase in street crimes over the last decade. . . . An addict can be forced to commit two or three burglaries a day to maintain his habit."[78]

Senate Bill 2637 had three main purposes, according to testimony of Attorney General Mitchell before the Senate Subcommittee to Investigate Juvenile

Delinquency, of which Senator Dodd was the chair. The measure was meant to "[1] provide more meaningful regulation over legitimate sources of drugs, [2] to strengthen law enforcement against illicit drug traffic, and [3] to eliminate some of the inconsistencies in the present regulation of drugs."[79] It also increased Justice Department involvement in drug education and research. As had been recommended by Congressman Poff and in line with the decision reached in the 8 July meeting, the administration maintained a penalty structure in the final legislative proposal that closely followed existing federal law, though abolishing the death penalty where it had been applicable to sales of heroin to minors. President Nixon's advisors were open to further revisions in the penalty structure but, in the furtherance of strong law enforcement, included in the bill what was known as the "no-knock" provision. This title allowed federal narcotics officers to enter premises without warning if first they obtained a warrant stating that they had reason to believe that evidence would be destroyed if they announced their presence and purpose. Although several states had similar laws, giving federal agents "no-knock" authority was extremely controversial. Liberals denounced the provision, and the administration complained that "the only thing that was reported in the media was that we would be kicking in doors without announcing authority and purpose."[80] Interestingly, this item had appeared previously in Senate Bill 1895 introduced by Senator Dodd, a Democrat.

The professionals at HEW rallied to oppose the measure that seemed to confer ownership of the drug issue on the Department of Justice once and for all. They allied themselves with those members of Congress, such as Senator Harold E. Hughes (D., IA) and Senator Ralph Yarborough (D., TX), who objected to treating drug abuse solely as a subject of criminal law rather than principally as an object of public health. Always careful to identify their remarks as personal and not indicative of administration thought, HEW officials advocated the greatest possible relaxation of the penalty structure, an increased emphasis on marijuana research, and expansion of addiction treatment and urged that drug abuse education be the responsibility of HEW and not Justice.

Criticism from HEW executives (for example, Stanley Yolles, director of the National Institute of Mental Health, and Sidney Cohen, director of NIMH's Division of Narcotic Abuse and Drug Addiction),[81] from a number of prominent senators, and from the press, and possibly the bitter experience of Operation Intercept (the administrations' first attempt at high-profile border interdiction), eventually led to a modification of the administration's tentative penalty structure along the lines of the original Justice Department draft. It fell to John Ingersoll, director of the Bureau of Narcotics and Dangerous Drugs, to present the new structure to Congress, which he did on 20 October in testimony before the Senate Subcommittee to Investigate Juvenile Delinquency. In spite of Congressman Poff's warning, the net effect of the new version was to ameliorate considerably the punitive nature of the bill. Mandatory minimum sentences were removed (except in the case of a continuing criminal enterprise), and possession of narcotics and dangerous drugs was classified as a misdemeanor rather than a felony.[82] The problem then faced by the White House was how to prevent the more flexible penalties from doing just what they had feared when the measure was being discussed in the Spring—make the administration appear to be "soft" on narcotics. John Ehrlichman instructed Egil Krogh to "get with Jeb Magruder immediately to coordinate the Administration's justification for reducing narcotics penalties for first offense to a misdemeanor so that the rationale will be easily understood by the average newspaper reader. It may be that Ingersoll or even the Attorney General should have a press conference on this right away in order to make a full explanation. As it is now, it looks like we're coming down soft on narcotics and we should scotch this immediately."[83]

A bipartisan leadership meeting to which representatives of the print media were invited was convened on 23 October. At the meeting, Ingersoll stoutly defended the proposition that "we will see more and better enforcement of the law under the new approach than at the present."[84] He also emphasized the importance of "no-knock" authority for his agents and the bureau's plans to attack drug trafficking at its highest levels as international conspiracies. This policy of concentrating the bureau's resources on long-term strategies to undermine high-level trafficking at the expense of more immediate and visible action against narcotics-related street crime (an approach advocated by both the Prettyman and Katzenbach Commissions) would later prove to be a point of political vulnerability for Ingersoll himself, but the administration's immediate need had been met. The impression of less-than-forceful commitment to punishing narcotics offenders, made all the more perilous by the very recent and embarrassing unraveling of Operation Intercept, had been contained.

OPERATION INTERCEPT: SORTIE AND RETREAT

In March of 1969 a Special Presidential Task Force Relating to Narcotics, Marihuana, and Dangerous Drugs had met for the first time. Its declared purpose was to "conduct a comprehensive study of marihuana with specific emphasis on the Mexican border problem."[85] Subcommittees on health, resources, and enforcement met during April and May, and a report was completed by early June. According to the transmittal letter to the president from Treasury Secretary David Kennedy and Attorney General Mitchell, the report was "a direct result of your pledge to the American people on September 16, 1968, at Anaheim, California."[86] The work of the task force had very likely been spurred on by rising public concern about unrest on college campuses across the nation.[87] May 1969 had seen widespread student disturbances, some provoked by arrests of students on drug charges, some related to the civil rights movement, and some related to antiwar protests. It was widely believed that students were quickly becoming the primary consumers of cannabis and that students were causing a lot of trouble.

In hindsight, the *Task Force Report* seems to serve these sorts of beliefs rather than to present objective analysis of a situation or a selection of policy alternatives. According to the report, cannabis use among young people was growing at a truly startling rate. It pointed out that in "1967 alone there were over 2,000 more arrests for marihuana violations than in the previous six years alone."[88] In dealing with the old questions of whether marijuana use leads to addiction to other drugs and whether there is a link between marijuana and crime, its authors engaged in some curious logical leaps. To wit:

> The evidence [tends] to show that only five percent of habitual marihuana users progress to heroin addiction. . . .
>
> In view of the foregoing, it must be concluded that regular and continuous use of *cannabis* can and does produce psychological dependency and marked susceptibility to progression to stronger reality concealing drugs.[89]

And this:

> The President's Commission on Law Enforcement and Administration of Justice has observed:
>
> > One likely hypothesis is that, given the accepted tendency of marihuana to release inhibitions, the effect of the drug will depend on the individual and the circumstances. It might, but certainly will not necessarily or inevitably lead to aggressive behavior or crime. The response will depend more on the individual than the drugs.
>
> While perhaps it cannot be statistically proven that marihuana or other dangerous drugs may be the cause of originating crime, nevertheless the use of marihuana or dangerous drugs is related to increased criminal activity.[90]

The first recommendation offered in the *Task Force Report* was that smuggling across the Mexican border should be brought under control through strict inspection and surveillance, more enforcement personnel, better detection equipment, and more funding for intelligence and evidence gathering. (These measures corresponded closely to those promised by candidate Nixon in his Anaheim address.) A second feature of the proposed attack on marijuana smuggling was to encourage Mexico to take stronger enforcement and crop control measures within its own borders. Third, the report urged more effective prosecution and punishment of violators. President Nixon concurred "in the basic conclusions and in the essential recommendations of the report" and ordered "immediate steps calculated to make a frontal attack on the narcotic, marihuana and dangerous drug traffic across the Mexican border."[91]

The end result of the deliberations of the action task force created by this presidential directive was Operation Intercept, a massive attempt to throttle cross-border drug traffic. How the plan was actually formulated is not clear from documents in the National Archives. In any case, the political and social atmosphere of the summer of 1969, as policy makers went about their work, was as charged as it had been in the spring. The "war on drugs" officially began on July 14; a month later the news media carried the spectacle of upward of 400,000 young people celebrating sex and drugs and rock 'n' roll at a massive gathering at Bethel, New York, to be remembered as "Woodstock." (Although one estimate put the number of pot smokers at the festival at "90% of those present," the police made "fewer than 100 arrests on narcotics charges.")[92]

News of a plan to declare Tijuana and possibly other border towns off-limits to military personnel (as the task force had recommended) began leaking to the press in late August, alarming business people on both sides of the border and inspiring the Mexican authorities to increase drug control efforts. On 9 September a detailed report on Operation Intercept appeared on the front page of the *New York Times* alongside a report on President Nixon's meeting with Mexican President Gustavo Díaz Ordaz at the new Amistad Dam on the Rio Grande. The article quoted extensively from the *Task Force Report,* including the observation that, should soldiers and sailors be forbidden to visit border towns, "the effect on the local economy would be substantial. Such action could be considered as an inducement for better drug control along the border."[93] White House planners found themselves scrambling to organize an announcement of the operation on their own terms. Herbert G. Klein, Nixon's director of communications, assured the president in a memo dated 13 September that "we have things in good order now"; the whole press corps had been brought up-to-date by Assistant Attorney General Richard Kleindienst and Eugene Rossides, assistant secretary of the treasury for enforcement, at a press conference the previous day.[94] A series of briefings was scheduled for the coming week in preparation for the official launch of the program. Klein told the president, "I am sure we will have some complaints because of the economic losses this will create along the border by virtually stopping tourism. I think the theme on the major war on narcotics has such power though that 'Operation Intercept' will be widely applauded by the public. I think we will earn the support from the community along the border through these briefings."[95]

Operation Intercept was officially begun at 2:30 P.M. on Sunday, 21 September 1969, under the operational control of Myles Ambrose, commissioner of Customs, and the general direction of Richard Kleindienst and Eugene Rossides. The following day Secretary Kennedy of Treasury and Attorney General Mitchell briefed the press on the first day of the operation and indicated that it would continue for some time.

Meanwhile, the 1,700-mile border with Mexico from San Diego to Brownsville, Texas, was clogged with irate travelers, and business owners were furious. The U.S.-Mexican Border Cities Association protested, and the Mexican government and press expressed indignation. Radio Station KVOZ in Laredo, Texas, complained bitterly. "In spite of a unanimous chorus of criticism from at least three Congressmen who represent this area . . . in spite of comments of protest from the Mexican Government—including the President himself. In spite of numerous calls, telegrams and letters into Washington to every conceivable bureau of government that might alter or review Operation Intercept—the attitude has been one of unbending inflexibleness."[96]

To judge from this evidence, the optimism expressed by Herbert Klein had not proven to be justified. Closer to the mark was a report done in the Budget Bureau that reached Egil Krogh's desk on 29 September. That document sharply criticized the original *Task Force Report* as "a grossly inadequate basis for Presidential decision and the policy line laid down in the Report seems likely to result in embarrassment to the President in an area of extreme importance to him."[97]

Nevertheless, the administration remained committed to the operation. A progress report submitted by Commissioner Ambrose on 6 October showed that Customs had made eleven seizures of narcotics at border ports that included 14½ ounces of heroin, ¼ ounce of cocaine, and small quantities of other substances.[98] He reported forty-five seizures of marijuana, peyote, and hashish (1,830 pounds 36 ounces of marijuana plus 9,892 cigarettes and 7 seeds, 60 pounds of peyote, and 78½ ounces of hashish). In addition, two marine seizures were accomplished, yielding 165 pounds of marijuana, 1,000 "pills," and small amounts of LSD, cocaine, and hashish. Searches of aircraft turned up another 1,000 pounds of marijuana. Ambrose's assessment of the effects of the operation on public opinion and upon the supply of marijuana and other drugs within the United States was rather different from what one might gather from the radio and newspaper reports cited above.

> Throughout the border community (United States and Mexico), the general populace supports Operation Intercept; but retail merchants have been very vocal in their criticism, citing as their main complaint loss of business up to 65 percent. It is important to note, however, that local exchange banks, which rely heavily upon monies tendered by the firms claiming the reduction of sales, report only a 1 percent reduction in volume of money exchanged.
>
> Civic groups such as the P.T.A., Rotary, Lions, and Chambers of Commerce in Mexico and the United States have supported Intercept and have proposed that Mexico join the effort by starting a cleanup of the Mexican border area. In addition, at least one of the Mexican Federal Judicial prosecutors has unofficially endorsed the program as required and long overdue to point up to the central government the urgent need for enforcement emphasis in the Mexican border communities. Numerous other Mexican officials have offered their support on a local level.[99]

And further:

> Information has been obtained from narcotic enforcement offices (city, state, and federal) regarding marihuana, heroin, and dangerous drugs availability throughout the United States from Honolulu to New York, Miami to Chicago, and along the border. It was consistently reported that Mexican marihuana is virtually unavailable or in very limited supply, and significantly higher in price.
>
> Mexican heroin is also very scarce in most communities sampled, and the price is markedly higher. Local police in some areas have reported that dangerous drugs are largely being obtained by the use of false prescriptions.[100]

But even before this report reached the president, moves were under way to arrive at some sort of understanding between the United States and Mexico to reduce the most damaging effects of Operation Intercept. A meeting of officials from both countries was held on 8 October, but U.S. representatives refused to accede to Mexican appeals to open the border. Then overnight everything changed.

Planners were caught between opinion leaders to their left who felt that the whole thing was a fiasco and those on the right who might see a change in policy as capitulation. It is also likely that they realized that, believing such input as the assessments of Herbert Klein and Commissioner Ambrose, the executive branch had miscalculated the willingness of the public to suffer discomfort and delays in the name of marijuana control. They had not sufficiently appreciated the implications of the BOB report or the poll data that indicated fairly low public concern about drug issues, nor had they correctly assessed the possibilities for extremely negative reaction on the Mexican side of the border. As so often happens, a complex environment had resulted in imperfect decision making. The resolution that was chosen and announced on 10 October was to rename the effort "Operation Cooperation." U.S. border interdiction efforts would be scaled back, and Mexico promised to undertake stronger control measures of its own.

It is possible that this frustrating experience eased the way for the administration's changed position on marijuana penalties in the Comprehensive Drug Abuse Prevention and Control Act. The obvious danger of appearing to retreat from a commitment to an uncompromising fight against drug abuse focused on marijuana may have lent further support to then emerging plans for eradication of heroin as a clearer, more reliable policy objective.

THE COMPREHENSIVE DRUG ABUSE PREVENTION AND CONTROL ACT OF 1970: THE POLITICS OF PASSAGE

The fall of 1969 saw a number of events that bore directly or indirectly on the drug abuse issue. Reports of drug-related deaths appeared in the media, a massive antiwar protest at which marijuana was openly consumed took place in November, and in December President Nixon hosted a Governors' Conference at which drug abuse was the main topic under discussion. Also at this time, the animosity of the White House staff toward HEW had solidified. Egil Krogh had complained as early as July of the leaks and sandbagging tactics he thought were the modus operandi of the professionals in that department.[101] Consistent with a generalized effort to control the cabinet bureaucracy from the White House, by December he and his colleagues were embarked on a difficult and complex course of action designed to make both formation and implementation of drug policy functionally effective and politically reliable through reorganization as well as through the new legislation.[102]

On 16 December a revised bill, S. 3246, was reported out of the Senate Judiciary Committee. The new measure combined the administration bill (S. 2637) and the Dodd proposal (S. 1895). It also revised the penalty structure according to the new administration recommendations and according to "the harmfulness, abuse characteristics and their social implications of the several classes of drugs. For example, to impose the same high mandatory penalties for marihuana-related offenses as for LSD and heroin offenses is inequitable in the face of a considerable amount of evidence that marihuana is significantly less harmful and dangerous than LSD or heroin."[103]

During January 1970 the Senate wrangled over the "no-knock" provision, which it finally approved over the strenuous objections of Senator Sam J. Ervin, Jr. (D., NC). Senator Harold Hughes (D., IA) continued his support of HEW as the principal locus of drug abuse control and as ultimate arbiter of the classification of dangerous substances, in opposition to his Democratic colleague, Senator Dodd. He also favored further reductions in the penalties for drug possession, but the amendments he introduced were defeated. On 28 January the Senate unanimously approved the Controlled Dangerous Substances Act. At that point, the measure included (1) reduction of the penalty for simple possession of narcotics to a misdemeanor punishable with up to one year in jail and a maximum fine of $5,000; (2) the "no-knock" provision; (3) a four-level drug classification system; and (4) authorization for a commission to study marijuana use and abuse.

The bill was still profoundly disturbing to health professionals both within and outside the government. They felt that it would imperil the authority of the health bureaucracy in the field of substance abuse and possibly even expose individual health practitioners and scientists to criminal prosecution or at least to both major and minor interference from law enforcement organizations. In April the American Medical Association objected to Justice Department registration and recordkeeping requirements that affected the activities of physicians and researchers, and to giving the attorney general the ultimate authority to classify drugs.[104] Later (June), physicians and scientists on the staff of NIMH and other HEW institutes signed a letter to Representative John Jarman (D., OK), chair of the House Subcommittee on Public Health and Welfare, that reiterated these objections.[105] The position of the Department of Justice was that the proposed law was meant only as a law enforcement measure, not as an all-encompassing solution to the drug problem, and that "researchers are not *sui generis* and must be held to the same high standards of others engaged in handling controlled dangerous substances."[106]

The administration did what it could to contribute to the ultimate triumph of Justice as the agency responsible for the bulk of narcotics control efforts. As will be discussed in greater detail, what was perceived at the White House as re-

President Nixon and Elvis Presley discuss drug policy while presidential aide Egil Krogh takes notes, December 1970. (Nixon Project, National Archives.)

calcitrance and disloyalty at HEW precipitated the departure under duress of three of that department's leaders in May and June. Public concern about both drug abuse and crime was rising at the time, which fact served to strengthen further the nearly instinctive preference of both the president and his staff for dealing with the Justice Department over HEW. The situation was made even more difficult by the fact that Republicans had a history of opposing transfer of drug control authority to Justice: they had, by and large, voted against moving all drug-related agencies (including HEW's BDAC) into the Justice Department in 1968, whereas Democrats had generally favored this reorganization. One possible explanation for this is that Republicans feared placing such responsibilities in the hands of President Johnson's attorney general, Ramsey Clark.[107] They had no such fears with respect to John Mitchell.[108]

In the House of Representatives, the conflict between proponents of locating the major thrust of drug control efforts in the Justice Department and advocates of the primacy of the health bureaucracy continued unabated through the spring and summer of 1970. The administration's bill had been introduced in the House in September 1969 as two bills (H.R. 13742 and H.R. 13743) because of disagreements over which committee should receive it, Ways and Means—which could be expected to favor Justice—or Interstate Commerce, whose health subcommittee was determined to include a title granting expanded research, education, and treatment resources to HEW. Both committees held hearings and executive sessions on the bills beginning in February 1970 while the Justice Department maneuvered to help Ways and Means gain control of the issue and to thwart Democratic support of HEW in the commerce committee. The situation was summed up by a Justice Department official as follows:

> [The health subcommittee of Interstate Commerce] displayed an antagonism toward the Administration's approach to drug control. Congressman Rogers, supported by other Democrats, indicated a clear intent to minimize the Attorney General's role in any legislation they acted upon.
>
> After a considerable lack of progress in getting the subcommittee to see our viewpoint in executive sessions, two steps became necessary:
>
> 1. Introduction of S. 3246 in a slightly revised version (H.R. 17463) by Chairman [Wilbur] Mills, at the Attorney General's request [6 May 1970]. . . .
>
> The real turning point occurred in July, 1970, when the Attorney General met with Chairman Mills and received the latter's promise to schedule hearings on H.R. 17463 and give the Department what it needed. Cooperation became more pronounced in the Commerce Subcommittee, which finally recommended to the

> full Committee a clean bill (H.R. 18583) on 7/22/70, just two days after Ways and Means began its hearings on H.R. 17463.[109]

The bill (H.R. 18583), containing elements of all three of its predecessors, was reported out of committee on 10 September. The measure still contained Title I, dealing with research and rehabilitation resources for the National Institute of Mental Health, and it divided narcotics and dangerous drugs into five schedules instead of the original four. This seems to have occurred because of Senator Dodd's insistence on including Librium and Valium among the dangerous drugs and because of pressure from the manufacturer of those drugs, Hoffman LaRoche, which did not want its products put into the same schedule as amphetamines and barbiturates.[110]

The Comprehensive Drug Abuse Prevention and Control Act of 1970 was finally approved by the conference of both houses on 13 October after some weeks of new attempts to include amendments favorable to HEW. One of these called for the creation of a new Institute for the Prevention and Treatment of Drug Abuse and Drug Dependence. The amendment was defeated, but the idea of the institute became a sort of "thing that wouldn't die": it came up again when the administration sought legislation creating the Special Action Office for Drug Abuse Prevention and, as will be seen, eventually took shape as the National Institute on Drug Abuse. The legislation in its final form did not include Librium or Valium at all, and the administration had to accede to inclusion of Title I, granting new money to community mental health centers administered by HEW and authorizing a number of grants for research and education. It was signed by the president on 27 October 1970.

With this legislation on the books, administration policy makers could devote their energies to the third aspect of drug abuse control—treatment and rehabilitation. The next major effort at crime control through a drive against drugs, the Office of Drug Abuse Law Enforcement, would emerge in late 1971. Its development would be motivated by organizational and political necessities similar to those that led to the establishment of the Special Action Office of Drug Abuse Prevention.

Chapter 3 The First Nixon Administration: Treatment and Rehabilitation

The third element of narcotics control policy developed during Richard Nixon's presidency addressed the problem of how to reduce demand for illicit mood-altering substances through treatment and rehabilitation of actual consumers and dissuasion of potential ones. By the spring of 1970, White House planners had come to view treatment and rehabilitation as integral parts of narcotics control policy, which itself was part of the campaign against crime. But this phase of the effort had to wait to receive the full attention of the policy staff until after drug law enforcement authority had been firmly established in the Justice Department through passage of the Comprehensive Drug Abuse Prevention and Control Act of 1970. After October the White House staff turned to making order out of what it saw as the administrative morass of drug treatment, rehabilitation, and education efforts as they existed in the various departments and agencies. They largely succeeded in gaining control of policy management by marginalizing the Department of Health, Education, and Welfare and establishing the Special Action Office of Drug Abuse Control in the Executive Office of the President; but because of the inertia that characterizes both the legislative process and the interests of the established bureaucracy, the success of the new entity was of limited duration and its freedom of operation quite circumscribed. What progress may have actually been made in controlling heroin abuse (for that became the principal objective of drug policy at the time) is an issue subject to multiple interpretations. The real size of the narcotic abuse problem was never satisfactorily established, either among military personnel or among the general population, and such hopeful developments as the spread of methadone maintenance were subject to political pressures that made it increasingly difficult to maintain their essentially medical and public health focus.

THE TURN TOWARD TREATMENT AND THE REJECTION OF HEW

There appears to have been some thought during the first year of the Nixon presidency that programs of education and information about the deleterious effects of drug use would be the most efficacious and politically appropriate federal response to the problem outside of law enforcement.[1] The House of Representatives launched its own initiative in this area in March of 1969 with the introduction of legislation that was to become the Drug Abuse Education Act. President Nixon was quoted in the press as saying, "I thought that the answer was simply to enforce the law and that will stop people from the use of drugs. But it is not that. When you are talking about 13-year-olds and 14-year-olds and 15-year-olds, the answer is not more penalties. The answer is information. The answer is understanding."[2] The administration's response to budgetary requests of the Department of Health, Education and Welfare offer some evidence of this thought. When HEW indicated that it wanted to shift treatment emphasis away from hospital care and toward community-based comprehensive treatment and rehabilitation centers and that it needed a budget amendment totaling $18.5 million to be devoted to research ($2.5 million), treatment and rehabilitation ($9.5 million), and education ($6.5 million),[3] only expenditures for education would be considered. These were to be drawn from previously frozen funds, not from new money. Egil Krogh wrote to John Ehrlichman, presidential assistant for domestic affairs, that "per the bipartisan leadership meeting, the President ordered a tripling of funds expended on drug abuse education. I have reviewed the proposals from the Office of Education and the National Institute of Mental Health. In both cases, I felt their presentations were spotty and not up to the quality we should require before authorizing an additional expenditure of 5.3 million dollars. This additional funding for drug education would be through release of funds now held in reserve as part of the 1970 cutback rather than wait for a supplemental request."[4]

But public awareness of, and media attention to, drug abuse increased throughout 1970[5]—particularly awareness of drug use among troops stationed in Southeast Asia—and the need for a more comprehensive narcotics policy became apparent. By May the emphasis had shifted away from education to an attack over a broad front including treatment, rehabilitation, and law enforcement, as well as the diplomatic initiatives discussed in Chapter 2. White House strategists were content to leave education programs with HEW but turned away from that agency when planning for development, management, and implementation of major initiatives. This is probably due to the lack of confidence in that organization evident in Egil Krogh's comments. The White House apparently felt that HEW had not proved itself either an effective agent of substance abuse control or a cooperative contributor to the overall political and organizational goals of the administration. A major contributing factor in this sentiment was undoubtedly HEW's lack of support for the Controlled Dangerous Substances Act, which was before Congress at the time. There seemed to be no way to achieve cooperation between HEW and the Justice Department on the provisions of the bill, and even when a compromise appeared to have been reached, the professionals at HEW would not testify in favor of the legislation. Krogh had complained to Ehrlichman and his aide, Kenneth Cole, in July of 1969 that "there is no such thing as a 'confidential memorandum' at HEW. Any effort by the White House aides to silence or mitigate the opposing testimony by an HEW official would, I am confident, be reported by the NEW YORK TIMES within a matter of days."[6]

Two groups within the White House in addition to members of the White House Staff devoted their energies to the search for narcotics policies that would be effective, organizationally sound, and politically profitable. The first of these was the Ad Hoc Committee on Drug Abuse headed by Football Hall of Fame coach Charles (Bud) Wilkinson. Just before his inauguration, Nixon had named Wilkinson special consultant to the president to develop recommendations to streamline the functions of special presidential commissions. By early 1970 he also had been made chairman of the Ad Hoc Committee, which was meant to foster coordination among the BNDD, NIMH, the Office of Economic Opportunity (OEO), and the Departments of Defense, Labor, and

HEW. One of the committee's first acts was to delay the release of $6.5 million in HEW funds in an effort to oblige that department to coordinate its anti-narcotics efforts with White House plans.[7, 8] Its major initiative in the general area of drug abuse education was to establish within HEW, but outside the Division of Narcotic Addiction and Drug Abuse in NIMH, a new National Clearinghouse for Drug Abuse Information, which was financed through the release of $290,000 of the frozen funds.[9] Karst Besteman, deputy director of the NIMH unit, "was upset over the lack of professionals on the Ad Hoc staff, and this lack of professional guidance was probably responsible for establishing the Drug Clearinghouse outside of the Division."[10]

The second unit confronting narcotics policy issues was the Drug Abuse Study Group, a part of the President's Advisory Council on Executive Organization (PACEO), which was also known as the Ash Council, after its chair, Roy Ash. The study group was to examine organizational alternatives for federal anti-drug programs. On 20 May the group submitted to the council a general description of the current state of the executive branch narcotics control organization. The group concluded that "no one agency, nor any one program, has demonstrated significant success in reducing drug abuse. One apparent cause is the lack of leadership."[11] The members observed that the division of responsibility between Egil Krogh, special assistant to the president in charge of drugs and crime, and Charles Wilkinson was not clear, and that "Mr. Krogh does not delegate authority to [Wilkinson's committee] because he doubts its competence and capabilities for decision making and innovative program planning."[12] Supporting what was then emerging as a consensus that "supply-oriented" (trafficking and foreign production) and "demand-oriented" (domestic consumption) control measures should be managed by different organizations, and exhibiting a clear understanding of the difficulties of teasing apart these two endeavors, the group wrote that "the effectiveness of . . . non-enforcement activities is adversely influenced by the organizational and philosophical constraints inherent in an enforcement agency and . . . all BNDD's resources should be directed to enforcement purposes. As a practical matter, however, this question is complicated by the President's inclination to look to the Attorney General for all drug abuse programs—law enforcement and otherwise."[13] The group also reported that coordination among the Office of Education, NIMH, and BNDD was far from ideal, and that the effectiveness of the National Clearinghouse for Drug Abuse Information might be compromised by BNDD's "reluctance to cooperate with a non-enforcement controlled information resource."[14]

Dr. Stanley Yolles, director of NIMH, was not at all in agreement with the direction that proposals for the organization of anti-drug efforts was taking in the spring of 1970. His assessment of the situation coincided with that of Besteman. He complained to the PACEO study group specifically about the Wilkinson committee and its assignment of new responsibilities to HEW (the Clearinghouse) without providing new funding. Generally, he felt that an interagency committee formed with BNDD during the Johnson administration had been functioning quite well until disbanded, he thought by Wilkinson. He also believed that his input and professional advice were being ignored by the White House staff in general and by Egil Krogh in particular.[15] He was firm in his belief that responsibility for drug control should lie with NIMH and BNDD. In essence, Yolles's position with respect to drug abuse control was that outlined in the NIMH report "Five-Year Program Plan for the Prevention and Treatment of Narcotic and Drug Abuse," published in 1967 (toward the end of the Johnson administration).[16]

In June 1970 Robert H. Finch, secretary of HEW, announced that Yolles had been dismissed. Yolles himself claimed that he had resigned. The *New York Times* reported that he had been forced out by pressure from presidential aides in the White House.[17] In his letter of resignation he accused the administration of "substitution of rhetoric for monetary support in federal drug abuse and alcohol programs" and of establishing the Department of Justice as the "final authority in medical determinations." Secretary Finch, in turn, declared that Yolles had "consistently shown a complete unwillingness to cooperate in this department's planning for more effective mental health programs." He added, "rarely, if ever, did he deign to participate or communicate with others in the department's efforts to bring better health to the mentally ill."[18] Dr. Joseph T. English, administrator of the Health Services and Mental Health Administration of HEW and Yolles's superior, had been forced out the previous month. He had not denied that he had been asked to resign, and, again, pressure from the White House staff was thought to be instrumental in his departure. Immediately thereafter, his job was reclassified as appointive rather than as a civil service position. On 6 June Secretary Finch himself was shifted to Nixon's staff and named "counselor to the president." His successor at HEW was Elliot L. Richardson. Dr. Yolles was replaced by his deputy Dr. Bertram Brown, but Dr. Brown did not enjoy materially better relations with the White House than had his predecessor, and John Ingersoll, the head of the BNDD, was also suspect. Both eventually came into conflict with the administration over its efforts to organize and direct the drug war.

DIFFERENT STROKES FOR DIFFERENT FOLKS

As these events were unfolding, Jeffrey Donfeld, Egil Krogh's assistant responsible for drug abuse affairs, went on a fact-finding mission during which he visited five narcotics abuse treatment programs and two individual experts in New York and, in Chicago, Dr. Jerome H. Jaffe, head of the drug abuse program of the State of Illinois Department of Mental Health. On his return, he submitted a memo to Krogh entitled "Different Strokes for Different Folkes."[19] In this document, Donfeld decried the lack of professional standards and quantified results exhibited by the approaches to narcotics treatment that he encountered. His most favorable comments were related to the program supervised by Drs. Vincent Dole and Marie Nyswander operating out of the Beth Israel Medical Center in New York and to Dr. Jaffe's agency in Illinois, both of which depended to a greater or lesser degree on methadone maintenance as the central treatment modality.

From the point of view of Donfeld and his associates in the Nixon administration, the fundamental difference between the Dole and Nyswander approach and that of Jaffe was one of political and practical applicability. Dole believed that "all ingestive behavior is in some way responsive to the biochemical state of the body,"[20] and that lifelong use of methadone was as acceptable a medical response to opiate addiction as insulin was to diabetes. He did not see his method as a stopgap measure or as an unfortunate but necessary way station on the road to total abstinence. The philosophy that Dr. Jaffe brought to federal policy was more heterodox and thus less vulnerable to charges that government was either getting into the narcotics business through a back door or attempting to sedate troublesome social deviants. As Donfeld explained in his June memorandum, the Jaffe program recognized both the relationship between crime and drug use and the moral and political difficulties associated with maintaining addicts indefinitely on a substitute narcotic. Jaffe advocated a "multimodality" approach that attempted to tailor elements of different treatment techniques to various types of needs, but "[Dr. Jaffe] cautions that the political price of methadone will be escalated by the blacks who will argue that you are trying to addict them, i.e., 'If it were middle-America that was hooked on heroin, you would have group therapy.' Therefore, Jaffe sells his mixed modality approach though he believes that 90% of the addicts will require methadone. The balanced program is political protection."[21] Jaffe's three goals, according to Donfeld's analysis, were to "a) prevent crime, b) develop productive, tax-paying people, and c) stop the use of *illicit* drugs."[22]

Methadone clinic in New Haven, Connecticut, June 1973. (U.S. News and World Report Collection, Library of Congress.)

Donfeld concluded his report with a recommendation that an advisory group of nongovernmental experts be formed that would develop an outline for a national drug rehabilitation and prevention program based on an agenda of nine items: (1) At whom should the effort be directed (heroin addicts, middle-class psychedelic devotees, etc.)? (2) Which treatment modalities would be the most effective? (3) What human resources would be needed? (4) What evaluation systems would be needed in order to generate meaningful data on success rates? (5) What would the proposals cost? (6) What administrative mechanism would be required? (7) Where would program units be located? (8) Should prevention of drug use be part of the program? (9) What would be the political and social hazards of a major methadone program? Months later, after the legislative dust raised by the Comprehensive Drug Abuse Prevention and Control Act of 1970 had settled, his recommendation would be put into effect.

THE PACEO STUDY

A week after Jeffrey Donfeld submitted the report on his fact-finding mission and following the preliminary memorandum of the Drug Abuse Study Group, the report of the full PACEO on federal organization to control drug abuse was submitted to the president. The essence of the report was that all non-enforcement or demand-oriented programs should be consolidated in a new administration (Drug Abuse Training, Education, and Rehabilitation Administration—DATERA) to be located in the Public Health Service and responsible to the assistant secretary for health and scientific affairs in HEW. The council stated, "In its activities designed to reduce demand, we have found the efforts of the Federal Government to be fragmented, poorly organized, inadequately coordinated and in urgent need of improved management."[23]

The recommendations of the Ash Council were, in general, well received by the White House, but were destined to undergo a process of transformation primarily owing to the perceived need to bypass the existing health bureaucracy and to sharpen the focus of all anti-narcotics initiatives. To begin with, the Controlled Dangerous Substances Act, at that time the centerpiece of the administration's narcotics policy, had not become law and would not be until October. Egil Krogh envisioned some areas of conflict—in both spirit and substance—between the reorganization idea and the dangerous substances bill and thought it would be unwise to begin touting rehabilitation before the essentially enforcement-oriented measure had passed. Above all, he did not want to undermine the attorney general's position as ultimate authority on the classification of dangerous substances—a possibility presented by the Ash Council's proposal to remove all research activities from BNDD. However, he was most interested in shifting the focus of federal policy away from enforcement and "towards drug abuse treatment, education and research," consistent with the PACEO report. He told Jeffrey Donfeld:

> I see real trouble in spinning off the non-enforcement research arm of BNDD. This seriously undermines the position which vests responsibility in the Attorney General for categorizing dangerous substances in the four categories. A shift now, of course, would bring the house down in the House of Representatives, where the Controlled Dangerous Substances Act of 1970 has not gotten to the hearing stage yet. As I understand it from John Dean, we will be getting hearings before the House Ways and Means Committee on the total bill starting July 24. Thus, it would not be sensible to start pitching a somewhat counter-productive proposal for reorganization until we have gotten the bill enacted. Please think about the strategy we would pursue in getting the bill enacted and shifting the federal policy towards drug abuse treatment, education and research.[24]

Another consideration was the advantage of avoiding, if at all possible, the delegation of authority to an unresponsive and headstrong health bureaucracy.[25] The main focus of criticism from Krogh and others throughout that year was NIMH. As late as April 1971 Krogh was still recommending a new DATERA-type agency to be located within HEW but at a higher level than NIMH.[26]

It seems quite clear that the emerging focus on non-law-enforcement measures did not represent a redefinition of drug abuse as a purely public health problem. It appears to have been meant as part of an effort to place all narcotics control measures in the service of a generalized attack on crime and to move away from Great Society liberalism as exemplified by HEW and its 1967 report.[27] While all those involved considered drug policies aimed at controlling demand and those aimed at supplies of illicit substances to be functionally discrete, and while a determined effort was made to maintain this distinction in the interest of simple and effective organization, *conceptually* the administration's view was unitary. Treatment and rehabilitation policy was thought to contribute to lower crime rates, to a morally justifiable posture vis-à-vis disadvantaged populations, and to the public perception that the administration was actively confronting a vexing social problem.[28] Conversely, good law enforcement was designed, at least in part, to drive non-pusher addicts off the streets and into treatment. By getting a maximum number of addicts out of circulation and into treatment programs, the administration could mount a concerted attack on what it saw as a principal cause of crime and social unrest while simultaneously demonstrating concern for victims of narcotics addiction.

THE JAFFE COMMITTEE REPORT

During the summer of 1970 methadone maintenance began to show signs of success in the District of Columbia's Narcotics Treatment Administration under the direction of Dr. Robert DuPont, whose efforts were highly praised by Dr. Vincent Dole, the methadone pioneer from New York.[29] Egil Krogh, while acknowledging the lack of "hard data," was optimistic,[30] and the strong impression of success lent further impetus to the growing support among White House staff members for a full-scale national treatment program based on methadone maintenance. By early October, a new drug education and rehabilitation program was on the agenda of the president's Domestic Council. It was listed under "*Crime*" in a synopsis of issues under consideration by the council developed by John Ehrlichman's aide, Kenneth Cole. The synopsis indicates that the council expected a report from Egil Krogh that would address "the advisability of closing the Lexington Drug Rehabilitation Center; moving drug responsibilities in the area of education, rehabilitation, research and training from HEW to Justice; evaluation of the Ash Council Report that suggested creation of a new drug abuse training, education and rehabilitation administration; a greatly expanded media campaign, and a national methadone program."[31]

On 23 October Krogh forwarded a timetable to Cole covering development of final recommendations on the rehabilitation program for the council's and the president's consideration.[32] Krogh's timetable assigned Dr. Bertram Brown of NIMH to head a government task force to study the issue in detail. A second parallel report was to be developed by a group of outside experts, which he hoped would be headed by Dr. Jerome Jaffe.

Jeffrey Donfeld, who had been charged by John Ehrlichman to find the best person to head the outside task force, had no doubt that Dr. Jaffe was by far the best man for the job. He recalls that Jaffe "had governmental experience . . . , he had credentials from a prestigious medical school, he had research know-how, and he seemed to know everybody in the business and everybody in the business knew him."[33] His view of the contribution that treatment and rehabilitation of the heroin addict could make to crime reduction provided much-needed justification for treatment as a function of a law and order approach to drug control. He believed, as Donfeld remembers, that "there ought to be a sufficient amount of treatment capacity in the United States so that no addict could claim that he committed a crime because he didn't have access to treatment. In other words, it was an idea to strip away an excuse which the anti-law-enforcement establishment used, and also it was out of genuine concern for that segment of the population, to try to bring about treatment capacity.[34] This concept cleverly encouraged those with great hostility toward drug users to champion treatment as a way to call their bluff. It was one of the most successful strategies to garner support for treatment programs among those who favored a law enforcement approach. Dr. Jaffe himself stated that "any strategy had to deal with both [heroin and crime]."[35]

On 27 October the Comprehensive Drug Abuse Prevention and Control Act of 1970 was signed into law, and the next day Dr. Jaffe agreed to lead the outside group of experts. Dr. Jaffe's recollections of the circumstances surrounding the drive for a new narcotics policy and supporting organization illuminate the conflicts of theory and practice between the existing bureaucracy and the administration: "It wasn't that the government wasn't funding some things—it was. But the funding had strange philosophical underpinnings. There were still overtones of the Great Society: Just give money to the community, everything will be fine, it's a sociological issue. There was still talk about legalization."[36] He emphasizes his own conviction that treatment does work to reduce crime as well as individual suffering and that "there does seem to be some general evidence of the efficacy of therapeutic communities and methadone maintenance," although he observes that there were few outcome studies in 1970.

While Jaffe's group worked on its report, Jeffrey Donfeld went about building a case for methadone maintenance as the principal federal strategy against heroin addiction. There were many legislators and bureaucrats who believed that putting the federal government into the business of distributing opiates was morally questionable as well as dangerous; the possibilities of misuse and diversion to the black market were too great. Donfeld was confronted by objections of this sort from agencies that might be affected by large-scale adoption of such an approach and urged the Jaffe committee to provide information to counter the criticisms. He himself composed a synopsis of arguments both for and against in which those in favor seemed quite compelling indeed.[37] His general approach was one of cost versus benefit: even in the face of accidental deaths, some diversion of supplies to the illicit market, and the questionable morality of replacing one addictive substance with another at taxpayers' expense, the benefits to society of reduced crime and improved public health and the benefits to individuals of increased employability and decreased risk of personal trauma, disease, and death far outweighed the costs.

The Jaffe committee produced a report that responded carefully and quite specifically to the needs articulated by Donfeld and his colleagues. It identified adult heroin addiction (not cocaine) and abuse of psychedelics among youth as the most appropriate focus for federal intervention. It concurred with those in the administration who had studied the issue and who believed that support for expansion of methadone was the most efficient and least costly way of reducing illicit opiate use and the attendant problems of crime, disease, and death. It is obvious from the report that the committee was constantly aware of the political problems that methadone maintenance might engender, but the group also saw significant political advantages to the approach. "We recommend that any Federal statement *avoid* embracing methadone as an addiction panacea. Rather, such a statement should accept methadone as an effective way of minimizing (1) the crimes committed by addicts to get money for heroin, and (2) the profits of the heroin pushers and high-ups. The point can also be made that this is a humane approach from the point of view of the addict himself, permitting him to become a productive and self-respecting member of the community. Meanwhile, law-enforcement efforts will continue unabated, and so will the research for effective alternatives to methadone."[38] The Jaffe recommendations emphasized that methadone, to be both effective and politically palatable, should be incorporated into a multimodality program in which its own disadvantages would be partially overcome by the advantages of other methods of treatment and rehabilitation, and, in turn, methadone would contribute to overcoming some of the limitations of other components. For example, psychotherapy, which the committee members felt had not proved useful in addiction treatment, might be used to help addicts with afflictions other than addiction, again while they were stabilized on methadone. The very high per-patient costs of other program types might also be reduced by low-cost methadone maintenance.[39]

In considering prevention efforts the group was somewhat circumspect. Their apparent disagreement with earlier administration thought on the subject may have coincided with then-current skepticism with respect to education as a means of prevention and a reluctance to attach any real importance to the Drug Abuse Education Act, which had been signed by the president on December 3 and which authorized $58 million over the next three years for various education programs to be administered by HEW. The Jaffe committee was loath to recommend substantial investment in "education aimed at discouraging all experimentation [because] it may be counterproductive."[40] The members endorsed supply control as the principal method of drug abuse prevention (as opposed to treatment of existing cases) and law enforcement as the only available means to that end. However, they emphasized that supply control was only one element among others that would make up a comprehensive approach. "We would prefer to give priority to primary prevention rather than treatment. The only established method of prevention, however, is the effort to make drugs less available. This effort should continue—but it is clearly not enough. . . . As it has become apparent that even long periods of imprisonment do not deter most addicts from returning to heroin use following release, additional approaches to the heroin problem had evolved to supplement (not to replace) efforts at controlling drug availability."[41] The heart of the Jaffe committee report was a recommendation that federal support for addiction treatment consist of intervention on three levels: support for current programs with waiting lists in urban areas; support for new ambulatory programs; and support for multimodality comprehensive programs.[42] A limited number of comprehensive service centers for youthful drug abusers should also receive federal assistance. Interestingly, the committee did not see fit to devote a great deal of time or space to issues of marijuana use and control, and cocaine was not mentioned, for it was seen as a minor problem at the time. An outline of seven legislative alternatives for cannabis control was offered, but, as is perfectly understandable, it did not appear to be based on a detailed knowledge of the debate surrounding the penalty structure of the Controlled Dangerous Substances Act. The committee deferred to the study group on marijuana that was to come into being as a result of that same legislation.[43]

In a responsible and determined effort to develop hard data on drug use and abuse, the Jaffe committee proposed a system of data banks associated with ten regional drug offices that would report to a single federal agency. (Recognition that important data were not available and that programs should be carefully monitored to learn their effectiveness was a widely held belief in the early stages of planning.) This agency would be the administrative mechanism that would centralize responsibility for the entire federal drug control effort. This proposal dovetailed with that of the PACEO report of the previous spring, although Dr. Jaffe and his colleagues did not feel that it was appropriate for them to advocate either location of this new body in any existing agency or creation of an entirely independent structure.[44] Other proposals covered development of human resources through training grants to universities, discontinuation of federal activities at the narcotics treatment facility in Fort Worth, Texas, and using the Lexington, Kentucky, installation primarily for research.

The budget summary submitted by the Jaffe group called for total expenditures of approximately $39.5 million of which $23 million would be devoted to heroin programs.

THE NIMH REPORT

The report submitted by the interagency group headed by Bertram Brown of NIMH was, as the Domestic Council later pointed out, "a National Institute of Mental Health staff report for, in reality, the other participating agencies did not contribute to the development of the report."[45] The document was obviously produced with a very different set of criteria in mind than had been in mind for the Jaffe report. It was a testament to the fundamental belief among NIMH professionals that drug abuse was exclusively a public health problem and to their disinclination to adjust their thinking to what might actually be accomplished given the realities of public opinion and the balance of political power. Depending on one's perspective, Brown and his colleagues might be credited with the courage of their convictions or faulted as bureaucratic Luddites bent on bringing the wheels of progress to a grinding halt. To begin with, NIMH placed most of its emphasis on research. The authors of the report felt that not enough was known about drugs or drug abuse to embark on an extensive national treatment program. For example, they were quite skeptical of methadone and felt that "reaction to the economic and social costs of heroin addiction in the ghetto has been by and large more considered, but evidence of over-reaction to the specter of the violent addict can be read in the somewhat premature willingness of professionals and public officials to accept methadone maintenance as an established treatment and the pell-mell rush to get thousands of addicts on the drug without due consideration of the possible long-term consequences."[46] They were also cautious about establishing a federal bureaucracy to treat and rehabilitate drug addicts without sufficient study of relationships with state and local entities.[47] They agreed with the Jaffe committee on the dubious merit of educational programs aimed at high-risk youth, but explained their doubts in the characteristic vocabulary of 1960s and 1970s criticism of traditional education, which was sure to antagonize the White House. They claimed that "recent surveys indicate that most schools are preoccupied with order, control and routine for the sake of routine; that students essentially are subjugated by the schools; that by practicing systematic repression, the schools create many of their own discipline problems; and that they promote docility, passivity and conformity in their students."[48]

Working as they did at a moment of great self-confidence and optimism among mental health professionals, the Brown group believed that the only way to really attack drug abuse was through fundamental social change, not crash programs born of exaggerated ideas of the size of the threat. The three objectives for national drug abuse treatment articulated in the report were to (1) minimize the adverse consequences of drug abuse; (2) minimize progressive involvement with drug abuse; and (3) minimize recruitment. The defense of these goals read as follows.

> Since some of the recommended actions involve a reordering of values some may be tempted to view the recommendations as unattainable. This is not the case. The program recommendations pertaining to Goal 1 . . . are within our capability. Since Goal 2 . . . is a new concept, programs to accomplish this would by definition be experimental in nature. The experimental programs recommended are, however, based on an understanding of the nature of addiction and psychology of human behavior. Many of the programs suggested for use in the prevention of recruitment are also experimental because attempts to control the abuse of drugs by reducing the psychological need for them is a new concept. A national program must try new approaches, evaluate their effectiveness, disregard those that do not work and utilize those that do.[49]

Criticism of the NIMH report was centered around the fact that, as Dr. Jaffe remembers, "it was not a document designed for saying, 'Here are some positive steps to take.' It was sort of 'We do research, we like research, give us more money for research.'"[50] The Justice Department felt that the report

> does not respond to the problems and issues identified by the Task Force in its discussion on November 9 as represented by the minutes of that meeting, nor is it responsive to Mr. John Ehrlichman's charge of October 29, 1970, to Dr. Bertram S. Brown. The statement of the issues in the report is not realistic in light of present law or public attitudes and concerns, It does not represent the problem in a comprehensive social context.
>
> One of our major concerns is the advocation of a "peaceful coexistence" with the problem. The repetition of the word *minimize* in the three goals in Chapter III is typical. The assumption that reducing the supply of drugs will not significantly reduce the problem is not substantiated by the available data and the experience of other nations such as Japan, India and even the United States with morphine. Surely our number one goal with regard to heroin should be to eradicate the sources of supply that are extracting over $2 billion annually from the American public, to say

> nothing of the incalculable loss in ruined lives and deaths. Heroin is no respecter of persons—anyone can become addicted if the drug is available. Use is spreading to the college campus. We cannot afford to remain blasé about its use.[51]

While this memo may represent just the sort of black-and-white, alarmist thinking that those at NIMH believed was inappropriate and counterproductive, it does much to reveal the "cultural" context from which any workable drug policy would have to emerge. In the final analysis, the Jaffe report was limited in scope, practical, and offered a politically useful course of action, and the NIMH document, however well intentioned and possibly correct in its basic assumptions, as Egil Krogh observed, "emphasize[d] the grandiose, synergistic analysis of drug abuse. This is not decisive nor marketable in a P.R. sense."[52]

Such attitudes and remarks are interesting, not for what they may say about some basic cynicism on the part of policy planners but rather for the light they shed on the relative weight of electoral politics in the ultimate decision to take any given course of action—among alternatives, the one that seems to offer simple, clear, action-oriented means and ends that can be communicated easily tends to be favored over one presenting complex analysis and/or a less decisive course of action that may be more difficult to explain or lack obvious commonsense appeal.

A PLAN TAKES SHAPE, AN AGENCY IS BORN

Three fundamental documents upon which drug treatment and rehabilitation policy would be based were composed by the Domestic Council staff (probably almost exclusively by Jeffrey Donfeld) between January and March 1971. The first of these, the *Domestic Council Staff Report on National Drug Programs,* a thoughtful analysis of the work of the NIMH and Jaffe committees, was submitted to John Ehrlichman by Egil Krogh on 12 January along with the two committee reports. The second, the *Domestic Council Summary Option Paper on a National Drug Program,* distilled the first. Yet a third refinement of the policy choices under consideration was in the *Domestic Council Decision Paper: Narcotic Addiction and Drug Abuse Programs,* completed on March 19.

The *Domestic Council Staff Report* showed a surprising degree of sympathy with much of the fundamental analysis of the drug problem in the NIMH study. Donfeld and his colleagues seemed inclined to accept an essentially medical definition of the phenomenon while struggling to couch proposed solutions in terms that would make them morally and politically acceptable.

> If the misuse of all drugs—illicit drugs as well as alcohol and tobacco—were discussed in only medical and public health terms, the problem of drug abuse would not take on an inflated importance requiring an undeserved federal response for political purposes. . . . If, however, the moral disapprobation of drug use were lifted, the ambivalent might be more apt to use drugs. . . .
>
> If the misuse of drugs is viewed with proper perspective, it is *not* in actuality a paramount national problem. If this analysis is accepted and if we know little about how to cope with it, then the response (funding) should be titrated to the need and the capacity to spend money effectively rather than to the outcry.
>
> However, because of the political significance of the problem, visible, hard-hitting programs must be highlighted in order to preclude irresponsible criticisms. Focus should be on the federal support of local efforts. [Emphasis in original.][53]

This report suggests that the three goals identified by NIMH be conceived as subgoals to a larger national goal of reducing all kinds of addiction and drug use as well as the harmful effects of these behaviors on individuals and society.[54] "Treatment, rehabilitation, prevention and law enforcement activities are all instrumentalities to achieve these goals. This is not an either/or situation. The law enforcement effort to interdict and destroy illicit distribution systems can be pursued at the same time that a compassionate climate is fostered for the youngster involved with drugs and his troubled parents."[55] The semantic problem presented by the less-than-forceful implications of the word "minimize" that the Justice Department had objected to could be overcome by substituting the more absolutist word "prevent." The key point of disagreement between NIMH and the Domestic Council staff (as well as with the Jaffe committee) was advocacy of methadone maintenance. The Donfeld group pointed out that "in 1972, citizens will be looking at crime statistics across the nation in order to see whether expectations raised in 1968 have been met. The federal government has only one economical and effective technique for reducing crime on the streets—methadone maintenance."[56]

The *Domestic Council Summary Option Paper on a National Drug Program* analyzed the issues raised in the staff report and offered short statements of costs, advantages, and disadvantages. At the end of the paper a budget outline was provided that showed that the NIMH proposals would cost significantly more than those of the Jaffe committee if funded at a moderate rather than a minimal level. It was also suggested that NIMH was inappropriate as the administrative locus of any new program because the "primary orientation of NIMH is toward professionals and psychiatrists not other approaches; the Institute's target populations have historically been non-poor; existing staffing and administrative support is inadequate for additional programs; administrative actions required for consolidation require long lead time, thus hindering program effectiveness. Philosophically, NIMH orientation could not accommodate non-mental health approaches necessary for a multi-disciplinary approach to drug abuse."[57]

The third document in this group, the *Domestic Council Decision Paper: Narcotic Addiction and Drug Abuse Programs,* narrowed the previous options to seven questions and offered "multiple choice" answers, which were submitted to the attorney general and the secretary of health, education, and welfare for their consideration. Mitchell and Richardson coincided in four of their choices and diverged on three. They both believed that (1) the theme for national policy goals should combine the goals of short-term reduction and long-term eradication of drug use; (2) that additional anti-drug initiatives should be undertaken in the current fiscal year; (3) that the initiatives should be funded at a "moderate" level of $60 million; and that (4) a "significant pilot study" of methadone maintenance should precede any large-scale support for this treatment (although Mitchell was willing to entertain much greater expenditures on methadone than was Richardson). The differences between the two cabinet officers on which target population should be emphasized were merely of degree: Richardson favored more or less equal attention to all drug-abusing groups, whereas Mitchell wanted to include all of them while concentrating a majority of resources on the drive against heroin use. The same might be said of their thoughts on resource allocation: both favored a comprehensive approach to spending the recommended $60 million, but the attorney general would allocate $28 million to methadone treatment services, the secretary favored $3 million; the attorney general favored spending $4 million on programs for experimenters and moderate users, the secretary $12 million. With respect to the administrative mechanism for new drug-abuse programs, Mitchell advocated vesting authority in one "lead agency" in a sort of primus inter pares arrangement with other agencies. Richardson naturally favored a new agency within NIMH.[58]

Egil Krogh relayed the opinions of Justice and HEW to John Ehrlichman on 27 April in preparation for a meeting to decide on the organizational structure for the drug effort. The meeting was apparently inconclusive,[59] and Krogh issued a plea for action on the issue "in order to mount an effective Administration anti-drug program which will maintain the President's initiative through November 1972."[60] He was willing to consider a new HEW entity either within or outside NIMH, but two events occurred during the following days that certainly played a part in, if not determined, the ultimate resolution of how and where to establish the drug-abuse rehabilitation agency. First, both John Ehrlichman in his notes and H.R. Haldeman, Nixon's chief of staff, in his diary entry for 24 May record that Richard Nixon stated that he wanted all drug authority taken out of HEW, adding that the agency's personnel was "all on drugs there anyway."[61] Then, on 25 May, Democratic Senator Edmund Muskie (ME) introduced a bill (S. 1945) that called for an Office of Drug Abuse Control in the Executive Office of the President. Muskie's proposal included in the oversight capacity of this office "stimulation" of research programs, development of methadone maintenance programs, and formulation of a plan for coordination of drug abuse control programs that included law enforcement and international initiatives. By the 27th, the administration had consolidated its plan for the new drug agency.

In a detailed memorandum for John Ehrlichman on the proposed organization for the development and implementation of anti-narcotics policy, Egil Krogh proposed the creation of a Special Action Office for Drug Abuse Prevention (SAODAP) to oversee all federal-demand-related programs from the Executive Office of the President. He also outlined the creation of a body that was to become the Cabinet Committee for International Narcotics Control, the responsibilities of which were to be "(1) Set policies to be executed by the new agency; (2) Set policies for the inter-relations of law enforcement agencies and new agency; (3) Set policies which relate international considerations to domestic considerations."[62] The executive director of this committee was to be Egil Krogh himself.

What appears to be either an earlier version of the same memorandum or a version prepared specifically as background for a meeting with HEW Secretary Richardson indicates that interagency conflict continued to be a factor. BNDD, the Office of Economic Opportunity, and the Office of Education were all opposed to the idea of a new super agency.[63]

John Ehrlichman's notes of the 27 May meeting with the president indicate that Krogh's suggestions were well received. Krogh made the point that the SAODAP approach kept control of the operation within reach of the White House. He also made a case for the use of methadone maintenance as the most important element in any approach to heroin control. Prompted by the president's insistence that law enforcement be kept out of the purview of the new office, Krogh expressed the opinion that addicts on methadone did not commit crimes at the same rate as others. Dr. Bertram Brown was also criticized in this meeting as having diverged from the accepted line on drug control. HEW executive labor director Frederic V. Malek felt that Brown should be dismissed. Secretary Richardson disagreed.[64]

On 1 June the president held a televised news conference in the East Room of the White House during which he announced a "national offensive" against drug use among both military personnel and the general population. He detailed four objectives for his new policy: (1) reduce the supply of heroin at its source; (2) prosecute narcotics "pushers"; (3) increase treatment and rehabilitation facilities; and (4) undertake an ambitious campaign to inform the public of the dangers of drug use. He also emphasized his opposition to legalizing marijuana and intimated that he believed there was a connection between use of cannabis and use of other drugs.[65]

By 10 June, plans for SAODAP were in place. Jerome H. Jaffe was welcomed as the director designate at a meeting at which the delicate mix of approaches to the drug problem that was to be the Nixon administration's policy was discussed.[66] Contrary to earlier thoughts on the issue, Dr. Jaffe's office was to concern itself with the problem of drug abuse among U.S. servicemen stationed abroad.[67] Dr. Jaffe comments insightfully on how drug use among soldiers in Vietnam contributed to consideration of treatment as an element in a policy mix that had previously consisted almost exclusively of punitive measures. "The great thrust of federal policy up until, certainly, into the 60s, when it began to change a little bit, was "once an addict, always an addict." You've got to do anything you can to discourage it, prevent it . . . because you can't cure it. Now suddenly you have these wonderful heroes [G.I.s]. Now what are you going to do? Well, maybe you ought to believe those people who say they can return and get better, or you're in big trouble."[68] The estimate that 10 percent of servicemen in Vietnam were addicted to hard drugs seems to have been accepted by those attending the meeting, and the need to identify users through urine tests was expressed. However, it was to be emphasized in all public statements that the problem was a national one and neither confined to service personnel nor a direct result of U.S. involvement in Southeast Asia. The faint hope was expressed that perhaps returning G.I.s would not relapse into heroin use once they found themselves in the home environment.[69] The president warned Jaffe that he could expect trouble from HEW and that he should not be tolerant.

On 17 June the legislation was conveyed to Congress with a special presidential message and was introduced by Senator Charles Percy as Senate Bill 2097 the next day. President Nixon's message emphasized the responsibility of the federal government to coordinate the anti-drug effort in the face of the "lim-

President Nixon welcomes Dr. Jerome H. Jaffe as head of the Special Action Office for Drug Abuse Prevention, 21 March 1972. (U.S. News and World Report Collection, Library of Congress.)

ited capacity of States and cities to deal with the problem" and set forth the priority that would be accorded to heroin use. Although the speech was primarily designed to introduce the new legislation establishing SAODAP, the president devoted approximately equal time to issues of supply control and law enforcement. Along with funding for SAODAP, his budget requests included $25.6 million for anti-narcotics activities of the Bureau of Customs and the Internal Revenue Service within the Treasury Department and requests for new personnel and training money for BNDD.[70]

THE LEGISLATION

While Jerome Jaffe and his staff set to work as authorized by executive order, the effort to establish SAODAP in law occupied White House staffers. The fact that there was wide bipartisan support in both houses of Congress for a number of versions of the SAODAP legislation is indicative of the degree of consensus among a majority of voters and their representatives that the drug problem had to be addressed at the federal level. As with the Comprehensive Drug Abuse Prevention and Control Act of 1970, the length and complexity of the process of seeing the administration's bill into law was due to disagreements, not over whether to establish a new system of federal oversight of narcotics control policy, but over the form and extent of such a system. Senator Edmund Muskie's bill has already been mentioned and Senator Harold E. Hughes (D., IA) introduced a similar but longer and more detailed bill (S. 2217) on 30 June. The essence of this measure was to allocate to the "Office of Drug Abuse Prevention and Treatment" sweeping oversight and coordination powers over drug-abuse control programs of the Departments of Defense, State, Justice, Housing and Urban Development, Treasury, Labor, and HEW; the Civil Service Commission; the Veterans Administration; and the Office of Economic Opportunity. However, Title III of the measure resurrected the idea of an "Institute on Drug Abuse and Drug Dependence" within HEW that would plan, coordinate, and implement research, training, and education initiatives. The measure called for large appropriations for grants and contracts to states, localities, and public and private institutions for drug abuse and dependence programs. The Community Mental Health Centers Act was to be expanded to make funding contingent upon provision of drug prevention and treatment at those facilities.[71] In short, under this construction, the new office was meant to be a powerful centralizing force for program management, but the money would go to HEW for implementation.

The administration, with its desire to control the bureaucracy and to translate successful programs into success at the polls, wanted the office to have substantial powers over a clearly defined and limited set of activities. It stuck to its conviction that an organization based on discrete functions made the most sense. The Congress was fighting to protect its budgetary prerogatives and its power bases in the affected cabinet agencies by limiting the power of the new body but broadening its scope to include, for example, oversight and evaluation of narcotics law enforcement. One example of administration efforts to rein in the Congress was formal establishment, already mentioned, of the Cabinet Committee on International Narcotics Control (29 August 1971), one of the rationales for which was to "head off the Democratic effort to put diplomatic, intelligence, and law enforcement functions in narcotics under the authority of the proposed Special Action Office on Drugs, now pending on the Hill."[72]

In September, the Senate Government Operations Committee attempted to introduce language into the bill that would, among other things, (1) give the director of SAODAP more authority over Department of Defense drug control activities than the Nixon people thought prudent (specifically budget control, probably inspired by the Murphy-Steele report [27 May 1971]); (2) require the administration to follow government reorganization procedures rather than simple notification to institute the office; and (3) include compromise language that would give the SAODAP director "policy, planning and objective setting" authority over law enforcement and international activities.[73] But the White House was determined to get the bill through without any changes.[74] John Meagher, who was in charge of the administration's congressional strategy for the bill, was at his wit's end, to judge from the analysis of the bill he submitted to Krogh. In Meagher's judgment the new Senate version of the bill gave the director of the proposed office far too much authority, reaching into the activities of the CIA, BNDD, and OMB. He referred to the approach as "Czarism." He was particularly appalled that the bill gave Jaffe authority to "represent the United States in negotiations with foreign governments and before international organizations, as the President may designate."[75] He summed up the situation, saying, "Frankly, I don't think we can live with this bill at all and think we should emphasize that this is a 'supply side' bill whereas ours is 'demand oriented.' The Wager [Robert Wager, member of the staff of the Senate Government Operations Committee] theme is that the drug problem in America is still basically a law enforcement one rather than a rehabilitation treatment, education one. I think we should put this onus on the Democrats and, in the process, make the President look like the good guy. We might think about this vis-à-vis a Jaffe statement."[76]

Paul Perito, assistant director of SAODAP, was also upset by the difficulties posed by lack of legislation:

> In all deference to the law enforcement community, the record is absolutely clear that law enforcement alone cannot solve drug abuse and drug dependence. Our society's continuing reliance upon such enforcement has led us into a state of self-delusion and allowed us the luxury of avoiding the compelling and unpleasant evidence underlying our Nation's addiction problem. . . .
>
> If the Senate staffs persist in what seems to be their present objective, i.e., the union of the international and national law enforcement communities with the medical and scientific communities in the treatment of drug abuse problems [he later refers to this as the "Muskie-Humphrey-Hughes approach" (S. 1945, 2217, and 2155)], then surely we will ensure the continuity of the health care delivery system's inability to respond to the national health care epidemic; and unfortunately, thousands of sick addicts, desirous of treatment, will remain neglected and/or untreated.[77]

Throughout October, problems continued to crop up. In a briefing paper Krogh wrote for John Ehrlichman, he discussed how Democrats in the Senate continued to advocate inclusion of budget authority over Department of Defense drug programs in the powers of the director of the SAODAP. The White House did revise the language of its bill to accommodate the senators' desires by requiring the DOD to itemize funds related to drug abuse control, but considered the changes cosmetic. Then the DOD began objecting to the new version on the grounds of national security, and the specter of a floor fight was raised.[78] The bureaucracy and its allies in Congress once more threatened the administration's chosen approach to the drug problem. There was great fear that other agencies would try to wiggle out from under SAODAP if they perceived that the DOD was successful in doing so. SAODAP's time and money were both running out.[79] Meanwhile, the National Institute of Mental Health was moving to sabotage the bill (from the point of view of the White House) as the issue dragged on and the administration's position weakened. Dr. Jaffe wrote to Egil Krogh in desperation, reporting that NIMH staff were refusing to provide information requested by SAODAP and were raising questions about the propriety of SAODAP's methods of compensating personnel detailed from other departments and reporting, too, that Bertram Brown was providing less-than-helpful testimony to Congress.[80]

As October came to an end, the White House was fighting to get rid of the drug abuse institute in HEW, which was termed "totally unacceptable,"[81] and was willing to accept the program of grants to states and localities if that was what it took to get congressional support for its elimination.[82] On 1 November a *New York Times* headline read, "White House and Senators Deadlocked over Scope of Office on Drug Abuse."[83] The article noted that Representative Paul G. Rogers (D., FL), continuing the role he had played in the struggle over the Comprehensive Drug Abuse Prevention and Control Act, had introduced legislation that would place treatment and rehabilitation programs under the control of three hundred NIMH community mental health centers and that a total of seventy-nine drug abuse bills were before Congress.

A compromise bill that broadened the scope but narrowed the powers of SAODAP was reported out of the Senate Committee on Government Operations in mid-November. It provided the director of the new office with more law enforcement involvement in the form of the ability to recommend to the president policies for BNDD and the State Department, but it significantly altered the budget authority requested by the administration. The committee reported,

> The original Administration bill proposed that the Director's powers over these programs should go considerably beyond the budget and funding authority granted here. Authority was requested to transfer money from one program to another, to operate programs, and to replace the leadership of ongoing programs. In making the determination that the Director's authority should go only this far the Committee was mindful that no powers are granted here that go beyond those already vested in or exercised by the Office of Management and Budget [OMB]. It was felt that to go beyond these powers over funding would involve the Special Action Office in direct operations to a degree which would be detrimental to the overall policy responsibilities with which it and the Director are charged. Furthermore, to have granted authority for the Director to transfer funds from one program to another as the Administration requested, would, in our judgment, have granted powers to the executive branch that more properly reside in the Congress.[84]

The bill had to proceed to review by the Committee on Labor and Public Welfare. Senators Muskie and Hughes were expected to ask the committee to amend the bill by adding the sections from their bill that established the National Institute on Drug Abuse and Drug Dependence.[85] The version of the bill that was approved by the Senate on 2 December by a vote of ninety-two to zero was ambitious indeed. It allocated a total of $1.5 billion to the fight against drug abuse. Senators Muskie and Jacob Javits (R., NY) had succeeded in including coordinating powers over law enforcement in the mandate of the Special Action Office as well as the title establishing the drug abuse institute in HEW. This was to be the principal conduit through which programs would be implemented and the money would be spent. Although SAODAP officials were quoted as expressing satisfaction with the bill,[86] the administration's feelings about it are probably more accurately reflected in a memo from Jaffe to Caspar Weinberger, head of the Office of Management and Budget, regarding proposed cuts to the SAODAP budget. "(1) In the forthcoming Senate-House conference, the position of those attempting to uphold the Administration's position (essentially the House bill) on drug abuse prevention will be seriously weakened. If the Senate version prevails as a result, the President would be faced with the choice between (a) vetoing a bill containing his own SAODAP idea, or (b) accepting a legislative mandate for spending running substantially in excess of a *billion* dollars for a new grant program and a new health institute."[87] On 4 February 1972 the House unanimously passed its version of the SAODAP bill, which drew closer to the administration's objectives, and on 15 March the final version was issued by the joint conference. On 21 March the resulting Public Law 92-255, the Drug Abuse Office and Treatment Act of 1972, was signed into law.

How successful had the Nixon administration been in preserving the essence of S. 2097 as it had been introduced eight months earlier? As with most affairs of politics and public policy, victory had a considerable price. For one thing, the president had wanted to limit spending to $155 million in keeping with attempts to cut the cost of government, but programs added by Congress brought final authorized appropriations to approximately $1 billion, including $800 million to be spent by HEW on formula and special project grants and contracts.[88]

One of the most interesting provisions of the original bill was its "sunset clause": Section 14, paragraph b of S. 2097 as written in June 1971 established that "this Act shall terminate on June 30, 1974, unless extended by the President, in which case it shall expire on June 30, 1976, or such earlier date after June 30, 1974, as the President may prescribe and publish in the Federal Register." Why this was done in a matter of debate. Jeffrey Donfeld recalls that "we had come to the conclusion that if we could not achieve what we set out to achieve within a finite period of time, we didn't want to be part of the problem. We did not want to set up a monument to ourselves by establishing yet another bureaucratic entity. If we couldn't do it in—what was it?—five years, the damn thing ought to self-destruct. And I don't think there are too many administrations that can take credit for that kind of foresight."[89] Jerome Jaffe attributes the inclusion of the sunset clause to the need to assure Congress that the executive branch was not intent on usurping any of its powers. "This super group in the White House with power to move things, despite what Congress wants to do—you have this kind of czar-like capacity to say, 'No, it's going to be here'—is encroaching on Congress, it's encroaching on OMB, encroaching on the secretaries. Now I think people were sufficiently concerned that things are not organized, and we've got to get them together, so they said, 'Let's do it, but let's make sure it doesn't go on indefinitely.' And I fully understood that that was the compromise."[90] Egil Krogh's memory of that aspect of the SAODAP effort closes the gap between the administration's original position and what was in fact legislated. "We put a three-year time limit on SAODAP. It was to do its job and then stop. And then hopefully at that point the policies that it had put in place, the priorities that had been established, could be carried out by the departments and agencies."[91] The law as enacted eliminated the power of the president to extend the life of the office but added a year to its de jure existence by stipulating an expiration date of 30 June 1975. At the same time, the law retained the National Institute on Drug Abuse (NIDA) in HEW that had been anathema to the White House planners, but this body was to come into existence by 31 December 1974, overlapping SAODAP by only six months. So the administration had its Special Action Office that would attempt to devise and coordinate a powerful attack on narcotics abuse outside the channels of the health bureaucracy at least in time for the 1972 presidential elections, but HEW would, in the end, inherit its mandate in the form of NIDA.

SAODAP AND VIETNAM

The first major task undertaken by SAODAP, operating under the authority of an executive order, was to oversee DOD programs aimed at identifying and detoxifying narcotics-abusing service personnel before they could be returned from Vietnam to the United States. The concerted drive against narcotics use in Southeast Asia had begun in early June 1971, when Richard Nixon had issued what amounted to an ultimatum to Secretary of Defense Melvin R. Laird. He began by telling Secretary Laird that "drug abuse in the Armed Forces, especially heroin addiction, has reached intolerable proportions both in real terms and as a political issue. Swift action is required for the identification and treatment of heroin addicts."[92] On 11 June, the president sent Laird a list of actions to be undertaken, including identification of drug-using servicemen departing from Vietnam, detoxification and treatment, and research and planning activities.[93] Jerome Jaffe calls the quick military response to this directive "amazing" (urine testing in Vietnam began on 18 June). The measures taken were decisively implemented and at first appeared to be largely successful in gauging the extent of opiate use among the troops and in keeping addicted servicemen from being discharged while still actively using narcotics. Jaffe stresses that the program was a simple one set up to test only those soldiers scheduled to leave Vietnam so they would not be discharged while still addicted.

On 17 July he reported to the president after a trip to Vietnam to judge the efficacy of the military drug-testing and detoxification program. He stated that the number of men seeking treatment had risen and that the number of addicts seemed to be well below the original estimate of 10 percent. Dr. Jaffe was careful to point out that only those men scheduled to leave Vietnam had been tested, that they all knew beforehand that testing would take place, and that those tested did not represent a proper random sample of all service personnel in Vietnam. "To date the cumulative percentage of heroin positive tests is about 4.5%, or about 1,000 men of the 22,000 tested. With all the foregoing caveats in mind, Mr. President, I believe that this is a reasonable estimate of the problem. Furthermore, I don't believe that the entire 4.5% consists of confirmed narcotics users, but includes at least a certain number of experimenters who were caught in the screening net."[94]

The president was told in later discussion that the number of men found positive by using TLC (thin layer chromatography) was only 1.72 percent cumulatively, but that for technical reasons Dr. Jaffe felt that this was an unrealistically low figure and should not even be published.[95, 96]

But, as has been pointed out, the facts regarding the use and abuse of drugs are elusive, and the effect that any course of action may have on the size and shape of the problem is always a matter of debate. Both large events and small variables influence the whole in unanticipated ways. For example, there were reports that Army Regulation 635-212 (known as "two-twelve"), which provided for the discharge of soldiers unfit for service, was being used to release servicemen who were active heroin users without detoxification or rehabilitation. This eventuality had probably not been anticipated by SAODAP planners, although Dr. Jaffe had recognized some of the shortcomings of military drug treatment programs for active duty personnel in his report to the president of 17 July. Jaffe said, and the *New York Times* reported, that some heroin-using soldiers were "de-toxed" for four to seven days and could then be sent back to their units, where they often resumed using the drug. Soldier-addicts could also volunteer for a two-week rehabilitation program, but only once. "Two-time losers [were] also candidates for the two-twelve."[97]

A follow-up study of the DOD intervention in Vietnam was done for SAODAP between May and September of 1972 by Lee N. Robins and others of Washington University in St. Louis. The study, which was exclusively of army enlisted men who had returned to the United States in September 1971, turned up both good news and bad news, neither of which seems to be closely related to the testing program itself. In fact, the data suggested that at least some drug users were not detected by the screening program at all. The study supported the conclusion that servicemen who had returned to the United States were not dependent on heroin in any large numbers and that they were not contributing in any significant way to crime rates or burdening the treatment system. Given the overwhelming concern with heroin that was the hallmark of federal drug policy at the time, and the fear—articulated by Jeffrey Donfeld and Jerome Jaffe—that addicted ex-soldiers might pose a threat to social order, the finding that heavy heroin use was not prevalent among returning veterans was a cause for celebration. After the hard-won success of securing the cooperation of the Defense Department and other concerned agencies and with the obvious justification that the results of the study provided to their efforts, SAODAP staff were not particularly struck by the fact—also reported in the study—that the returnees did continue to use other substances, particularly alcohol and non-opiate drugs, and that they were not particularly interested in quitting. The authors declared that "rather than giving up drugs altogether, many had shifted from heroin to amphetamines or barbiturates. Nevertheless, almost none expressed a desire for treatment."[98]

The data also indicated that heroin dependence among the follow-up group had been much more prevalent while in Vietnam than among the group reported on by Dr. Jaffe, and more so than Congressmen Murphy and Steele had reported the previous May. The authors of the study disclaimed the validity of any direct comparison between their data (applicable only to those army enlisted men returned to the States in September 1971) and other published estimates of the extent of drug use among all American military personnel in Vietnam.[99] Even so, the numbers are arresting. "Over all, one out of five (20 per cent) of all Army enlisted men returning in September 1971 said that they felt that they had been 'strung out' on heroin while in Vietnam. While we cannot be certain that all who said they were addicted actually were so, all had used narcotics regularly for more than one month, and 83 per cent for more than six months, suggesting that the figure of 20 per cent is realistic."[100]

At the same time, the study discovered that whereas many of the returned men had used opiates at some point since their return, very few showed any sign of dependence. (Some of those who did had not been detected as drug users prior to their departure from Southeast Asia.) They concluded, "Contrary to conventional belief, the occasional use of narcotics without becoming addicted appears to be possible even for men who have previously been dependent on narcotics. The returnees' lack of interest in obtaining treatment for drug use perhaps reflects this experience with successful voluntary abstinence and light use."[101] This was not to be the only time that attempting an accurate measure of the drug problem proved to be unexpectedly complicated.

MEASURING THE ADDICT POPULATION

Title III of the Drug Abuse Office and Treatment Act of 1972 enjoined the president to establish a Strategy Council composed of the director of SAODAP, the attorney general, the secretaries of HEW, state and defense, the administrator of the Veterans Administration, and any other officials that he might deem appropriate. The principal task of this council would be to submit to Congress an annual strategy report covering the accomplishments and plans for all federal agencies involved in the struggle against drugs. An important element of the strategy was to be "an analysis of the nature, character, and extent of the drug abuse problem in the United States."[102] In other words, the council was expected to provide, among other things, some measure of how many drug abusers there actually were in the country. (The council didn't function as intended until the Carter administration and even then had an erratic existence.) The answer to this question proved to be no less ambiguous and perhaps even more politically perilous than the issue of how many soldiers were dependent upon opiates.

The first federal agency to make an attempt to track the size of the addict population was the Federal Bureau of Narcotics, predecessor to the Bureau of Narcotics and Dangerous Drugs, which was created in 1968. The FBN had relied on reports from local police to arrive at a total for the nation. This method yielded a total of 62,045 known narcotics addicts in 1968.[103] BNDD officials made the reasonable assumption that a considerable number of narcotics abusers would not be known to the police and tried to develop a method that would estimate that unknown population based on the known one. They produced estimates of 315,000 "addict/users" in 1969, 524,000 in 1970, and 559,000 in 1971. Differences among various uses of the term "addict," as well as among statistical methods, seem to have contributed greatly to the confusion. John Ingersoll, director of BNDD, wrote to PACEO in January of 1970 saying that, based on estimates of total consumption of heroin in the United States, there were between 148,000 and 180,000 *addicts* in the country in June of 1969.[104] In June 1971, he reported at a bipartisan congressional briefing on the president's drug message that there were 300,000 *heroin addicts* in the United States.[105] The larger figures apparently reflect the application of the word "addict" to any heroin user and an attempt to include these in the estimate. The effect of this sort of blurring is apparent in the following quotation from the administration's public information files. "In an effort to give a more responsive estimate of the number of heroin addicts in the United States, the Bureau of Narcotics and Dangerous Drugs employed the 'capture-recapture' method for estimating the total addict population for 1969. Among the factors considered in this method are new, recorded addicts, those in hospitals, jails and other institutions, and those who have died or been rehabilitated. . . . If we assume that 60% of the estimated 560,000 heroin addicts steal property to support their habit, more than $18 billion worth of property is stolen each year to pay for heroin addiction."[106] Then there is this from material prepared by Egil Krogh for testimony before a Los Angeles grand jury (emphasis is added).

1. Federal drug abuse agencies estimate the number of heroin *users* at from 515,000 to 560,000. Estimates of heroin consumption range from four to six tons a year. . . .
4. The Bureau of Narcotics and Dangerous Drugs (BNDD), which produced the estimate of 560,000 *addicts*, also reports that heroin *users* probably spend from $3 to $50 a day to support their habit. BNDD puts the average addiction cost at $30 a day. That means a daily narcotics expenditure of more than $16,750,000.[107]

Dr. Jerome Jaffe, in an interview with a *New York Times* reporter who quoted the BNDD's "addict/user" figure for the time of 559,000, said, "They are such crude estimates that the fewer times we mention them, the better." He added that SAODAP preferred a more conservative estimate of 300,000.[108] Some felt at the time that Dr. Jaffe was attempting to put the best face on the situation as the presidential election approached—which is possible—but it is also true that, given both the semantic and statistical difficulties of the issue, there is little reason to doubt that his estimate was a valid interpretation of the scarce data available.

Whatever his initial motivation might have been, Dr. Jaffe had accepted the BNDD approach by the time he testified before the House Committee on the Judiciary in October—with the election a mere month away.

> When we began work in 1971, we confronted the fact that no one could provide a reliable estimate of the size of the problem—nor an acceptable way of going about it. At that time, for planning purposes, we took the least unreliable number available—an estimate of 300,000–350,000 addicts. Other estimates were higher and lower.
>
> Since then, we have reviewed carefully all the estimating methods in use. We are still not satisfied with any, but we now know enough to revise our planning estimate. On the basis of two or three different methods, we believe the number of heroin addicts and users must be revised to between 500,000 and 600,000. Please note that I said "revise" and not "grown." There had been much confusion on this point. None of the estimating techniques in general use until recently have been of any use in estimating growth rates.
>
> The research indicates major epidemic growth took place from 1965 to 1969; during this period, the number of new addicts grew at an accelerating rate. Since 1969, the rate of increase has slowed.
>
> I would be happy to tell you how the estimates are figured.
>
> The BNDD estimate is based on a dilution principle which is a capture, recapture technique. In other words, you look at who was arrested in one year as an addict and are then released in a subsequent year; you see how many people are rearrested and you look to see how many are old ones and how many are new ones; on that basis you try to figure out how many addicts and users are really out there.[109]

The acceptance of the estimate of 500,000 to 600,000 addicts and users presented a political problem to the administration. The decision on how to handle the apparent growth in the size of the heroin problem had been made during the summer[110] and is reflected in Jaffe's testimony. Richard Harkness, who was in charge of public information on the drug issue at the time, had told Egil Krogh that "we should emphasize at every opportunity the fact that the figures come from a revision of our statistical procedures: there can be no valid comparison with prior estimates."[111] How successful were efforts to avoid embarrassing—and usually inaccurate—comparisons? Judging from the following from the *New York Times,* not very. "The estimated number of heroin addicts in the United States has multiplied 12 times in the last 10 years, an official of the Justice Department's Office of National Narcotics Intelligence said yesterday.

Dan McAuliffe told the annual convention of the National Association of Citizen Crime Commissions that there were an estimated 600,000 heroin addicts in the country today compared with 50,000 10 years ago. He said that while the rate of heroin addiction is far higher now, it is increasing at a slower rate."[112]

When the first *Federal Strategy for Drug Abuse and Drug Traffic Prevention* was presented to Congress under the terms of the Drug Abuse Office and Treatment Act of 1972, the problem of measuring the size of the heroin problem remained as knotty as ever. The *Strategy,* published in June of 1973, reiterated Dr. Jaffe's testimony of the previous October.

> Any estimate of the extent of the narcotics problem in the United States must recognize that not all who use narcotics are narcotic addicts. This need to differentiate among users creates major difficulties in estimating the size of "the problem."
>
> There is no entirely satisfactory method for estimating the number of heroin addicts in the United States. After considering the results of several methods, our best estimate placed the number of addicts and users, in 1972, between 500,000 and 600,000. But we know the population also contains ex-addicts and many who are temporarily abstinent as well as addicts and active users. The difficulty is in knowing how many people fall into each category.[113]

The problem did not go away—in some ways it got worse. An incident that occurred in the summer of 1974, which can only be called the birth of a factoid, provides an example. In the autumn of 1973 Dr. Jaffe's successor, Robert L. DuPont estimated that the number of active heroin addicts had been reduced by 50 percent.[114] The following year he testified that "the *active pool of heroin users* was 630,000 in 1971 and 610,000 in 1972. The 1973 estimate fell slightly to 580,000 *narcotic users,* of which about 40 percent or 250,000 are estimated to be *active heroin users.* These 250,000 active heroin users are one measure of the unfinished task before us" (Emphasis added).[115] Although this statement was made in October of 1974, it seems likely that it reflects information that had been available earlier. On 11 July, Senator Walter Mondale (D., MN) introduced an amendment to the Controlled Dangerous Substances Act to limit foreign aid to countries deemed uncooperative in efforts to curtail production of opium poppies. He was motivated by the recent decision by the government of Turkey to allow resumption of poppy cultivation. As evidence of the success of the poppy ban he declared that "since [1971] the number of estimated heroin addicts in this country has dropped by 60 percent from something like 600,000 to 250,000. In the Nation's capital the number of heroin addicts had dropped from an estimated 16,000 to 2,000."[116] Senator Packwood (R., OR) repeated the estimate later the same day.[117] Two days later, the editorial page of the *New York Times* enjoined the government of Turkey to reconsider its action and declared unequivocally that "since the ban, the number of American addicts has dropped about 60 percent."[118]

CONCLUSION

The architecture of drug abuse control policy in the Nixon administration emerged from the political decision to act against crime; the nature of the drug problem itself required bringing public health measures into the service of public order; and the nature of the administration's practical and political goals required that public health initiatives, like enforcement measures, be closely controlled by people not likely to have conflicting loyalties. The structure had a number of strengths: treatment and rehabilitation did enjoy funding levels not seen since that time,[119] and problems of drug use in the military were addressed seriously, if imperfectly. But the political necessity of dealing with a difficult social issue in ways that would be understandable and acceptable to the electorate, and probably the president's personal antipathy toward the leaders of HEW and BNDD as well, led White House planners to accept a fairly simple cause-and-effect interpretation of the relationship between drug use and crime and to favor alternatives that tended not to address the problem in its full complexity.

Chapter 4 The Second Nixon Administration: Drug Abuse Control

The overriding concern of the Nixon organization during 1972 was the fall election. Reports of a burglary at the headquarters of the Democratic National Committee in the Watergate building, in Washington, D.C., which began to appear on 18 June and which involved some people associated with the Committee to Re-elect the President (CRP), had no apparent effect on political or programmatic plans related to the narcotics problem. The "Watergate caper," as H.R. Haldeman refers in his diaries to the affair that led to the president's resignation, was to remain a background issue through the November election in spite of indictments handed down in September against G. Gordon Liddy and six others associated with the break-in and steadily increasing press coverage of irregular activities carried out by the staffs of CRP and the White House. Richard Nixon was reelected in November of 1972 with 60.7 percent of the popular vote, a margin of victory second only to that of Lyndon Johnson over Barry Goldwater in 1964. It must be allowed that the administration's approach to law and order issues in general and to drug abuse and related crime in particular played a part in the victory.

THE OFFICE OF DRUG ABUSE LAW ENFORCEMENT

Probably the most controversial of Nixon's 1972 initiatives was the Office of Drug Abuse Law Enforcement (ODALE). The office was ostensibly designed as a tool to enable the federal government to assist local governments to enforce drug laws and oblige addicts to enter treatment (either out of desperation caused by reduced supplies or as an alternative to incarceration), thereby reducing street crime. Some have suggested that ODALE was part of a byzantine White House plot to use drug control legislation as a platform for a domestic secret police in the service of a sort of palace coup.[1] Such scenarios are best left to novelists. The more likely impetus behind the creation of ODALE was the need to show decisive action against crime in an election year and to circumvent what was seen as bureaucratic inertia and unwillingness to "get with the program" at the Treasury Department and the Bureau of Narcotics and Dangerous Drugs—a situation comparable to that which existed at HEW and which had, in part, motivated the creation of SAODAP. The idea was to select a number of cities thought to have a significant drug problem and to establish in them teams made up of federal and local prosecutors and law enforcement agents whose task it would be to hound drug pushers to earth making use of special grand juries, prosecute them, and convict them. The origins of the approach are obscure. Myles Ambrose, commissioner of Customs until January 1972, when he became the head of ODALE, believes the idea originated with him and describes its inception as follows.

> I submitted to the White House a proposal, probably in 1970. It was the result of a memorandum that I then got from the secretary of the treasury, Charls Walker, acting on behalf of the cabinet group that were discussing ideas for increasing the enforcement activities and what we should do—they wanted independent ideas from senior officials. . . . I said we needed some shock treatment—not long-lasting but immediate shock treatment utilizing whatever resources we had available. . . . I suggested we emulate to some extent the strike forces, which were having a considerable impact on . . . organized crime. And then a year later, I got a call . . . to come over and talk to them about it, which I did. And from that, Bud [Egil] Krogh and Geoff Shepard . . . —we evolved a program which we called ODALE, which was of eighteen months' duration.[2]

But there are indications that similar ideas had been in circulation for some time. Daniel Patrick Moynihan cited James Q. Wilson as the source of one of these. "Attorney General Clark seems to have had some success with his 'strike force' concept in attacking organized crime in Buffalo. Wilson, at all events, feels that a dramatic, visible, openly experimental effort to cut down street crime in the worst precinct of, say, the ten largest cities in the nation might very well do just that, would advertise [the president's] concern and very likely end up producing important knowledge as to how it might be done elsewhere."[3]

Michael Sonnenreich, deputy assistant counsel to BNDD, forwarded a suggestion to Egil Krogh in early January 1971 for a secret, White House–based drive against major traffickers,[4] and Ed Harper, special assistant to the president on the Domestic Council, declared himself "fascinated by Sonnenreich's 'gang buster' approach to the problem." Harper thought, "What might be the best thing to do is to set up a special unit to do this, perhaps in the Justice Department (FBI?)."[5]

Then there was Gordon Liddy. Liddy had joined the Treasury Department at the behest of House Minority Leader Gerald Ford[6] but had run afoul of Eugene Rossides and had been forced out of Treasury in April 1971. After the publication of the Pentagon Papers in June, he and Howard Hunt, an ex-CIA operative, had been recruited by Egil Krogh to form the later infamous "Plumbers" unit in the White House. That September, they had burglarized the offices of Dr. Lewis Fielding, a psychiatrist who had treated Daniel Ellsberg, the man responsible for releasing the Pentagon Papers to the *New York Times.* John Ehrlichman recounts that "G. Gordon Liddy was Krogh's protégé. When Liddy worked at the Treasury Department, a time came when his boss, Eugene Rossides, was about to fire him. Earlier Liddy had worked on a law-enforcement task force that Krogh oversaw, so when he got into trouble Liddy came to Krogh for help. Krogh disliked Rossides. Unfortunately, he took the occasion to thumb his nose at Rossides by bringing Liddy into the White House."[7]

On 10 November 1971 Liddy sent a detailed, footnoted plan for a federally sponsored attack on street-level drug traffic to John Ehrlichman (through Egil Krogh). How long he had spent hatching this plan or with whom he had discussed it is not clear.[8] In any event, it is clear that the thirteen-page document he submitted had required a great deal of thought and preparation. He began by citing a Louis Harris poll to the effect that the American people wanted to see forceful action against foreign producers of drugs, effective rehabilitation programs for addicts, and really tough pursuit of drug dealers.[9] He believed that "our efforts [in the last area] have been invisible, both in terms of responding to the objective requirements of the problem and the subjective imperative of the electorate in 1972." He went on to say that "what is needed is a method and a vehicle for achieving media-dominated nationwide disruption of street-level trafficking in a manner defensible as safeguarding individual rights."[10] He then built an argument for using the grand jury as a mechanism for a full-scale assault on the narcotics business based on the history of Thomas E. Dewey's campaign against organized crime in New York in the 1930s.

Liddy's proposal was complete in every detail—mission, budget, funding source (the Law Enforcement Assistance Administration [LEAA]), and organization chart. Here is the heart of it all:

> Exploiting the special prosecutor and "black ribbon"[11] grand jury concepts, the President would create a Special Assistant to the Attorney General for Drug Trafficking Suppression, and direct him to empanel special grand juries throughout the United States, wherever the affliction of drug abuse is severe. Seated as a member of the Cabinet Committee on International Narcotics Control, his charter would extend for one year, and although limited to trafficking in heroin and cocaine, would extend to all enforcement phases of the problem including, but not limited to, retail, wholesale and international trafficking and related unlawful acts in advance of such trafficking; e.g. official corruption.[12]

Liddy recommended that Myles Ambrose be appointed to the special assistant attorney general post and that the plan be announced on television in December. And so it was—in a manner of speaking. At a meeting at Nixon's residence in Key Biscayne, Florida, on 3 December the president approved both the initiative itself and Myles Ambrose as its head.[13] On 6 December another meeting was held to welcome Ambrose to his new role, and the proceedings were filmed by a camera crew from NBC television.[14] When the NBC film was aired on 21 December it caused an uproar at Justice. While Ambrose had given Eugene Rossides some idea of what was to be broadcast that night[15] (though not, one would suppose, of Liddy's part in it), John Ingersoll, head of BNDD, knew nothing about the new law enforcement office or Ambrose's appointment. Ingersoll believes that John Mitchell had not been informed either.[16] All of this developed against a background of intense personal and professional animosity between Ingersoll and Ambrose, whose agencies had long competed for dominance in narcotics law enforcement.[17] Resistance in both departments hardened when Ingersoll and Rossides were told that they would be expected to detail agents from BNDD and Customs to the new unit. Justice Department officials including Ingersoll and Jerris Leonard, administrator of LEAA, advised the attorney general that they would be willing to see a campaign mounted against lower-level trafficking but that a new organization was not needed to accomplish such a mission. They told the attorney general that they believed that "to create an additional apparatus for a task that the Department

Myles Ambrose, head of the Office of Drug Abuse Law Enforcement and former commissioner of Customs, 14 March 1972. (Library of Congress.)

of Justice is now equipped to undertake would be wasteful of time and effort, and more serious, would involve a substantial risk of failure."[18]

Nevertheless, plans proceeded apace for what was referred to at that point as the Drug Trafficking Suppression Program (an adaptation of Liddy's terminology). The first official notice of the effort appeared in Nixon's State of the Union address on 20 January 1972. The program was formally announced on 28 January. Closely following Liddy's proposal, the program was to make use of the combined efforts of grand juries, federal prosecutors, specially designated agents from BNDD and the Bureau of Customs, and local law enforcement officials in twenty-four major cities. Its mandate was to remain in force for eighteen months.

The story of ODALE parallels that of SAODAP but is rather more dramatic, perhaps owing to the inherently rough-and-tumble environment of law enforcement. It seems obvious that Myles Ambrose's tough, can-do style appealed to President Nixon and his staff as they cast about for someone to make a forceful public impression of action against drug trafficking in time for the 1972 election.[19] It appears to be equally clear that John Ingersoll's measured leadership of BNDD as well as his seemingly complicated and drawn-out attempts to curtail the activities of shadowy international drug rings rather than home-grown traffickers grated on the nerves of administration planners hungry for political hay. Much the same could be said of the contrast between Jerome Jaffe's clear-cut proposals for methadone maintenance versus the complex and apparently inconclusive approach of Bertram Brown's task force. And the reactions at BNDD and Customs to the new office were also similar to those of NIMH toward SAODAP. They didn't like it one bit. Treasury was particularly aggrieved given its history of conflict with Justice. It now seemed that yet another power center was being established in Justice that, on top of every-

John Ingersoll, head of the Bureau of Narcotics and Dangerous Drugs, and Attorney General John Mitchell, 24 February 1971. (U.S. News and World Report Collection, Library of Congress.)

thing, would have authority over Customs agents detailed to its service. To make matters worse, Eugene Rossides' twin nemeses, the White House staff and the Justice Department, had co-opted his erstwhile deputy, Customs Commissioner Ambrose. John Ehrlichman was obliged to attempt a reconciliation. He wrote to Secretary of the Treasury Connally,

> Please understand that this is an undertaking by the President, not by the Department of Justice. Mr. Ambrose is working for the President, not the Attorney General.
>
> Therefore, Mr. Ambrose will draw upon both Departments for personnel and funds, as contemplated in the budget.
>
> In his Presidential capacity, Mr. Ambrose will direct personnel of both Departments. He will certainly consult with both. But, in view of our past experience, neither will have a veto. Interdepartmental disputes will, as always, be referred to the President for final decision.
>
> On-going review of the program will be conducted for the President by an OMB Task Force and both you and the Attorney General will be furnished the reports.[20]

Nothing seemed to work. Egil Krogh informed Ehrlichman on 10 March that "we are now four weeks behind in our efforts to utilize the [Customs] computer facilities with no end in sight. Ambrose is convinced Rossides is intentionally sitting on this matter, having had it referred to him by Secretary Connally."[21] A month later twenty-six Customs agents had finally been assigned to ODALE duty and a qualified agreement had been reached regarding computer time and secretarial assistance. But Customs still did not want to lend any of its minority agents to ODALE for undercover work, and Rossides was doing everything he could to protect IRS agents, who were busy with a program to prosecute drug traffickers on tax charges, from being plundered for ODALE duty.[22] Krogh foresaw operational as well as political disaster if the Treasury Department could not be persuaded to support ODALE. "The DALE program was designed to take our best drug spokesman (Ambrose) and put him in charge of a short term, high impact program to dramatically illustrate to the public President Nixon's all-out law enforcement war on heroin. The DALE program can limp along without Treasury's enthusiastic support, but it will never be able to convince the voting public that real progress is being made. This is a clear policy choice and if we cannot muster Treasury's enthusiasm, we will have to content ourselves with another mediocre program in a vitally important political area."[23]

A partial solution to the impasse seems to have been found in allowing Rossides to elevate the public profile of the IRS program to a level similar to that of

ODALE, and for Ambrose's replacement at Customs, Vernon Acree, to also share the stage. John Ingersoll of BNDD was increasingly marginalized. It probably didn't help him that John Mitchell, who had consistently taken Ingersoll's part when his capacities were questioned, had left the Justice Department in January to go to the CRP. Gordon Liddy had gone with Mitchell.

THE NATIONAL COMMISSION ON MARIHUANA AND DRUG ABUSE

As ODALE gradually found its footing, the first of several potential threats to the administration's chosen position on drug abuse emerged. On Wednesday, 22 March 1972, the National Commission on Marihuana and Drug Abuse, which had been established the year before, as required by the Comprehensive Drug Abuse Prevention and Control Act of 1970, submitted its first report. The atmosphere created by the president's activities of the previous two days gave some indication of how the report might be received. On Monday, President Nixon declared drug abuse to be "public enemy Number One" during a press conference in New York City, and he took the occasion to underline his faith in law enforcement as the principal weapon against this so-called public enemy. On Tuesday the president signed into law the Drug Abuse Office and Treatment Act, which formally established SAODAP.

Thus the moment was not a very opportune one for the report, which was detailed and many-faceted and which generally advocated a calm reappraisal of the nature and consequences of marijuana use. It reflected an increasingly widely held belief among a visible and vocal minority of citizens, including youth (the Gallup poll of that same month estimated that 29 percent of youth between the ages of eighteen and twenty-nine years had tried marijuana) and some members of the scientific, medical, intellectual, and political professions that cannabis did not represent a sufficient threat to public health and safety to justify the penalties associated with its use and possession, particularly in state law. (In Texas, marijuana possession was classified as a felony punishable by two years to life in prison.) But the opinion of a majority of Americans, which the commission duly reported, was rather different. "The threat which marihuana use is thought to present to the dominant social order is a major undercurrent of the marihuana problem. Use of the drug is linked with idleness, lack of motivation, hedonism and sexual promiscuity. Many see the drug as fostering a counter-culture which conflicts with basic moral precepts as well as with the operating functions of our society. The 'dropping out' or rejection of the established value system is viewed with alarm. Marihuana becomes more than a drug; it becomes a symbol of the rejection of cherished values."[24] Although cautious and thoughtful and rejecting the extreme of outright legalization of cannabis along the lines of the post-Prohibition alcohol model, the commission did align itself with the mainstream minority opinion. Its central recommendation read as follows.

> The commission is of the unanimous opinion that marihuana use is not such a grave problem that individuals who smoke marihuana, and possess it for that purpose, should be subject to criminal procedures. On the other hand, we have also rejected the regulatory or legalization scheme because it would institutionalize availability of a drug which has uncertain long-term effects and which may be of transient social interest.
>
> In general, we recommend only a decriminalization of possession of marihuana for personal use on both the state and Federal levels. The major features of the recommended scheme are that production and distribution of the drug would remain criminal activities as would possession with intent to distribute commercially; marihuana would be contraband subject to confiscation in public places; and criminal sanctions would be withdrawn from private use and possession incident to such use, but at the state level, fines would be imposed for use in public.[25]

The fact that this recommendation was hardly radical, was more a logical extension of, rather than a departure from, the position the administration had finally taken with respect to the penalty structure in the Comprehensive Drug Abuse Prevention and Control Act, and had been developed by a panel headed by Republican stalwart Raymond P. Shafer, former governor of Pennsylvania, did little to improve its marketability among members of the administration. It was too complicated, too difficult to explain in the context of intensifying election-year efforts to paint the administration as uncompromising in its fight against crime in general and drug crime in particular. It was simply not feasible to tease apart heroin from marijuana, legalization from decriminalization, then explain the difference to the public, 81 percent of whom, according to the Gallup Organization, opposed "legalization" of marijuana.[26] It was yet another analogue of the NIMH report of December 1970: it dealt with the issue on a level of complexity that made it at best useless, at worst destructive, to the policy direction and the estimate of political necessity to which the administration was committed. A glimpse of this process is gained from an "eyes only" background paper dated April 1972. The paper reviews some polling data on the nature of the electorate and states, "To successfully put across the President's involvement with substantive issues, we need to put together his strong personal characteristics, what we know about the people's basic concerns and values, and the President's approach to the issue in a few, simply understood, simply demonstrated themes about each of the major issues."[27] This document then presents an outline of issues and themes that should be used to communicate the president's positions. For example:

DRUGS

Themes

1. The President wants to help young people caught on drugs.
2. He wants to stop pushers.

Events

1. Meet with some young people who have come off drugs and are now fighting drugs.
2. Establish a regular, high visibility report on the success in fighting drug pushers.

CRIME

Themes

1. Drugs cause crime.
2. The President's helping good cops fight crime.
3. The President's helping building respect for law and order.

When asked about the Marihuana Commission's report at a press conference, Mr. Nixon stated, "I oppose the legalization of marijuana and that includes its sale, its possession and its use. I do not believe you can have effective criminal justice based on the philosophy that something is half legal and half illegal. That is my position, despite what the commission has recommended."[28] And that was that.

DRUG POLICIES, PUBLIC INFORMATION, AND PRESIDENTIAL POLITICS

With the advent of the ODALE program and related SAODAP, Customs, and IRS efforts, the rejection of the Marihuana Commission's report, and constant emphasis on the relationship between drug use and crime—even in the development of treatment strategies—the administration's preelection posture was decidedly to "get tough." Whatever the operational achievements of narcotics control initiatives, the April memorandum makes clear that constant and favorable communication of the effect of those initiatives on public order was crucial to the effort to elect Richard Nixon to a second term. Some of the initial attempts to gain attention for the president's anti-narcotics programs were transparently political and had little to do with the real work of such agencies as SAODAP and ODALE. One of these was an anti-drug conference for celebrity athletes held at the White House in February. Another was the "Heroin Hot Line."

The hot line had a toll-free number available to citizens who wished to provide anonymous tips on drug-trafficking activity to the federal authorities—specifically ODALE. It was initially to be announced by the president in a national television address, but that idea was abandoned, and the president's press secretary, Ron Zeigler, announced the program at a press conference on 7 April. Great pains were taken to assure the press that no information would be used for blackmail or police harassment, though the assurances met with some skepticism.[29] In September, Robert Feldcamp, public information officer for ODALE, submitted an analysis of the hot line to Myles Ambrose that painted a rather rosier picture of its results than his own figures seemed to warrant. For example, he reported 6,741 calls in which some conversation was elicited from the caller, but there were over 33,000 calls in which no conversation took place. (Feldcamp interpreted this large number in positive terms as an indication of wide public awareness of the hot line.) He claimed that "there have been hundreds of investigations across the country resulting from Hotline calls," but could cite only eleven arrests as examples of concrete results.[30] Representative Lester Wolff (D., NY) claimed that a study by the General Accounting Office showed that the hot line was ineffective, but Ambrose, as might be expected, stuck by Feldcamp's interpretation.[31]

Even as the Heroin Hot Line got under way, the ad hoc, somewhat gimmicky approach to public information that it represented was replaced with the beginning of a more polished campaign under the direction of Richard Harkness. Harkness was an old media pro who had retired in 1970 from a long and distinguished career in both print journalism and television. In 1948 he broadcast the first televised network news program from Washington for NBC and later won an Emmy award. While working as special consultant to Nelson Gross at the State Department, he had impressed Egil Krogh by orchestrating very favorable coverage of the administration's war on drugs in the April 3 issue of *U.S. News and World Report.* Krogh brought Harkness onto the White House staff and set him to work to organize a coordinated public front for all government officials involved in the drug effort. Among many other organizational details, he established a narcotics "situation room," where members of the press could view dramatic photographs and graphic statistical evidence of drug busts, treatment programs, and the like. By August, his "Operation Inform" was in full swing. A briefing book on narcotics issues for the use of all departmental personnel had been produced, interviews in major news media with the administration's designated spokespersons had been scheduled with special emphasis on appearances in ODALE cities, information to counter unfavorable press reports had been gathered, and a grand design for the operation had been established. The interlocking relationships among various parts of the drug control program, all with the aim of crime prevention, were to be emphasized along with the huge increases in budget allocations that had developed over the course of Nixon's first term.[32] By this time, the drug issue seemed to be firmly harnessed to the Nixon election bandwagon, and the president could "express satisfaction that Mr. Harkness was on the team" to organize press coverage of such events as a 24 July meeting held to report to the president on law enforcement.[33]

The July meeting included Eugene Rossides, Myles Ambrose, and Customs Commissioner Vernon Acree (John Ingersoll was reportedly on vacation). The three officials displayed a chart that showed that federal arrests for drug violations had nearly doubled since 1969. The president expressed the opinion that the public enemy was "on the run" and that the statistics should be doubled again in the coming year.[34] At the press conference following the meeting, Ambrose described his progress in getting ODALE under way in glowing terms. The program was, he said, "fully operational" in thirty-three cities (up from the original twenty-four), with other sites planned. Not to be outdone, Eugene Rossides declared that the "IRS tax investigation program is all pervasive, institutionalized, nation-wide. It is not hit or miss, it is highly structured, working closely with the two Federal agencies, the Bureau of Narcotics and Dangerous Drugs, and the Customs and all of the state and local police departments to select the targets."[35]

But the news was not uniformly positive. In a situation that was somewhat analogous to that created by the Marihuana Commission report, the Harkness operation had to deal with two challenges presented from within the administration itself. The first of these was the need to explain the BNDD's revised calculation of the number of opiate addicts in the country, which seemed to indicate that the situation had worsened considerably. As noted earlier, attempts to keep interpretations of the statistics under control were only partially successful, and the balancing act required in order to claim important gains in the war on drugs while simultaneously declaring that the problem was much greater than previously thought was delicate indeed. Program planners strove to show that, although there were many more opiate addicts than had been supposed, there had been no increase in the real numbers, only an improved estimate. This rationale was then used to support a request for a $135.2 million supplement to the drug budget, thus highlighting the importance of the problem as well as Nixon's commitment to dealing with it.[36]

Another hurdle that the public information campaign had to clear was the publication of the *World Opium Survey, 1972* under the auspices of the Cabinet Committee on International Narcotics Control. Released to the press on 16 August, the report seemed less than optimistic about the possibility of controlling international supplies of heroin. While claiming that "efforts of the US Government and others to interdict and eliminate the international traffic in heroin are beginning to have an impact on international trafficking," the survey went on to say that "despite the rising pace of seizures, the international market seems still to have adequate supplies to meet the demand in consuming countries."[37] This point of view was not politically helpful, no matter how fundamentally accurate, especially given the fact that the Turkish poppy moratorium had just taken effect. Adding a touch of salt to the wound, release of the opium survey coincided with publication of a book entitled *The Politics of Heroin in Southeast Asia* that purported to document CIA involvement in the opium trade.[38] The administration's response was to emphasize the achievements of SAODAP in increasing treatment capacity throughout the country and its contribution to reductions in addict crime, to draw attention to the fact that federal expenditures to fight narcotics had increased from $65.7 million in fiscal 1969 to the $594 million budgeted for fiscal 1973 (exclusive of the $135.2 million supplemental request), and to claim that drug seizures by federal agents had created a veritable heroin "drought" on the East Coast.[39] As indicated, the real existence of this shortage was the subject of some debate. Eugene Rossides claims that not only was there a shortage but that it was due to his IRS traffickers program,[40] while others, especially Democratic presidential candidate George McGovern, questioned the existence of such a shortage.[41]

Still, the general thrust of the attack on drug abuse and attendant crime held together. A collaborative structure consisting of ODALE enforcement and SAODAP treatment programs began to emerge that, besides sensibly linking treatment alternatives with arrests, was an ideal vehicle for channeling federal largess to key local areas.

SAODAP AND ODALE: FEDERAL PROGRAMS GO LOCAL

The immediate goal of SAODAP-ODALE collaboration was the expansion of treatment programs in cities that ODALE had targeted for its strike force effort. The operative assumption was that treatment needs would increase as addicts were deprived of their supplies of narcotics because of either reduced availability or incarceration.[42] The first of these programs, the "Waiting List Project," was described as a "standard mechanism for the prompt buy-up of waiting lists for drug treatment and rehabilitation services and [standardization of] the level of treatment throughout the Nation."[43] Allocation of $4 million for expansion of treatment facilities resulted in an increase of 2,880 treatment slots in seventeen municipalities by July 1972.[44] Methadone programs were contracted in New York, Baltimore, San Antonio, Chicago, Indianapolis/Gary, San Francisco, Miami, New Orleans, Denver, Seattle, Atlantic City, Los Angeles, Boston, and Buffalo. Therapeutic communities in Miami also received federal contracts. True to the pattern most dramatically exemplified by NIMH, the agencies directed to implement SAODAP policies applied their own priorities to the tasks. The results were often not what SAODAP had intended. In this case, besides creating routine difficulties in the handling of paperwork, OEO signed treatment expansion contracts in Des Moines (therapeutic community), Providence (therapeutic community), and Corpus Christi (methadone), contrary to the directives of SAODAP.

The second major collaboration between SAODAP and ODALE was Treatment Alternatives to Street Crime (TASC), the theoretical basis of which was the now familiar proposition that "a major portion of property crime in America is committed by opiate-dependent persons."[45] Sixteen cities where ODALE had established, or was in the process of establishing, law enforcement programs were slated to receive money from LEAA and technical assistance and training from SAODAP to establish TASC programs. There is evidence that TASC came in handy as a vehicle for political favors and probably to further bend the resources of the bureaucracy to the political will of the White House.[46] The first two cities to receive "demonstration grants" were Wilmington, Delaware ($500,000 on April 14), and Philadelphia ($1 million on May 20), whose Democratic mayor, Frank Rizzo, had endorsed Nixon on 12 April. In July, apropos of possible TASC intervention in Miami, Baltimore, Atlanta, Newark, Indianapolis, Portland, San Francisco, and Austin, Jeffrey Donfeld asked Walter Minnick:

Public service billboard in New Haven, Connecticut, June 1973. (U.S. News and World Report Collection, Library of Congress.)

1. What friend in the state or city should be officially informed that we intend to enter the city with the assistance noted above?
2. What friend, possibly the same as #1, should invite the SAO team into the city and get credit for our presence and getting the federal dollars into the city?
3. What friend, possibly the same as #1 and #2, should I side with in the event of TASC policy disputes within the city structure?[47]

Testimony before the Senate Watergate Committee in the spring of 1974 revealed that Frederic V. Malek, at the time special assistant to the president, had developed a secret plan to improve "departmental responsiveness in support of the President's re-election" and had observed that flexible funds were available in many departments that could be "rechanneled to impact more directly on target groups or geographic areas."[48]

RESULTS

Whatever hopes may have been entertained for SAODAP and ODALE programs, both political and programmatic results were mixed and difficult to interpret. At the end of August, Wilmington and Philadelphia were still the only two sites to which TASC grants that had actually been made.[49] The First *Federal Strategy for Drug Abuse and Drug Traffic Prevention,* published in the spring of 1973, stated that "grants have been approved in 10 cities and are pending in several others; four programs are operational."[50] The SAODAP annual report, dated 15 June 1973 and covering the period from March 1972 through March 1973, indicates that there were TASC projects "operational in five major metropolitan areas."[51] This report also counted among the successes of the office (1) expansion of treatment programs, (2) reduction of drug abuse in the military, and (3) increased research in both pharmacological and sociological approaches to drug addiction. The report noted that "although precise measures of the number of active heroin addicts are not yet available, analyses of available data clearly indicate a slow-down in the rate of growth of heroin addiction and a likelihood that over the next year or two many communities will experience an actual decrease in the number of active heroin addicts. Other indicators of deaths and crimes associated with narcotics use also support the view that the heroin problem is not as acute as it was less than two years ago."[52] Although this view is not indefensible in the context of the data on which it was based, it proved to be optimistic.

If one looks specifically at federal support for the much-discussed methadone maintenance treatment modality, the actual number of patients enrolled in this sort of program fell short of both the external pronouncements and the internal designs of policy staff. Methadone maintenance programs grew at a much slower pace than did drug-free treatment—a situation that reflects the intense ideological competition between maintenance and drug-free treatment advocates. In October 1971, after SAODAP had been in operation for four months, there had been approximately equal numbers of clients in maintenance and nonmaintenance programs directly funded by the federal government (10,398 and 10,219 respectively).[53] By March 1973 there were more than twice as many clients in nonmaintenance programs as there were being treated with methadone (48,825 versus 23,716). These programs included those run by NIMH, the Department of Defense, the Office of Economic Opportunity, the Veterans Administration, the Department of Housing and Urban Development, the Bureau of Prisons, and the Law Enforcement Assistance Administration. This outcome may have been partially due to lack of complete acceptance of the methadone component of the multimodality approach within the bureaucracy. The fact that drug-based therapy for opiate dependence was, and still is, controversial provided some opportunity for the implementing agencies—whose biases favored drug-free treatment—to limit methadone use. Dr. Vincent Dole, the methadone pioneer and medical scientist, saw the multimodality concept as a major mistake. In his words, "There entered into the field a kind of hybrid thinking, with methadone being considered only a limited expedient. This type of attitude was adopted and expanded into an official view by the federal government, and it was incorporated into their regulations by 1974. The goal of treatment was not rehabilitation but abstinence."[54] But Dr. Dole was not obliged to operate under the political constraints that, rightly or wrongly, Dr. Jaffe and his colleagues saw as defining their activities, or under the limits imposed on those activities by the necessity of dealing with the federal bureaucracy. The federal strategy, as articulated in March 1973, was that "The long-term goal of [methadone] treatment should be withdrawal from all narcotic drugs, although we recognize that this may not be possible for all clients; On the basis of current information the maintenance approach should be used only with confirmed addicts—of at least two years' duration—and that those who have been using narcotics for shorter periods should be treated by other approaches; We believe that methadone is only one of several drugs that can be used in oral maintenance programs and that the utility of other drugs should be explored."[55]

In spite of mixed federal support for various treatment options, press reports during the period leading up to the 1972 presidential election contributed to the impression that methadone was making a significant contribution to reducing criminal activity among addicts. In March, Dr. Robert Dupont of the District of Columbia Narcotics Treatment Administration stated that crime rates had declined in the District coincidentally with the implementation of large-scale treatment programs.[56] In New York, Mayor John Lindsay's health services administrator reported that repeat arrests of male methadone patients who had been in treatment for thirteen months or more had declined by a truly startling 96 percent.[57] There can be little doubt that methadone, however controversial, had made many converts at every point on the political spectrum, primarily for its apparent effectiveness in reducing addict crime.

REORGANIZATION AND RETRENCHMENT

After the presidential election of 1972 federal drug abuse control policy became subject to a process of de-emphasis that was to continue until the end of the Carter administration eight years later. While it is quite clear that the drug issue became a far lower priority for the administration of Gerald Ford than it had been for that of his predecessor, and that some of the fundamental assumptions that had guided Nixon's policy makers were seriously questioned, if not rejected outright, by Ford's staff, what is less obvious is that both public interest in, and policy staff attention to, the drug issue had begun to decline as early as the summer of 1972. Major shifts in the structure of the policy-making apparatus in late 1972 and early 1973 coincided with, and responded to, that change in the political climate, as well as to the ever-increasing demands of the developing Watergate affair.

Peter Goldberg, writing in his capacity as senior policy analyst for the Drug Abuse Council, dated the de-emphasis of the drug issue to 12 September 1973, when President Nixon declared that "we have turned the corner on drug addiction in the United States."[58] He went on to attribute the policy shift to four factors: first, the fact that the election had passed, thereby relieving the political pressure that had, until that time, been a primary driving force behind drug policy making; second, no significant number of addicted Vietnam veterans had appeared on the streets; third, public interest in the issue was decreasing; and fourth, "new avenues of response to the use of illicit drugs . . . had in their combined effect failed to measure up to the original expectations, and it seemed unlikely that any further improvement would result from an expanded or intensified effort in these areas."[59] Goldberg's view probably does not date the diminishing importance of drug abuse as a policy priority early enough (nor does he consider the ultimately unsuccessful attempts of drug hawks in Congress and of the president himself to return to extremely harsh penalties for trafficking offenses). The Gallup Organization registered a significant decline in public concern about drugs beginning in May 1972,[60] and a dramatic realignment of the administration's policy staff, including responsibilities for narcotics policy, took place in December: the Domestic Council was reduced to a skeleton staff; responsibility for drug policy was assigned to a small office in OMB under the direction of Walter Minnick, who had headed the coordinating subcommittee of the Cabinet Committee on International Narcotics Control; Egil Krogh moved into the Transportation Department; and Jeffrey Donfeld went to an obscure office in the Department of the Interior. Responsibility for drug issues from the White House side fell to Geoffrey Shepard, associate director of the Domestic Council and Krogh's deputy until Krogh's departure. All those who retained responsibility for some part of narcotics control policy development became involved to a greater or lesser degree in a plan for a complete reorganization of drug law enforcement. This effort, which was to become Reorganization Plan 2 of 1973, was part of a move away from the organizational philosophy of Nixon's first term, which was to centralize authority in the White House and to limit the power of cabinet agencies. Now, bureaucracies were reorganized and experienced staffers were dispersed in a effort at control from within. The special law enforcement offices, which after the elections lost their political luster, were merged with the troublesome Bureau of Narcotics and Dangerous Drugs and given a new identity as the Drug Enforcement Administration in the Justice Department. SAODAP's term was to expire in 1975, but the unit began to operate on a lame-duck basis after the resignation of Jerome Jaffe in July of 1973. Under his successor, Dr. Robert DuPont, most of its activities and personnel began to move to the new National Institute on Drug Abuse in HEW, where another reorganization was under way: among other changes, the old Division of Narcotics and Drug Abuse (DNADA) evolved into NIDA and slowly subsumed SAODAP.

REORGANIZATION PLAN 2 OF 1973: EARLY BACKGROUND

Problems of bureaucratic organization and jurisdictional rivalry between the Federal Bureau of Narcotics and the Bureau of Customs had plagued federal anti-drug efforts since the inception of the two agencies. (Customs districts and activities were first authorized in 1789, but a separate Bureau of Customs was not established within the Treasury Department until 1927. The FBN came into existence in the same department in 1930.) The 1968 attempt to solve the problem by transferring narcotics law enforcement authority to the Justice Department (Reorganization Plan 1 of 1968, which created BNDD) only made things worse. What had been a dispute between two offices of the same department, adjudicated when necessary by the secretary of the treasury, became an interdepartmental conflict ultimately resolvable only by presidential authority. The Nixon administration inherited this bureaucratic nightmare along with additional difficulties: the personality conflict between John Ingersoll, the quiet, cautious director of BNDD, and the flamboyant, take-no-prisoners Customs commissioner, Myles Ambrose; the combative style of Assistant Secretary of the Treasury Eugene Rossides, Ambrose's boss; and animosity among Rossides, Ingersoll, and the White House staff. The circumstances associated with the creation of ODALE and the management of the IRS program to prosecute drug traffickers on tax charges were only the most outstanding examples of the conflict.

The principal bone of contention between Customs and the narcotics bureau, both in its BNDD incarnation in the Justice Department and in its previous identity as the Federal Bureau of Narcotics in Treasury, had been the felt need in both agencies to pursue smuggling conspiracies from their origins overseas through ports of entry and, in some cases, on to delivery of the "goods" at their destinations in the cities of the United States. Although there had been sundry directives and memoranda of understanding over the years that had attempted to establish the primacy of the narcotics bureau in matters of drug smuggling at any point not specifically a border or port, Customs had consistently challenged the validity of such documents. The President's Advisory Council on Executive Organization (the Ash Council), having been asked to address the problem, provided President Nixon with the following summary.

> In 1962 the Assistant Secretary of Treasury for Law Enforcement, James A. Reed, relieved Customs of that part of the job of collecting overseas intelligence on traffic in narcotics that it had been performing and assigned this function to the Bureau of Narcotics, then also a part of the Treasury Department. In June of 1969, the Assistant Secretary of the Treasury for Law Enforcement, Eugene Rossides, instructed Customs overseas agents to begin supplying their bureau with intelligence on traffic in narcotics. BNDD, now part of the Justice Department as the result of Reorgan-

> ization Act Number [1] of 1968, objected to the Rossides instruction. The Department of State had delayed transmission of the instruction to Customs overseas agents pending clarification of the overseas role of each bureau.[61]

PACEO's recommendation was essentially that narcotics law enforcement in all its forms be clearly designated the province of BNDD and that Customs should play a secondary, cooperative role. Here again, personal chemistry contributed to the ultimate failure of any attempted solution to stick. The president himself initially favored unification of all federal law enforcement agencies in the Department of Justice[62] in spite of the Ash Council's reservations about concentrating investigative and prosecutorial functions in the same department.[63] But, as John Ehrlichman observed in his memoirs, "Nixon had more confidence in John Mitchell than he did in [Secretary of the Treasury] David Kennedy. (But in later years, when John B. Connally was its secretary, the Treasury Department began to win all its jurisdictional battles with the Department of Justice.)"[64]

The Ash Council proceeded to study the question of appropriate organization for the entire drug control program, but its final report addressed only the question of organization of "demand" efforts. It may be that the council was deflected from analysis of enforcement organization both by presidential disinclination to consider its concerns and by White House staff members determined to settle the question on their own terms. Egil Krogh and Jeffrey Donfeld told PACEO researchers, "The BNDD/Customs dispute is firmly settled. The only other White House action may be a formal memo to Secretary Kennedy from the President."[65] That memo, designating BNDD as the only legitimate law enforcement authority with respect to both domestic and foreign drug control, was written and sent to Secretary Kennedy, but as pointed out earlier, in a classic case of the limited control of policy makers over the behavior of determined bureaucrats, neither Kennedy nor Customs Commissioner Ambrose nor Eugene Rossides ever really accepted the terms of the memorandum. The successors to Kennedy and Ambrose (John B. Connally and Vernon Acree) did not conform to the directive, either. The Office of Drug Abuse Law Enforcement was supposed to circumvent interdepartmental bickering, make up for BNDD's lackluster style, and unify all domestic drug enforcement personnel in time for the 1972 elections, but its debut was anything but smooth, and controversy over its "no-knock" authority, which came to a head in early 1973, contributed to the impetus behind a major and permanent reorganization.

REORGANIZATION: INITIAL PROPOSALS

An excellent overview of the background, development, and immediate effects of Reorganization Plan 2 of 1973 can be found in Patricia Rachel's book on the subject, and her findings are heavily relied upon here.[66] However, Rachel's study does not address in any depth the effects of the administration's growing preoccupation with the Watergate affair. As the trial of the seven Watergate conspirators opened in January, top White House aides would surely have had little time to deal adequately with delicate and complicated issues of narcotics organization (H.R. Haldeman's diaries give a good sense of this). This situation probably materially contributed to what Rachel identifies as one of the principal weaknesses of the plan—a lack of in-depth analysis of the actual effects of bureaucratic rivalry and of then-current narcotics law enforcement procedures. The effects of the Watergate scandal and the attendant resignations on White House resolve and coordination may also have been at least partly responsible for the inability of staff members to impose discipline on insubordinate Customs officials who sought to sabotage the plan in Congress. (The contrast between the administration's weakness in this situation and its purging of HEW officials in the spring of 1970 is dramatic.) Nor does Rachel incorporate in her study the indications that the drug issue no longer occupied the position of foremost importance that it had before the presidential election. Nevertheless, she points out very effectively that the antagonism between Customs and BNDD was a source of considerable pressure on the administration to push forward with the drug reorganization. The dispute was public knowledge as well as political ammunition for the administration's opponents in Congress: both the General Accounting Office and the Library of Congress had issued studies critical of drug policy implementation, and on 21 January Senator Abraham Ribicoff (D., CT) introduced legislation aimed at rationalizing federal narcotics enforcement, principally by assigning most of the responsibility to the Federal Bureau of Investigation.

Serious consideration of a reorganization of federal narcotics law enforcement began at least as early as October 1972, when Egil Krogh forwarded to Mark Alger of OMB a memo he had received from Walter Minnick that outlined some suggestions for drug reorganization. Oddly enough, Minnick's original recommendation resembled, to some degree, the concept of a drug czar that the administration had so vigorously resisted in its negotiations with Congress over the SAODAP legislation in 1971 and early 1972. (Minnick referred to the idea of having a "drug 'boss.'") He envisioned three deputies reporting to the "boss": one would be in charge of "demand"; one would oversee law enforcement and would simultaneously serve as assistant attorney general; and one would be responsible for international drug control and would carry the title of assistant secretary of state. Although this outline was not ultimately considered, Minnick's fundamental appreciation of the difficulty of a coordinated approach to drug control policy implementation did guide the thinking behind the options finally presented. He emphasized that "the sad history of the past twenty years makes clear that only through an outright merger can the Customs/BNDD dispute and like divisive competition among existing drug enforcement organizations be eliminated permanently. Creating a single merged drug enforcement agency will make it be possible for the first time to develop a coordinated, high-impact program where everyone 'pulls together' as one team."[67]

Planning for reorganization of the drug effort began in earnest in December. A study group to consider the issue was formed including John Ehrlichman, Roy Ash—by then head of OMB—Attorney General Richard Kleindienst, and Secretary of the Treasury George Shultz. Each of these men appointed a representative to a task force charged with developing a reorganization plan. Rachel identifies the members of this group as Mark Alger of OMB, Donald Santarelli for the Justice Department, Edward Morgan of Treasury, and Geoffrey Shepard of the White House Domestic Council.[68] However, there is considerable evidence to support Walter Minnick's contention that he was responsible for actually drafting the alternatives that were eventually presented and for seeing the plan through Congress.[69] This also fits with the responsibilities he assumed in December 1972 as head of the Drug Policy Management Office at OMB.

After a number of contretemps that included a furious reaction from George Shultz to the possibility of moving all drug enforcement authority from Customs to Justice[70] and what amounted to a refusal from L. Patrick Gray, acting director of the FBI, to consider the possibility of locating drug enforcement in his bureau,[71] Mark Alger forwarded a detailed option paper on drug trafficking enforcement to Roy Ash.[72] It included seven options the first four of which were variations on a theme of establishing a new, comprehensive drug law enforcement agency in the Justice Department. Option 5 was that of giving the FBI principal responsibility for narcotics enforcement; the opposition to the idea of that bureau's acting director was duly noted. Option 6 offered the possibility of locating both domestic and international drug law enforcement in the Treasury Department under the dual authority of Customs (overseas jurisdiction) and a new entity for domestic enforcement. Option 7 was, essentially, to do nothing—to wait, to study the situation, and to determine whether the problem was "really structural and not the result of personalities or rapid growth over the past few years." In spite of the fact that one thorn in their sides had been removed with the resignation of Eugene Rossides on 20 January, the arguments against this approach were overwhelming to policy makers for whom it was imperative to get something done. Morale in all existing narcotics law enforcement agencies was low and getting lower as rumors about the reorganization flew; reappointment of agency heads for the new term could not be delayed much longer; and, most important, the president's authority to reorganize without formal legislation was due to expire on 31 March.

Reducing the seven options to three final possibilities for the president's consideration would take until early March, which caused a certain amount of anguish to Geoffrey Shepard as he watched Senator Ribicoff stir up the press with his own proposals involving the FBI.[73] Simultaneously, confirmation hearings on the nomination of Patrick Gray as permanent FBI director became increasingly embroiled in questions about the relationships among the bureau, the rest of the Justice Department, and the White House and how Gray had handled information related to Watergate. Yet even in the midst of all this, enough of the president's attention remained focused on the problem of crime and drugs for him to urge cabinet officers and staff members to "take a very hard line. We have to move in this area. Step up penalties on drugs and so on."[74]

THE HEROIN TRAFFICKING ACT OF 1973

Why the spring of 1973 seemed an appropriate moment to revise the penalty structure of the Comprehensive Drug Abuse Prevention and Control Act of 1970 is an issue open to several interpretations. One might cite this as evidence that drug policy did indeed remain a priority in the second Nixon administration. Given the strains introduced by the Watergate affair, the declining importance of the drug menace in the public mind, and the disarray in the agencies charged with enforcing drug laws, this argument does not seem particularly powerful. It is more likely that the impetus for seeking legislation to increase penalties for heroin trafficking was its appeal as a way to divert public attention from the growing scandal and as further justification for strengthening drug law enforcement through reorganization. In addition, as Goldberg observes, treatment had played itself out as a political issue by this time, and treatment programs were in the process of being reabsorbed into the health bureaucracy.[75] Still another factor contributing to the renewed appeal of tough anti-narcotics laws was, as H.R. Haldeman points out in his diaries, that the president was anxious to "figure out other ways of getting on TV and getting TV domination": the Vietnam peace negotiations had concluded in January, the withdrawal of American combat troops would be completed on March 29, and thus the conflict would no longer provide a reliable source of dramatic announcements.[76] Additional motivation to emphasize the administration's unyielding posture with respect to drugs was provided by the proximate release of the final report of the Commission on Marihuana and Drug Abuse. It could be expected that this document would fortify the conclusions of its predecessor—which it did.

The president had expressed a desire to increase penalties for drug trafficking as early as June 1971, when planning for SAODAP was in full swing and the Comprehensive Drug Abuse Prevention and Control Act, with its relatively moderate penalty structure, was less than a year old,[77] but no specific action had been taken. Then, on 10 March 1973, Nixon raised the issue again, calling for mandatory minimum sentences for heroin-trafficking offenses in a speech that included a call to restore the death penalty for certain federal crimes. He gave details of his proposal in his State of the Union speech of 14 March, declaring, "These are very harsh measures, to be applied within very rigid guidelines and providing only a minimum of sentencing discretion to judges. But circumstances warrant such provisions. All the evidence shows that we are now doing a more effective job in the areas of enforcement and rehabilitation. In spite of this progress, however, we find an intolerably high level of street crime being committed by addicts. Part of the reason, I believe, lies in the court system which takes over after drug pushers have been apprehended. The courts are frequently little more than an escape hatch for those who are responsible for the menace of drugs."[78]

The president also reiterated his opposition to any sort of legalization of marijuana in anticipation of the final report of the National Commission on Marihuana and Drug Abuse, which was due later the same month. His legislation was not formally introduced in Congress until 20 March, by which time there was a whole array of similar proposals before both houses. The bill was referred to committee and did not emerge during the remaining sixteen months of the Nixon presidency. Even under better circumstances, the bill would probably not have been passed in this length of time—sixteen months passed between the introduction of the Comprehensive Drug Abuse Prevention and Control Act and its passage. The SAODAP legislation required nine months to

Members of the National Commission on Marihuana and Drug Abuse, 22 March 1973. (U.S. News and World Report Collection, Library of Congress.)

gain passage, but this was during a period of intense policy-staff commitment to the narcotics problem and a generally favorable climate in Congress. In 1973 the combination of intensifying congressional determination to uncover the facts of the Watergate affair and waning concern on the part of the public and its representatives probably greatly reduced the importance placed on passage of the new heroin-trafficking legislation by all parties. Nixon attempted to revive the measure in February of 1974 by introducing supplementary legislation that withdrew a provision for life imprisonment on a second conviction for heroin trafficking and revised mandatory minimum penalties yet again, but to no avail. By the time the Ford administration had established itself, the social and political climate, to say nothing of the character of national leadership, had changed sufficiently to make the measure unpalatable, and it was allowed to die.

REORGANIZATION: THE PLAN AND ITS IMPLEMENTATION

On 22 March (just as the White House attempt to cover up the involvement of top aides in the Watergate scandal began to collapse) the National Commission on Marihuana and Drug Abuse presented its final report, *Drug Use in America: Problem in Perspective.* The report observed that "public policy, as presently designed, is premised on incorrect assumptions, is aimed at the wrong targets, and is too often unresponsive to human needs and aspirations. . . . Drug policy can be thus summed up: increased use of disapproved drugs precipitates more spending, more programs, more arrests and more penalties, all with little positive effect in reducing use of these drugs."[79]

On the 28th, President Nixon's reorganization plan was presented to Congress—it would take effect in sixty days unless either house passed a resolution rejecting it. Patricia Rachel documents in detail what happened to the plan over the next two months. Her analysis is careful and complete and supports the contention that the nature of political power, the nature of bureaucracy, and the influence of personality create a degree of complexity in the process of policy development and implementation that makes clearly successful outcomes difficult in the extreme.

Reorganization Plan 2 of 1973 consisted of three main elements:

1. Created the Drug Enforcement Administration, combining ODALE, ONNI [Office of National Narcotics Intelligence], BNDD, and Customs narcotics agents in a new agency in Justice;

2. Transferred to the Attorney General (from the Secretary of the Treasury) intelligence, investigative, and law enforcement functions relating to the suppression of illicit traffic in narcotics, dangerous drugs or marihuana. Included in the transfer were approximately 500 Customs agents (Section 1 of the plan);
3. Transferred to the Secretary of the Treasury functions vested by law in the Attorney General regarding inspection of persons and papers at ports of entry. Included in the transfer were approximately 1,000 INS inspectors (Section 2 of the plan).[80]

It was this last provision, which sent Immigration and Naturalization Service inspectors to Customs and which, to some extent, was designed to compensate that agency for the loss of five hundred of its agents to Justice, that nearly scuttled the plan. Recalcitrant Customs officials (who escaped both discipline and dismissal by a weakened administration) and the labor union that represented the interests of INS employees succeeded in mobilizing support in Congress, and the House Government Operations Committee recommended disapproval of the plan on 22 May, thus forcing the White House to negotiate for the life of its proposal in a crisis atmosphere.[81] The result of these negotiations was abandonment of section 3. On 6 June, Roy Ash submitted draft legislation that would render that section inoperable.[82] This had the effect of pacifying INS and gaining congressional acceptance of the plan, but it left a poisonous residue of resentment in the Bureau of Customs, which was to lose five hundred agents with no compensatory transfer of INS personnel, as well as the power and prestige associated with narcotics law enforcement. Rachel records several statements by Customs officials that bear dramatic witness to their determination not to get out of the narcotics business and to make life as difficult as possible for the new drug agency. One in particular makes the point: "But they left the door open in regard to border enforcement and we grabbed at the chance to reassert ourselves, to make it clear that we could not follow the policy of the administration."[83] Former Customs commissioner Acree also indicates that the ambiguity of the language that described the border interdiction role of Customs was used to strengthen the bureau's patrol force.[84]

And so the Drug Enforcement Administration came into being on 1 July 1973. The new organization, in addition to facing a hostile bureaucratic environment and a corps of confused and unassimilated agents, was leaderless. John Ingersoll of BNDD resigned after it became painfully obvious that he would be passed over for the top job at the new agency. Myles Ambrose also resigned. He declares that he had never intended to continue in government service after the expiration of ODALE's mandate in spite of reports in the press that he was a candidate for the DEA post.[85] In any case, it is unlikely that his candidacy would have been successful in the face of allegations that he had accepted the hospitality of a wealthy Texas rancher who was suspected of heroin smuggling and illegal arms dealing. His position had been further compromised by two incidents in which ODALE agents, using their controversial "no-knock" authority, had broken into houses they mistakenly thought to be occupied by drug traffickers and had mistreated the occupants.[86] The administration's eventual choice to lead the new DEA was John R. Bartels, who had been Ambrose's deputy at ODALE and who had, previous to a stint in private law practice, served in the criminal division of the Justice Department. The appointment was not a fortunate one. Bartels did not have strong administrative talents, had no political connections to speak of, and appears, with the benefit of hindsight, to have been breathtakingly naive.[87] In any event, he faced problems that would have severely tested the most skilled administrator: a truly vicious campaign of obstruction and sabotage by the Customs Bureau,[88] dissension in his own ranks among ex-Customs agents and BNDD agents who were now supposed to work together as DEA agents, and resentment among former BNDD management personnel who felt that John Ingersoll had been ill used. The turmoil in the Justice Department during the fall of 1973 (which included the resignations of Attorney General Elliot Richardson, in office only since the spring, as well as his deputy, William Ruckelshaus) certainly did nothing to improve working conditions. It would take three years, a scandal, and several congressional hearings before the new agency gained anything like a state of operational equilibrium.

TURNING THE CORNER ON DRUGS

On the day the nomination of John Bartels as administrator of the DEA was announced, President Nixon told attendees at a conference on Treatment Alternatives to Street Crime, "We haven't solved the [drug problem]—we've got a long way to go, but we've turned the corner."[89] His statement was based on the belief among NIDA officials, particularly the new director, Robert DuPont, that "there are now growing signs of success in our struggle against heroin addiction."[90] DuPont reported "notable progress in the heroin area" to the House Subcommittee on Public Health and Environment and stated, somewhat confusingly, that "whatever the number [of heroin users] was 2 years ago,

President Nixon announces, "We have turned the corner on drugs." John Bartels (*left*) of the Drug Enforcement Administration and Robert DuPont of the National Institute on Drug Abuse listen, 11 September 1973. (Nixon Project, National Archives.)

it is likely to be about half that nationally at this point. Thus there may have been as much as 50 percent reduction in active heroin users though I would not want to give you an estimate of what the actual number of addicts may be."[91] John Bartels, who also testified before the same committee, cited significant increases in heroin prices and declines in purity since 1970 that would indicate increasing scarcity of the drug on American streets. Data on addiction rates in Washington, D.C., and New York showed dramatic declines in new heroin use after 1969, a rising average age of arrestees and patients in treatment, and declining numbers of deaths due to overdose and medical complications of drug addiction in these key cities.[92]

But the statistics were not unambiguous. Leon Gibson Hunt wrote in 1974 that "aggregate treatment program data do seem to show that the peak period of new heroin use occurred everywhere in the U.S. about 1968, but when local data are corrected for addicts' delay in entering treatment, this synchronous national 'epidemic' becomes a sequence of local peaks ranging from 1967 to the present."[93] Data from a National Household Survey indicate that lifetime use of heroin among young adults remained constant between 1972 and 1974 and that lifetime use among youth nearly doubled during the same period.[94] This survey is often criticized for measuring only the household population, from which large numbers of heroin users might well be excluded, but correcting for that effect would only increase the estimate of heroin use.

Not surprisingly, the administration committed itself to a guardedly optimistic interpretation of the available data—good news was at a premium in the fall of 1973. In October Vice President Spiro Agnew had been forced from office, President Nixon's attempt to fire Watergate Special Prosecutor Archibald Cox had precipitated the resignations of the attorney general and his deputy, and the House of Representatives had begun to consider impeachment, and on 17 November President Nixon had felt compelled to assure the American people that he was "not a crook." What is surprising is that the drug control program held together at all. That it did is probably testimony to the tenacity of such second- and third-level staffers as Frederic Malek, at the time deputy directory of OMB, Walter Minnick, his deputy in charge of the Office of Federal Drug Management, and Geoffrey Shepard of the Domestic Council. This was the atmosphere in which what may have been the last significant drug policy meeting of the Nixon administration took place. Geoffrey Shepard sent a preparatory memorandum to Melvin Laird, who had replaced John Ehrlichman as chief domestic advisor, outlining three policy issues to be resolved by the assembled cabinet officers: (1) a shortage of medicinal opium; (2) the flow of heroin from Mexico; and (3) the emerging problem of polydrug abuse. He also indicated to Laird that "President Nixon sees the enforcement initiatives as the most politically important aspect of this Administration's work on drug abuse. With the void in Justice, Cap Weinberger [secretary of health, education and welfare] expects to chair the meeting with the President. It is vitally important that you assert your interest in running the meeting to keep the balance."[95] The meeting was finally scheduled for 27 November, and Frederic Malek composed a brief for the president in which he indicated that the purpose of the gathering would be "to obtain publicity for the successful drug program and to provide it policy direction for the coming year."[96] Malek recommended against discussing possible steps to alleviate the shortage of medicinal opium at this meeting because the subject was "too complicated," and established as a major issue to be addressed the question of what steps could be taken to get unrepentant heroin users, who would not volunteer for treatment, out of circulation. The meeting itself, to judge from Geoffrey Shepard's record of it for the President's Meeting File, was something of an anticlimax.[97] It was preceeded by a press photo opportunity and was opened by the president, who assured the group of his commitment to the continuing success of the anti-drug effort. He and Secretary of State Henry Kissinger excused themselves after fifteen minutes, and the remaining officials, led by Laird, continued deliberating for forty-five minutes. They reached the following conclusions:

1. an outreach program should be aggressively pursued to bring non-volunteer heroin addicts into treatment;
2. existing treatment should be maintained;
3. existing facilities should be opened to non-opiate abusers, but there should be no public commitment to solve the nation's polydrug abuse problem;
4. approval in principle of the international initiatives proposed by Ambassador [to Turkey, William] Handley;
5. no decision is made on the magnitude or source of additional budget resources to implement the approved initiatives. Resource issues will be worked out jointly by OMB and the affected agencies.[98]

Unfortunately for the administration's hopes for favorable publicity, press coverage of the meeting was scant. Malek was moved to write an opinion piece for the *New York Times* in which he complained of what he saw as a lack of interest among the media in "good news." His article reveals how the Nixon administration wanted its handling of the drug problem to be viewed and shows the contrast between that desire and the impression of demise given by the material examined here.

> - Narcotics-related crimes are down.
> - There is a decline in the rate of new heroin addiction across the country. In New York it has been cut by 30 per cent since 1972, and in Washington, D.C., the number of new addicts in 1972 was 100, down from a peak of 2,700 in 1969.
> - International and domestic law enforcement has caused a heroin shortage along the Eastern seaboard since 1972. The result in New York City is that many addicts have been involuntarily detoxified because of their inability to get drugs of sufficient purity.
> - Drug seizures and arrests have markedly increased along with a massive rise in drug treatment facilities. Not only are addicts being taken off the street but they are also being placed into previously unavailable treatment programs. . . .
>
> Not long ago, our papers, journals and airwaves were filled with reporting on the dimensions of a heroin problem which annually killed hundreds of people and contributed to startling levels of crime in our nations's cities and suburbs. That crisis was confronted by the President, and we have definitely turned the corner on heroin abuse. The American people have the right to know that this is one problem which is steadily being solved—just as they were once informed that it was a problem threatening our entire society.
>
> It is a pleasure to be able to cite this heartening progress. It is too bad that this information surfaced on the editorial page as an opinion instead of on the front page as some good news.[99]

1974—THE END

In his State of the Union speech on 30 January 1974, President Richard Nixon repeated his assertion that "we have indeed turned the corner on hard drugs." He proceeded to announce supplementary legislation to the Heroin Trafficking Act then before the Senate Judiciary Committee and the House Committee on Interstate and Foreign Commerce. As mentioned, the new proposals retreated somewhat from the penalties he had proposed the previous year and undoubtedly represented recognition of the difficulty in gaining passage of such laws at that time. A newly harsh approach to drug trafficking penalties was not without support in Congress—Senators Herman Talmadge (D., GA) and Birch Bayh (D., IN) had tried to outdo the president with a draconian drug-penalties amendment to the Omnibus Crime Control and Safe Streets Act the previous year, but that bill was no more successful than the president's.

Throughout the spring, Walter Minnick's Office of Federal Drug Management issued biweekly bulletins on "drug developments" that give evidence of unflagging efforts to communicate what were considered to be the administration's successes in the struggle against drug abuse, but there were few opportunities for optimism. The report for 1 June noted that SAODAP was concerned about the possibility that medium-sized cities were experiencing localized outbreaks of heroin use and that, in the midst of that office's attempts to verify the data, the Drug Abuse Council, a private research organization funded by various foundations, had released information that confirmed them. The authors of the report expressed relief that the press did not seem to be interested in the implications of the Drug Abuse Council study.[100] The report for 15 June reproduced an assessment of the heroin situation for the first three months of 1974 from the DEA Statistical Services Division that documented an increase in heroin availability and purity and a decline in price. Accompanying this disturbing trend was an increase in heroin-related deaths.[101] Part of this phenomenon was probably due to increasing amounts of Mexican heroin on the market, but the report also noted an increase in health problems associated with other drugs—amphetamines, barbiturates, and hallucinogens. In mid-July the Turkish government announced that it would no longer adhere to the ban on opium poppy production. The same month, the Department of Defense suspended its urinalysis program in response to a decision by the U.S. Military Court of Appeals that held that evidence gathered through mandatory urinalysis amounted to self-incrimination.[102]

On 27 July 1974 three articles of impeachment against Richard M. Nixon passed the Judiciary Committee of the U.S. House of Representatives. The president announced his resignation on 8 August.

Chapter 5 The Ford Administration: The White Paper on Drug Abuse

The repercussions of President Richard Nixon's resignation for the direction of drug policy were profound. The change in national leadership itself interacted with evolving changes in the social climate to create a new, and newly complex, political environment. The first of these new circumstances was a natural aversion among President Gerald Ford's advisors to Nixon-era initiatives. The second was the belief among those concerned with the issue that drug policy had to be reevaluated. Social mores seemed ever more tolerant of all drugs, and scientific opinion, in concert with this widespread unwillingness to condemn drug use out of hand, supported a more nuanced interpretation of the varying effects and consequences of consumption of various psychoactive substances.

The rise in heroin use that began to appear in 1974 coincided with these political and social changes, with the change in presidential style, and with new appreciation of fiscal limits on policy implementation. This coincidence provided a curious symmetry to the drug policy enterprise as it developed over the next several years. There were bad drugs, principally heroin, that caused misery, disease, and crime and should be resisted with all the force of the law. Then there were not-so-bad drugs that, if not exactly harmless, could be used in moderation in much the same way as alcohol and therefore should not be allowed to absorb a major share of scarce time, effort, or money. In a stunning example of our limited ability to understand complex issues, even with ample information available, when we are breathing in with the air the attitudes and opinions of a particular historical moment, cocaine was included with marijuana in this not-so-bad group—at great cost to American society just a decade later.

A glimpse of the emerging priorities and style of the new administration can be gained by looking at how administration staffers made use of a July 1974 memorandum written by Robert DuPont (who had replaced Jerome Jaffe as head of SAODAP and was in the process of assuming leadership of the new National Institute on Drug Abuse [NIDA])[1] to prepare questions and answers on drug issues for the new president's use in responding to the press.[2] For the most part, the staff used DuPont's language verbatim, providing only a slightly more positive cast to the information. For example, they replaced "the active heroin population has been reduced" with "the active heroin addict population has been halved," and left out DuPont's reference to the possibility of increased crime.

DuPont Memo, July 1974	"Questions and Answers," August 1974
In the late 60's this country was gripped by an epidemic of drug abuse—notably heroin addiction. Addicts numbered in the hundreds of thousands and drug-related street crimes—muggings, robberies, purse snatchings—were soaring. In Southeast Asia, over 35% of our troops had experimented with heroin and 20% were considered addicted. . . .	When President Nixon entered office in January, 1969, the country was gripped by an epidemic of drug abuse, notably heroin addiction. Addicts numbered in the hundreds of thousands and drug-related street crimes—muggings, robberies, and purse snatchings—were soaring. In Southeast Asia, over 35 percent of our troops had tried heroin, and 20 percent were addicted. . . .
Results have been dramatic: the active heroin population has been reduced; drug-related street crimes declined substantially in 1973; the epidemic of drug abuse among our Vietnam troops did not come home with them.	Results are dramatic. The active heroin addict population has been halved and drug-related street crimes are down substantially. The epidemic of drug abuse among our troops in Viet Nam did not come home with them; today, only a

	small percentage of those who served are civilian addicts.
Recent developments, however, suggest the possibility of significant slippage in our efforts, which, if unchecked, could lead to a new wave of addiction, drug-related crime and damage to major international policies. In part, this may have been caused by over-confidence at the initial results and the understandable desire to turn attention to other serious matters once the immediate urgency was removed. Unfortunately, we may find ourselves very soon in a frightening situation.	Recent developments, however, indicate that some slippage may be occurring, which, if unchecked, could lead to a resurgence of the drug abuse problem. There has been a very recent upsurge in treatment demand, particularly in the West and in medium and small cities across the country.
Mexican heroin is flooding the United States, especially throughout the Southwestern parts of the country.	Mexican brown heroin has spread far beyond its traditional Southwestern area and now is estimated to supply over 60 percent of all the heroin available in the country. And the prospect of renewed Turkish opium production could significantly worsen the supply situation, depending on the effectiveness of the controls implemented.

The following excerpts appear in DuPont's memorandum but have no counterparts in the presidential document. Significantly, DuPont made only one passing reference to cocaine, while none is made in the notes for President Ford.

Since then significant progress has been made. The federal budget has increased almost tenfold in the past six years; more than 400 federally funded community treatment programs exist throughout the country; and more than 160,000 people are in treatment (over half in federally-funded programs). . . .

Cocaine is finding its way into the United States in increasing proportions.

The U.S.-Mexican border may be the world's busiest drug trafficking geographical area.

Turkey has rescinded its former opium poppy production ban and is getting ready to plant an opium crop. We must now expect heroin from this crop to again find its way into the United States.

Prime indicators of opium use such as heroin overdose deaths and property crime rates are up nationally, in some cases significantly, such as Cook County, Illinois, which reported a hundred percent increase in overdose deaths between the years 1972 and 1974; Southern California which has seen an increase in overdose deaths from 29 in 1971 to 105 in 1974.

THE FORD TRANSITION

When Gerald Ford took office in August 1974, he inherited a cabinet bureaucracy riven with conflict and a confused and demoralized White House staff. The historical dissension between the Customs Bureau and various succeeding Justice Department drug agencies had been exacerbated by Reorganization Plan 2 of 1973, and the new Drug Enforcement Administration was experiencing a management crisis that came close to destroying the agency.[3] There were also disagreements between the Justice Department and the Treasury Department about the value of IRS involvement in tax fraud investigations of people suspected of drug trafficking, which IRS Commissioner Donald C. Alexander discontinued in October of 1974.[4] Another high-profile Nixon initiative that had been suspended was the drug-testing program in the armed forces.[5] Among those responsible for "demand"-oriented programs run through the Department of Health, Education, and Welfare, there was unease and confusion about the merger of the White House–based Special Action Office for Drug Abuse Prevention with the Division of Narcotics Addiction and Drug Abuse in NIMH that created the National Institute on Drug Abuse.

A note from Edward Johnson of the Office of Management and Budget (who had replaced Walter Minnick as head of the Office of Federal Drug Management in OMB) to Dale McOmber, assistant director for budget review of the same office, gives some indication of the sense of disorientation—even dread—among the drug policy staff as the Ford administration tried to gain its footing. The note, dated 9 August 1974, the day after Nixon's resignation, read, "Administration's highly successful drug abuse program starting to drift. New Turkish poppy production, major increases in Mexican heroin traffic and a new surge of patients entering an overtaxed treatment system threaten prior successes."[6] In much the same terms, OMB's Office of Federal Drug Management, in its August 16 "Drug Developments" memo, outlined a deteriorating situation on both the international and domestic fronts: "Every day of inaction dims the already gloomy prospect of selling a workable control program to Ankara"; and, "The discussion seemed to revolve around a shared belief that the program seemed to be losing momentum, and general malaise about our inability to clearly articulate where we were and where we were going. . . . General uneasiness about the confident prediction all of us were making several months ago: perhaps they went too far."[7] In October, the "general malaise" was still palpable. "Speaking bluntly, some of the people in our own organizations are growing disheartened, feeling that national attention seems to be drifting to other issues."[8] It appeared that the "corner" in the road toward effective control of narcotics abuse had not been "turned" after all. Estimates of increased heroin use such as that of the Drug Abuse Council gained increasing credibility and, mirabile dictu, a large percentage of the American public seemed not to care much. One staff member wrote, "In general the Gallup results show a peak of concern over drugs in 1973, while the Harris peak is 1972. All show a sharp decline of interest in 1974, which, considering 8% unemployment and 12% inflation is no surprise."[9]

An overview of answers to Gallup's question "What do you think is the most important problem facing the country" for 1974 through 1976 shows that "the high cost of living" and related worries consistently topped the list by huge margins. At the beginning of Ford's presidency, in August 1974, "dissatisfaction with government" was mentioned by 4 percent of respondents, and "drugs" was mentioned by 2 percent, along with crime, and unemployment. By October 1976, 33 percent of those surveyed were most worried about unemployment, and 1 percent cited drugs as the most important national problem (Table 5-1).[10]

Table 5-1 The Most Important Problem Facing the Country: Gallup Results, 1974–1976

	16 August 1974	30 September 1974	14 October 1974	3 March 1975	21 July 1975	5 January 1976	11 October 1976
High cost of living	72	73	73	56	44	45	43
Unemployment	2	2	3	20	21	23	33
Dissatisfaction w/ govt.	4	5	6	7	7	3	7
Crime	2	4	3	5	5	8	5
Foreign policy	3	1	2	5	1	5	7
High food prices	5	8	6	4	5	2	1
Moral decay	1	1	1	3	5	4	4
Energy crisis	1	2	3	7	3	3	1
Drugs	2	1	no mention	2	2	2	1

THE SUPPLY SIDE—THE DEA IN 1974 AND 1975

The first major obstacle to a meaningful remedy to the stagnation of the federal anti-narcotic enterprise was the sorry state of the law enforcement bureaucracy. The Drug Enforcement Administration had a less-than-propitious beginning in the spring of 1973, with a history of bureaucratic sabotage and personal bickering that preceded and accompanied it. The leadership vacuum during the agency's first year and a half contributed materially to a situation in which the stated overall policy of the DEA to pursue major players in the illicit drug trade evaporated as individual agents still operated on the assumption that their own success depended on number of arrests made and quantity of drugs seized.[11] Rather than following the model established by BNDD, the agency's activities more closely resembled those of the discredited ODALE—from whose leadership the DEA administrator, John R. Bartels, had been chosen. The competing estimates of the success of drug control programs up to that time were another key influence on the credibility and effectiveness of the DEA. The Customs Bureau's evaluation of DEA's modus operandi was predictably negative.

> In [a *Washington Post* article of 15 April 1975] Mr. Bartels states that the supply reduction strategies, combined with the Turkish opium ban, plus aggressive DEA en-

President Ford meets with (*left to right*) Geoffrey Shepard, John Bartels, Sheldon Vance, and Robert DuPont after signing the Drug Abuse Prevention Week Proclamation, 18 October 1974. (Gerald R. Ford Library.)

> forcement, have been extremely successful in creating a shortage of heroin in major eastern cities for the past 2-year duration. We maintain that, much to the contrary, the Turkish opium ban was, indeed, an unfulfilled pipe dream.
>
> It would be infinitely more productive to assist and advise local police narcotics officers in fighting the internal traffic by providing training, equipment, and funding, without DEA operational manpower. Present DEA activities reflect a "big brother" concept to low-level enforcement activities precipitating many of the internal problems encountered in a "buy and bust" operation. However, they are mindful that the statistics on low-level arrests are needed to justify their activities for high-level appropriations from Congress for the infiltration of narcotics traffic.[12]

By the fall of 1974, relations between DEA and Customs and among the top managers of the DEA were reaching a nadir and the Senate Permanent Subcommittee on Investigations, under the direction of Senator Henry M. Jackson (D., WA) had opened an inquiry into corruption and mismanagement at the agency. Within the DEA, an extraordinary conflict was developing between Administrator Bartels and Acting Assistant Administrator Andrew C. Tartaglino, who was allied with the head of the Office of Inspection, George Brosan. This messy affair is recorded in detail in a report on the hearings held by Senator Jackson's committee beginning in June 1975. To begin with, Tartaglino had come to the new DEA from its predecessor agency, BNDD, where he had worked closely with John Ingersoll; Brosan was a Customs man, whereas Bartels had been Myles Ambrose's deputy at ODALE. These facts alone did not bode well for a harmonious working relationship among the three men. They also seem to have differed profoundly about how internal integrity investigations and routine background checks on potential appointees should be conducted. Bartels testified to the Senate subcommittee that he felt that Tartaglino and Brosan had resisted resolving allegations against drug enforcement personnel in a timely fashion.[13] Early in his tenure, Bartels had objected to Brosan's handling of the Office of Inspection, particularly with reference to unresolved integrity allegations against senior DEA officials, including William J. Durkin, the assistant administrator for enforcement.[14] Whatever the sources of their mutual antipathy, the matter came to a head in September of 1974.

On 7 September Bartels asked Dr. Mark Moore, who was analyzing DEA operations in his capacity as planning officer while on leave from the Kennedy School of Government, to conduct a study of the effectiveness of the Office of Inspection. (Shortly before this, Tartaglino had sent Bartels a memorandum to the effect that the Office of Inspection had a backlog of unresolved integrity cases, and requested additional personnel: Bartels had rejected his request.)

Bartels then left for Europe on agency business in the company of DEA Public Affairs Director Vincent Promuto (also a former ODALE official). During his absence, information came to Brosan's attention, through William Durkin, that Promuto, a former professional football player, had been seen in the company of people of less-than-sterling reputations, including convicted felons and a woman who figured in DEA files as an associate of drug traffickers and possibly a prostitute. Brosan, in consultation with Tartaglino and Durkin, decided to open an integrity investigation of Promuto in his and Bartels's absence, feeling that they could not adequately discuss the issue with Bartels while he was traveling with the subject of their concerns.[15] When Bartels returned, Brosan briefed him on the situation and later testified that Bartels had reacted angrily.[16] Shortly thereafter, Bartels relieved Brosan of primary responsibility for the investigation.

By November, Tartaglino had come to believe that Bartels was actively impeding the investigation of Promuto's activities.[17] He composed a memorandum for Deputy Attorney General Lawrence H. Silberman in which he "alleged, first, that DEA Administrator Bartels was indifferent to personnel integrity problems, second, that DEA's image was being tarnished in the law enforcement community because of integrity problems, some of which Tartaglino spelled out in detail; third, that Bartels had intimidated the Acting Chief Inspector [Brosan] and, in so doing, had impeded a personnel integrity inquiry; and, fourth, the situation had deteriorated to such a low point that he, Tartaglino, wished to be assigned to another job outside DEA."[18] On 20 December, Bartels relieved Tartaglino and Brosan of their duties, and they were assigned new ones in the Justice Department.[19] Silberman was essentially sympathetic to Bartels and felt that the investigation of Promuto should not have begun in his absence.[20] Nevertheless, Silberman recommended to the new attorney general, Edward H. Levi, that Bartels be replaced because of what he considered to be extremely poor management. Bartels hotly defended himself both overtly and covertly—through open statements and leaks to reporters expected to be friendly. He suspected the hidden hand of the Customs Bureau in the affair and wrote to Richard Parsons of the White House staff about unfriendly reportage.

> This continuous series of articles falsely alleging massive corruption and mismanagement are starting to have a serious effect on morale. The constant repetition of the corruption allegation, for example, gives the impression of a revealed truth despite the prior investigative judgments to the contrary by Deputy Attorney General Silberman and the FBI. These stories from Jackson's Committee of possible transfer

> of jurisdiction, furthermore, have been printed throughout the world and affect foreign cooperation. These allegations apparently by Senator Jackson's staff, Mr. Tartaglino, and certain dissident Customs agents have recently led to a strong agent movement for unionization within DEA to defend their integrity, professionalism, and careers.[21]

This was on 27 May. On 30 May 1975, Attorney General Levi requested John Bartels's resignation.[22] Levi then chose Deputy Assistant Attorney General Henry S. Dogin to serve as acting administrator. Dogin remained in the post until the appointment of Peter Bensinger in early 1976.

DEA AND CUSTOMS

One of Dogin's first and most demanding tasks was to negotiate a truce between DEA and the Customs Bureau—an achievement that had eluded all his predecessors. In February 1974, Nixon policy staffers were still struggling with what they thought they had solved with Reorganization Plan 2. James B. Clawson of the Treasury Department told Kenneth Cole, presidential assistant for domestic affairs, that

> problems of interface between the responsible agencies still exist. They are the result of an escalating series of operational misunderstandings and confusion as to the respective roles of the principal law enforcement agencies at port of entry and along the borders between ports of entry. . . .
>
> The basic DEA mission requires an extensive professional investigative effort which should not be diluted by diversion to performance of Customs interdiction responsibilities. It should contribute intelligence and information to Customs as to whom and what to watch for. However, this type of data is not forthcoming in any volume from DEA.[23]

At the end of 1974, coincident with the escalation of managerial tensions within DEA, the situation with respect to Customs was, if anything, worse. In a telephone conversation with an unnamed Customs official, a White House staff member learned that

> Customs is planning to use any and every opportunity to attack DEA, INS and the law enforcement components of the DOJ [Department of Justice]. It appears to be a twofold strategy. They are working on a paper to present to the White House to alert the President that the law and order bureaucracy established under Nixon may be a grave liability in the Presidential sweepstakes for '76. In this paper, they will propose that the law enforcement functions included in DEA, INS and FBI be removed

> from the DOJ leaving Main Justice as an organization of bureaucratic lawyers only. . . .
>
> The second approach would be directly to the Hill working through their friends in Congress. The approach there would be to take all criticisms of the Reorganization Plan No. 2 and find some Hill sponsors to take the law enforcement issue away from the Republican Party. The plan to attack on every nickel and dime issue or point of contention between DEA, INS and Customs because they believe that the DOJ law enforcement agencies are not doing the job or not doing the job efficiently. Furthermore, they plan to do this because they have nothing to lose.
>
> It's going to be a no-holds-barred affair. . . . They will use the Inspection/Internal Security situation.[24]

From the point of view of the White House, the fact that Senator Jackson began public hearings on DEA right after Bartels was fired had at least something to do with the activities of the Customs Bureau. "We believe that the corruption exposé is a means to an end, that being the ultimate revamping of the powers and jurisdiction of DEA. In response to this, the Sub-Committee may issue a series of recommendations for the distribution of present DEA powers among other agencies, primarily Customs and the FBI. It is our estimation that the Sub-Committee feels DEA has too much power, and by exposing its internal chaos and ineffectiveness, it can provide the impetus for reorganization."[25]

Negotiations and recriminations between the two agencies and their parent departments continued throughout the summer, most concentrated, if only symbolically, on the issue of how Customs could operate without authority to gather intelligence overseas, a problem referred to in the Clawson memorandum and which dated back to the days of the Federal Bureau of Narcotics. DEA was supposed to be sharing its intelligence with Customs, but that arrangement did not seem to be working to the satisfaction of the latter agency. Throughout the drug policy review process, which will be addressed below, the sniping continued. There were leaks to the press, apparently from the Customs Bureau, though that was not certain,[26] and attempts to influence the deliberations of the Drug Policy Review Task Force. Speaking of various policy options put forward as possible solutions, one member of the White House staff informed Richard Parsons that

> from my discussions with Jon [Jonathan C. Rose, Office of Policy and Planning, Department of Justice] it appears that he would like to see whether or not the new initiatives which Hank Dogin has underway will succeed or not before exploring options which include expanding Customs' role. (Dogin's initiatives are essentially embodied in Option No. 1.) As a fallback position, Jon would probably accept Op-

> tion No. 2, which retains DEA as the sole [intelligence] collection source overseas. I believe that both Options 1 and 2 could probably work with reasonable people. However, given the depth of the DEA/Customs antagonism, and the current obstinant [*sic*] stances which they are taking, it is doubtful whether either is a realistic solution to the problem.[27]

Although Dogin was making "substantial progress in removing the tired deadwood and in clearing up many of the outstanding integrity investigations,"[28] his efforts had still not produced the hoped-for truce with the Customs Bureau. In October, James Cannon, executive director of the Domestic Council, drafted an overview of the conflict for the president. Cannon was not in the least sympathetic to the Customs position. He told President Ford that

> Customs has never accepted constraints on its activities, and has always managed to overturn, subvert, or simply ignore the decision which constrained their activities. In this, they have been assisted by an almost missionary zeal, and by strong allies in Congress and the press. In the latest situation—created by Reorganization Plan No. 2 of 1973, which created DEA by combining BNDD, the office [of] Drug Abuse Law Enforcement, and the Office of National Narcotics Intelligence from Justice and by transferring approximately 500 agents and support personnel involved in drug investigations from Customs to the new agency—their attempts to overturn the President's and Congress's decisions have been strengthened by the fact that the new DEA was almost immediately put on the defensive concerning allegations of mismanagement and worse.[29]

At last, in December, a memorandum of understanding was completed and signed by Henry Dogan and Vernon Acree, commissioner of Customs. Interpreting Acree's recollections of the period, it seems likely that he was finally willing to strike a bargain primarily because the legacy of Nixon and Ambrose was no longer a force in the DEA. Acree regarded John Ingersoll as "a gentleman and a professional" with whom he could have worked well—and in fact had done so during the short time that his tenure as Customs commissioner and Ingersoll's as director of BNDD had coincided. He did not feel the same way about Myles Ambrose, whom he called "flamboyant," or any of Nixon's drug enforcement policy staff, whom he saw as inexperienced.[30]

The seven-page memorandum of understanding spelled out in detail that the DEA was to have "primary responsibility for investigation and intelligence gathering related to drug smuggling and trafficking," whereas Customs was responsible for "interdiction of all contraband, including all drugs at the land, sea, and air borders of the United States."[31] For the agreement to work as intended, a close cooperative relationship would have to be maintained between the two agencies to facilitate the exchange of information and the transfer of jurisdiction over cases that required surveillance before, through, and beyond border points. The arrangement should probably be counted as a success. In the ensuing years the relationship between DEA and Customs rarely functioned without hitches, but neither did it reach the depths of animosity and dangerous rivalry that existed before 1975.

NIDA AND SAODAP—THE DEMAND SIDE

The state of drug abuse treatment and prevention programs during the summer of 1974 was a second bureaucratic difficulty facing the new administration. While not subject to the sort of turmoil that reigned among the law enforcement agencies, the drug treatment bureaucracy was also in a state of flux. The Special Action Office for Drug Abuse Prevention began the process of transformation into the National Institute on Drug Abuse through merger with the Division of Narcotic Addiction and Drug Abuse of NIMH. Though there was some suspicion between the career civil servants of DNADA and the veterans of the White House SAODAP, the atmosphere was certainly not poisonous.[32] The principal dilemma for the Ford White House was whether it would be wise to extend SAODAP's mandate after its legislated termination date of 30 June 1975. There were many, both in the executive branch and Congress, who felt that removing drug treatment policy oversight from the White House would indicate lack of presidential commitment to the issue. Robert DuPont, at that point chief of both NIDA and SAODAP, felt that the SAODAP performed an irreplaceable political and organizational function and should be extended in some form. With a series of memos and reports on the social and political costs of reduced federal attention to the narcotics problem, he lobbied OMB and the Domestic Council through the summer and fall of 1974 in favor of maintaining some significant drug policy office in the White House. Certainly the idea that public perception of a lack of presidential interest in the drug issue could be damaging was accepted in the White House, although the real need for a White House drug policy office was not generally agreed upon.

During the winter and into the following spring DuPont continued to press his case. In one communication to President Ford, he wrote, "The legislatively scheduled termination of the Special Action Office for Drug Abuse Prevention on June 30, 1975, has serious consequences for the Administration in terms of its ability to effectively coordinate the Federal drug abuse prevention effort and to maintain the current momentum in dealing with drug abuse in the United States. The successive reductions in the drug abuse prevention budget for FY-75, and 76, coupled with the termination of the White House Special Action Office, would signal a decline in the Administration's attention to the nation's drug abuse problem at an unfortunate time."[33] However, cabinet departments most involved in drug abuse programs opposed extension. Continuation of the White House office also did not fit with President Ford's determination to devolve program management authority to those departments. Paul O'Neill, deputy director of the Office of Management and Budget, opposed any extension of SAODAP.

> We recommend against extension of the Special Action Office. We have canvassed Defense, HEW, Labor, VA [Veterans Administration] and Justice at the policy level on extending the Special Action Office. The agencies are in uniformly strong opposition to extension. . . .
>
> The office was created to oversee and coordinate the rapid increase in the Federal support for drug treatment capacity; it did that job reasonably well. Treatment capacity is, however, stabilizing. Moreover, virtually all civilian drug abuse programs are located in HEW and the major substantive policy decisions concerning drug abuse treatment have already been made. We see no need for a separate agency in the Executive Office of the President. The "serious consequences" referred to by Dr. DuPont are not specified in his materials.
>
> Nevertheless, we recognize the possible need—for political reasons, as well as to handle whatever coordination functions remain—to continue visible White House leadership of the drug abuse prevention program.[34]

Kenneth Cole held a similar view.

> OMB correctly points out that all the major substantive policy decisions concerning drug abuse treatment have already been made, and recommends against continuation or creation of any separate agency in the Executive Office. OMB does, however, recognize the possible need to continue visible White House leadership in this area.
>
> A Special Assistant role has usually been the answer for this type of problem but naming DuPont would only aggravate the situation by singling out one particular area of drug abuse (in DuPont's case, treatment) for emphasis. Moreover, both OMB and the Domestic Council staff have specialists on drug abuse already doing the non-public policy and management staff work. The need really is for an occasional visible spokesman at the White House to speak to the worsening drug situation.
>
> Yet a candid political analysis would suggest that having President Ford do a significant number of drug abuse statements and initiatives would be too reminiscent of the previous Administration. One promising solution would be to ask VP Rocke-

> feller to chair the existing Domestic Council Committee on Drug Abuse. As a former Governor of the State worst ravaged by heroin, he has both familiarity and experience with the problem. Most advantageous of all, policies or initiatives advocated by Rockefeller could not be attacked as "blindly following the Nixon hard line on drugs."[35]

By mid-March DuPont had changed his position somewhat. He seemed to have recognized the likelihood that the OMB view would prevail in the end in spite of some attempts in Congress to extend the life of SAODAP through legislation. He began advocating an approach that combined a higher policy profile for NIDA, establishment of a cabinet committee for drug abuse, and a role for himself as special assistant to the president.[36] "An incremental approach to continued coordination of the Federal drug abuse prevention activities provides the best available solution to the termination of the Special Action Office for Drug Abuse Prevention. The three increments would: integrate the technical expertise of the National Institute on Drug Abuse through the Director; establish the National Institute on Drug Abuse as the lead agency for Federal drug abuse prevention activities; and create a special Cabinet Committee on Drug Abuse to integrate activities of HEW, VA, DoD, BoP [Bureau of Prisons], LEAA, and Department of State."[37]

Richard Parsons of the Domestic Council lent support to DuPont and pointed out some problems with Kenneth Cole's position to his boss (James M. Cannon, executive director of the Domestic Council and assistant to the president for domestic affairs). He believed that the political danger of appearing to retreat from a full presidential commitment to the fight against drugs might be greater than that posed by hewing too closely to the Nixon precedent.

> In my view, however, Cole's statement of the options [in his memo to Donald Rumsfeld of 7 January] is not complete and his ultimate recommendation fails to adequately deal with the situation we are currently facing. My reasons are as follows:
>
> 1. At the time Cole wrote his memo there was little Congressional or media focus on the fact that despite the massive Federal effort of the last six years, the drug problem is getting worse. This new focus can be seen in the fact that
>   - the Senate Subcommittee on Alcoholism and Narcotics has scheduled hearings on possible extension of the SAODAP authorizing legislation;
>   - The Senate Permanent Subcommittee on Investigations has scheduled hearings on the overall effectiveness of the Drug Enforcement Administration;
>   - NBC News recently did an eight-minute piece on the growing heroin problem and involving the so-called "Mexican connection"; and
>   - Commentary will shortly publish an article by James Q. Wilson, entitled

"Heroin," which indicates that we have not "turned the corner" on the heroin problem.

2. There has been little, if any, review of the effectiveness of existing Federal drug abuse prevention programs, strategies or policies. Despite a tenfold increase in Federal funding since 1968, the problem has not gone away; indeed, it has gotten worse. Perhaps it's time to review our approach to see if we are doing something wrong or could be doing something better.
3. The Domestic Council Committee on Drug Abuse is a farce. It has met only once (the organization meeting) and has never functioned as a Committee. Nor is there a Working Group of the Committee. Therefore, reliance on the Committee to articulate and coordinate domestic drug abuse initiatives would clearly signal a lessening of Administration commitment to the overall prevention effort, with potentially disastrous results both politically and programmatically.[38]

Robert DuPont had brought a draft of the James Q. Wilson article to Parsons's attention a few days earlier.[39] The piece focused sharply on the narcotics situation and made a strong case that much of the conventional wisdom with respect to patterns of heroin use, availability, and price between 1970 and that spring of 1975 was flawed. Of particular importance was Wilson's emphasis (in agreement with Leon Gibson Hunt of the Drug Abuse Council)[40] on the spread of heroin use from large cities to small cities during the first years of the decade. Thus, he maintained, although it was true that there had been a heroin shortage on the East Coast during that period, and it was true that the combination of vigorous law enforcement and treatment availability had much to do with declining drug abuse indicators, use patterns were simultaneously spreading to new areas. Wilson also contended that the emerging presence of Mexican heroin in the U.S. market was not immediately or primarily the result of the breach created by the Turkish opium ban. He claimed that Mexico had been a major source for heroin used outside Asia since the 1940s and that heroin addicts used to Asian heroin did not easily or quickly adjust to the Mexican product. He made the argument that the East Coast law enforcement and treatment model was a good one; that it could have been applied to other areas but that "nobody noticed" the spread to small cities and towns; and that, in spite of the danger of political gamesmanship, "the costs of failing to provide Presidential leadership are ever graver: law enforcement will continue to be muddled by bitter jurisdictional quarrels, the support and direction of treatment programs will sink down into obscure, business-as-usual bureaucratic niches, and our foreign-policy objectives will not be sufficiently sensitive to our domestic drug concerns.[41]

But none of these concerns prompted any quick or public presidential response. The White House staff and the Executive Office of the President, particularly the Office of Management and Budget and its Federal Drug Management unit under Edward Johnson, were well aware that heroin use was increasing in spite of more than six years of intense government effort. The president had been informed that

> increased drug abuse, especially heroin, is becoming a major potential problem in America. Enforcement efforts are spread thin, with increases in the supply and purity of heroin. All national drug indicators show an upward trend in drug use for the first time since 1971 and there are now waiting lists for treatment in thirty states. . . .
>
> More cities and all areas of the country have emerging heroin problems. Studies indicate that epidemics rippled from large cities to medium and small-size cities throughout the country in the early 1970's; new epidemics are again breaking out in some cities on both coasts of the U.S.; and former addicts are again becoming active users.[42]

PREPARING THE WHITE PAPER ON DRUG ABUSE

The president's staff also knew that the situation could prove to be a political liability, but that public concern about drugs per se was not high relative to other issues, particularly about economic problems. Above all, they did not want to let Robert DuPont "use the Strategy Council[43] and the March 24th hearings as leverage to force a premature decision."[44] The solution to this problem, as well as to enduring questions about the direction of drug law enforcement policy, was to give DuPont some of what he wanted and hold off on any other decisions pending a complete policy review of all existing drug control programs. The study would be carried out by a Domestic Council Task Force under the direction of Vice President Nelson Rockefeller and would address both political and programmatic concerns. It would "signal continuing interest; blunt Congressional criticism; revitalize drug management; and provide answers regarding appropriate level and structure of Executive Office drug management."[45] OMB and the Domestic Council jointly agreed in principle that NIDA should be designated the lead agency for treatment and prevention activities and that DuPont should be "given a WH [White House] title of some sort."[46]

When Robert DuPont did testify before the Senate Subcommittee on Alcoholism and Narcotics on 24 March, his prepared statement reflected the administration's position that "a separate agency to provide coordination in the Executive Office of the President is no longer necessary, since the main policy and coordination issues have been resolved."[47] In his response to senators' questions, however, he candidly acknowledged his personal support for a White House drug policy office to continue some of SAODAP's oversight functions and his belief that, if such a body were established by law, it would "meet with substantial success." He continued: "I do not think it is a situation in which the administration is saying, 'If you force such an office down our throats, we will never use it at all.'"[48] Events would prove him wrong in this respect.

Plans for the drug policy review were outlined for the president in a final decision paper which included the observation that such a review "could also be an important component of a comprehensive program to combat crime."[49] The president approved the memo on 21 April.

Leading up to official organization of the Drug Policy Review Task Force, Richard Tropp[50] wrote a memo for Richard Parsons and other members of the Domestic Council that bears a relation to Jeffrey Donfeld's Domestic Council staff reports of early 1971 and the establishment of SAODAP. The same sort of doubt with respect to the real size and importance of the drug problem is expressed both in the Donfeld documents and the Tropp memo, but there are fundamental differences in historical circumstances and associated points of view. It bears repeating that Donfeld and his colleagues' central assumption was that there was indeed a strong relationship between drug abuse and crime. They were convinced, working in the absence of major previous initiatives and facing what they saw as a new situation, that both treatment and law enforcement could reduce crime rates and bring political credit to their administration. Their estimates of the true dimensions of the problem or of its importance relative to, for example, alcohol abuse did not alter the fundamental utility, for them, of their calculus. And for a while, their premise seemed to be correct, for massive infusions of federal funds at all levels of the drug control effort coincided with declining levels of new heroin use and lower indices of major crime.

On the other hand, to Parsons and Cannon and their staffs, things seemed to be getting worse. They saw that drug abuse appeared to be increasing in spite of unprecedented growth in narcotics control programs and resources to fund them during the previous administration. Given these circumstances, they disagreed about the political wisdom of high-profile presidential announcements of drug control initiatives and felt that the assumptions that had guided Nixon policy were, at the very least, open to question. Tropp had serious doubts about the relationship between drug abuse and crime rates. He also questioned the efficacy of methadone. He suggested a basic premise upon which to found the activities of the Domestic Council drug policy review.

> A healthy amount of data suggests that the Domestic Council drug abuse study may profit by starting with the hypothesis that nothing that the Federal government has tried works, either in demand reduction or supply reduction. Two questions then follow:
>
> - What specific exceptions to that hypothesis does the evidence support, and what kinds of continued or new Federal investment do those exceptions warrant?
> - If the evidence supports no exceptions, why not simply disinvest from drug abuse programs altogether, save for limited funding for experiments?
>
> Even if the tone of the final report which goes to the President bears no resemblance to the initial hypothesis, I suspect that vigorously articulated skepticism at this stage will generate—from agencies and from outside consultants—more precise data and more reflective analysis than we would otherwise receive.[51]

Briefing notes for a meeting with Vice President Rockefeller summarized the situation and made the case for the political and practical utility of the drug policy review.

> In short, we had only a temporary, and to a large degree regional, improvement, based mainly on the combined effects of the Turkish opium ban and the success of French police in destroying a number of drug networks centered in Marseilles. . . .
>
> Program spokesmen began mentioning these changed trends in late summer, 1974, but the statements about "turning the corner" had effectively turned public attention off. Then, Watergate and the energy crisis soon came to dominate the news, keeping attention off drugs.
>
> The "grace period" is over. While Congress and the press were slow to pick up trends, attention and criticism is now resounding with a vengeance, The tone has been generally questioning—almost hostile.
>
> Skeptical about claims of success
> Distressed about news of renewed threat
> Concerned about continuing Administration commitment
> Attacking drug management . . .
>
> Major questions remain.
> Drug abuser population could be as large—or larger—than ever.
> Most "treated" addicts return to drug abuse and must cycle through treatment again.
>
> Major program management problems remain.
> DEA management
> NIDA effectiveness

Treatment/manpower rehabilitation interface
Lenient courts
Intra-program rivalry
CONCLUSION
The drug problem is far from solved.
Visible signals of White House attention are required.
The Special Review meets these needs without automatically endorsing past programs.[52]

In the midst of these preparations for the drug policy review, President Ford delivered a special crime message to Congress. The message nicely illustrates Ford's attempt to base his political credibility on some of the same issues that had served Nixon well while simultaneously distancing himself from his predecessor. In fact, by this time, Ford's desire to be "un-Nixon" appeared to be winning out over arguments in favor of a more forceful "law and order" stance linking crime and heroin abuse. After using the phrase "domestic tranquility" several times, the president said, "I do not talk about law and order. . . . I turn to the Constitutional guarantee of domestic tranquility."[53] He did mention the latest estimate of the value of property crime supposedly committed by addicts to finance their habits and advocated mandatory minimum sentences for a number of federal crimes, including narcotics trafficking. The president then went to some length to emphasize that the federal government is constitutionally limited in its law enforcement role and that states and localities must bear the major burden of crime control. After a perfunctory reference to treatment for the "hapless victims of narcotics traffickers,"[54] Ford cited the new drug policy review as evidence of his commitment to drug abuse prevention and control. "Recent evidence suggests an increase in the availability and use of dangerous drugs in spite of the creation of special Federal Agencies and massive Federal funding during the past six years. I am deeply concerned over these developments and have, therefore, directed the Domestic Council to undertake a comprehensive review and assessment of the overall Federal drug abuse prevention, treatment and enforcement effort to ensure that our programs, policies and laws are appropriate and effective."[55]

THE 1975 FEDERAL STRATEGY

In June 1975, the newest edition of the *Federal Strategy for Drug Abuse and Drug Traffic Prevention* was completed and forwarded to the Drug Policy Review Task Force. The document reveals a subtle but quite perceptible shift in tone from its immediate predecessor, which was put together in the waning months of the Nixon administration. For one thing, the 1975 *Strategy* did not address cocaine as a discrete issue at all and mentioned it only in association with heroin. The 1974 edition's treatment of cocaine, while not extensive, did evince some low-key alarm. For example:

> As a drug of abuse, cocaine has been available for decades in the United States. Over the last few years, the nonmedical use of cocaine appears to have increased, particularly among those who use other drugs such as heroin. At the present time, it is not possible to estimate the extent of use nor is it possible to estimate social cost since cocaine is rarely used in isolation. Its powerful euphoric effects lead many experimenters to repeat the experience and high doses of cocaine may produce a toxic psychosis similar to that produced by amphetamines. Cocaine can be inhaled or injected to provide the user with a stimulating, euphoric effect. The duration of its effect is short, lasting approximately fifteen minutes.[56]

And, with reference to the rank of cocaine trafficking among law enforcement priorities, the *Strategy* explained that "increased demand for cocaine has increased its attractiveness to traffickers, and it has now become a significant element in the total illicit drug trade. In 1974, many of the techniques applied so successfully against the clandestine manufacture and distribution of opiates will be employed to suppress cocaine traffic."[57]

There is also a difference between the two *Strategies* in their treatment of the delicate issue of how the law should treat marijuana possession and use. The 1974 report seems uncomfortable with the new tolerance toward cannabis, saying, "The controversy surrounding [marihuana] has not diminished. Studies of its long-term toxicity and related health risks were initiated in the last few years but are not yet complete. Until the time that these studies or others demonstrate that marihuana does not create hazards to the public health and safety, federal policy will be to eradicate its illicit cultivation and harvesting, and otherwise to limit its availability within the United States."[58] As the 1975 *Strategy* makes quite plain,

> Given the scarcity of resources and the size of the drug abuse problem, DEA seeks to deflect State and local government units from making large numbers of retail marihuana arrests. Since marihuana arrests are increasing by more than 30 percent per year in most of the States, there is a real danger of swamping local criminal justice systems with these lower priority arrests. In view of the fact that most local marihuana enforcement activity is not associated with increases in heroin and other high-

> priority enforcement activity, DEA's Task Force Program, partially funded by LEAA, seeks to refocus State and local efforts on high-priority drug abuse trafficking, including large-volume trafficking in marihuana. Such refocusing would avoid needlessly stigmatizing many casual users of marihuana while increasing heroin-related enforcement activity.[59]

The 1975 *Strategy* sought to convey what was seen as a newly realistic appraisal of what American citizens could expect the federal government to do to control drug abuse. In an adjustment to the fact that, over several years of intense federal effort, drug abuse had not fallen back to pre-1960, or even pre-1968, levels, Americans were informed that they should accept that complete eradication of all drug use was not only unlikely but perhaps not even desirable as a policy goal. "We are helping individuals to function in our society, whether drug-free or not, and are moving in a generally forward manner toward accepting drug abuse as a problem the society can and has to live with. Our intolerance of the addict's addiction; our impatience with those individuals whom we think should 'know better' than to abuse drugs, yet do; and our invidious ranking of abusers of alcohol as socially more acceptable than abusers of barbiturates are all gradually being seen from more informed and experienced perspectives."[60]

PROGRESS AND DISSENSION

At the Drug Policy Review Task Force meeting on 16 July, the outlines of what would be the principal recommendations of the group's report became apparent—and they reflected further acceptance of the attitudes and priorities expressed in the 1975 *Strategy* in official circles. Edward Johnson, speaking for the working group, "emphasized the need to carefully distinguish among drugs and to focus on high levels of abuse so that government efforts are focused on those parts of the drug problem which have the greatest social cost in terms of criminal acts, poor health, economic dependence, and other adverse effects." He went on to say that "opiates remained the most serious problem, that the illegal use of psychoactive drugs was a fairly close second, and that marijuana and cocaine were somewhat lower priority."[61]

Richard Parsons addressed the problem of how to deal with the resistance in the treatment community and in Congress to the termination of the SAODAP presence in the White House.

> Mr. Parsons said that his contacts with the Hill convinced him that the treatment community and their supporters were afraid that treatment would lose the dignity a special office in the White House had provided, and that they were concerned that attempts to coordinate treatment and rehabilitation from NIDA might be stifled by the HEW bureaucracy. Dr. [Theodore] Cooper said that he felt these concerns could be overcome if NIDA were given adequate budget resources, strong leadership, which he feels Dr. DuPont provides, and some sign of visible Presidential intent, such as the designation of the Director of NIDA as a special assistant to the President.[62]

By the end of August, Parsons was able to report to James Cannon that the "outline and substance of the White Paper [as the task force report came to be called] was becoming clear."[63] He remarked that the report would draw "heavily on the lessons learned over the past six years of dramatic and sometimes frantic expansion of the Federal program." He went on to list ten points that he expected to be made in the report, which can be arranged into three categories:

1. Management: have a balanced attack on supply and demand; increase participation of state and local governments; strengthen cabinet management by removing White House program responsibility; improve interagency cooperation and follow-up; and make better use of limited resources through strong federal leadership.
2. Political style: establish realistic objectives and move away from talk of war and victories.
3. Establishing priorities: focus resources on drugs that cause most damage to individuals and society, and concentrate federal enforcement efforts on major international traffickers and wholesalers.

Parsons also explained that the task force participants had not agreed on everything they had discussed. Their disagreements reflected the principal drug-related bones of contention that were being fought over in all the branches of government as well as in the larger society. The first of these disagreements was that some members of the group wanted the president to support decriminalization of marijuana—something Parsons felt was too hot to address directly. He advocated a statement that cannabis did not seem to be as damaging as other drugs but felt that President Ford should be kept off that particular hook. In the end, the White Paper did not mention decriminalization and steered clear of the marijuana issue, offering some data on usage levels and expressing some worries about stronger cannabis products, like hashish, while defending assignment of a low priority to both enforcement of anti-pot laws and treatment of pot users. The Treasury Department representatives in particular objected to this de-emphasis, for they felt that their efforts to interdict marijuana smuggling were very important to overall drug enforcement and disruption of smuggling rings.[64]

The second area of contention was that the controversy surrounding the expiration of SAODAP's mandate was generating pressure on the task force to recommend re-creation of that sort of oversight office in the Executive Office of the President. But the policy review group stuck to the administration point of view that more vocal presidential and vice-presidential leadership and small organizational adjustments would be most in keeping with Ford's goals. The Department of Health, Education, and Welfare was not particularly happy about this and said as much in its criticism of the draft report. That department's representative, Theodore Cooper, assistant secretary for health, commented that the paper seemed to be recommending more, and more complicated, organizational structures than had been in place under SAODAP. The *White Paper* proposed that (1) the Strategy Council be given additional responsibilities; (2) a Cabinet Committee on Drug Abuse Prevention be created to assume some of the coordinating functions of SAODAP; and (3) a small professional staff be maintained in OMB to oversee federal policy.

Third was the calamitous hostility between the Drug Enforcement Administration and the Customs Bureau. At the time of Parsons's memo, Henry Dogin had been at DEA for about three months, and Senator Jackson's investigation was continuing. Parsons reported that although the task force generally supported the validity of Reorganization Plan 2, he "fully expect[ed] Customs to torpedo this aspect of the report and, possibly, call the whole endeavor a whitewash."[65] He was not far wrong.

On the same day that David R. Macdonald, assistant secretary of the treasury for enforcement, operations, and tariff affairs, submitted his department's criticism of the draft *White Paper*,[66] a leaked story appeared in the *Chicago Daily News* that quoted directly from the draft and discussed the dismay among Customs officials, who felt that the document had given their agency short shrift.[67] The newspaper quoted its sources as describing Customs Commissioner Vernon D. Acree as "'bitter, hurt and angry' over the selection of DEA to be the sole agency for narcotics control." It went on to assert that Acree had "submitted a number of 'position papers' to the Task Force, but these were all but ignored." Macdonald, in his official departmental response to the *White*

Paper draft, did not express this sense of wounded pride, but rather discussed inconsistencies between what he and his colleagues felt was the low-key optimism of the draft and what they saw as the facts of the worsening drug abuse situation and the inadequacy of the steps that had been taken to correct it. They worried that "the United States can suffer only tragic consequences by practicing selective law enforcement. Enforcement must be even-handed and comprehensive to be effective and corruption-free. To diminish efforts against marijuana and cocaine can only erode further respect for law and law enforcement officers."[68] They also felt that Reorganization Plan 2 had denied "flexibility" to the federal government in adapting its law-enforcement resources to the changing needs of drug interdiction. Herein lay a fundamental, perhaps irreconcilable difference between the Customs point of view and that of DEA. Customs saw the border as the most obvious point of vulnerability in narcotics commerce. "The most effective and efficient means of interdicting the drug traffic is to seize the high-value, concentrated narcotics at the borders of the Customs territory of the United States. The common law right of search and seizure by the U.S. Customs Service is broader than that of any other U.S. enforcement agency. Effective drug interdiction at the borders is dependent upon the gathering of intelligence abroad concerning potential shipments and the application of all enforcement tools to accomplish the actual seizures at the border."[69]

The DEA perspective, articulated in Henry Dogin's analysis of the *White Paper* draft, is in marked contrast.

> It is at the foreign source and the domestic points of delivery where the greatest opportunities for penetration exist. . . .
>
> . . .The actual crossing of the U.S. border with the contraband goods is the point of least vulnerability for the large, organized criminals. . . .
>
> The disputes between Customs and DEA] have been exacerbated in recent months because of the Customs Service's dissatisfaction with the jurisdictional determinations expressed in the Reorganization Plan and its hope of returning the previous state of affairs as a result of the present study and similar inquiries being conducted by a Senate Subcommittee.[70]

The final *White Paper* did not resolve these issues, but it did include shortened versions of the two agencies' criticisms as appendixes to the document. As mentioned, a memorandum of understanding was signed by Customs and DEA in December which did serve to ameliorate, for the most part, the ill-feeling between them, although it did confirm the primacy of DEA in narcotics control law enforcement.

THE FINAL REPORT

The White Paper on Drug Abuse: A Report to the President from the Domestic Council Drug Abuse Task Force occupies a pivotal place in the history of federal narcotics policy. For the first time, a public presidential document on drug policy eschewed absolutist rhetoric, tried to accommodate increasing social tolerance of drug consumption, and recognized the fact that the "drug problem" was not monolithic—that different drugs have different effects and pose different dangers to their users. As pointed out earlier, the new perspective could be seen emerging in the 1975 federal strategy report, but what was really new about it was not so much its content as that the official climate of opinion had changed enough to accept it. After all, many of the same ideas had been expressed in the reports of the Commission on Marihuana and Drug Abuse in 1972 and 1973, which Richard Nixon had rejected. It may be significant that Raymond Shafer, who had chaired the Marihuana Commission was, at the time the *White Paper* was written, assistant to Vice President Nelson Rockefeller and attended some of the meetings of the task force as Rockefeller's representative. Richard J. Bonnie, professor of law at the University of Virginia, was another leading participant in both undertakings. For whatever reason, there are enough passing similarities between the *White Paper* and the final report of the Marihuana Commission, *Drug Use in America: Problem in Perspective,* to provoke some observations.

First, the *White Paper's* advice that law enforcement efforts be concentrated on major traffickers and development of conspiracy cases closely parallels the Marihuana Commission's recommendation that "federal agencies concentrate primarily on the top of the illegal distribution network: importation, exportation and large volume foreign and domestic traffic."[71] It will be remembered that President Nixon sought to discredit this approach (which was defended by Director John Ingersoll of the Bureau of Narcotics and Dangerous Drugs) by establishing ODALE to circumvent BNDD.

Another important point of agreement between the two documents can be found in a comparison of the following two passages.

Drug Use in America	*White Paper on Drug Abuse*
Recognizing that some degree of psychoactive drug use seems to be inevitable in all societies, policy makers must determine whether this society should maintain a posture of undiffer-	We must be realistic about what can be achieved and what the appropriate Federal role is in the war against drugs. We should stop raising unrealistic expectations of total elimination of drug abuse

A Cabinet Room meeting to discuss drug problems with members of Congress and the White House staff, 22 December 1975. (Gerald R. Ford Library.)

> entiated disapproval, or whether it should try to channel use toward less harmful substances and behavior. Our laws have already made alcohol the preferred social drug. That historical fact should not prevent further evaluation of the wisdom of this preference. While continuing to disapprove use in general, society might find it efficacious to make an integrated set of availability decisions, reflecting the relative risk potential of various substances. (p. 410)

> from our society. At the same time, we should in no way signal tacit acceptance of drug abuse or a lessened commitment to continue aggressive efforts aimed at eliminating it entirely. (p. 5)

That Americans should learn to live with some level of use and even abuse of psychoactive substances—as urged by the Marihuana Commission report, the 1975 *Strategy,* and the *White Paper,* had been utterly unacceptable to Richard Nixon (and would be later to Ronald Reagan). There was no room for those who publicly espoused this thought in the councils of power in the Nixon White House. What was now so different that President Ford saw fit to allow the idea to reemerge? As was pointed out with respect to the operating assumptions of Nixon's drug policy staff, there was at the time no reason to suppose that a combination of energetic law enforcement and expanded treatment capacity emphasizing methadone maintenance would not have the desired effects on drug abuse. Gerald Ford, however, could not be so optimistic. He faced a discouraging situation: new agencies, new programs, and large budgets were in place, and still all indications pointed to increasing use of illicit substances, particularly heroin. In the absence of a proven cure and in the face of softening public attitudes toward at least some drugs, accommodation seemed to be the only sensible course. In addition, Ford's whole approach to governance, which he later called "new realism," was essentially a commitment to cut federal spending to the bone. (Ford vetoed fifty-nine spending bills and was overridden twelve times).

The *White Paper* was not, however, a monument to political courage, nor did it ultimately "signal continuing interest; blunt Congressional criticism; revitalize drug management; and provide answers regarding appropriate level and structure of Executive Office drug management"[72] as its drafters had hoped. It mostly avoided such politically "radioactive" issues as marijuana decriminalization and any major departure from the traditional law-enforcement-based approach to narcotics control—for one thing, it endorsed mandatory minimum sentences, which the Marihuana Commission had rejected. One also suspects that it was designed, at least in part, to take some of the political steam out of the issue and to do whatever possible to prepare the public to receive calmly the mounting evidence of increased drug abuse and not to pin the blame for it on Gerald Ford. De-emphasizing cocaine would fit well into this scenario: use might be going up, but—unlike heroin—it was being used by otherwise law-abiding people and, as far as anybody knew, was not such an awful substance anyway.

After some confusion about the appropriate date for its release, the *White Paper* was made public on 14 October.[73] President Ford immediately lent strength to the impression among some members of Congress and the press that he was not willing to face facts by putting off a clear statement of his position on the recommendations of the report, although he praised it as "realistic and comprehensive."[74] Instead, he asked the cabinet departments to submit their reactions to the final version by 15 December 1975. It is a little hard to see what he expected to gain from such a request—other than time—as the agencies had already commented on the final draft. Edward Johnson continued to worry. "Frankly, Paul, the alleged absence of *personal* Presidential interest in the drug program is an impression still held by a surprising number of people both inside and outside government. This reflects, I suppose, the contrast between President Nixon's frequent (and often bellicose) public statements on the subject, and President Ford's significantly less public stance."[75] Richard Parsons alerted James M. Cannon to a *Washington Post* editorial that complained, "Since the task force report, President Ford has been silent on the subject of drug abuse and how it should be dealt with. His task force produced a report that was widely admired for its candor and its pragmatic tone. If the President were to match that tone with utterance of his own, we might get past the arguments to some results."[76] Parsons advised his boss that "this kind of criticism is becoming more and more frequent, both in the media and on the Hill. In light of this fact, you might want to 'nudge' the Cabinet officers who have been asked to respond to the White Paper to ensure that they meet the 15 December deadline."[77]

By the end of December all departments had responded in generally positive terms. Theodore Cooper, writing on behalf of HEW, was perhaps the most critical, wondering, as health officials often did, how the goals of the report could be reached without significant increases in budgetary resources.[78]

As *The White Paper on Drug Abuse* was being prepared for publication, NIDA director Robert DuPont had released new data on levels of drug use in the United States during the previous year.[79] The data were the result of four surveys, two of which, *Public Experience with Psychoactive Substances* (the Household Survey) and *Monitoring the Future: Continuing Study of the Life Styles and Values of Youth* (the High School Seniors Survey), have been conducted periodically up to the present. The third was *Veterans' Drug Use Three Years After Vietnam* by Lee N. Robins. This was Robins's second follow-up study of Vietnam veterans, whom she had first studied in 1972. The fourth report was entitled *Drug Use Among Young Men in the United States* and was "based on interviews with a national sample of 2,510 Selective Service registrants from ages 20–30 in 1974." It was conducted by Dr. John O'Donnell of the University of Kentucky at Lexington.[80]

All the studies reported increased drug use among their subject populations. The Household Survey reported that "the trend toward earlier introduction to drug use is definitely upward. The only aspect of the trend that seems to have stabilized is in current use among the 19–25 age group."[81] The survey of young men found "no indication of any recent decline in the annual prevalence of use of any drug, with the possible exception of psychedelics. This means that there is no basis to suggest that the drug epidemic has ended; indeed, for several drugs, notably cocaine, the data are consistent with a continuing increase in use."[82]

In the face of these indications of continued increases in the levels of drug use, particularly among the young, it is difficult to appreciate how President Ford could be simultaneously praised for the "realism" of the *White Paper* and criticized for lack of resolve to control narcotics use. One has to consider the beliefs of the large percentages of respondents who reported very little or no drug use. Lloyd Johnston and his colleagues, authors of the High School Seniors Survey, remarked on the generally conservative views of their subjects with respect to use of any illicit drug except marijuana and pointed out that "it would be quite erroneous to conclude from the increase in illicit drug use since 1969 that using a wide array of illicit drugs had become the 'in' thing to do. Less than a quarter of the seniors have gone beyond experimenting once or twice with any of the illicit drugs other than marijuana, and the large majority still feel that the use of such drugs is improper and unwise. In fact, over 70% say they would forbid their own children from using any illicit drug except marijuana."[83]

Marijuana was indeed a special case—as it had been since the mid-sixties. Only one third of Johnston's young respondents felt that cannabis use should continue to be a crime. Their elders did not generally agree[84] although a trend toward liberalized pot laws was gaining strength at the state level, and presidential advisors were increasingly nervous about the willingness of the health professionals at HEW to "flirt with" endorsements of decriminalization.[85] The Johnson administration had had a similar problem with the statements of Dr. Goddard. Nixon's unequivocal condemnation of all drugs and his rejection of the Marihuana Commission's report generally succeeded in keeping public dissent among his appointees and their staffs to a minimum in spite of strident and politicized marijuana militancy among some segments of the population.

CONGRESS, THE WHITE PAPER, AND INTERNATIONAL DRUG CONTROL

Meanwhile, Congress continued to agitate for a specific and detailed administration response to the *White Paper.* In late October Senators Williams, Ribicoff, Hathaway, Javits, Percy, and Schweiker invited Vice President Rockefeller to discuss the *White Paper* with their Committees on Labor and Public Welfare and Government Operations. The vice president declined.[86] At the same time, Congressman Charles Rangel (D., NY) wrote a long letter to the president urging him to take whatever unilateral or bilateral action might be necessary to stem the flow of heroin from Mexico and to prevent reemergence of Turkey as a major supplier of the drug.[87] Rangel and his colleagues in both houses of Congress seemed convinced that the key to heroin control was diplomatic action aimed at narcotic source countries. Senator Charles Percy wrote to Secretary of State Kissinger in October and again in November about the influx of Mexican heroin. He told Kissinger: "I reiterate my firm belief in the importance of your personally interceding in this matter lest the complacency which seems to prevail today compared to the declaration of President Nixon that drug abuse in the nation's No. 1 domestic enemy thwart any immediate redress to what has become an even more urgent domestic problem."[88]

In late November, a bipartisan group of eighty-five House members wrote to the president to tell him of their concern about rising heroin abuse indicators and to request that he meet with them to discuss the "impending epidemic."[89] The president replied to Rangel's October letter on 9 December, telling him about recent contacts with Mexico and Turkey and agreeing to meet with a congressional delegation to discuss drug control initiatives, particularly high-level contacts with foreign leaders. When the president met with Rangel's delegation of seven representatives, they assailed him with complaints that the problem was worsening in both inner cities and border states, that the administration, and particularly the State Department, seemed to lack the determination to pressure Turkey and Mexico to control opium production, and that Ford himself had to make a better show of concern for narcotics control.[90] The president tried to reassure them. He promised that the Drug Policy Review Task Force would undertake a review of what was being done to control trafficking across the southwest border. Several days later he made a public statement endorsing the *White Paper* and declaring that he had directed Secretary of State Kissinger to negotiate improved drug control cooperation with Mexico.[91]

In early January of 1976, DEA administrator Henry Dogin followed up on President Ford's December meeting with Rangel and his colleagues with a long letter detailing recent administration drug-control efforts aimed at Mexico, Turkey, France, Thailand, and Burma. He argued that the "traffic in morphine base from Turkey and heroin from Marseille to North America is at its lowest level in 30 years" and that lower-grade heroin from Southeast Asia might be a greater threat.[92]

Later that month, New York Congressmen Lester L. Wolff (D.) and Benjamin A. Gilman (R.), both of whom had been signatories to the November letter to the president, told the press that they believed that a billion dollars' worth of Mexican heroin and cocaine were coming into the country each year and that they were disappointed in Mexico's crop eradication efforts.[93] To judge from minutes of a meeting of the Drug Policy Review Task Force held on 6 January and from a document titled "International Narcotics Control"—undated but probably from about the same time—domestic policy advisors were indeed quite concerned about the "emergency situation in this country in drug abuse,"[94] but dramatic presidential pronouncements on the issue were still considered inappropriate given the posture of reassessment and restraint they judged to be the best strategy in the face of the worsening situation. The tone that Gerald Ford continued to seek for his entire administration, a tone intended to bolster his credentials as an honest and reliable leader, was one of "new balance," which meant "promising [the American people] no more than we can deliver, and delivering all that we promise."[95] Still, Ford did have to answer the agitation in Congress for stronger measures against foreign drug producers and smugglers. An "International Narcotics Control Assistance Program," through which "grants of equipment and training are used to enable foreign governments showing the commitment to do so to more effectively control narcotics abroad—so as to cut down on amounts reaching the United States," was already in place.[96] The emphasis of this program, in accord with the *White Paper*, was heroin control, to which 80 percent of the program funds were allocated, the remaining 20 percent being devoted to cocaine traffic. The countries receiving the bulk of the aid were Mexico, Burma, and Thailand.

The results of the promised study of drug smuggling across the nation's southwestern borders were typically Fordian. James Cannon reported to the president that

> I came back with the impression that the "solution" to the problem [of drug trafficking across the Southwest border] lies in doing better what we now do, rather than in dramatic—and expensive—new initiatives. There is considerable room for improvement in the way we manage existing resources, particularly in more fully utilizing the resources of all Federal departments and agencies available along the border.[97]

THE OFFICE OF DRUG ABUSE POLICY

The hope that the *White Paper* would satisfy Congress that the executive branch was adequately addressing drug policy management was also proving to be illusory. Ford's domestic policy staff had succeeded in preventing legislative extension of the Special Action Office for Drug Abuse Prevention beyond June 1975, but the autumn saw several new congressional attempts to establish a White House drug policy office. The domestic policy staff were "opposed to [an Office of Drug Abuse Policy] because it sets up another advocacy office, because it detracts from Cabinet management, because it raises fake expectations of actual influence, and because its immediate predecessor did not work well."[98] (On this last point, it had been the administration's contention that "on major disputes, SAODAP has required Domestic Council and OMB intervention, which is also available to NIDA.")[99] Senate Bill 2017, which proposed amendments to the Drug Abuse Prevention and Treatment Act of 1972 that would create a White House "Office of Drug Abuse Prevention Policy," was headed for conference. James M. Cannon wrote to Senator Charles Percy, who was to participate in the conference on the legislation and who had supported the White House position on SAODAP extension, detailing White House objections to S. 2017. He called such an office "unnecessary and improvident in a time of fiscal restraint."[100] Percy's reply indicates that he was distinctly underwhelmed by the *White Paper* and that he felt that there should be a high-level person in charge of drug policy coordination whose appointment should be subject to Senate confirmation and who should have access to the president.[101]

After some discussion of technicalities, the conference report was approved by the Senate and was sent to the House of Representatives for consideration.

James Cannon, Domestic Council director, leads a discussion on drug abuse problems during a Cabinet Room meeting, 7 April 1976. (Gerald R. Ford Library.)

It passed the House in late February 1976, and the bill was sent to the president for signature. Administration staffers were in a quandary: they were convinced that an Office of Drug Control Policy in the White House was unnecessary and inappropriate to Ford's management and budgetary goals, but they did not feel that a veto of a drug bill could be sustained in a election year.[102] James Cannon advised the president as follows.

> Inevitably, the programmatic rationale for disapproving the bill would be misunderstood by a substantial segment of the general public, who would view the veto as an indication of diminished Administration interest in the drug abuse problem. While this erroneous impression could ultimately be corrected, I have no doubt that a veto would detract from your solid accomplishments in this area. Moreover, at a time when we are attempting to educate members of the Congress on the dimension and seriousness of the drug abuse problem so that we can enlist their support in our efforts to combat it, a veto of this bill would, in my judgment, be counterproductive. Finally, enactment of the bill is necessary to permit the appropriation of additional needed funds for Federal drug abuse treatment programs. For this reason, the Department of Health, Education, and Welfare has recommended approval of the bill.[103]

Cannon suggested a way out that he hoped would allow the president to approve a drug bill in an election year and at the same time avoid implementing it. He offered the possibility that the president could sign the bill, thus approving the provisions to fund NIDA treatment and prevention programs, but not seek appropriations for the policy office. He thought that "if we can persuade the respective appropriations subcommittees not to fund the office, we can avoid actual creation of the office without forcing a major confrontation with the Congress on this issue."[104] This option was adopted, and the president signed the bill on 20 March 1976, stating as he did so that "I do not intend to seek appropriations for the new Office of Drug Abuse Policy [ODAP] authorized by the bill."[105] Needless to say, Congress was not pleased. The election year had begun in earnest, and criticism of Ford's perceived unwillingness to speak out forcefully on narcotics control policy had to be dealt with. The president had taken some steps in that direction early in the year and in fact had been advocating mandatory minimum sentences for certain drug-related crimes since the beginning of his term. Even so, he had insisted on the limited role that the federal government could legitimately play in local law enforcement and had tried to avoid perfervid anti-drug, law-and-order oratory. But as the spring progressed, his public statements on the narcotics question began to take on a distinctly aggressive character.

SHOWING "INTEREST": CRIME AND DRUGS

In mid-February Ford had told a gathering of the Federal Bar Association that "the increasing use of hard drugs contributes to the soaring crime rate. In this case, our Federal responsibility is very, very clear. I have directed all Federal law enforcement agencies—in particular, the Drug Enforcement Administration—to intensify the drive against major narcotic traffickers." He added that he supported mandatory prison sentences for convicted drug traffickers, for "these merchants of death deserve nothing less."[106] Later that month the president released a statement to publicize his meetings with leaders of drug source nations and members of Congress "to assure them of my full commitment to curbing the illicit traffic in drugs, I want to take this opportunity to pledge to the American people an all-out Federal effort to combat the drug menace."[107]

After the president's announcement that he planned not to request funds for ODAP, the domestic policy staff prepared a lengthy briefing for him, representatives of the cabinet departments, and all of Ford's principal policy advisors on the background and current state of federal drug control efforts. The staff reported that "in 1974 the crime rate increased a whopping 17 per cent. It increased an additional 9 per cent last year."[108] They also passed on the latest estimates of numbers of users of various drug types of drugs.

> We believe that approximately 2,000,000 people use heroin on an occasional basis. However, only about 400,000 of these users are addicted to heroin. . . . Barbiturates, tranquilizers and amphetamines are used without medical supervision by some 7 to 8,000,000 Americans. We estimate that slightly more than half of these users are in serious trouble because of the use of these drugs. . . .
>
> We know less about cocaine than we do about most other illicit drugs because widespread use of cocaine is relatively new. . . . At the present time approximately 2,000,000 people use cocaine on an occasional basis. Evidence is that very few are suffering adverse consequences. . . .
>
> An estimated 30,000,000 Americans have used marihuana at least once. We believe that some 12 to 13,000,000 people currently use marihuana. . . .

Although the picture that Richard Parsons painted for the briefing audience was generally gloomy, he focused on three "very real successes," two of which had to do with crime control and all of which had had their major impacts during the previous administration. One was the break-up of the heroin pipeline from Turkey through France to the United States. The second was the reduction of narcotic addiction among returning Vietnam veterans. The third area where Parsons claimed success for federal drug-control programs was in the

Treatment Alternatives to Street Crime program. He went into some detail in order to explain recidivism rates in TASC cities and claimed that "the average [number of people who commit additional crimes during the period they are in the TASC program in] all TASC cities was 10 percent, compared to an 18 percentage average for all offenders generally."[109]

> Mr. Cannon summarized the more promising initiatives which were being considered: (1) a special message to Congress on drug abuse; (2) re-instituting the IRS enforcement program; (3) more vigorous prosecution by U.S. attorneys; (4) better interdiction; and (5) an expanded program to alert the public to the dangers of drug abuse and to create a national commitment to dealing with it. . . .
>
> The President asked the Attorney General [Edward H. Levi] to describe the problems Justice had and to outline what could be done to improve the situation. The Attorney General said that four problems existed, and that action was underway in each of them: (1) strengthen DEA leadership—he had appointed a new administrator; (2) following up on White Paper recommendations regarding priorities—he understood DEA was giving this top priority; (3) focusing prosecution on top-level conspiracy—a very difficult problem; and (4) interdiction—to be discussed by others.[110]

President Ford seemed particularly irritated that the IRS traffickers program had been suspended. As noted earlier, IRS Commissioner Donald C. Alexander had ended the program in October 1974. He was sensitive to allegations that his agency had engaged in civil rights abuses, particularly with respect to the tax status of nonprofit organizations whose political activities had angered the Nixon administration. After Watergate testimony revealed that his Special Services Staff had compiled dossiers on the operations of numerous such organizations as well as individuals, he dismantled the staff. In this context, when various public interest groups challenged the IRS policy of seizing the assets of traffickers suspected of tax evasion, Commissioner Alexander thought it best to curtail the program. "The President again said that he didn't accept the rationale for stopping the IRS program aimed at major drug traffickers. Attorney General Levi said that the stated rationale was nonsense, and the President said that he felt the public would applaud any program which took the profit out of drug trafficking. Mr. Parsons noted that public opinion polls showed that the American people were extremely supportive of government efforts to deal with the criminal aspects of drug abuse."[111]

Following the briefing, James Cannon's suggestion that the president prepare new narcotics control legislation and submit it to Congress with a special message was adopted. Cannon wrote a detailed decision paper for the president including all the options for legislation as well as for the organizational structure of policy coordination and implementation that had been discussed at the briefing and/or were suggested by the *White Paper.* Among these was the question of mandatory minimum sentences. Ford's proposal of the previous year for such a law had been appended to the Criminal Justice Reform Act, but that measure was stranded in Congress and would not be acted upon until after the elections at the earliest, so a new bill would have to be introduced to cover narcotics sentencing. Another problem was bail jumping, which was particularly troublesome in cases of alien traffickers who had plenty of money and no incentive to stick around. Cannon's decision paper proposed legislation authorizing judges to deny bail in certain circumstances as a way to deal with that. The paper also contained suggestions meant to reduce money laundering, strengthen forfeiture powers, and require timely reporting of vessel arrivals to Customs.

But the thorniest question for federal drug control management continued to be how to coordinate policy from within the White House without abandoning Ford's commitment to strong cabinet management and at the same time head off any congressional attempts to force funding of ODAP. Revitalizing the defunct Strategy Council was one option, although the attorney general was strongly opposed to the idea, fearing that law enforcement activities would again come under the purview of the White House in the manner of ODALE.[112]

> The Department of Justice strongly objects to the proposal that a Strategic Council on Drug Abuse to be chaired by the Assistant to the President for Domestic Affairs be re-established and given expanded responsibility for coordinating drug abuse programs. Law enforcement is, of course, a major aspect of the Federal government's drug abuse program. In our view it is inappropriate to place—or appear to place—any of the responsibility for law enforcement decisions involving the Department of Justice in the White House or anywhere other than in the Department under the authority of the Attorney General. There is a rather long and dismal history of past violations of this principle in prior administrations—and I feel very strongly about this.[113]

The attorney general suggested that two separate cabinet committees be formed, one to coordinate law enforcement programs and another to look after prevention and treatment.

President Ford initialed Cannon's paper in favor of all the proposals and noted his support for the attorney general's idea for two cabinet committees to oversee drug policy. He presented his legislative package to Congress on 27

April along with a special message in which he emphasized that he was determined to combat the "staggering" cost of drug-related crime to the nation, which he now estimated at $17 billion a year—up from the $15 billion he had cited in his crime message of the previous year. His two oversight committees were to be called the Cabinet Committee for Drug Law Enforcement, to be chaired by the attorney general, and the Cabinet Committee on Drug Abuse Prevention, Treatment, and Rehabilitation, to be headed by the secretary of health, education, and welfare. He directed the secretary of the treasury to revive the IRS program to prosecute major traffickers on tax charges, and he urged ratification of the 1971 Convention on Psychotropic Drugs aimed at international control of amphetamines, barbiturates, and other similar synthetic substances. He mentioned his diplomatic contacts with the leaders of Columbia, Mexico, and Turkey but did not offer any specific initiatives other than promises of liaison, nor did he make mention of Parsons's and Cannon's February visits to border states.

RETURN TO ODAP

Congress was not to be so easily thwarted in its attempt to force a drug policy office on the president. In mid-May the Senate passed a supplemental appropriations act with an amendment to fund ODAP.[114] Edward Johnson, head of federal drug management in OMB, was convinced that the determination in Congress to see the office established had much to do with distrust in Congress and in the professional treatment community of the HEW bureaucracy. Speaking of an organization and management study of NIDA, he complained to James Lynn, OMB director, that

> despite numerous meetings about this report with a host of HEW officials, no significant progress has been made in implementing any recommendations in over seven months. No one ever says "no"; instead, each meeting simply raises another set of bureaucratic impediments and notes more reviews which are necessary before any action can be taken. No one ever focuses on whether the recommendations are right or not; rather, the discussion always seems to focus on protecting the turf of ADAMHA [Alcohol Drug Abuse and Mental Health Administration], or H (Health), or P (Planning), or GC (General Counsel), or C (Comptroller), or some other organizational entity. This is a classic case of excessive layering stifling initiatives intended to improve the delivery of services to constituents. . . .
>
> My concern is two-fold. First, there is no question but that these delays have both added to the Congressional resolve to establish ODAP and dissipated some of the

President Ford reads a statement before signing his Message to Congress on Drug Abuse, flanked by (*left to right*) Robert DuPont, F. David Mathews, Edward Levi, and Peter Bensinger, 27 April 1976. (Gerald R. Ford Library.)

> momentum generated by the White Paper. Second, and perhaps more important, I suspect I have seen a pattern in which a large and entrenched bureaucracy is able to effectively stifle any management improvement initiatives by throwing a blanket of multiple reviews and repeated references to "departmental policy" over it. If this is true, then any changes we manage to force through are probably only temporary.[115]

In spite of congressional resolve and bureaucratic obfuscation, the president's advisors began to consider a proposal to rescind the $250,000 earmarked in the spending bill for ODAP. Johnson worried that OMB Deputy Director Paul O'Neill was "digging in his heels against the tide," and decided to warn him of some of the implications of a rescission.

> It is important for us to recognize that ODAP was initially proposed and doggedly pursued because supporters of drug abuse prevention and treatment believed that those activities would slip in priority if left up to HEW. Further, they doubted that NIDA would have sufficient authority or motivation to either be responsive to their constituents, or to earn the respect and cooperation of VA, Defense, Prisons, et al. All the rest—the need for a spokesman responsive to Congress; the need to coordinate law enforcement with treatment; and so on—is secondary to this deep-seated fear that the HEW bureaucracy would somehow "bury" drug abuse prevention and treatment.
>
> I have reluctantly concluded that they are probably right. I still believe that their proposed solution to the fundamental problem—a high profile advocacy office—is incorrect and that the current arrangement (relying on Domestic Council and OMB) has a better chance of making real progress. But the reality is that HEW has thus far done more to confirm their concerns than allay them, and the President's decision against revitalizing the Strategy Council didn't help. In that environment, I doubt a rescission stands a chance of being sustained, and expect that the Congress will independently provide funds for FY77 and 78, as well.[116]

Richard Parsons of the Domestic Council told James Cannon that he felt much the same way.

> As you will recall, when the legislation establishing ODAP came to the President, he decided to approve the bill because, among other things, this was the unanimous recommendation of all of the Republican Congressional leaders, based on the fact that a veto of the bill could not be sustained. It is my personal view that the proposed rescission would similarly not be sustained. I assume, therefore, that the real reason to propose a rescission of the $250,000 is to permit the President to make a political statement concerning the proliferation of government agencies and outline his attempts to decrease the size of the Federal bureaucracy. In my view, this is not the place where the President should make his stand.

He gave three reasons: "the intense public interest in doing something about the drug abuse problem; the apparent Congressional interest in addressing this matter; and the relatively small amount of money involved."[117]

In the end, O'Neill recommended rescission to the president. He apparently agreed with the argument, outlined in his memo along with opposing views, that "ODAP is an unnecessary office which adds another layer of bureaucracy. Its establishment would be inconsistent with your attempts to decrease the size of the Federal bureaucracy. . . . An additional and duplicative mechanism is not needed and detracts from your emphasis on cabinet management."[118]

On 7 June Ford approved the recommendation. In his message to Congress proposing the rescission, President Ford insisted that "ODAP represents an unnecessary expense for the taxpayer and adds to the Federal bureaucracy. Furthermore, I believe the establishment of this Office is an encroachment on my responsibilities as Chief Executive to organize the Executive Office of the President to carry out, as effectively as possible, the programs and laws which are established by Congress."[119]

THE 1976 CAMPAIGN

At the time that President Ford made the decision to shelve the ODAP issue once more, he was already nearly assured of the Republican presidential nomination in spite of a determined challenge from his party's right led by Ronald Reagan. Former governor Jimmy Carter of Georgia was the likely Democratic nominee, and the only issues that seemed to offer traction for the two principal candidates were economic recovery and improving government efficiency to reduce wasteful spending. They left direct involvement in complicated and emotionally charged conflicts over abortion and gun control to Reagan. The candidates mostly avoided the subject of illegal drugs in spite of consistent and fairly detailed press coverage throughout the summer of cocaine use, manufacture, and smuggling and the by-then-routine reports of well-known people being busted for possession of one or another drug. When they had to face the fact that their own children had used marijuana, both Carter and Ford expressed concern, understanding, and admiration of their sons' candor. Carter did intimate that he would consider federal decriminalization of marijuana if elected, while Ford remained opposed to the idea. There were other differences, mostly of style, between the candidates from which voters might be expected to draw some conclusions about their respective attitudes toward drugs, or at least toward people who used them. Carter seemed to be making a concerted effort to counter his image as a straight-laced Southern Baptist by cultivating the endorsements of rock bands, one of which, the Allman Brothers, was embroiled in the trial of its manager for cocaine trafficking. On a more formal level, a Carter campaign advisor, Dr. Peter G. Bourne, told *U.S. News and World Report* that decriminalizing heroin possession was an idea that should be considered. Although he recognized that such a measure would not be politically possible at that moment, he said, "Unless we're willing to accept a steadily worsening condition, we really have to look for new alternatives."[120]

Such a consideration was far outside Gerald Ford's thinking. Just that April he had delivered perhaps his strongest message ever on the need for renewed efforts against heroin and had established two new committees to coordinate those efforts. His aides knew, and the *White Paper* recognized, that the problem was not going to go away any time soon and that talk of decriminalization of anything could only stir up controversy that would be difficult to control. Dick Parsons informed James Cannon in August that

> for FY 1977, the President has requested $780 million for the Federal drug program. In FY 1974, however, the Federal drug budget was $782 million. What has happened over the past three years is that the massive budgetary increases of the early 1970s (when the Federal drug budget went from less than $100 million in FY 1969 to almost $800 million in FY 1974) have been completely absorbed by the bureaucracy. We are now operating at close to maximum capacity and, simply put, we aren't going to get much more out of the program without putting more into it.
>
> I note by way of historical perspective that the only time we have made truly significant (or at least dramatic) progress in reversing the drug abuse trend was in late 1972–early 1973. I note also that crime decreased for the first (and only) time in the last 20 years during that period. I believe it is more than coincidence that this dramatic progress, which the former President hailed as "turning the corner on drug abuse," came on the heels of a massive increase in Federal spending to prevent and treat drug abuse (from $223 million in FY 1971 to $511 million in FY 1972).[121]

Better to change the subject.

Carter and Ford secured their parties' nominations in August, and in September and October one vice-presidential and three presidential debates were held in which a total of about four sentences were devoted to the drug issue. In the first presidential debate Jimmy Carter cited what he considered to be the excessive number of federal agencies involved in drug treatment as an opportunity to streamline government. Gerald Ford said he thought that progress could be made against crime and drug abuse without significant spending increases (regardless of what his staff may have thought). In the vice-presidential debate between Democrat Walter Mondale and Republican Robert Dole, only Senator Mondale broached the subject, saying that the Drug Enforcement Administration was "totally demoralized" and that "a national effort that really makes sense" was needed to stop "the importation of those death-dealing imported illegal drugs."

CONCLUSION

After Jimmy Carter's narrow victory in the November election, President Ford and his staff had time to reflect on their short spell in office. Their view of what had been accomplished to control illegal drug use and what remained to be done was summed up in the 1976 federal strategy report, which was published in November. The new report recapitulated the *White Paper* and noted those areas in which some progress had been made. James Cannon interpreted the report optimistically for the president. "The Strategy documents the fact that we have made substantial progress in revitalizing the Federal drug program and in implementing most of the recommendations contained in the *White Paper on Drug Abuse.* Encouragingly, it notes that the overall level of drug abuse in the United States, which was increasing at the time you took office, has leveled out and remained relatively stable in the last year."[122] The 1976 strategy report is most notable for its insistence on the *White Paper's* contention that drug policy makers must recognize the different social effects of different drugs and the limits upon federal funds to control them and must establish priorities accordingly. It declared valid the *White Paper's* emphasis on heroin, on focusing federal law enforcement on major traffickers, and on "greater selectivity and targeting of Federal efforts in both supply and demand reduction, so that scarce resources are used where the problem is most severe and where the greatest impact can be made."[123] In a peculiar twist, it discussed significant steps that had been taken to deal with increasing cocaine traffic from Colombia, then seemed to try to explain away the apparent divergence from the established priority of heroin. "Questions have been asked about these 'cocaine initiatives' in light of the fact that cocaine is a lower priority than heroin or the 'dangerous drugs.' However, the drug priority concept does not mean that all efforts should be devoted only to the opiates, barbiturates, and amphetamines which have higher social costs. Attention must be given to all drugs to keep them from expanding into major problems."[124] The last chapter of the document, "The Open Agenda," was almost entirely devoted to criminal justice issues, including what sanctions should be applied to marijuana possession. The Ford strategists persisted in their opposition to decriminalization of cannabis, but had to recognize the need to study alternative approaches "in light of the widespread recreational use of marihuana and the relatively low social cost associated with this type of use."[125]

In retrospect, it appears that Ford's *White Paper on Drug Abuse* may have had a lasting impact in spite of its failure to reach any of its immediate political goals. It accurately, if cautiously, reflected informed thinking at the moment that America was ready to reconsider its approach to marijuana and a belief that cocaine was unlikely to develop into a major threat to the nation's health and safety. The priorities it advocated in good faith would inform the direction of drug policy in the succeeding administration and set the stage for backlash.

Chapter 6 The Carter Administration: The End of Accommodation

When Jimmy Carter entered the White House in January 1977, he was met with an energy crisis, increasing inflation, and a federal budget he considered too large. To emphasize the determination he had expressed in his campaign to streamline the government, he cultivated an image of parsimony and simplicity, ostentatiously slinging his carry-on bag over his shoulder when he traveled and cutting White House perks—much to his staff's discomfort. Because social and political circumstances had changed significantly since drug abuse had emerged as a major public concern more than a decade earlier, drug policy development and implementation during the Carter presidency were particularly subject to presidential cost-cutting priorities. Carter's advisors felt confident that they were moving in a direction increasingly approved by the public and one that would reduce the exaggerated fear of drugs that characterized the past while simultaneously avoiding extravagant expenditures on drug control.

The majority of "expert" opinions at the time generally reflected the belief first articulated in Ford's *White Paper* that at least grudging toleration of some use of some drugs was the most humane and certainly the most fiscally appropriate course. Cocaine use was seen as, first, exotic, and second, no more threatening to social or personal health than was the more familiar marijuana—which was seen as more of a political problem than a health problem. Heroin, the hard drug par excellence, maintained its primacy in the minds of most bureaucrats and elected officials, many of whom claimed that crop eradication would eventually reduce heroin traffic to a trickle. Even so, there were a few in the administration who were less than enthusiastic about this approach and worried that the president might be misled by overly "sanguine"[1] estimates of the social and personal consequences of drug use and the efficacy of poppy crop eradication. Their disagreements were muted at first, but by the summer of 1978 the balance of public opinion and political power shifted in their favor and signaled the impending end of the era of even tentative acceptance of recreational consumption of mood-altering substances.

The career of Dr. Peter G. Bourne as Jimmy Carter's advisor on health matters and, for the first year and a half of the administration, head of drug policy formation in the White House, describes nearly exactly the trajectory of drug policies and attitudes toward them during the period in which drug use and acceptance peaked among middle-class voters. Bourne had headed then-governor Carter's drug program in Georgia. He had also brainstormed much of Carter's strategy for achieving the presidency and had been a key figure in his campaign. Naturally, Bourne took on the drug issue as his responsibility from the outset.

Even before Carter's inauguration, Bourne had begun advocating establishment of the White House Office of Drug Abuse Policy that Gerald Ford had so determinedly resisted, and was briefly successful. In his capacity as director of the office, he supported continued attention to the world heroin problem, cautiously advanced marijuana decriminalization, and interpreted the available information on cocaine in such a way as to defend de-emphasis of that substance in allocation of federal budgetary resources. But, for all his intimacy with Carter, Bourne found that he could not deflect the zeal of the Office of Management and Budget to carry out Carter's cost-cutting imperatives. ODAP fell victim to OMB's stringent reorganization initiative after only one year of existence. In a compromise of sorts, the role of the office was to be taken up in November 1977 by the White House Strategy Council on Drug Abuse, a group composed of appropriate cabinet secretaries and some nongovernmental or "public" members. The Strategy Council had impressive statutory responsibilities and rights, but in fact served as a facade behind which White House staff and cabinet bureaucrats developed and implemented drug policy. Bourne himself was forced from office a few months later under circumstances that would effectively destroy any further attempts at a less than totally condemnatory federal drug control effort. This pivotal event, combined with later accusations of cocaine use among other close Carter aides, contributed to the impression that the White House was becoming careless and irresponsible with regard to drugs. In turn, the embarrassment led to a determined effort on the part of presidential staffers to reduce the salience of the drug issue in public debate. This atmosphere also made it possible for those aides and departmental bureaucrats who were inclined to do so to establish bona fides with emerging anti-drug groups, collectively known as the Parents' Movement, who were becoming increasingly vocal in support of more punitive drug control policies.

In the midterm elections of 1978, the defeat of Congressman Newton I. Steers in suburban Maryland's Montgomery County after he had endorsed marijuana decriminalization, was a shock to many in Congress and the administration.[2] Perhaps it was the Parents' Movement that represented the wave of the future; maybe the marijuana issue would not be so easily resolved along the lines recommended in 1972 by the President's Commission on Marihuana and Drug Abuse.

THE SHORT LIFE OF ODAP

Very early in the administration, Bourne had advised Carter that it might not be wise to resist congressional pressure to establish ODAP in the White House in spite of his own reservations about the office. Carter himself initially wanted whatever entity might be set up "out of the White House."[3] By early January 1977 Bourne told Carter

> The over-riding issue, of considerable urgency, is the need for a decision on the establishment of the Office of Drug Abuse Policy (ODAP). The office is mandated by law, and although its establishment runs counter to your desire to reduce the size of the Executive Office of the President, the Congress is insistent on its immediate establishment. There is a major need for coordination in this area. It is currently being handled very effectively by Dick Parsons on the Domestic Council with staff back up from three people detailed to him from OMB. He estimates that it takes 30 per cent of his time. I believe the optimal arrangement would be to continue something along the same lines with someone assuming Parsons's functions, and the continued detailing of the same three people from OMB. This may not be possible in light of the strong Congressional desire to establish ODAP, in which case the current role of the Domestic Council would become redundant.[4]

By the end of the month, the president had decided by go ahead with ODAP,[5] and it was officially announced on 14 March 1977.[6] At the same time, he abolished the three cabinet committees on drug policy set up by President Ford and authorized revitalization of the dormant Strategy Council to replace them (this last body would not be activated until November).

> The Federal Government currently supports a widely diversified, and to some degree fragmented, program to reduce the abuse of illicit drugs in the United States. The program is currently spread among eight Cabinet Departments, over 40 Federal organizations, and totals nearly $800 million annually for enforcement, demand reduction and international initiatives.
>
> Because of the diverse range of the drug abuse program, the President has recently established the Office of Drug Abuse Policy in the Executive Office of the President to provide policy guidance and oversight responsibilities to the total program. Additionally, the President has charged the new Office with the responsibility of leading his reorganization efforts in the drug abuse area. He has further indicated that he expects that ODAP will be fully supported by the affected Departments and agencies and the Office of Management and Budget in its undertakings.[7]

Bourne set to work providing the new president with monthly narcotic reports, in which he expressed optimism about controlling the flow of heroin from Mexico and worried about the implications of increased poppy cultivation in Afghanistan, a problem that would come to dominate White House drug policy planning at the end of the administration. "The one bleak spot is Afghanistan where opium cultivation has increased dramatically this year. This is not yet affecting the international market, but we have asked Secretary [of State Cyrus] Vance to express our concern in the strongest terms to President Daoud. We may need to involve you at some stage."[8] He also began to resist the reorganization plans emanating from the Office of Management and Budget, under the direction of Bert Lance, that were decidedly not in "full support" of ODAP. OMB, as quickly became clear, had slated ODAP for elimination regardless of congressional opposition. In the narcotic report of 10 June, Bourne's difference of opinion with OMB about the necessity of continuing the existence of the drug policy office, which, after all, had been established only in March, was solidifying into outright hostility.

> The issue of whether to have or continue the ODAP is a policy question and not a reorganization issue. Either we wish to have a drug abuse program which is coordinated and integrated for maximum impact and efficiency, or we will be satisfied with having each of 20 different agencies going their own way with no national plan or strategy—similar to the way energy has been treated in the past. . . .

> Any move to establish a date for the termination of ODAP will be interpreted as a lack of interest in the drug problem. Such action would be harmful to the program and contradictory to a strongly expressed Presidential and Congressional mandate.[9]

OMB's position was that "the Office of Drug Abuse Policy was created by the Congress to carry out specific functions within a rigid time frame. The office was authorized through September 30, 1978. ODAP will have completed its reorganization and policy mandates prior to that date and as a result should be eliminated by the end of this fiscal year."[10] But Bourne was correct that Congress would not be happy about the move to abolish ODAP and that the reorganization would do nothing to enhance the president's credentials as a drug foe in spite of Burt Lance's assurances to the contrary.

The apparent tendency of OMB to bypass Bourne in the planning process did not contribute to his cooperation with the enterprise, either.

> There is considerable negative reaction to the phase out of ODAP on the Hill. Much of this could have been avoided had I been briefed by the reorganization team on this decision and had the opportunity to defuse congressional displeasure myself before they and I read about it in the newspapers. Their concern centers around the following:
>
> - The office was implemented 3-14-77 with a splash to the Congress reversing Ford's previous refusal to implement the office. Even though implemented with only 50 per cent of the intended staff they were pleased.
> - The swearing in of myself and my deputy did not occur until June 1st—six weeks later the office is abolished.
> - It is quite unclear what the subsequent mechanism for coordinating drug policy will be.
> - Signal of deprioritization—public statements and the drug message give high priority to drug abuse—phase out of ODAP seems to refute this.[11]

At this point, Bourne was bucking for continuing ODAP at least until its funding would run out in September of 1978 rather than when the reorganization plan would wipe it out (October 1977). Handwritten notes from Carter on Bourne's memo indicate that the president thought that "sounded okay," and Bourne thought a push for ODAP could be included in the president's drug message that was being planned for midsummer. But in the end, Carter deleted references to ODAP from the draft message and replaced them with "my staff,"[12] and as the weeks passed, the OMB reorganization team gained greater control of the situation and Bourne became increasingly irritated.

For one thing, the information that OMB provided to the president on the value and legal status of ODAP was, in Bourne's opinion, erroneous. Bert Lance had informed the president that [the reorganization plan] provides for each of [the functions of ODAP] to continue when ODAP is terminated.

The policy development and program coordination responsibilities will be handled by the Presidential Adviser on Drug Abuse, the Domestic Policy Staff, and the Strategy Council on Drug Abuse. (The Strategy Council is an interagency coordinating group that has rarely met.) Drug abuse issues will be handled within the Policy Management System much as other priority domestic issues are to be handled. The coordinating group will meet regularly, staffed by the Domestic Policy staff, to develop solutions for specific problems and broad policy. By retaining a highly visible White House drug adviser, you will demonstrate your continuing commitment to solving the drug abuse problem. As you recall, you have also asked Dr. Bourne to develop and maintain an Administration policy for solving drug abuse problems.

We expect the ODAP staff to finish its pending reorganization projects in January 1978, and have planned to leave the office in place until these projects are complete. Future drug abuse related reorganization efforts will be handled by the OMB President's Reorganization Project.

By placing drug abuse policy development, coordination, and reorganization activities within the normal EOP [Executive Office of the President] channels and for handling such work, we believe that drug abuse issues can be handled equally efficiently and can be better integrated with related concerns. By retaining a White House adviser, you can assure overall guidance and sufficient priority to these issues. . . .

Although the congressional opposition to eliminating ODAP is vocal, it is limited and we do not believe that Reorganization Plan No. 1 will be vetoed. The key defenders of ODAP are Senators Hathaway, Percy, and Javits and Congressmen Lester Wolff (D-N.Y), Ben Gilman (R-N.Y.), Peter Rodino (D-N.J.), Paul Rogers (D-Fla.), and Charles Rangel (D-N.Y.).[13]

Bourne angrily rebutted the Lance memo, but his advice did not carry the day.

The Strategy Council is *not* "an interagency coordinating group that has rarely met." It is a Cabinet Committee mandated by law to develop U.S. Strategy in the narcotics area, it has never met. The "coordinating group" (Strategy Council) will *not* "meet regularly," but probably only annually to determine the federal strategy as required by law. I doubt members of the Cabinet would be willing to meet more frequently.

While placing drug abuse policy development and coordination within "normal EOP channels" is a reasonable management approach, it is exactly the approach which the Nixon and Ford Administrations used, and the approach to which the Congress reacted negatively in establishing ODAP. The two years of Congressional argument over this issue have not been addressed. [Emphasis in original.][14]

Much of the "Congressional argument" took place in the sessions of the House Select Committee on Narcotics Abuse and Control, which had been established in July of 1976 and was chaired by Congressman Lester Wolff. The committee heard testimony from ODAP and OMB officials and came to this conclusion.

> The effect of the Reorganization Plan was to eliminate the Office of Drug Abuse Policy in the Executive Office of the President. The committee expressed unanimous opposition to the termination of the Office of Drug Abuse Policy and developed information from the witnesses that termination was based upon a management analysis rather than a review of the impact this would have on drug issues. The committee expressed its opposition to the policy of terminating a high-level policy office created by statute without consultation with Congress. Negotiations between committee members and the Office of Management and Budget to extend the Office of Drug Abuse Policy for an additional year beyond December 31, 1977, were fruitless, however. ODAP will continue to function into 1978 as it concludes its seven major drug abuse studies.[15]

Any doubt that may have remained in Carter's mind with respect to congressional support for ODAP must have been dispelled by a letter he received in October from eight representatives.

> Mr. President, we do not question your commitment in fighting drug abuse. However, we do question the manner in which OMB arrived at its decision to recommend the termination of the one agency within the EOP that could assist you in formulating and developing a comprehensive, coordinated national drug abuse policy . . . a policy that is urgently needed. . . .
>
> Mr. President, since OMB did not consult with the top narcotics administrators or with Members of Congress, and since OMB did not have any narcotics experts on its staff, it did not arrive at an informed and objective decision regarding ODAP's effectiveness in formulating a comprehensive, coordinated national drug abuse policy and in fulfilling the Congressional mandate stipulated in P.L. [Public Law] 94-237. . . .
>
> Mr. President, P.L. 94-237 does not contain any termination date with regard to ODAP's life existence; there is no sunset clause in this legislation. Rather, under section 211 of the Act, ODAP's authorized appropriations expire on September 30, 1978, at the end of that fiscal year. However, the life of that office continues statutorily, subject to reauthorization of funds. Obviously, if the Congress declined to reauthorize appropriations for this office, ODAP would cease to exist. But this is not the same as saying that ODAP is statutorily terminated at the end of fiscal year 1978. Apparently, the distinction between the "termination" of ODAP's existence and the "expiration" of its appropriations was not properly explained to you, if it was explained at all. . . .
>
> Mr. President, why didn't OMB provide you with the alternative option of re-

> taining ODAP within your Executive Office, particularly when you activated the office only last March? Under Dr. Bourne's leadership, ODAP has just begun to fulfill its Congressional mandate. Some members of the Select Committee are still at a loss for a clear rationale upon which OMB based its decision to scrap ODAP.[16]

But in spite of this fervent congressional opposition, Bert Lance was correct in his contention that Congress would not reject Reorganization Plan 1 of 1977 in its entirety only because the plan abolished ODAP. (An executive order dated 27 March 1978 finally terminated the office as well as the Domestic Council and the Economic Opportunity Council and formed the domestic policy staff along with implementing other provisions of the reorganization.)[17] The Strategy Council on Drug Abuse was convened for the first time in November 1977 with the thought that, consistent with Lance's views, it would take over some of the coordinating and policy articulation functions of ODAP. "It was decided at [the first Strategy Council meeting] that the structure of the Strategy Council would be issue-related. There would not be standing committees, but the Department of State would take the lead on international issues, the Department of Justice on criminal issues, the Department of HEW on health-related issues, and appropriate ad hoc committees would be formed around each particular problem to stay in existence only until a specific task is completed."[18]

MARIJUANA POLICY UNDER BOURNE

At about the same time that President Carter was being bombarded with his advisors' conflicting views on the Office of Drug Abuse Policy, he was also dealing with congressional proposals to decriminalize marijuana possession in federal law and with the practical implications of the willingness he had expressed very early in his presidential campaign to consider such a step. The supporters of these initiatives agreed that imprisonment of large numbers of middle-class youths for possession of cannabis for personal use was inappropriate. Most of them also believed that pot smoking was not very harmful and wanted to appear in tune with the popular sentiment that decriminalization was a measured and defensible response to what was already a fact of life. Just after the Carter inauguration, Senators Jacob Javits (R., NY) and Alan Cranston (D., CA), and Congressman Edward Koch, (D., NY) told the new president,

> We are . . . reintroducing legislation tomorrow [S. 601 and H.R. 432, 95th Congress, 1st Session] providing that the possession and not for profit transfer of one ounce or

> less of marihuana would be punishable at the Federal level by a civil fine of not more than $100. Commercial sale of the drug for profit would remain a criminal offense. . . .
>
> Public attitudes towards marihuana smoking have changed dramatically over the past few years. Eight states have enacted decriminalization statutes—including California—and the issue will be considered this year in forty state legislatures. Where stiff jail penalties were once demanded for someone caught with a small amount of marihuana, many public opinion polls confirm that civil fines are now favored by a majority of our citizens, and fines rather than imprisonment are routine in almost all jurisdictions today.[19]

Such congressional and public support that there was for the notion of decriminalization—that is, removal of criminal penalties for possession of quantities of marijuana consistent with personal use—was, in large measure, guided and informed by the inspired lobbying of the National Organization for the Reform of Marijuana Laws (NORML) and its zealous and peripatetic founder, Keith Stroup. Stroup had a gift for political activism and for collecting powerful and colorful allies. Hugh Hefner's Playboy Foundation provided considerable funding, and such national figures as former attorney general Ramsey Clark and John Finlator, former deputy administrator of the Bureau of Narcotics and Dangerous Drugs, were vocal sympathizers. Stroup enjoyed the support of a number of young journalists and congressional staffers as well as a motley assortment of Yippies and dopers. He also forged close working relationships with Thomas Bryant, head of the Drug Abuse Council (a policy analysis organization funded by various foundations) and with Peter Bourne.

Although it was undoubtedly true, as Senator Javits and Congressman Koch believed, that "public attitudes towards marihuana smoking [had] changed dramatically over the past few years," there was opposition to reduced marijuana penalties both within and without the administration. A tension existed between those who favored marijuana decriminalization and those, like Stuart Eizenstat, head of the president's Domestic Council, who had serious questions about its implications. The unease within the administration was only a microcosm of what Wolff's committee was hearing from its witnesses. In April, Bourne testified before House Select Committee on Narcotics Abuse and Control in favor of decriminalization of marijuana at the federal level, with the details of penalty structures to be left to states. His estimate of the importance of the marijuana issue to the society at large reveals a certain lack of appreciation for its emotional power. "There was minimal adverse reaction to my statement on marijuana decriminalization before the House Select Committee on Nar-

Stuart Eizenstat, domestic policy advisor in the Carter administration, 9 May 1979. (U.S. News and World Report Collection, Library of Congress.)

cotics. . . . It is a low priority issue, and no longer raises the passions it did a few years ago. I plan to minimize our emphasis on it."[20] The committee reported Bourne's testimony as follows: "Dr. Peter Bourne, Director-Designate of the Office of Drug Abuse Policy, presented the administration's policy on marijuana decriminalization. As a national policy, the administration discourages the abuse of all drugs, including alcohol and tobacco. However, it takes the position that present Federal criminal penalties as they apply to the possession of small amounts of marijuana for personal use do not effectively deter the use of marijuana and are more harmful than marijuana abuse."[21]

Other witnesses were skeptical about the direction that cannabis law enforcement was taking even in the absence of new legislation. "Chief [Edward] Davis [of the Los Angeles Police Department] asserted that in some cases, due to political pressures, some police departments have virtually ceased to enforce marihuana laws just as some departments have ceased collecting information on terrorists. He added that although the costs are lower now, there will eventually be a high price to pay for these decisions.[22] Further, Chief Davis . . . emphasized that his department had been unable to realize a cost saving even after California reduced the penalties for the possession of small amounts of marihuana for personal use."[23]

Much to the dismay of law enforcement professionals like Chief Davis, the judiciary and the treatment community were often on the opposite side of the controversy. "Dr. Jerome Hornblass, a proponent of decriminalization, pointed to a survey conducted by the Addiction Services Agency of New York City, which concluded that the majority of New York City's judges and directors of drug treatment programs believe New York's stringent drug law has not been successful in deterring drug abuse."[24]

At the same time, opinions among White House advisors were similarly divided, though rather less polarized. Bourne was working on background material for a presidential message on drug abuse in which he was advocating a statement by the president in favor of cannabis decriminalization but not any new legislation other than that before Congress. Bourne's July draft for the president's message on drug abuse was consistent with this attitude, but just as Bourne's estimate of the importance of ODAP was at variance with that of other close advisors to the president, his way of thinking about marijuana policy was not shared by everyone on the White House staff. Stuart Eizenstat declared himself "very concerned about the marijuana section of [Bourne's draft]."[25] Indeed, some of the language that appears in the discussion of marijuana is quite remarkable for its resemblance to the rhetoric used by marijuana advocates. In fact, one author claims that the very phrases that Eizenstat objected to were written in collaboration with NORML.[26] Eizenstat told the president:

> In general, I believe the section on marijuana is written in an almost laudatory tone, which I believe is unfortunate. Sentences such as "marijuana has become an established fact throughout our society, and the sky has not fallen," "research studies indicate it may have beneficial uses in the treatment of certain types of illness," and a suggestion that the states should repeal their criminal prohibitions, "thus bringing to a close an unhappy and misguided chapter in our history" almost seem to be a positive recommendation of the drug.

> Further, I would disagree with the statement that "the evidence to date shows that the medical damage done by marijuana as it is used in our country today is minimal." From what I have seen, the studies on medical damage are very mixed, some indicating the contrary. During the campaign you said, "I don't approve of the use of marijuana. The medical effects of persistent use of marijuana still concern me very much." When you were asked if you thought the use of marijuana is more harmful than liquor, you said, "I think so. I can't say for sure. One of the bad things about marijuana is that quite often it is used in an environment consistent with much more habit-forming drugs. I don't think there's any evidence that marijuana is habit-forming, but no adequate study of marijuana's final effects has yet been conducted." (September 3, 1976, Plains, Ga.).[27]

It may be a measure of President Carter's true opinions about marijuana that he took Eizenstat's advice and marked for deletion all the phrases in the draft drug message that seemed to downplay the dangers of pot smoking.[28] One dramatic example of the distance that Bourne was willing to go down this road, but where Carter and Eizenstat at least were not willing to follow, is the following passage, which the president deleted: "My hope is that all states will soon follow suit and repeal their criminal prohibitions against [marijuana consumption], thus bringing to a close an unhappy and misguided chapter in our history."[29] The contrast between the language Bourne used, or allowed to be used, with respect to marijuana and his recommendations for heroin control indicates the clear distinction he drew between the substances. Bourne was apparently in favor of very severe measures to punish heroin traffickers that, from Eizenstat's point of view, were probably not constitutional (revoking passports of "known traffickers" and a form of preventative detention for major dealers) or that were opposed by the Justice Department (sentencing guidelines that seemed to be approaching mandatory minimums).[30, 31]

A similar situation developed with respect to the administration's attempts to articulate cocaine control policy. Bourne's vision of what was then known of the effects of cocaine, of the scope of the market for the drug, and of the future direction of cocaine control was forced through the filter of the policy-vetting process and emerged quite changed, though not entirely vitiated.

PETER BOURNE AND COCAINE POLICY

A background paper on cocaine that Peter Bourne wrote for Carter in December of 1976, as the transition team prepared for Carter's presidency, details some of the evidence pointing to a burgeoning cocaine market but reflects the opinion of Bourne and many of his contemporaries that the drug itself did not pose a serious threat. He expressed just the sort of doubts about the wisdom of spending money on coca eradication in Bolivia that Ford's strategy report had tried to deflect just the previous month.

> [Cocaine smuggling] not only has created new ethnic networks of smugglers among Cubans, Colombians, and other Latin Americans in the United States, but it also fuels the existing heroin trafficking networks. . . . Although there may be some potential for serious medical consequences from cocaine, for all practical purposes at the present time there are none. This has caused a serious dilemma among our policy makers. . . .
>
> The major justification for our policy with regard to cocaine and the effort to push the crop substitution program in Bolivia was based on an erroneous assumption by those in policy making positions, particularly in the State Department, that cocaine was of far greater medical consequence than it is. The policy was also based on concern about the immense profits made from cocaine trafficking, and its fueling effect on the existing illicit heroin trafficking market as well on organized crime. The immense profits being made from cocaine are of course in part related to the fact that it is illegal. And the effect on organized crime is something comparable to what we have seen during prohibition with alcohol.[32]

Bourne's estimate of the cocaine situation had not changed materially by the following June (1977), when he wrote a secret (later declassified) memo to President Carter on aid to Latin American countries that were the sources of the cocaine being smuggled into the United States.

> We are spending more than $7 million now in Colombia, Peru, and Bolivia to support law enforcement activities with little evidence that we are reducing the flow of cocaine to this country. We have a potential obligation for an additional $45 million for crop substitution programs in Bolivia (a commitment made by Kissinger). Peru is pushing for similar amounts of money, and Colombia is complaining because we have failed to deliver 3 helicopters we promised. . . .
>
> It is estimated that 40 tons of cocaine a year come into the U.S. from Colombia, bringing half a billion dollars back into the Colombian economy, equal to the amount they currently derive from coffee.[33] [This remark also appears in the 1976 cocaine policy paper.]

Late that month, Bourne again alluded to the possibility of opium poppy cultivation in Colombia.[34] During July, he developed a policy paper on cocaine that was submitted to officials on the White House staff, the heads of DEA and Customs, Mathea Falco of the State Department's office for international narcotics matters, and Robert DuPont, director of NIDA, for comments.[35] Dr.

DuPont felt it would be wise to "recast the discussion on the nature and consequences of cocaine use in a way that is less sanguine." He went on to say, "At a minimum we should note that over 6 million Americans have used the drug and 1 million currently use it, and it can cause acute toxic reactions and even death in unusual but no longer rare cases in this country. The powerful reinforcing properties of the substance are well known as is the toxicity of high dose, regular use."[36]

The following table presents a comparison between Peter Bourne's draft for the cocaine policy paper and the final version, which seems to have been completed toward the end of September.[37] The final report is presented in its entirety in the right column, and Bourne's draft is in the left column, broken up so that similar paragraphs can be compared directly to their versions in the later document. The two versions agree on many points—for example, that current penalties for cocaine violations should not be changed but that federal agencies should not publicly appear to be reducing attention to cocaine control. In some cases the two versions directly contradict each other, as in "users do not develop irresistible compulsive urges to use the drug as is the case with heroin" in the original document, versus the final version in which the following appears: "Cocaine, however, is a powerfully reinforcing drug; in other words, given a ready supply, use can easily become compulsive. At high doses, cocaine can cause acute toxic reactions and even death." In other cases the changes are quite subtle. For example, the element of doubt about the dire consequences of increased cocaine availability that is introduced into the draft paper by the phrase "We do not, however, have adequate scientific data to substantiate this belief and we should make every effort to increase our studies in this area" was excised from the final document. A dramatic difference in emphasis between the two versions lies in the complete removal of all of Bourne's long discussion of Latin American coca cultivation, law enforcement, and the diplomatic ramifications of these activities. In its place, the final policy paper includes several paragraphs that place in stark relief the economic value of the cocaine trade, its tie-in to heroin trafficking, and the political consequences of this criminal commerce for Latin America. Also eliminated from the final version of the paper was Bourne's observation that "perhaps the overriding consideration in the development of federal policy should be credibility. The past failure of marijuana policy was in large part due to an attempt to sell the American people a bill of goods about the health hazards of marijuana which were patently untrue. We must absolutely avoid the same pitfall with cocaine."[38]

The clear impression that one takes away from this comparison is that of tension among various offices, departments, and individual members of the administration as each sought to define the drug abuse problem and the most appropriate measures to deal with it. Peter Bourne was placing the strength of his influence with the president behind a drug strategy based on an optimistic estimate of the present nature and future course of the market for cocaine and the efficacy of policies then in place to control it. Many of his colleagues were not so sure.

Bourne's Draft	Final Policy Paper
	EXECUTIVE SUMMARY **Cocaine** Under the leadership of the Office of Drug Abuse Policy, the principal drug abuse representatives from the Department of State, the Department of Justice, and the Department of Health, Education and Welfare have been working towards formulating a coherent national policy on cocaine. The resulting policy statement considers both short- and long-range domestic and international issues. The report maintains that while the current health hazards of cocaine use should not be overstated, the potential adverse consequences if use increases should be emphasized. The critical factor underlying this apparent lack of severe health consequences is the high price of the drug, which restricts the general level and extent of use. The major focus of domestic cocaine strategy, the report concludes, must be to maintain the high price of the drug while curtailing its availability. Cocaine should be assigned a higher international priority, since international drug smuggling is strictly an economic phe-

nomenon, and cocaine is one of the most profitable drugs. The tremendous profits support criminal elements both in the United States and abroad and the illicit traffic is seriously undermining the political and economic stability of a number of Latin American countries. The Cocaine Policy Statement is attached.

COCAINE POLICY

(Page 1) Cocaine use appears to be increasing dramatically in the United States. Approximately a ton a week of the drug is smuggled into the country, and it sells for up to $100 per gram. Use of this drug is predominantly, although not exclusively among the more affluent and educated segments of American society.

Domestic Policy Considerations

Recent National Institute on Drug Abuse surveys indicate that over six million Americans have used cocaine illicitly and that one million Americans are current users. Cocaine is an expensive drug, used generally by the more affluent segments of society. The latest DEA reports indicate that one gram of cocaine sells for $750.

If cocaine were more freely available at lower cost in the United States, use would probably increase and the public health consequences might well be grave.

Because cocaine is short acting and not physically addicting, users do not develop irresistible compulsive urges to use the drug, as is the case with heroin. As a result there is very little if any cocaine inspired crime aimed at obtaining money by any means to buy the drug. Similarly, deaths directly related to cocaine use are exceptionally rare, numbering less than 20 per year as compared to more than 2,000 per year from heroin.

At present levels of use, cocaine causes relatively few health and social consequences. Unlike heroin and the barbiturates, cocaine is not physically addictive. Cocaine related deaths in the United States number only 20 a year as compared to over 2,000 heroin related deaths. Cocaine is controlled under Schedule II of the Controlled Substances Act and has legitimate, although limited, medical uses, primarily as a surface anesthetic.

Cocaine, however, is a powerfully reinforcing drug; in other words, given a ready supply, use can easily become compulsive. At high doses, cocaine can cause acute toxic reactions and even death. If cocaine were more freely available at lower cost in the United States, use would probably increase

	and the public health consequences might well be grave.
(Page 8) We also need to monitor very closely changes in the incidence and prevalence of cocaine use, and changes in the pattern of use, such as an increase in intravenous consumption, which might portend serious new health consequences	Every effort should be made to increase our knowledge of the effects of compulsive, high dose cocaine use. Changes in the incidence, prevalence, and patterns of cocaine use should also be monitored closely. For example, an increase in intravenous consumption of cocaine might portend serious new health consequences.
(Page 1) In the past, the basis of our policy with regard to cocaine has been unclear, as have been our objectives and the priority we attached to cocaine relative to other drugs. There has also been considerable ignorance about cocaine and its pharmacology and the health hazards it posed among officials shaping that policy. This represents a first draft of a policy paper to be formulated jointly by the principal agencies in the drug field, and summarizes the results of an initial meeting to review this topic.	
(Page 7) ***Use of Cocaine*** There is no reason to reduce the penalties for (Page 8) possession of cocaine. Unlike marihuana, cocaine possession has not resulted in incarceration of large numbers of otherwise law abiding young people, There is also some reason to believe that the law may help discourage use.	Domestic penalties for simple possession of cocaine should not be reduced at this time. Unlike marihuana, cocaine possession laws have not resulted in inducting large numbers of otherwise law-abiding young people into the criminal justice system. There is also some reason to believe that the law may help to discourage use.
(Page 8) Our public position should be to not overstate the current health hazards, but at the same time to make clear the much more serious potential consequences if usage should escalate.	While the current health hazards of cocaine use should not be overstated, the potential adverse consequences if use increases should be emphasized.

(Page 8) The present policy is based on the belief that while present use levels cause minimal health problems, reduction in price and increased availability would cause substantially greater levels of use and corresponding increases in deaths and other health problems. We do not, however, have adequate scientific data to substantiate this belief and we should make every effort to increase our studies in this area.

It must be understood that the critical factor underlying this apparent lack of severe health consequences is the high price of the drug, which reflects its relative scarcity, and restricts the general level and extent of use.

(Page 7) Domestically singling out cocaine for special attention by law enforcement agencies seems to offer little practical benefit. At the same time it should not be assigned a lower priority in any public way. . . .

Domestic law enforcement agencies should not publicly assign cocaine a low priority, but at the same time cocaine should not be singled out for special attention since such an approach seems of little practical benefit.

(Page 7) Although the overall quantity of cocaine being seized is small as a percentage of the total coming to the United States there was a feeling, particularly on the part of Customs, that an increase in manpower would not necessarily lead to a proportionate increase in seizures. Better intelligence and closer coordination with law enforcement officials in Colombia and other countries was more likely to greater seizures of the drug.

In Fiscal Year 1976, only 1500 pounds of cocaine were seized, a small percentage of the estimated total coming in the U.S. Increases in the numbers of Customs agents would not necessarily lead to substantial increases in seizures: better intelligence and closer coordination with Latin American law enforcement officials might prove more effective.

(Page 2) Our national drug policy can be characterized as having two major objectives:

(1) To reduce the use of all drugs for non-medical purposes
(2) To keep to a minimum the health, social, and economic costs of drug use where it does occur.

Where these two objectives may be in conflict, the second objective takes precedence, and should be considered the more important goal.

With regard to cocaine there is general consensus that we have largely achieved the second objective. The number of people dying from or suffering from adverse effects of cocaine are minimal, and drug related crime by cocaine users is close to zero. Obviously we would like to eliminate cocaine deaths entirely, yet we should regard our present policy as in large measure successful and be cautious about changing too hastily that policy.

The key to that policy appears to be our ability to keep the price of cocaine high and the availability relatively low with the intended result that the level of use, while extensive, is not excessive. The negative aspect of this current policy is that by keeping the price high we also maintain an extraordinary profit incentive for those who traffic in the drug,

The major focus of our cocaine strategy must be to maintain the high price of the drug while curtailing its availability.

(Page 3) What are the strategies for keeping the supply low and the price high?

The source—With other botanically derived drugs, particularly heroin, the key to our national strategy is, wherever possible, to destroy the plant source at its point of cultivation or as soon after harvesting as possible. The extraordinarily extensive cultivation of coca in the Andean countries, as well as the centuries old culturally accepted practice of coca leaf chewing in the region make crop eradication or crop substitution, in our estimation, completely unfeasible at the present time.

(Page 7) The cocaine market has a fi-

Efforts in the international area, particularly in cooperation with the major producing and transit countries—Colombia, Peru, Bolivia, and Ecuador—are critical in this strategy.

eling effect in maintaining trafficking organizations either when heroin is unavailable or in addition to heroin. Priorities should be based on the magnitude of the trafficking operation and not what drug is involved.

International Policy Considerations

International drug smuggling is primarily an economic phenomenon. The pharmacological distinctions among heroin, cocaine, and marihuana are irrelevant; the critical factor is the economic value of the drug in the illicit distribution network, In this context, cocaine should be given a higher priority in the international arena. The profits derived from the illicit cocaine traffic are enormous. One kilogram (2.2 pounds) of pure cocaine obtained for medical purposes from a legitimate pharmaceutical wholesaler costs $1,250. The same kilogram would be worth almost three-quarters of a million collars if sold at street prices. Hundreds of pounds of cocaine are smuggled into the United States every week.

The tremendous profits in the cocaine traffic support organized crime and criminal elements both in the United States and abroad. In addition, the illicit cocaine traffic is seriously undermining the political and economic stability of a number of Latin American countries, as well as corroding the independence and integrity of their judicial systems. In Colombia alone, cocaine accounts for half a billion dollars of the annual gross national product, about the same amount as do coffee exports. Furthermore, the criminal networks which distribute cocaine can also distribute marihuana or heroin, virtually interchangeably. The focus of international concern, therefore, must be on reducing the strength of these networks both by curtailing the supplies of illicit drugs available to them and by coordinating law enforcement efforts to disrupt the major trafficking networks.

THE PRESIDENT'S DRUG MESSAGE—2 AUGUST 1977

Planning for a presidential message on drugs had gone on while issues of administrative structure and cocaine and marijuana policy were under discussion. The first draft of the drug message had come out of Peter Bourne's office in April. In contrast to its later iterations the message was at first conceived in very general terms. It did not mention specific drugs but rather gave a broad outline of diplomatic initiatives to reduce the world supply of drugs. It touched on domestic law enforcement measures to punish traffickers; spoke of the necessity to "cut through imagery and look at facts in order to concentrate on the most dangerous drugs"; advocated controls on the use of barbiturates and dangerous drugs in medical practice; and advocated treatment of victims of drug addiction, and abuse prevention through social programs. The draft ended with a admonition that speaking of stopping drug use in absolute terms would be deceptive.[39] Stuart Eizenstat questioned whether such a message was a good idea before specific legislative proposals had been developed—something that he said would be forthcoming in about six weeks. President Carter scribbled at the top of the memo, "Wait for specifics."[40]

About a month later, with a view toward developing "specifics," Bourne circulated a long outline to cabinet people concerned with drug abuse. He sketched a series of "themes," "policies," "legislation" proposals, and "administration" needs. These he organized under "Reorganization," "Demand Activities," "Executive Office and Cabinet Oversight," "International Activities," and "Law Enforcement." Under reorganization, Bourne highlighted what he saw as his own responsibility for the administrative structure of drug policy. Significant among his policy suggestions was the idea that the problems of heroin addiction had perhaps been overemphasized to the detriment of treatment and prevention of polydrug and barbiturate abuse. He addressed the issue of marijuana decriminalization as follows:

> We feel that the damage, the medical damage demonstrated at this point as being caused by use of marijuana in the quantities in which is currently being used in this country, does not warrant making it a criminal offense for simple possession. We should not move toward decriminalization of other drugs. I think the evidence with marijuana, the situation with marijuana, is quite different from other drugs. Perhaps one reason, apart from the medical aspect, is that marijuana can be grown throughout this country. Despite very intensive efforts to control it over several years, it is clear that we are completely incapable of doing that. This is not the case with drugs like heroin, which have to come from outside the United States, where it appears we have a reasonable chance of controlling the drug at the source. I do not see any reason at this time to consider decriminalizing other drugs.[41]

Bourne felt that it was essential to identify the primary goal of international narcotics activities as "source control," including crop eradication and substitution, in spite of the fact that he had made the point in his draft for the cocaine policy paper that "with other botanically derived drugs, particularly heroin, the key to our national strategy is, wherever possible, to destroy the plant source at its point of cultivation or as soon after harvesting as possible. The extraordinarily extensive cultivation of coca in the Andean countries, as well as the centuries old culturally accepted practice of coca leaf chewing in the region make crop eradication or crop substitution, in our estimation, completely unfeasible at the present time."[42]

The following spring, in the 1978 annual report of the Office of Drug Abuse Policy, Bourne framed the problem as follows: "There are serious problems in attempting to reduce coca cultivation. Coca is legally grown in Peru and Bolivia, is a part of the Indian history and culture and has extensive legitimate local use. In addition, the coca bush is extremely hardy, easy to grow and harvest, and lives for nearly 40 years. Both major producing countries are poor, and coca is a principal cash crop for many of the people. Obviously, we cannot expect instant changes."[43] His colleague at NIDA, Robert DuPont, disagreed with his assessment of the applicability of a crop eradication policy to coca plants.

> Unlike marihuana and heroin (our two large-scale use drugs from plant sources), cocaine comes from plants which are now narrowly distributed in the world—the Andes Mountains in Western South America. Also, unlike marihuana and heroin, the coca plant is a perennial, making its cultivation much less flexible. After all, it takes

100 days or less from seed to harvest for poppies or marihuana. It takes 3 to 5 years for a newly planted coca bush to become productive. These characteristics—narrow geographical distribution and multi-year cultivation—make coca much more vulnerable as a plant to eradication than either marihuana or poppies.[44]

Carter's drug message as delivered on 2 August 1977 synthesized the advice that the president had received from Bourne and the criticism of that advice from others, such as Eizenstat and DuPont. Carter followed Bourne's blueprint in that he avoided special emphasis on cocaine, except for mentioning it in the larger context of international drug control. He highlighted the importance of controls on amphetamines and barbiturates and expressed support for decriminalization of marijuana.

The president devoted the first major section of the message to international cooperation and crop substitution and eradication. Additionally he referred to revitalization of the Strategy Council, inactive since 1972, as the body to be responsible for articulating and evaluating federal drug policy as required by the

President Carter announces his administration's drug policy with Peter Bourne, 2 August 1977. (Courtesy: Jimmy Carter Library.)

Comprehensive Drug Abuse and Control Act. (This body would be convened in November.) In the final analysis, he closely paralleled Gerald Ford's message of more than a year earlier and gave strong indications that he accepted the basic tenet of Ford's *White Paper*—namely, that in consideration of limited federal resources and the intractable nature of addiction, policies should aim to minimize social damage rather than seek to wipe out all illicit drug use. Carter went on to endorse some of the legislation introduced during Ford's tenure while skirting issues such as mandatory minimum sentences and denial of parole by offering to study these proposals.

Ford, 27 April 1976	Carter, 2 August 1977
Law enforcement officials estimate that as much as one half of all "street crime" . . . is committed by drug addicts to support their expensive habits. In simple dollar terms, drug abuse costs us up to $17 billion a year.	Many communities remain unsafe because of drug-related street crime, and the immense profits made in the illicit drug traffic help support the power and influence of organized crime. . . . The estimated cost of drug abuse in America exceeds 15 billion dollars each year.
. . . I will submit to the Congress this week legislation which will require mandatory minimum prison sentences for persons convicted of trafficking in heroin and similar narcotic drugs. . . . I shall submit to Congress legislation that would enable judges to deny bail if a defendant arrested for trafficking heroin or dangerous drugs is found (1) to have been previously convicted of a drug felony. . . .	I am directing the Attorney General to review the adequacy of the penalties for major trafficking offenses and give me his recommendations within 90 days. I am directing the Attorney General to study the necessity for and constitutionality of proposals which would deny pre-trial release to certain persons charged with trafficking in drugs posing the greatest threat to health, and to give me his recommendations within 90 days.
. . . I shall ask Congress to raise to $10,000 the ceiling for administrative forfeitures.	I support legislation raising from $2,500 to $10,000 the value of property which can be seized and forfeited from drug violators by administrative action.
The delay in U.S. ratification of the [1971 Convention on Psychotropic Drugs] has been an embarrassment to us.	I urge the Congress to adopt legislation implementing the Convention on Psychotropic Substances, and I urge the Senate to ratify this treaty promptly.

The Federal program to control drug abuse is as diverse as any in government, involving some seven Cabinet departments and seventeen agencies. It is vitally important that the efforts of these departments and agencies be integrated into an effective overall program but that responsibility for specific program management rest with the appropriate departments and agencies	Because the federal effort is currently divided among more than twenty different and often competing agencies, I have directed my staff to coordinate Federal action and to formulate a comprehensive national policy.
Accordingly, I am today establishing two new Cabinet Committees—one for drug abuse law enforcement and the other for drug abuse prevention, treatment and rehabilitation	This will end the long-standing fragmentation among our international programs, drug law enforcement, treatment and rehabilitation, prevention, and regulatory activities. I will also seek the counsel and active involvement of members of the Cabinet and heads of major independent agencies on all drug abuse policy questions through a revitalized Strategy Council on Drug Abuse.

The media found Carter's endorsement of cannabis decriminalization proposals to be the most interesting aspect of the message. The *Washington Post* ran a front-page article on the subject that, quite fairly, pointed out that Carter had endorsed pending legislation rather than introduced a new proposal and that he did not say anything to encourage the states to adopt similar measures.[45] Several days later the same paper published a story on pot use in the District of Columbia under the headline "The Heat Is Off for Marijuana Users: De Facto Decriminalization Result of Change in Public Opinion."[46]

SUMMER OF 1977 TO JULY 1978

For the next year, Peter Bourne continued to manage the drug policy of the Carter White House. After ODAP was finally phased out by executive order in March of 1978, he stayed on in his capacity as special advisor to the president for another four months. As such, he continually expressed his concern to the president about the threat of heroin and his belief in the efficacy of international efforts to control opium poppy crops. As will be seen, the insistence that heroin posed the principal, perhaps even the only, real drug threat to American public health and life—and the conviction that choices had to be made, that eradication of all drug use was impossible—continued to drive drug control policy until the end of the Carter presidency.

Immediately after the president's August 1977 message, Bourne spoke at a press briefing where he underlined the importance to the administration's policy of drug crop eradication, specifically opium poppies. In his estimation, eliminating drug crops where they were grown held more promise as a method of reducing domestic availability than border interdiction. Bourne told the press corps that

> we feel in many ways the weaker link in the chain in terms of stopping drugs [weaker than stopping traffic at the border] is prior to the point at which they are put on an airplane, particularly with heroin. If one is going to stop the traffic, one's chances of doing it are far greater when it is still in the form of opium and in the ground, growing. . . .
>
> That does not mean we are not going to make an effort also to go after those planes, but in terms of effectiveness of the overall strategy, going after the opium poppy as near the source as possible . . . is the key to what we are trying to do.[47]

Over the next several months, three reports were produced all of which reinforced the administration's commitment to drug crop control and the primary role of the DEA in all foreign operations, especially investigation and prosecution of major international traffickers. On 7 September 1977 the first of seven interagency reviews ordered by ODAP was completed. Titled *Border Management and Interdiction,* it reaffirmed the choice of "control at the source" over border control as the preferred method of supply reduction and recommended creation of a new Border Management Agency that would consolidate the functions of Customs, INS, and other agencies concerned with contraband of various sorts.[48] The study reopened the old wounds at the Customs Bureau that had been inflicted by Reorganization Plan 2 of 1973. Robert Chasen, commissioner of Customs, echoing sentiments expressed by his predecessor with respect to Ford's *White Paper,* commented,

> Reorganization Plan No. 2 had the effect of disrupting the Customs narcotics law enforcement effort. That effort, prior to the reorganization, was a continuum which included the investigation of cases abroad, interdiction at U.S. borders and related follow-up investigations. The reorganization constructed barriers and created gaps along the continuum by placing the investigators in one agency and the interdiction force in another. The result has been that the investigators are functioning with less

than total involvement by the interdiction force, while the interdiction force is handicapped by the lack of a closely coordinated investigative capability.[49]

His colleague at the DEA, administrator Peter Bensinger, predictably justified the conclusions of the study, as had Henry Dogin before him, also with respect to the *White Paper.*

We believe that much of the controversy associated with drug interdiction centers on its relative priority within the overall U.S. drug supply reduction strategy. The role of border drug interdiction is essential; however, its relative importance must be placed in juxtaposition with the value of programs aimed at removing the foreign source, financing, etc., and the disruption of drug trafficking systems. Border interdiction is a deterrent to drug smuggling; it is a defensive rather than an offensive strategy. Its effectiveness, however, is handicapped by the need to expeditiously process a tremendous volume of cargo, passengers, baggage, and vehicles.[50]

When the official review of DEA's mandate, *Supply Control: Drug Law Enforcement, an Interagency Review,* was released in December, it also reiterated the priorities established in Gerald Ford's *White Paper* and incidentally resurrected the word "minimize," which had been specifically rejected in the Nixon Administration.

Given the enormous profits realized through illicit drug transactions, stopping *all* illicit drug activities is an unreachable goal. Consequently, a more realistic objective is to *minimize* the rate at which drugs reach the illicit market. During FY 1977, the Federal Government dedicated approximately $350 million in more than a dozen separate Government agencies to minimize the flow of illicit drugs. . . .

Since all drugs are not equally dangerous and all drug use is not equally destructive, our current national strategy specifically places the highest priority for control of those drugs that are individually and socially more destructive, e.g., heroin and barbiturates. Moreover, with a finite number of resources available to devote to the problem, the Federal government has articulated a policy of directing drug investigative resources at major national and international illicit drug producers and distributors. At the same time, this strategy for control of illicit drugs is designed to regulate and safeguard the availability of legitimate drugs for proper medical purposes. [Emphasis in original.][51]

Further confirmation of the emphasis on source control and the primacy of the DEA in all matters of drug control came with the *International Narcotics Control Policy Report* submitted on 31 March 1978.

The report recommends initiatives to (1) reduce supply by (a) seeking international commitments and financial support for projects to reduce poppy and coca cultivation, (b) in developing measures to improve an attack on the financial aspects of trafficking and procedures for arrest and prosecution of offenders overseas through further mutual assistance and extradition treaties; (2) reduce demand through (a) providing greater assistance to foreign governments in developing demand reduction programs, (b) reviewing drug treatment services provided to U.S. citizens abroad; (3) exploring the feasibility of greater use of regional efforts to control drug trafficking and abuse; (4) developing specific Narcotics Action Plans for countries affected by the supply of and/or demand for drugs; (5) assessing the scope of the drug control problem through a comprehensive compilation of all existing data; and (6) improving the conduct of U.S. overseas programs through (a) systematic communication of drug-related policies to key embassies and missions, (b) developing an improved DEA foreign personnel system, (c) evaluating U.S. training programs provided to foreign drug control personnel, and (d) sensitizing narcotics control personnel to demand reduction techniques and opportunities.[52]

MIDSUMMER NIGHTMARE—1978

The summer of 1978 marked the end of an era, although the dimensions of the change were not perceived at the time. The confidence that at least marijuana would soon be quasi-legal was such that a *New York Times* writer could declare that "aggressive enforcement against marijuana use has ended, and 60 percent of the respondents in a recent Gallup Poll support decriminalization, with 28 percent favoring outright legalization."[53] But that state of affairs would last only a political heartbeat. Lester Wolff's committee kept up the heat on the administration to pay more attention to cocaine, and the odd symbiosis between Keith Stroup and Peter Bourne would soon profoundly change the career paths of both men.

Bourne's ignominious departure from the White House would make the Carter administration's accommodationist drug policy untenable. The way would open for leaders who were more aware of, and sympathetic to, emerging grass-roots rejection of fine distinctions among the dangers of different drugs. The notion that the risk of personal and social damage posed by some drug use was at least marginally acceptable was slowly becoming a political liability. Stroup himself would lose power over the movement he had so cleverly orchestrated to appeal to moderate voters, and NORML would be left much weakened at the moment that middle-class parents were getting fed up with official and scientific temporizing in the face of youthful drug experimentation. The administration's campaign for decriminalization of cannabis would be abandoned.

Keith Stroup, executive director of the National Organization for Reform of Marijuana Laws, in his office, 15 April 1975. (U.S. News and World Report Collection, Library of Congress.)

The controversy that set the stage for the Bourne fiasco was, paradoxically, one that began as a rallying point for congressional and media support for pot smokers. Since early 1977 stories had been circulating in Congress and the White House that the Mexican government was spraying marijuana crops in the Sierra Madre with an herbicide called paraquat and that the spraying program had at least some support from DEA and the State Department.[54] Keith Stroup, worried about the possibility that his constituents might be poisoned (and perhaps seeing the fund-raising possibilities of a good controversy), discussed the issue with Peter Bourne and with an aide to Senator Charles Percy.[55] At about this time, the Carter administration was claiming credit for a decline in heroin-related deaths, which they attributed to U.S.-sponsored chemical destruction of Mexican poppy crops.[56] On 12 March 1978, Joseph Califano, secretary of health, education, and welfare, released a report that had originated at NIDA that indicated that significant lung damage might result from smoking paraquat-contaminated joints.[57] On 22 March, Bourne told President Carter that "last summer" the question had been raised about the health implications of the Mexican spraying program and that he had asked for studies. He also informed the president that NORML was now planning to sue the government to stop the program and that Senator Percy wanted to hold hearings on the issue. Bourne was quite firm in his conviction that not only did it make no sense for the administration to oppose the program but also that it had limited power to do so.

> Despite the criticism I see no reason to change our policy. We are committed to discouraging the use of marijuana. To pressure the Mexican government to stop using Paraquat to protect the health of Americans would be a tacit government statement that marijuana without Paraquat was safe, a position we have never taken. Our critics would like us to treat marijuana the same way we would farm products imported for consumption that were contaminated. If we did we would in fact be giving marijuana quasi legal status which we cannot do. Mexico regards marijuana, because of the vast amounts of money made from it, as their number one drug problem, not opium. We cannot dictate to them what they can or cannot do about it.
>
> Unless you have feeling to the contrary I plan to enforce this policy, and should Percy be foolish enough to hold hearings I plan to take the position that he is implicitly sanctioning the use of marijuana.[58]

Keith Stroup was already angry with Bourne over what Stroup perceived as personal slights and political waffling on the part of his erstwhile ally in the White House. He was furious about the administration's position on the paraquat issue and was planning a full-scale legal assault on the program.[59]

In early June, NORML's request for a injunction to stop the spraying program was dismissed, but Stroup soon had his chance at revenge. In July, Peter Bourne, in what can charitably be termed a lack of appreciation for the sensitivity of his position, wrote a prescription for Quaaludes for a member of his staff on which he falsified the staffer's name to protect her identity. Through a series of completely fortuitous events, the matter became public. In the ensuing furor, Bourne thought it best to request a leave of absence. Then Stroup, who knew that rumors were rife that Bourne had used cocaine at a NORML party the previous December, refused to deny the rumors when asked about them by members of the press. The columnist Jack Anderson broke the story on morning television the day after the Quaalude disaster had appeared. In spite of his denials, Bourne had to resign. He had been the indispensable supporter of marijuana decriminalization within the administration, and the manner of his going put an end to any further White House sponsorship of relaxed drug laws. Stroup himself had sabotaged the decriminalization of marijuana and therefore had the distinction of having both given life to the movement and leaving it moribund. (As it turned out, Stroup's organization was outraged that he would use an accusation of drug use—just what NORML argued was a private matter—against an ally, and he was forced from his leadership position later that year.)

COCAINE AND MARIJUANA AFTER BOURNE— THE VIEW FROM THE HOUSE

Peter Bourne's resignation came at a crucial moment. Patterns of drug use were changing, and awareness was growing in Congress and the public that, in spite of claims of success against heroin, federal countermeasures were doing little or nothing to stop youthful experimentation with marijuana or to stem the influx of cocaine from South America. For example, the *Annual Report* for 1977 of the House Select Committee on Narcotics Abuse and Control had reported that "despite all attempts to stem the flow of cocaine before it enters the United States, trafficking continues to flourish and is becoming increasingly sophisticated in its techniques and methods. The strong relationship between overwhelming growth of cocaine use in this country and the easy availability of the substance in South America must be the focal point of any effective attack on this problem."[60]

In June the Wolff committee had sent a telegram to Bourne and his cabinet colleagues in charge of drug control to the effect that south Florida was becoming a traffickers' paradise. "House Select Committee has just completed extensive investigations and hearings in south Florida. What we have seen and heard convinces us that this area is in the midst of a catastrophic and overwhelming drug disaster. Therefore as in any other natural disaster faced by this nation this situation must be countered by whatever means are necessary and whatever materiél is necessary to cope with this problem. This situation is so serious we must take immediate action to stem the tide of illegal drugs into the United States through south Florida."[61]

The Wolff committee believed that

> marihuana from Colombia is dispatched by the tonload in all manner of vessels, some foreign flag, some American, destined for south Florida. Seizures of marihuana at the Miami airport have quadrupled over the past 6 months. Almost daily, tons of marihuana and kilos of cocaine were interdicted, yet it is clear from testimony given to the committee that these seizures represent only the tip of the iceberg. Despite dedicated and heroic efforts by Federal, State and local law enforcement personnel, the committee estimates that less than 5 percent of the total contraband coming into south Florida was seized prior to the committee's hearings. The committee found, among other things, that fortunes were being built on the drug trade; that relatively young persons with no visible means of support were paying huge sums of money, hundreds of thousands of dollars in cash on individual transactions, for pleasure boats, homes and other expensive properties; that the drug trade was so pervasive that many millions of dollars in cash were being diverted by the Federal Reserve System to the Miami district in order to meet the demands of the illicit drug trade. The committee discovered that the total gross dollar value of the drug trade in south Florida was at least $7 billion annually, of which the majority represented sales of marihuana and at least $500 million, sales of cocaine.[62]

The congressional group had heard testimony from Frederick A. Rody, Jr., the DEA regional director, that

> "South Florida has become inundated with marihuana and cocaine smuggling and trafficking." Seizures by the Coast Guard, Customs and DEA, in the past 6 months, represent "more drugs than were collectively seized by the U.S. Federal law enforcement community during the entire previous year." Mr. Rody indicated to the committee the dimensions of drug trafficking and the economics associated with the trafficking. He emphasized that the revenue loss to the United States in untaxable income is incalculable. He concluded that the smugglers are better equipped and have more financial resources than the entire drug law enforcement community.[63]

Careful official distinctions among tolerable drugs and intolerable ones—really only heroin—would soon collide with these emerging perceptions that absolutely no good could come of any drug use and especially not marijuana use among the children of middle-class voters. Just days before Bourne's resignation, the White House responded to the committee's concerns with a memorandum outlining what was termed the Southeast Initiative. The document detailed new measures that had been undertaken to improve interdiction, border management, and legal controls on money laundering in southern Florida and the Carribbean, but it mentioned cocaine only in the opening paragraph and did not indicate any real appreciation for the possible consequences of the apparently increasing availability of that substance.[64] The administration continued to emphasize what it saw as its success in dealing with heroin. At the close of the Ninety-fifth Congress President Carter drafted a letter of support to Lester Wolff in which he listed the successes of his overall drug control program.

> The heroin purity rate is at its lowest level, 4.9%, down from 6.6% in 1976.
> Heroin overdose deaths are down 27% from 1977 and 73% from 1976. In 1977, 1,000 fewer people died from heroin overdoses than in 1976.
> Our cooperation with the Mexican Government has brought about a 20% decline in the amount of Mexican heroin available in the United States.
> Statistics indicate a steady decline in barbiturate and other sedative/hypnotic overdose deaths.
> International cooperation has permitted us to work with other governments in seizing huge quantities of marijuana on the high seas.[65]

OUTSIDE THE BELTWAY

In addition to congressional agitation, the angry voices of parents concerned about glamorization of marijuana use and trivialization of its ill effects were reaching the White House. Lee Dogoloff, who had been Bourne's deputy and had replaced him as head of the drug policy unit of the domestic policy staff, seemed more receptive than his predecessor had been to the emerging reaction and began to orchestrate some changes in the vocabulary used to communicate the administration's substance abuse control efforts.

In his January 1979 State of the Union address, President Carter again cited statistics to support the claim that the heroin situation was vastly improved, but some new language had found its way into the message. The president made passing reference to a new drug policy focus on "the behavior of the individual" for the coming year. Lee Dogoloff explained in his exit interview at the end of the Carter term that individual behavior within the context of the fam-

Peter Bourne welcomes Lee Dogoloff as deputy director of the Office of Drug Abuse Policy. (Courtesy: Jimmy Carter Library.)

ily was to be the new focus for treatment and rehabilitation programs.[66] This suggests that the demands of the middle class were beginning to affect the policy response to the drug problem as a whole, regardless of the specific drug in question. Policy and health officials were apparently recognizing that potentially powerful groups of voters were becoming measurably less willing to tolerate casual drug use. "Today in the United States there are 110,000 fewer addicts than there were in 1975. One thousand fewer Americans died of heroin overdoses in the 12-month period ending June 30, 1977, than in the previous 12 months. Seizures of illegal drugs are at their highest level ever. . . . In 1979 we will look more to the behavior of the individual who turns to drugs. We will stress financial investigation and a means of prosecuting those individuals responsible for the drug traffic, and will rely heavily on enlisting foreign cooperation in the overall drug program."[67]

By March of 1979, more changes began to appear in the tone and content of pronouncements by officials charged with narcotics control policy. Lee Dogoloff, testifying before the Senate Subcommittee on Alcoholism and Drug Abuse, repeated the president's statements about changing individual behavior as well as prosecuting traffickers and encouraging international cooperation against drugs. Even more significantly, he also highlighted what he called the administration's concern "about increases in the consumption of marijuana and cocaine." He went on to stress the importance of providing effective antidrug information to adults responsible for counseling and educating young people.

> One of our major concerns is the increased drug abuse among our youth. The latest survey results show that one in nine high school seniors smokes marijuana daily, and that this figure is probably quite a bit higher in urban areas. . . .
>
> In the coming year we hope to undertake a number of initiatives to deal with this and other issues that confront us. The three most important areas that we will concentrate on are, first, an adolescent drug abuse campaign to provide accurate information about adolescent drug abuse to parents, teachers, and other key youth leaders so that they will be prepared to firmly discourage drug abuse by adolescents with whom they come in contact.
>
> Secondly, increased financial investigation as a means of prosecuting individuals for drug trafficking, and thirdly, a plan to enlist foreign cooperation in the overall drug program.[68]

At the same time, he reported on the achievements of the Southeast Initiative against cocaine and marijuana.

> In an effort to halt the enormous quantities of marihuana and cocaine entering the country through the Southeastern United States, the Executive Office initiated, during the summer of 1978, a major interdepartmental effort against drug trafficking in that area. . . .
>
> Since the beginning of the Southeast Initiative, over 987 tons (1,974,680 pounds) of marihuana have been seized by the U.S. Coast Guard. This represents a three-fold increase over 1977 seizures during the same period (325 tons or 650,000 pounds). . . .
>
> The U.S. Customs Service has seized over 780 pounds of cocaine in Florida, Georgia, and the Carolinas during this July through December period. These 780 pounds of cocaine represent a 45% increase over the amount of cocaine seized during the first six months of 1978.[69]

On 30 March Stuart Eizenstat and Lee Dogoloff underlined the shift in direction of federal drug policy in a memorandum for the president. "We have had considerable success in reducing the availability and the effects of heroin on American society. While we do not intend to reduce our effort directed at heroin, it is time to place more emphasis on helping people, rather than on specific drugs. During our program to reduce adolescent drug use, we will assess the opportunities which may arise for your personal involvement and will advise you accordingly."[70]

THE STRATEGY COUNCIL AND THE 1979 FEDERAL STRATEGY REPORT

At the time of Dogoloff's March memo, the Strategy Council[71] had been in official existence for about a year and a half, although the full group had met for the first and only time in November of 1977. (The public or nongovernmental members had met twice.)[72] After ODAP was scheduled to be phased out, President Carter and his staff envisioned the Strategy Council as a major component in the post-ODAP federal drug policy apparatus.[73] At least in part, it was meant to satisfy Congress that the provisions for publication of a specific and measurable plan for drug abuse control included in the Comprehensive Drug Abuse Prevention and Control Act of 1970 would be adhered to.[74] Development of this plan was the official charge to the council. However, the fact of the matter was that the plan, *The Federal Strategy for Drug Abuse and Drug Traffic Prevention,* as it was eventually titled, was mostly drafted by the White House drug policy staff and the "Principals Group."[75] This body consisted of the commandant of the coast guard, the commissioner of Customs, the administrator of DEA, the assistant attorney general in charge of the Criminal Division of Justice, the director of NIDA, the assistant secretary of state for narcotics matters, and a special assistant to the secretary of health and human services.[76] Other policy documents—notably a five-year plan for drug control that was initiated in the fall of 1979 and the 1980 *Annual Report on the Federal Drug Program*—were similarly developed by policy professionals in the White House and cabinet departments and presented to the Strategy Council more or less as faits accomplis. Congressman Wolff and some members of the council would later complain publicly about this modus operandi.

The Principals Group cobbled together the *Strategy* from such sources as the cocaine policy paper of the fall of 1977, the president's message on drug abuse and State of the Union address, and the memorandum that NIDA director Robert DuPont had composed in response to Peter Bourne's cocaine policy draft. Various versions were circulated to the members of the Strategy Council for comment. By January of 1979 Dogoloff was able to report that the *Strategy* was "in the final stages of completion."[77] The final document was forwarded to the president on 2 April 1979[78] and published on 20 May.

The 1979 *Federal Strategy* followed many of the themes that had made their appearance in federal drug control policy in the Ford administration, most prominently "that total elimination of the drug abuse problem is unlikely,"[79] but it also reflected significant movement away from the tone and emphasis of the Bourne era as expressed in the 1978 ODAP *Annual Report*—which was itself partially a product of the exchanges among White House staff members working on marijuana and cocaine policy during the summer of 1977. Worries about cocaine and reaction against complacent attitudes toward youthful pot smoking were now being expressed in official documents more clearly and with fewer qualifications, and some problematic language was disappearing. Here is a comparison of key points and language.

ODAP Annual Report, Spring 1978	*Strategy,* Spring 1979
. . . ODAP, while continuing to assign top priority to heroin as the major cause of death and drug related crime also gave significant attention to the sedative/hypnotics. (p. 16)	
The damage to the world community and the United States of international drug trafficking is strictly an economic phenomenon. The pharmacological dis-	International trafficking, however, is strictly an economic phenomenon, where there are no priorities except the value of the drug shipment. Our pur-

tinctions, for example among heroin, cocaine and marihuana, become irrelevant when million dollar drug shipments are moved from one country to another.(pp. 16–17)

pose is to restrict cocaine availability and maintain a high price for the drug. Efforts to reduce cultivation and trafficking in coca and cocaine in the producing and processing countries are the most effective ways to use our resources to prevent cocaine-related morbidity and mortality at home. (p. 32)

Heroin availability in the U.S. has sunk in the last twelve months to its lowest level in seven years, with a national average retail purity of five percent and a price of $1.69 per milligram pure. As a result, heroin-related deaths are at the lowest level since this data was available in mid-1973. Deaths have declined over 40 percent since July 1976, and heroin-related injuries show a similar decrease. There has been a drop in the crime rate nationwide of approximately nine percent, some of which can be attributed to a decrease in heroin use. (p. 17)

Heroin purity has declined from 6.6 percent in the first quarter of calendar year 1976 to 4.2 percent in the third quarter of 1978. The price per milligram of pure heroin has risen in the same time period from $1.26 to $1.96. This increase in price and decrease in purity is significant because it is generally believed to reflect a decline in availability brought about by international and domestic control efforts. Heroin overdose deaths in 1977 are down 63% from 1976. In more tangible terms, approximately 1,000 fewer people died from heroin overdoses in 1977 than in 1976. During the same period, emergency room episodes related to heroin declined by 40%. Both heroin-related deaths and emergency room visits are at the lowest reported level since data became available in mid-1973. Current data (September 1978) indicate that the number of heroin addicts has declined since 1975 by 100,000 from 550,000 to 450,000. The data strongly suggest that the heroin problem is decreasing. (p. 10)

The policy of this Administration is to discourage all illicit drug use. However, in applying this policy the penalties against possession of a drug should not be more damaging to an individual than the use of the drug itself. The Administration has supported legislation to

The past use of incarceration as a sanction against marihuana use has been erratically applied, often with an extremely harsh punishment doing more harm to the individual than the drug itself. Therefore, Federal strategy supports a reduction in the severity of the amend the Federal law to reduce the penalties regarding simple possession of marihuana for personal use. (p. 28)

Cocaine . . . has qualities which make it problematical to categorize within the framework of a national drug policy. It is difficult to detect its use since it produces few overdose deaths, or emergency room episodes, when used infrequently, and by sniffing or "snorting" it up the nose. Cocaine-related deaths number only about 20 a year contrasted with over 2,000 heroin-related deaths. However, cocaine has the potential for causing severe health consequences if use patterns and consumption levels alter, particularly if there is a trend toward intravenous use and frequent administration. At high doses, particularly when used chronically, cocaine can cause acute toxic reactions with psychosis, erosion of the nasal mucosa and even death. Because it is one of the most reinforcing drugs, consumption levels can tend to increase rapidly if cocaine is more available and less expensive, easily leading to compulsive use if there is an adequate supply. (p. 29)

While the current health hazards of cocaine use should not be overstated, the potential adverse consequences if use increases should be emphasized. It must be understood that the critical factor underlying this apparent lack of health consequences is the high price of the

Federal criminal penalties for personal possession and use. The penalties should not be lifted altogether, however, as this could be misconstrued to mean we condone marihuana use and could, furthermore, undermine our Federal policy, which is to discourage marihuana use. (pp. 51–52)

There are, however, several important things we do know about the health consequences of cocaine use. We know, for example that cocaine can kill—not commonly but occasionally and not predictably. Despite the street lore to the contrary, death can occur even when the drug is snorted rather than injected. We also know that cocaine is the most powerfully reinforcing of all abused drugs. Although not physically addictive in the sense that opiates are, there is good evidence to show that the desire to continue using cocaine is remarkably strong if the drug is available.

drug, which reflects relative scarcity and restricts the general level and extent of use. (p. 30)

The recent attention that cocaine has received in the media is of great concern, as is the advertising effect of all the cocaine paraphernalia now on sale—the gold razor blades and fancy coke spoons. American should not be led to believe that cocaine is a harmless drug. However, it is difficult to convey to the American people a realistic warning about cocaine use since there are currently few visible health hazards, and one does so at the risk of being discredited and disbelieved. (p. 30)

Domestic law enforcement agencies should not single cocaine out for special attention since that approach seems of little practical benefit. In Fiscal Year 1976, only 1,500 pounds of cocaine were seized, a small percentage of the estimated 15–17 tons coming into the U.S. Increases in the number of enforcement or interdiction personnel would not necessarily lead to substantial increases in seizures.

There are serious problems in attempting to reduce coca cultivation. Coca is legally grown in Peru and Bolivia, is a part of the Indian history and culture and has extensive legitimate local use. In addition, the coca bush is extremely hardy, easy to grow and harvest, and lives for nearly 40 years. Both major producing countries are poor, and coca is a principal cash crop for many of the people. Obviously, we cannot expect instant changes. (p. 31)

Cocaine is the principal psychoactive ingredient of the coca bush, which unlike marihuana and opium, has been geographically restricted to the Andes Mountains of South America. The production and shipment of cocaine have been largely limited to Peru, Bolivia, Colombia, and to a lesser extent Ecuador. In cooperation with the governments of these countries, Strategy 1979 encourages all efforts to control the drug within these source and primary transit countries. (p. 54)

Our policy is not merely one of crop substitution. It places emphasis on the broader concept of rural development and we are working closely with the U.N. and the international financial institutions and are hopeful for long-term, lasting progress. (p. 32)

Chewing coca leaves has long been an accepted cultural practice of many of the peoples native to these countries and many of these people are currently dependent upon the coca bush for income. Reducing coca cultivation, therefore, will entail comprehensive and carefully designed programs to provide for income and crop substitution. (p. 56)

Although the authors of the 1979 *Strategy* took pains to point out the dangers of cocaine, they still did not imply that it should supplant heroin in established priorities.[80] The *Strategy* also reflected the new importance accorded to research into the baneful effects of cocaine. "In conclusion, the *Strategy* considers cocaine to be a priority drug exceeded only by heroin and barbiturates. The *Strategy* recognizes that the effort to reduce coca cultivation and cocaine trafficking in the source and processing countries is the most effective way to prevent an increase in cocaine-related deaths and injuries at home. The *Strategy* further recognizes that these efforts alone will not suffice and therefore encourages the research and scientific efforts necessary to adequately inform the American public of the health and social consequences of cocaine use."[81] The 1978 *Annual Report* had expressed the priority relationship among drugs in a less alarming way: "In summary, cocaine use in the U.S. has not created a need for extensive treatment and cocaine is placed in our domestic priority system below heroin and barbiturates which currently pose greater threats to life and health.."[82] Making reference to the concern for "behavior" that had appeared in Carter's 1979 State of the Union address, the *Strategy* explained that it

> no longer focuses primarily on individual drugs, but looks instead at drug-taking behavior. Chronic, compulsive drug abusers—of any substance—are those most in need of treatment and should receive Federal priority. The Strategy also recognizes that negative consequences can result from a wide variety of drug-taking behaviors—from occasional, recreational use to the misuse of prescription drugs—and recommends an increased sensitivity throughout the Federal health and social services delivery systems to drug-related problems. The Strategy recommends more specificity in treatment and prevention programs and planning, with increased attention paid to the unique needs of special populations, including youth, the elderly, ethnic minorities, rural populations and women.[83]

PARAQUAT AGAIN

It was in this atmosphere that the paraquat controversy that had been simmering for a year finally came to a head. The previous September, Senator Charles Percy's campaign to prohibit U.S. foreign aid to support herbicide use on cannabis crops had culminated in an amendment to the International Security Assistance Act of 1978. The amendment stated,

> (d)(1) Assistance authorized by this chapter may not be made available or used for any program involving the spraying of an herbicide to eradicate marihuana plants if the use of that herbicide is likely to cause serious harm to the health of persons who may use or consume the sprayed marihuana. This prohibition shall not apply if the herbicide is used in conjunction with another substance that will clearly and readily warn potential users and consumers of the sprayed marihuana that a herbicide has been used on it.
>
> (2) The Secretary of State shall inform the Secretary of Health, Education and Welfare of the use or intended use by any country or international organization of any herbicide to eradicate marihuana in a program receiving assistance under this chapter. The Secretary of Health, Education, and Welfare, on the basis of scientific information and testing and after receiving comments from the Secretary of Agriculture and the Administrator of the Environmental Protection Agency, shall promptly advise the Secretary of State if the use of that herbicide is likely to cause serious harm to the health of persons who may use or consume marihuana sprayed with that herbicide. If the Secretary of State is so advised with respect to any herbicide, the prohibition contained in paragraph (1) shall apply with respect to the use of that herbicide.[84]

The following June, Congressman Wolff and his Select Committee on Narcotics Abuse and Control heard testimony on paraquat from both governmental and nongovernmental experts. The committee came to the conclusion that "for a marijuana smoker to incur fibrosis of the lung from paraquat-sprayed marijuana, he would have to be an extremely heavy smoker, obtaining consistently contaminated marijuana for extended periods of time. This evidence disputes the finding of the Department of Health, Education, and Welfare that paraquat-sprayed marijuana is harmful."[85] Then, on 2 August 1979, the outgoing secretary of HEW, Joseph Califano, wrote to Secretary of State Cyrus Vance pursuant to the notification requirement of the Percy amendment.

> At my request, the Center for Disease Control (CDC) and the National Institute of Environmental Health Sciences (NIEHS) have investigated the health consequences of consuming paraquat-sprayed marijuana. Their findings, concurred in by the Sur-

> geon General, are that the smoke of paraquat-contaminated marijuana is likely to cause serious and in some cases irreversible lung damage when inhaled in sufficient quantities by marijuana users. There is a direct relationship between the amount of paraquat inhaled and the extent and severity of lung damage that results. Lung damage from intermittent or short-term exposure may be reversible, but frequent, high-level exposure over a long period of time can result in a severe form of damage called fibrosis.[86]

When the text of Califano's letter was released by HEW, Wolff was incensed[87] in spite of the fact that HEW's position on paraquat had been known since the previous year. Califano's official notification to Vance to the effect that paraquat was indeed dangerous would activate the provisions of the Percy amendment against Mexico. Thus, in Wolff's opinion, the campaign against Mexican heroin would be compromised because the amendment appeared to be applicable to "*any* program involving the spraying of marijuana" whether or not such a program also involved the spraying of other things, such as poppies. In the context of the public's increasing impatience with anything that implied tolerance toward any drugs or drug users, this situation was unacceptable. The congressman wrote to new HEW secretary Patricia Roberts Harris asking why the information presented to his subcommittee did not support the conclusion to which HEW had apparently come.[88] The government of Mexico (GOM) was also "outraged." Stuart Eizenstat and Lee Dogoloff wrote to Attorney General Griffin Bell asking him to talk to his Mexican counterpart.

> Although there has not been any public reaction, the Mexican Government has privately conveyed its outrage to us (see attached cable). Attorney General Flores, who heads the Mexican narcotics eradication effort, is particularly upset. They take exception to the claim that paraquat-sprayed marihuana is likely to cause serious health harm. They have informed us that they will continue to spray paraquat on marihuana since this is their domestic priority. Any reduction of assistance would result in lessened opium poppy destruction and increased availability of heroin in the U.S. Ambassador Lucey and the State Department believe strongly that elimination or even reduction in narcotics assistance to Mexico would have an adverse effect on our narcotics program, on overall GOM/U.S. relations, and on the President's September 28 meeting with President Lopez Portillo.[89]

Bell was supposed to tell Flores that, among other things, "we have looked into the possibility of altering Secretary Califano's decision and delaying the implementation of the Amendment but the law is quite specific. We are strongly committed to changing the legislation as soon as possible after the

Congress returns in September and have made this a high priority."[90] Bell did phone Flores on 10 August. The conversation seems to have gone well,[91] but Wolff was still angry. A 21 September memo for Eizenstat from Lee Dogoloff outlined the situation.

> On Thursday morning, September 20, I met with Lester Wolff about a number of issues. He is livid about Paraquat—believes that HEW misinterpreted the scientific data regarding the potential harm that marihuana sprayed with Paraquat might bring and is threatening to hold hearings, to call the head of the Center for Disease Control to account for his judgment and then to charge him with misfeasance of office and ask for his removal. He also threatened to bring a suit against the Government and, lastly, said that he will talk to Senator Percy about it. I am not sure whether he will pursue all or any of these efforts but I passed the information on to HEW and suggested that they have someone meet with congressman Wolff as soon as possible to discuss the basis of their decision, etc.

Dogoloff suggested some talking points for Eizenstat to address with Percy.

> You realize that some of the consequences, in terms of Mexican reaction, were not intended. However, the basic problem is that the legislative approach assumes that the Mexican decision to use Paraquat on marihuana can be controlled through U.S. funding. In fact, the opposite is true. The Mexicans purchase the Paraquat on their own and have sufficient equipment and expertise to continue spraying. In *their* opinion, the notion of passing a law to protect the health of people who are violating the law is ludicrous. They also are not receptive to a suggestion that they discontinue spraying marihuana—a drug which they see as their own priority in terms of protecting their own population. Also they are, by being a signatory to an international treaty, compelled to eradicate illicit narcotic crops. A nationalistic reaction by the Mexicans is likely, which may result in increased marihuana spraying (since that is their priority) and decreased opium spraying. [Emphasis in original.][92]

Five days later, Richard Williams, Dogoloff's deputy in charge of drug policy management and enforcement, reported to Stuart Eizenstat that Percy did not want to hurt the poppy program and had met with Wolff.[93]

The end result of at least the portion of the whole dustup that related to heroin was an amendment to the amendment, which replaced the words "for any program involving" with "for the purpose of," thereby applying the funding prohibition to marijuana spraying only. As Wolff's committee reported:

> There was much controversy concerning the implementation of the Percy Amendment due to the intertwined nature of both marihuana and opium poppy spraying by the Mexican government. The Select Committee was concerned that implemen-

> tation of the Percy Amendment would seriously jeopardize the successful opium poppy program, thereby increasing the risk that more Mexican brown heroin would enter this country. The Committee noted that the congressional intent by both Senator Percy and Chairman Wolff was not to jeopardize the opium poppy eradication program by a paraquat-related funding cutback.
>
> To solve this dilemma, the Select Committee staff negotiated an amendment with Senator Percy's staff at the Conference Committee meeting on the International Security Assistance Act of 1979. This amendment, which was adopted without objection, clarified the original Percy Amendment. It provided that no U.S. assistance could be used for the purpose of spraying marihuana with paraquat under a determination of health harm by the Secretary of HEW in the absence of an effective marker agent.
>
> As a result, this amendment safeguarded not only the opium poppy eradication program but the health of the U.S. citizen as well.[94]

The Carter administration never did resolve the issue of finding either an effective marker agent that would alert pot smokers to the presence of paraquat or an alternative herbicide that would pass muster at HEW. Throughout 1980 the Principals Group continued to worry about the lack of an acceptable product and the political implications of the law's apparently greater concern for the health of marijuana users than for the harm caused by the availability of even unsprayed marijuana.[95]

> Mr. Dogoloff . . . raised, at the request of Ms. Falco, the crop destruction issue for which we have begun to develop short term and long term strategies. With regard to the short term strategy, Mr. Dogoloff referred the principals to page seven of the Drug Abuse Message Draft dated March 12, 1980, which reads "Present law provides that we cannot assist source country efforts to destroy illicit marihuana cultivation if even only one or two users might potentially be harmed. We urge the Congress to consider amending this rigid standard to allow the government to take into consideration the harm the availability of marihuana now has on the health and well-being of the people of the United States.[96]

The Percy amendment had also confused the often-articulated priority assigned to crop destruction.

> Mr. Dogoloff and Mr. Bensinger argued that our principal strategy of effective control as close to the source as possible was not in effect being carried out if we are unable to work with foreign countries in eradicating drug-producing crops such as marihuana. Mr. Linnemann readily admitted that eradication is the most effective means of destroying crops though we may have several unanticipated problems in conducting a spraying program in Colombia. He noted that his reservations should

> not be interpreted to mean that the Department is not doing anything in this area. INM [International Narcotics Matters, a division in the State Department] is working towards the development of a marker for paraquat in accordance with the current legislation.[97]

THE PARENTS' MOVEMENT

The grass-roots movement to reject accommodationist drug policies was, by the summer of 1979, a force to be reckoned with. Much as the marijuana lobby coordinated by Keith Stroup and NORML had gained the sympathies of a number of bureaucrats, journalists, policy specialists, and legislative professionals, this Parents' Movement eventually succeeded in making itself heard by not just Lee Dogoloff but also people in Congress and officials at ADAMHA and NIDA. Angry and frustrated about casual acceptance of youthful drug experimentation, these mostly suburban parents felt that far too many politicians, health professionals, and fellow citizens had been seduced by overly sophisticated hairsplitting about the relative safety of this or that drug. They were deeply offended and even frightened by the siren song of hedonism and glamor sung by the likes of NORML and by the burgeoning drug paraphernalia industry that legally purveyed such items as gold razor blades for cutting coke "lines" and intriguing or humorous pot pipes and drug-related knickknacks.

That August, Lee Dogoloff made a trip to Naples, Florida, where he was distressed to discover that, just as Frederick Rody had told the Wolff committee, local law enforcement was totally unable to deal with marijuana traffic and consumption. Parents had reacted to what they saw as a crisis by forming groups to monitor absences from school and activities in playgrounds and parking lots.[98]

About the same time, the president received a number of letters from citizens who were beginning to rebel against what they saw as weak-kneed drug policies and pronouncements. These activists sought to influence the national substance abuse debate by lobbying for changes in the style and tone of drug education materials put out by the government. Where once the promoters of pot were able to influence the language of federal policy statements, angry parents now demanded that intellectuals and lawyers allied with the decriminalization lobby be barred from contributing to federally sponsored drug information literature.

Joyce Nalepka, a Maryland homemaker and organizer of the Coalition for

Concern About Marihuana Use in Youth, wrote a letter to the president that included ten specific requests for action by the federal government to control marijuana. Among these requests was "that the President of the United States call for an update of all written and audio-visual materials on drug abuse that are used or recommended for use by agencies of government or those using federal funds. This call should be aimed specifically at elimination of obsolete and inaccurate material, especially that positioning marijuana as a harmless drug."[99]

Dogoloff met with Nalepka and sixty members of her organization and gave quite detailed responses to their questions. He told her,

> In a draft letter which we have prepared for the Strategy Council on Drug Abuse (comprised of the Secretaries of Health, Education, and Welfare; State; Defense; and Treasury; the Attorney General; the Administrator of Veterans Affairs; and the Director of the Office of Management and Budget [Dogoloff did not mention the public members of the council]) I have asked for an update of all government materials which discuss marijuana to reflect the currently known dangers which the drug poses, particularly for children. In that this ambitious project may require a significant amount of time, the White House, together with the National Institute on Drug Abuse, has prepared a draft paper specifically on marijuana, to parents and other members of the general public, to alert them to these dangers and ensure that this information is promptly distributed. In this instance, we have neither the luxury of time nor the opportunity for esoteric debate. We must act quickly and seize every opportunity to assure the paper's widest distribution and media attention.[100]

Dogoloff later recorded that he had done as promised. "Since that time we have had numerous discussions with Mrs. Nalepka and others who attended the meeting and, as promised, have asked all the Cabinet Members of the Strategy Council on Drug Abuse to review and update the information in Federal publications on marihuana."[101]

The Parents' Movement also got its message to Congress. On 1 November 1979 the Select Committee on Narcotics Abuse and Control heard testimony from Sue Rusche, president of Families in Action of DeKalb County, Georgia, in which she related how her organization had been founded two years before in response to the discovery that sixth and seventh graders were smoking pot and using other drugs.[102] She was very upset about the drug lobby (NORML) and the growth of paraphernalia industry.

> Are we getting information or propaganda when the Liaison Task Panel on Psychoactive Drug Use/Misuse, chaired by NORML advisory board member Dr. Nor-

> man Zinberg, cites NORML in the report as a "moderately effective agent for public education" and recommends to the President's Commission on Mental Health the immediate decriminalization of marihuana, the eventual legalization of marihuana, the decriminalization of other psychoactive drugs, and an "immediate cessation . . . of the development of materials and programs aimed exclusively at prevention of all use"? . . .
>
> Last week a mother sent me a copy of NIDA's newest pamphlet for kids, "Let's Talk About Drug Abuse." The pamphlet cites NORML as a source for "general marihuana information. . . ." The mother also sent me a copy of one of the pamphlets recommended for further reading, "Drug Abuse: A Realistic Primer for Parents," published by the Do It Now Foundation. . . .
>
> Mr. Chairman, if we are to stem the tide of drug use among the Nation's children, this kind of nonsense must stop. Therefore, on behalf of parents all across the country, we call upon Congress to conduct a full-scale investigation of the drug paraphernalia industry, *High Times Magazine,* and the National Organization for the Reform of Marihuana Laws.[103]

Later, Sue Rusche wrote to committee chair Lester L. Wolff to inform him that "sometime during the week of the hearings, the National Institute on Drug Abuse stopped printing the pamphlet I cited in my testimony ('Let's Talk About Drug Abuse'). NIDA plans to rewrite the marijuana section and to delete all references at the end, including the National Organization for the Reform of Marijuana Laws and the Do It Now Foundation."[104]

The parents also enjoyed some success in promoting legislation to control the paraphernalia industry. In 1980 the Wolff committee issued a report in which it gave six recommendations for control of the paraphernalia industry, including enactment of model legislation at the federal level, state and local control legislation, possible scheduling as controlled substances things that are eaten, and more sophisticated programs for the education of youth.[105] Inveighing against the evils of the paraphernalia trade and championing the cause of parents fighting to protect their children, the committee reported that

> the young person today is confronted with peer pressure, with paraphernalia shops, with a generation of parents who themselves came of age during a time of increasing marihuana use, and with a national attitude bordering on nonchalance and permissiveness regarding drug use in general and marihuana use in particular.
>
> This socially pervasive attitude of permissiveness may also be a major contributing factor in the frightening levels of increase in polydrug abuse among our Nation's youth. Alcohol, PCP, cocaine, heroin, solvents, all form the deadly and nightmarish supplements to the joint smoked during recess in the school playground.[106]

David Musto, in the third edition of *The American Disease: Origins of Narcotic Control,* recounts the effect of the Parents' Movement on Robert L. DuPont, then head of NIDA—specifically through his contact with Marsha Mannatt, one of the founders of Parent Resources Institute on Drug Education (PRIDE).

> In Atlanta, Georgia, Marsha Mannatt had discovered in 1977 that parties for young teenagers were starting to become drug parties. After organizing parents there, she came into contact with drug abuse professionals but found them to be often hostile to her concerns and perceptions. She did receive encouragement from some experts, however, particularly Dr. Robert L. DuPont, then Director of NIDA, and her message spread. Under commission from NIDA, she wrote a handbook for parents' organizations, *Parents, Peers and Pot,* of which a million copies were distributed after it appeared in 1979. Dr. DuPont had previously been an advocate for decriminalization but changed his mind, and by the time of his departure from government in 1978, he firmly opposed marihuana and its decriminalization. He later stated that "it was parent power that changed my mind on marijuana."[107]

1980—HEROIN RETURNS

The year 1979 ended badly for Jimmy Carter, and his fortunes were not to improve in 1980. Rising interest rates increased the pressure to slash federal spending. In November of 1979 Iranian student militants stormed the American embassy in Tehran and took its occupants hostage. Later the same month Pakistani rioters torched the U.S. embassy in Islamabad. The Soviet Union invaded Afghanistan on 29 December. It began to look as if Carter could not count on his party's nomination to a second term. Then his chief of staff and most trusted aide, Hamilton Jordan, was accused of having used cocaine on two occasions in the past.

On top of everything, administration officials began to fear that heroin from that very area of the world that now seemed out of control would wipe out the gains that had been the cornerstone of their claims of success against drugs. Peter Bourne had been worried about heroin from Afghanistan since very early in the Carter presidency.[108] Now administration planners had to turn most of their attention to this new menace in an election year and in the midst of the anguish of the seemingly insoluble Iranian hostage crisis. Drug policy planners were also under threat of budget cuts emanating from both OMB and Congress. Under the circumstances, making an issue of cocaine must have seemed singularly unappealing—heroin was bad enough, but at least it offered a solid target whose dangers were well established and widely accepted. As for marijuana, even with the support of the Parents' Movement, the fledgling attempt to emphasize the risks of pot smoking lost some of its urgency.

A draft policy statement that seems to have circulated among domestic policy staff early in the year advocated cautious treatment of the rumors regarding Southwest Asian heroin.

> Despite the considerable press interest in U.S. seizures of heroin originating in Iran, Afghanistan, and Pakistan, there is insufficient evidence to support the emerging theory that we have a new "heroin epidemic" in the United States. Middle Eastern heroin is the major drug problem in Western Europe and remains a potential threat to the U.S. We have asked the heads of the drug agencies to avoid endorsing the "epidemic" theory until we have solid evidence of the effect on the U.S. as well as a coordinated response to the problem. We will have a report in late February from the working group created to assess the situation and will inform you of their findings.[109]

In spite of whatever desire there may have been among Eizenstat's people to handle the issues gingerly, others were not so circumspect. Attorney General Benjamin Civiletti expressed great concern about Southwest Asian heroin to the president. "While we have been able over the last three years, to reduce the number of addicts in the United States to approximately 380,000 and limit the number of heroin deaths and injuries to the lowest level in a decade, large supplies of Middle East heroin could reverse this progress by reducing the price of increasing the purity of heroin sold to users. A serious risk of attracting new users and a wave of destruction to the lives of our young people, who are most susceptible to addiction, would follow."[110] A "Talking Points" summary documented concern among White House staff about Civiletti's memo and insistently made the point that the appropriate course was "to devote current effort to collecting intelligence and minimizing effect of the threat within current agency resources."[111]

Lee Dogoloff informed the president of steps being taken to address the possible problem while avoiding a reaction that might be out of proportion to anticipated budgetary resources.

> Given the increased media attention and government-wide interest in the problem [of rapidly expanding production of opium in Afghanistan, Pakistan, and Iran], I would like to quickly outline our assessment of the problem and the steps we have taken to date to deal with it. . . .
>
> While our traditional epidemic indicator, the national average heroin purity, does not appear to be increasing dramatically, we (I and other members of the Principals Group) believe that we may be at the edge of a precipice with regard to the Middle

Eastern/South Asian heroin problem in the U.S. I have told the Principals, however, that mere "handwringing" will only raise anxiety levels and do little to serve the public good. I have, therefore, asked for additional information on the trends, traffickers, etc., as well as the steps we should take to address this problem. Once we have gained a more complete understanding of the problem, we will be able to undertake a Government-wide response to the problem which would include, at that time, widespread public statements on the issue. This should occur over the next 60 days.[112]

The organization put in place to gain a "more complete understanding of the problem" was the "Steering Group on Southwest Asia Heroin," which was supposed to coordinate the activities of ten subgroups, each meant to address what was thought to be a discrete aspect of the phenomenon. These were: Public Information, Pakistan Aid, Turkish Enforcement Assistance, European Enforcement Training, United States Border Interdiction, Foreign Intelligence, Domestic Impact, Domestic Enforcement, Treatment Preparation, and Overseas Personnel.[113] These groups, including something called the Heroin Strategy Task Force, worked on their assigned tasks until the end of July. At least some of their findings seemed to confirm the administration's estimate that Southwest Asian heroin did not appear to be causing an "epidemic," although there was legitimate cause for concern.

Nationally, heroin indicators show a relatively level trend following a significant decline between 1976 and 1978. . . .

Several heroin indicators, however, suggest a recent increase in heroin quality and availability. Much of the heroin newly available has been identified as originating in Southwest Asia. The increase appears to be restricted to specific areas of the country, particularly the Northeast/Mid-Atlantic corridor, and fluctuates from slight to dramatic.[114]

As of June 30, 1980, southwest Asian heroin accounts for 64% of bulk domestic seizures while Mexican brown accounts for 27% and Southeast Asian heroin—8% (see attachment). The average purity of bulk Mexican brown heroin with adulterants and diluents, is 8.3% while Southwest Asian heroin remains at 78% pure. Bulk Southeast Asian heroin is of high average purity, but does not represent a significant part of the domestic supply. . . .

Since the U.S. and Iran broke diplomatic relations, there has been a dramatic reduction of travel from Iran to the U.S.[115]

The Domestic Impact Group reported on heroin price and purity, as well as death and injuries, since 1973. Its data showed a low point in the third quarter of 1973 "due to Turkish opium poppy ban." Then a new high was recorded at the beginning of 1976 with "gradual tapering off, during Fall–Winter 1976, due to opium crop eradication in Mexico." A new low was reached in 1978, then a slight increase in middle of 1979, which "paralleled a resurgence of Southwest Asian heroin."[116]

The Public Information Group commented on the importance of communicating to the public that the administration was monitoring the situation and ready to act if necessary. "In addition to a briefing at the White House for selected members of Congress, each Department should make a concerted effort to communicate to the public the Administration's awareness and monitoring of the problem and what has been and is being done in response to it. Efforts should be made, for instance, to increase the number of op-ed pieces on the subject and public speaking on the problem should be increased. The emphasis should not be on recital of the facts—although continued accuracy is important—but on what the public can expect of the government under these circumstances."[117]

But it was all quite confusing, and the press remained convinced that a "tidal wave" was building just beyond the horizon. The *New York Times* editorialized:

> Through most of the 1970s, the addict population was steadily declining. Now the National Institute for Drug Abuse reports more and more people seeking treatment, particularly in the Northeast. New York State reports a 46 percent increase last year in the number of drug-related hospital cases, 11 percent in drug-related arrests and 77 percent in drug-related deaths. Yet $40 million—25 percent—has been sliced off a $160-million drug program that goes mostly to support treatment of addicts.
>
> Congress made clear, when it chartered the Strategy Council on Drug Policy in 1976, that it wanted the White House to steer both enforcement and treatment. That responsibility has better be taken seriously.[118]

ANNUAL REPORT ON THE FEDERAL DRUG PROGRAM, 1980

President Jimmy Carter was able to fend off a challenge to his candidacy from Senator Edward Kennedy, but as the summer ended and the election approached, Carter's reelection campaign was in serious trouble. Republican nominee Ronald Reagan had proved a skillful campaigner who offered an optimistic vision of the nation's future in contrast to Carter's rather intellectual concentration on what he saw as the difficulties lying ahead and his powerlessness to solve the endless hostage crisis in Iran. He even seemed unable to control the behavior of his own staff. Further support for the public perception that some members of the Carter team were not at all serious about drug abuse came in September when his national campaign manager, Tim Kraft, had to resign in the face of evidence that he had used cocaine. A few days later, the last major drug policy document produced by the Carter Administration, the *Annual Report on the Federal Drug Program, 1980,* was delivered to Congress. On its first page, the report lamented the permissive attitudes toward some drug use that seemed to have caused so much trouble.

> We have passed from a time when the nonmedical use of any drug was considered the first step toward certain drug addiction to the present situation where, unfortunately, drug abuse is looked upon by some with benign tolerance. The Administration has adamantly opposed the nonmedical use of any drug such as marihuana and cocaine. . . .
>
> In the past, Federal programs have concentrated on specific drugs with emphasis on heroin. Although we are still very concerned with heroin as the drug presenting the most serious health hazard to our citizens, the current strategy focuses more on the behavior of the individual who abuses drugs, and places a renewed emphasis on incorporating drug abuse services into the general health care system. . . .
>
> A major new emphasis on prevention, through greater parental involvement, has elicited overwhelming public support and is already showing positive effects. . . .
>
> The Administration is attempting to counter growing acceptance of drug use in our society, a disturbing trend which has resulted from the glamorization of the use of drugs such as marijuana and cocaine, and which has masked the issue of their effects. A permissive social attitude has posed particular difficulties for law enforcement officials.[119]

But the report came too late to influence a new critique published by Lester Wolff's committee on September 24, 1980 that could not have been helpful to the Carter election campaign.

> Drug abuse and drug trafficking, and the incidence of these phenomena, are chronic national problems that seriously threaten the health, safety and welfare of the American people and undermine social, economic and political institutions and values in our country. Virtually every community and school district in our nation is adversely affected by drug abuse and drug trafficking. The pervasive use of drugs in our society is reflected in the following statistics. Over 50 million Americans have used marihuana and 40 percent of these persons are current users. Approximately 375,000–450,000 of our citizens, including a disproportionate number of minority youth, are addicted to heroin and other narcotic drugs. An estimated 15 million Americans have

> used cocaine, 8 million have used PCP, 13 million have used inhalants, and 16 million have used hallucinogens. As more and more people turn to pills for the solution to life's problems, the abuse of prescription drugs in the United States has become a major health problem. Estimates of the number of persons who have used stimulants and sedatives non-medically are placed at 13 million and 11 million respectively. Over 45 percent of the drug-related deaths reported to the Drug Enforcement Administration (DEA) in 1979 were attributed to barbiturates and other depressants.[120] . . .
>
> The Committee also has investigated the alarming increase in drug abuse among our youth, a problem that is particularly disturbing because of the substantial risks drug abuse poses to the physical, emotional, intellectual and social development of children. Marihuana, the most widely used illicit drug among school-age children and young adults, can no longer be viewed as a harmless substance. Evidence continues to mount that smoking marihuana can lead to serious, and sometimes irreversible, physiological and psychological impairment. The risks are particularly high for persons in their formative years. Moreover, the potency of marihuana has increased substantially over the past 5 years. . . .
>
> Heroin from Iran, Afghanistan and Pakistan—the so-called Golden Crescent—poses the most recent and most dangerous threat to the United States. A virtual tidal wave of heroin from these countries—10 to 20 times the amount that fueled the heroin crisis of a decade ago—is pouring into cities such as New York, San Francisco and Washington, D.C. Although estimates of the number of heroin addicts and heroin-related deaths declined steadily throughout the latter half of the 1970's, these trends are certain to reverse under this new onslaught of Southwest Asian heroin. Drug-related deaths in New York City rose 77 percent from 1978 to 1979, and the City's treatment programs report an increased number of clients with heroin as the primary drug of abuse.[121]

Wolff's committee also took note of the way in which bureaucrats on the Carter staff in various departments had co-opted policy development and had, in effect, bypassed the Strategy Council and dodged once more the will of Congress in its continuing struggle to gain some sort of control of drug policy management.

> Unfortunately, the law [requiring that the Federal Drug Strategy be "reviewed, revised as necessary and promulgated . . . prior to June 1 of each year" (PL 94-237)] has not operated as Congress intended. As of September 1 of this year, no Federal drug strategy for 1980 had been issued. The congressionally mandated Strategy Council—a high-level body composed of 8 Federal representatives . . . and 8 non-Federal members charged with developing Federal strategy and evaluating progress in carry-

ing out the strategy—has remained largely inactive, despite President Carter's 1977 vow to revitalize the Council. Citing the infrequency of the Council's meetings, a recent (May 22, 1980) New York Times article by two of the non-Federal appointees to the Council concluded; We have grave doubts that the council can work as Congress and the President originally intended. The council apparently is a facade behind which bureaucrats alone continue to establish policy.[122]

TREATMENT AND REHABILITATION IN THE AUTUMN OF 1980

As the elections approached Lee Dogoloff was quite concerned about the implications that cuts in overall federal spending would have for drug abuse and control funding, especially given the possible repercussions of increases in availability of Southwest Asian heroin. He wrote to Stuart Eizenstat.

> The purpose of this memo is to advise you of anticipated short-falls in drug abuse treatment and treatment management services, which have been created by a combination of legislative action and budget decision, and to ask your assistance in urging the Department of Health and Human Services immediately to begin a review of the resources allocated to these areas. In addition, HHS should be developing alternative treatment strategies to be applied if the current increase in heroin availability now seen in the Northeast persists and spreads to other parts of the Country.
>
> Our greatest concern is the major reduction in the 95,000 Federal treatment slots funded annually over the past several years. Congress has directed that by Fiscal year 1981, 10% of the current treatment dollars funded by the National Institute on Drug Abuse (NIDA) should be dedicated to prevention activities. This will result in the loss of 9,000 treatment slots. The fiscal year 1981 budget revisions reduce the NIDA service budget by an additional 20% through the elimination of the $38 million formula grant program to the states. Approximately $18 million of the formula grant funds are currently used for treatment support. This will result in the loss of approximately 10,000 additional treatment slots.[123]

The Law Enforcement Assistance Administration, which had been the source of funding for Treatment Alternatives to Street Crime since 1972, was also slated for elimination. Dogoloff scrambled to find other agencies to provide funds and facilities.

> Given the unqualified success of the TASC program and its history, the Interdepartmental Drug Abuse Treatment and Rehabilitation Group has asked me to forward a request that you review the feasibility of accepting the transfer of the TASC program to the Department of Health and Human Services.[124]

> This potential loss of a very successful program [TASC] has concerned us greatly and we, therefore, brought it to the attention of the Treatment and Rehabilitation Steering Group of the President's Strategy Council.
>
> . . . We are trying to compensate for the loss of treatment slots by using alternative treatment facilities at the VA Medical Centers, the Community Mental Health Systems and the Community Health Centers in the four cities (New York, Newark, Baltimore, and Washington) hit hardest by the influx of Southwest Asian heroin.[125]

Stuart Eizenstat communicated this initiative to Congress in a special briefing in August.

> To meet the acute treatment situation in New York, Newark, Baltimore and Washington, D.C., the White House has asked the Veterans Administration to absorb the overflow of patients who qualify for veterans benefits from drug treatment programs supported by the States and the National Institute on Drug Abuse. Public Health Service hospitals and clinics, community health centers, and community mental health centers in these cities are also being alerted to the problem and asked to assist those centers which provide heroin treatment. This coordinated approach can serve as a model response system if the heroin influx spreads to other parts of the U.S.[126]

But the states wanted money. New York State was suffering the most from the lack of funding for drug treatment, and on 26 September a group of state officials met with Eizenstat to plead their case. Shortly thereafter, the domestic policy staff proposed $10 million in aid to the areas Eizenstat had singled out in August plus Philadelphia and Connecticut.[127] But the Department of Justice refused to support federal assistance to state and local law enforcement, and OMB wouldn't release the funds without approval from Justice. Eizenstat promised Lee Dogoloff that he would try to sway Deputy Attorney General Charles Renfrew, but noted rather forlornly, "I don't see how this can be scheduled before the election, realistically."[128] Eizenstat's recollection of these events is that, in fact, no such assistance to the states was ever approved.[129]

CONCLUSION

The Carter administration ended with an uncertain drug policy. In 1976 Jimmy Carter had been elected in spite of—not because of—his open-minded statements about marijuana, but over the next four years, the social and political climate gradually shifted as support for marijuana decriminalization evaporated, and the burgeoning Parents' Movement took possession of the drug debate. Perhaps if Carter had won the 1980 election he would have been able to appropriate the growing antipathy toward casual drug use in the service of a new policy. But as it was, the hard line on drugs was left for the Reagan administration to promulgate. Reagan would return to a policy reminiscent of Nixon's adamant rejection of liberalized drug measures and, unlike Nixon, would enjoy the political advantage of a steady decline in drug toleration among the public.

Appendix: Summary of Drug Control Policy, 1958–1974

ABA/AMA Committee 1958*	Prettyman Commission, 1963†	Johnson	Nixon and Ford	Carter
	1. That the President issue a directive to all federal executives who can play a part in combating the problem of narcotic and drug abuse to initiate immediately more aggressive action in the national interest. This recommendation is basic to all that follow.	Presidential statement—July 15, 1964**		
	2. That the President appoint a Special Assistant for Narcotic and Drug Abuse from the White House staff to provide continuous advice and assistance in launching a coordinated attack. The Special Assistant will have general coordinating authority and the organizational responsibility to follow through on the evaluation and the implementation of the Commission's recommendations.	Presidential statement—July 15, 1964**	SAODAP—1972–1973 (Jerome H. Jaffe) Cabinet Committee on International Narcotics Control (CCINC), etc. NIDA—1973 (Robert DuPont)	ODAP

	3. That a citizens' advisory committee be created for service from time to time. This committee should be composed of authorities from all facets of drug abuse and be drawn from all relevant disciplines and professions. It should critically review progress made toward the development and execution of a federal policy and program. The Special Assistant would serve as liaison between the President and the advisory committee.	In 1947, the National Research Council established the Committee on Drug Addiction and Narcotics, which became the Committee on Problems of Drug Dependence in 1965, then was spun off as an independent organization in 1977.	National Advisory Council on Drug Abuse—mostly honorific.	Strategy Council
The dissemination of accurate information about narcotic addiction has been neglected and even discouraged by some enforcement authorities. The Joint Committee feels that this matter should be studied critically, to determine whether a campaign of enlightenment might not produce good results.	4. That a core of information and educational materials be prepared by the Secretary of Health, Education, and Welfare to provide the public and all professions involved with accurate knowledge on narcotic and drug abuse to combat the misinformation that is so prevalent today.	PCLEAJ (Task Force on Narcotics and Drug Abuse): A core of educational and informational materials should be developed by the National Institute of Mental Health (Report, p. 20).‡	National Clearinghouse on Drug Information—January 1970	

(continued)

ABA/AMA Committee 1958*	Prettyman Commission, 1963†	Johnson	Nixon and Ford	Carter
The Joint Committee also feels that other preventative techniques can be devised which can aid materially in lowering the incidence of drug addiction.				
It is not possible to fully measure the worth of treatment and rehabilitation measures without more data than has yet been accumulated on the rate of relapse, and on the causative factors underlying both addiction and successful rehabilitation. The Joint Committee feels that large scale research in this area (complementing several limited studies which are already under way) would be highly desirable. Such research is absolutely indispensable to any thoroughgoing evaluation of present policies in dealing with narcotic addiction, as well as to the	5. That the Federal Council for Science and Technology, with the advice of an ad hoc committee of experts, design a comprehensive research plan covering all aspects of narcotic and drug abuse and that the National Institute of Mental Health earmark for narcotic and drug abuse research a specific amount from its extramural research budget for each fiscal year to finance the operation of the plan.	PCLEAJ (Task Force on Narcotics and Drug Abuse): The National Institute of Mental Health should devise and execute a plan of research, to be carried on both on an intramural and an extramural basis, covering all aspects of marihuana use (Report, p. 14).‡	NIDA—1973	

formulation of new approaches in dealing with this difficult problem.			
	6. That the Secretary of Health, Education, and Welfare establish a national reporting system to collect, collate, and analyze data on all forms of narcotic and drug abuse so as to obtain an accurate assessment of the problem. This should be set up on a cooperative basis with federal, state, municipal and private agencies participating.	Reorganization Plan 1, 1968	NIDA—1973 TASC—1972
	7. That the functions of the Bureau of Narcotics relating to the investigation of the illicit manufacture, sale, or other distribution, or possession of narcotic drugs and marihuana be transferred from the Department of the Treasury to the Department of Justice.	Reorganization Plan 1, 1968	

(*continued*)

ABA/AMA Committee 1958*	Prettyman Commission, 1963†	Johnson	Nixon and Ford	Carter
	8. That the responsibility for the investigation of the illicit traffic in dangerous drugs be transferred from the Department of Health, Education, and Welfare to the Department of Justice.	Reorganization Plan 1, 1968		
	9. That the functions of the Bureau of Narcotics relating the regulation of the legitimate importation, exportation, manufacture, sale, and other transfer of narcotic drugs and marihuana be transferred from the Department of the Treasury to the Department of Health, Education and Welfare. Narcotic drugs would be regulated under the power to regulate interstate and foreign commerce, not under the tax power; and the importation, production, sale, or other trans-	Drug Abuse Control Amendments of 1965 (BDAC) PCLEAJ (Task Force on Narcotics and Drug Abuse): Those states which do not already have adequate legislation should adopt a model State drug abuse control act similar to the Federal Drug Abuse Control Amendments of 1965 (Report, p. 9).‡ The recordkeeping provisions of the 1965 amendments should be amended to require that records must be segregated or	Comprehensive Drug Abuse and Control Act of 1970	

fer of marihuana would be prohibited except where expressly licensed for legitimate scientific purposes or for the emergency production of hemp.	kept in some other manner that enables them to be promptly identified and inspected. (Report, p. 10).‡	
10. That a unit be established within the Department of Health, Education and Welfare to determine the safety and efficacy of and to regulate all narcotic and dangerous drugs capable of producing severe psychotoxic effects which can lead to criminal or lawless behavior when abused. This unit would also regulate the legitimate importation, exportation, manufacture, sale and other transfer of narcotic and dangerous drugs.	Drug Abuse and Control Amendments of 1965 (BDAC) Research should be undertaken devoted to early action on the further development of a sound and effective framework of regulatory and criminal laws with respect to dangerous drugs.	
11. The Commission recommends a substantial increase in the number of federal enforcement personnel assigned to the	PCLEAJ (Task Force on Narcotics and Drug Abuse): The enforcement and related staff of the Bureau of Customs	Establishment of Drug Enforcement Administration with a staff of 3,000 from abolished agencies plus 500 special agents

(*continued*)

ABA/AMA Committee 1958*	Prettyman Commission, 1963†	Johnson	Nixon and Ford	Carter
	investigation of the illicit importation of and trafficking in narcotic drugs, marihuana, and dangerous drugs.	should be materially increased (Report, p. 9).‡	transferred from Customs.	
There is uncertainty at present both in the ambiguous provisions of some of our narcotic drug statutes and in the court decisions through which they have been applied. There is also doubt as to whether the premises on which our present narcotic laws rest are sound and validly conceived. A critical study in this area would make possible a thorough evaluation of present legal approaches to narcotic addiction. It should result in the formulation of better methods for dealing with the addict and more realistic and sounder means for controlling the illicit drug traffic.	12. That the penalty provisions of the federal narcotics and marihuana laws which now prescribe mandatory minimum sentences and prohibit probation or parole be amended to fit the gravity of the particular offense so as to provide greater incentive for rehabilitation. [Key to this recommendation was the concept that narcotics offenses could be separated into three categories: large-scale trafficking, generally by non-addicted criminals, small-scale sales, in-kind transfers or gifts among addicts; and simple possession for personal use. This distinction was to have	PCLEAJ (Task Force on Narcotics and Drug Abuse): State and Federal drug laws should give a large enough measure of discretion to the courts and correctional authorities to enable them to deal flexibly with violators, taking account of the nature and seriousness of the offense, the prior record of the offender and other relevant circumstances (Report, p. 12).‡ PCLEAJ (Task Force on Narcotics and Drug Abuse): Some part of the added personnel [in the Bureau of Narcotics] should be used to design and execute a long-range intelligence	Comprehensive Drug Abuse and Control Act of 1970	

a profound and lasting impact on the development of drug control statutes as well as on competing theories of law enforcement.]	effort aimed at the upper echelons of the illicit drug traffic (Report, p. 9).‡
13. That all non-narcotic drugs capable of producing serious psychotoxic effects when abused be brought under strict control by federal statute.	Drug Abuse Control Amendments of 1965 (All hallucinogens, including LSD, and most barbiturates and amphetamines) PCLEAJ (Task Force on Narcotics and Drug Abuse): Research should be undertaken devoted to early action on the further development of a sound and effective framework of regulatory and criminal laws with respect to dangerous drugs (Report, p. 6).‡
14. That the training school now conducted by the Bureau of Narcotics be more fully publicized among state and local law enforcement agencies, that in-service training sessions,	

(continued)

ABA/AMA Committee 1958*	Prettyman Commission, 1963†	Johnson	Nixon and Ford	Carter
	workshops and seminars be conducted in the areas where drug abuse is most prevalent, and that the federal government provide field training courses for the dissemination of current federal information on narcotics control to state and local law enforcement officers.			
	15. [That legislation be enacted] authorizing the use of wire tapping by federal enforcement officials in limited circumstances and under strict controls to detect and prevent the international smuggling of narcotics.			
	16. That the United States request the United Nations to establish a system of international control of the distribution of dangerous drugs. The Commission does not see the necessity			

	of new federal legislation to supplement the general smuggling law by expressly prohibiting the illegal importation of dangerous drugs into the United States.			
	17. That the United States invite the Mexican government to assist in the establishment of a Joint United States–Mexico Commission for consultation on the development of better methods to curb the illegal flow of narcotics, marihuana, and dangerous drugs between Mexico and the United States.	Johnson/Lopez-Mateos meeting	Nixon/Diaz-Ordaz meeting—September 1969	
	18. That the United States oppose, in its present form, ratification of the Single Convention on Narcotic Drugs, 1961, until there is a correction of those sections which weaken the control and limitation of world opium cultivation and produc-	LBJ seeks ratification of Single Convention on February 6, 1967.		Single Convention signed.

(continued)

ABA/AMA Committee 1958*	Prettyman Commission, 1963†	Johnson	Nixon and Ford	Carter
	tion as established in the Protocol of 1953.			
	19. That the Federal government encourage and increase assistance to states and municipalities to develop and strengthen their own treatment programs and confine its activities in the immediate future to research instead of maintaining extensive treatment programs.		SAODAP—1971 NIDA—1973	
[See above.] There is considerable uncertainty and confusion in the enforcement of existing drug laws. This may be inherent in the nature of the laws, procedures or administrative and judicial machinery which seeks to enforce them. A careful study of how existing laws are operating should provide invaluable guides for a rational drug control program in this country.	20. That federal regulations be amended to reflect the general principle that the definition of legitimate medical use of narcotic drugs and legitimate medical treatment of a narcotic addict are primarily to be determined by the medical profession.			

	21. That legislation be designed to provide authority for the Federal government to render direct financial and technical assistance to state governments (singly or acting together on a regional basis), to local governments, and to private nonprofit organizations for the establishment, maintenance, and expansion of broad treatment and rehabilitation programs and the training of staff and personnel to staff and operate the programs.	TASC—1972
. . . The Joint Committee feels that the possibilities of trying [some] outpatient facility, on a controlled experimental basis, should be explored, since it can make an invaluable contribution to our knowledge of how to deal with drug addicts in a community, rather than on an institutional basis.	22. [That federal assistance be given] to state governments, acting singly or on a regional basis, and to local governments for the construction of non-hospital treatment centers for narcotic and dangerous drug abusers and for new treatment units in existing state and local hospitals.	SAODAP—1971

(*continued*)

ABA/AMA Committee 1958*	Prettyman Commission, 1963†	Johnson	Nixon and Ford	Carter
	23. That the Public Health Service hospitals in Lexington, Kentucky, and Fort Worth, Texas, accept voluntary patients only for purposes of research study in the future.		Turned over to the Bureau of Prisons in 1974.	
	24. That the Bureau of Prisons establish a special treatment program for confirmed narcotic and drug abusers within the federal prison system.		See above	
	25. That a Federal civil commitment statute be enacted to provide an alternative method of handling the federally convicted offender who is a confirmed narcotic or marihuana abuser.	NARA—November 1966		

* *Drug Addiction: Crime or Disease? Interim and Final Reports of the Joint Committee of the American Bar Association and the American Medical Association on Narcotic Drugs* (Bloomington: Indiana University Press, 1961).

† President's Advisory Commission on Narcotic and Drug Abuse, *Final Report* (Washington, DC: GPO, 1963).

** "Statement by the President on Narcotic and Drug Abuse," *Public Papers of the Presidents of the United States: Lyndon Johnson* (Washington, DC: Federal Register Division, National Archives and Records Service, 1969), p. 860.

‡ Presidential Commission on Law Enforcement and the Administration of Justice (PCLEAJ), *The Challenge of Crime in a Free Society* (Washington, DC: GPO, 1967).

Notes

INTRODUCTION

1. D.F. Musto, *The American Disease: Origins of Narcotic Control,* third ed. (New York: Oxford University Press, 1999), p. 246.
2. Charles Reich, *The Greening of America* (New York: Random House, 1970).
3. As David F. Musto records in the latest edition of *The American Disease,* "I recall a talk in the early 1970s with James Markham, a highly respected reporter for the *New York Times* who reviewed the first edition of [*The American Disease*]. Having covered the *Times's* drug beat for a couple of years, he told me that he had planned to continue for one or two more in order to see the end of the problem before moving on to some other topic." (D.F. Musto, *The American Disease: Origins of Narcotic Control,* third ed. (New York: Oxford University Press, 1999), pp. vii–viii.

CHAPTER 1. THE JOHNSON ADMINISTRATION: DRUG ABUSE AS A POLICY ISSUE

1. I. Cisin, J.D. Miller, and A.V. Harrell, *Highlights from the National Survey on Drug Abuse: 1977* (Rockville, MD: National Institute on Drug Abuse, 1977), p. 15.
2. L.G. Hunt, *Recent Spread of Heroin Use in the United States: Unanswered Questions* (Washington, DC: Drug Abuse Council, 1974).
3. A.H. Cantrill and C.W. Roll, Jr., *Hopes and Fears of the American People* (New York: Universe Books, 1971).

4. President's Advisory Commission on Narcotic and Drug Abuse, *Final Report* (Washington DC: GPO, 1963), pp. 4, 5.
5. E.M. Brecher and editors of *Consumer Reports, Licit and Illicit Drugs* (Boston: Little, Brown and Co., 1972), p. 103.
6. Alfred Lindesmith had been critical of exclusive reliance on prohibitive measures for decades. In 1947 he published *Opiate Addiction* (Bloomington, IN: Principia Press) in which he devoted a chapter to "needed reforms." This book was reprinted in 1957, and in 1965 Lindesmith published *The Addict and the Law* (Bloomington: Indiana University Press).
7. Illinois Institute for Juvenile Research and Chicago Area Project, *Drug Addiction Among Young Persons in Chicago, October 1953,* quoted in *Drug Addiction: Crime or Disease? Interim and Final Reports of the Joint Committee of the American Bar Association and the American Medical Association on Narcotic Drugs* (Bloomington: Indiana University Press, 1961), p. 62.
8. Illinois Institute for Juvenile Research and Chicago Area Project, *Drug Addiction Among Young Persons in Chicago, October 1953,* quoted in *Drug Addiction: Crime or Disease? Interim and Final Reports of the Joint Committee of the American Bar Association and the American Medical Association on Narcotic Drugs* (Bloomington: Indiana University Press, 1961), p. 68.
9. Advisory Committee to the Federal Bureau of Narcotics, *Comments on Narcotic Drugs: Interim Report of the Joint Committee of the American Bar Association and the American Medical Association on Narcotic Drugs* (Washington, DC: GPO [1959]).
10. Memorandum, John Seigenthaler for Lee C. White, 28 December 1961, folder: "Department of Justice General," Box 13, Dean F. Markham files, Department of Justice—Department of the Treasury, Henry Giordano, J.F.K. Library.
11. President's Advisory Commission on Narcotic and Drug Abuse, *Final Report* (Washington, DC: GPO, 1963), p. 3.
12. W.B. Eldridge, *Narcotics and the Law: A Critique of the American Experiment in Narcotic Drug Control,* rev. ed. (Chicago: University of Chicago Press, 1967), p. 136.
13. The Gallup Organization commented on trends in opinions on legalization of marijuana use as follows:

> Between 1969 and 1977 the percentage of Americans who favor the legalization of marijuana rose sharply. Demographic analysis during these years showed that the sharpest rise in support was recorded among men, the college educated, and those under age fifty. However, the latest survey reveals a slight decline in support of legalization, with 24% in favor compared to 28% in 1977. When this measurement was initiated a decade ago, as few as 12% favored making marijuana use legal.
>
> Although the adult population as a whole is currently almost three to one in opposition to legalization, persons eighteen- to twenty-nine-years-old are closely divided in their views, with 45% in favor and 48% opposed. Opposition to making the use of marijuana legal is greatest among women, persons with less formal education, and residents of the Midwest and South. (G.H. Gallup, *The Gallup Poll: Public Opinion, 1979* (Wilmington, DE: Scholarly Resources, 1980), p. 195.)

14. W.B. Eldridge, *Narcotics and the Law: A Critique of the American Experiment in Narcotic Drug Control,* rev. ed. (Chicago: University of Chicago Press, 1967), p. 145.
15. Paper, Statements and Replies Concerning the Bureau of Narcotics, 26 June 1963, folder: "Treasury Department—Bureau of Narcotics," Box 13, Dean F. Markham files, Federal Agency file, J.F.K. Library, p. 3.
16. Paper, Statements and Replies Concerning the Bureau of Narcotics, 26 June 1963, folder: "Treasury Department—Bureau of Narcotics," Box 13, Dean F. Markham files, Federal Agency file, J.F.K. Library, p. 9.
17. Letter, James A. Reed for E. Barrett Prettyman, 22 May 1963, folder: "Department of Treasury, General," Box 13, Dean F. Markham files, Federal Agency file, J.F.K. Library.
18. Henry Giordano (interview, 27 May 1993) explained that there was much bad feeling between Customs and FBN, but that the difficulties were adjudicated within the Treasury Department. As will be seen, one of the unintended consequences of the removal of narcotics law enforcement from Treasury was that this conflict became the bureaucratic equivalent of open warfare between two cabinet departments, Justice and Treasury. The skirmishes continued for decades.
19. Memorandum, Dean F. Markham for the record, 11 December 1963, folder: "FG 727 Pres's Ad. Comm. on Narcotic and Drug Abuse, 11/22/63–2/29/64," Box 401, White House Central File, hereafter WHCF, L.B.J. Library.
20. Memorandum with attachment, James A. Reed for Walter Jenkins, 15 January 1964, folder: "FG 727 President's Commission on Narcotic & Drug Abuse 11/22/63–2/29/64," Box 401, WHCF, L.B.J. Library.
21. Memorandum with cover note, Dean Markham for Lee White, 1 April 1964, folder: "FG 727, 3/1/64–6/30/64," Box 401, WHCF, L.B.J. Library.
22. See especially *Domestic Council Staff Report on National Drug Programs,* January 1971, papers of Jerome H. Jaffe.
23. Memorandum, Herbert J. Miller, Jr., for Nicholas deB. Katzenbach, 27 February 1964, folder: "Department of Justice General," Box 13, Dean F. Markham files, Department of Justice—Department of Treasury, Henry Giordano, J.F.K. Library.
24. David F. Musto, *The American Disease: Origins of Narcotic Control,* third ed. (New York: Oxford University Press, 1999), p. 41.
25. Memorandum with attachment, Dean Markham for Lee White, 8 April 1964, folder: "FG 727, 3/1/64–6/30/64," Box 401, WHCF, L.B.J. Library.
26. Summary with attachments, 2 April 1964, folder: "Bureau of Narcotics and Dangerous Drugs [1]," Box 194, Ex. and Gen. FG 135-13, L.B.J. Library.
27. See especially *Drug Addiction: Crime or Disease? Interim and Final Reports of the Joint Committee of the American Bar Association and the American Medical Association on Narcotic Drugs* (Bloomington, IN: Indiana University Press, 1961); Isidor Chein, "Some Needed Research on Opiate Addicts," in *White House Conference on Narcotic and Drug Abuse: Proceedings* (Washington, DC: GPO, 1962), pp. 131–136; and Jill Jonnes, *Hep Cats, Narcs and Pipe Dreams: A History of America's Romance with Illegal Drugs* (New York: Scribner, 1996).
28. Lyndon B. Johnson, "Statement by the President on Narcotic and Drug Abuse, July 15, 1964," in *Public Papers of the Presidents of the United States: Lyndon B. Johnson* (Washing-

ton, DC: Federal Register Division, National Archives and Records Service, 1969), item 458, p. 860.

29. Richard Lindblad, "Civil Commitment Under the Federal Narcotic Addict Rehabilitation Act," *Journal of Drug Issues* 18, no. 4 (1988): 595–624. The author points out that it is one more measure of the change in public attitudes toward a definition of drug addiction as a disease that such a measure could be contemplated.
30. U.S. Congress, House of Representatives, Committee on the Judiciary, Hearing: Civil Commitment and Treatment of Narcotic Addicts (Washington, DC: GPO, 1995–1996), pp. 88–89.
31. Letter, [signed] Ramsey Clark for Charles L. Schultze, 25 October 1966, folder: "PL 89-793 HR 9167 11/8/66," Reports of Enrolled Legislation, Box 48, L.B.J. Library.
32. Letter, [Sec'y HEW] for Charles L. Schultze, 27 October 1966, folder: "PL 89-793 HR 9167 11/8/66," Reports of Enrolled Legislation, Box 48, L.B.J. Library.
33. Joseph Califano, *The Triumph and Tragedy of Lyndon Johnson: The White House Years* (New York: Simon and Schuster, 1991), p. 153.
34. Richard Lindblad, "Civil Commitment Under the Federal Narcotic Addict Rehabilitation Act," *Journal of Drug Issues* 18 no. 4 (1988): 600–606.
35. U.S. Congress, Senate, Committee on the Judiciary, The Narcotic Rehabilitation Act of 1966, Hearings, 25, 26, and 27 January, 12, 13, 19, 23, and 25 May, 14 and 15 June, 19 July 1966 (Washington, DC: GPO, 1966), p. 153.
36. See, for example, "Dream Stuff," *Time,* 28 June 1954, pp. 66–67.
37. R. Dobin, "Dr. Leary's Concord Prison Experiment: A 34-Year Follow-Up Study," *Journal of Psychoactive Drugs* 30 no. 4 (1998): 419–426.
38. John Marks, *The Search for the "Manchurian Candidate": The CIA and Mind Control* (New York: Times Books, 1979).
39. U.S. Congress, Senate, The Narcotic Rehabilitation Act of 1966, Hearings, 25, 26, and 27 January, 12, 13, 19, 23 and 25 May, 14 and 15 June, 19 July 1966 (Washington, DC: GPO, 1966), p. 168.
40. U.S. Congress, Senate, The Narcotic Rehabilitation Act of 1966, Hearings, 25, 26, and 27 January, 12, 13, 19, 23 and 25 May, 14 and 15 June, 19 July 1966 (Washington, DC: GPO, 1966), p. 170.
41. U.S. Congress, Senate, The Narcotic Rehabilitation Act of 1966, Hearings, 25, 26, and 27 January, 12, 13, 19, 23 and 25 May, 14 and 15 June, 19 July 1966 (Washington, DC: GPO, 1966), p. 239.
42. U.S. Congress, Senate, The Narcotic Rehabilitation Act of 1966, Hearings, 25, 26, and 27 January, 12, 13, 19, 23 and 25 May, 14 and 15 June, 19 July 1966 (Washington, DC: GPO, 1966), p. 416.
43. U.S. Congress, Senate, The Narcotic Rehabilitation Act of 1966, Hearings, 25, 26, and 27 January, 12, 13, 19, 23 and 25 May, 14 and 15 June, 19 July 1966 (Washington, DC: GPO, 1966), p. 337.
44. Memorandum, Joseph A. Califano for Nicholas deB. Katzenbach, 5 September 1966, folder: "Law Enforcement, Juvenile Delinquency, Narcotics," Box 17, Task Force Reports, L.B.J. Library.

45. President's Commission on Law Enforcement and Administration of Justice, *The Challenge of Crime in a Free Society* (Washington, DC: GPO, 1967).
46. President's Commission on Law Enforcement and Administration of Justice, *The Challenge of Crime in a Free Society* (Washington, DC: GPO, 1967), p. 225.
47. A. Leshner, "Addiction Is a Brain Disease and It Matters," *Science,* 3 October 1997, pp. 45–47.
48. President's Commission on Law Enforcement and Administration of Justice, *The Challenge of Crime in a Free Society* (Washington, DC: GPO, 1967), p. 228.
49. President's Commission on Law Enforcement and Administration of Justice, *The Challenge of Crime in a Free Society* (Washington, DC: GPO, 1967), p. 230.
50. Memorandum, General Government (Beck) for the Director, 25 November 1966, folder: "Law Enforcement, Juvenile Delinquency, Narcotics," Box 16, Task Force Reports, L.B.J. Library.
51. Draft, Narcotics Task Force: Proposed Language for President's Message, undated, folder: "Law Enforcement, Juvenile Delinquency, Narcotics," Box 17, Task Force Reports, L.B.J. Library.
52. R.J. Bonnie and C.H. Whitebread, *The Marihuana Conviction: A History of Marihuana Prohibition in the United States* (Charlottsville: University Press of Virginia, 1974), p. 223.
53. R.J. Bonnie and C.H. Whitebread, *The Marihuana Conviction: A History of Marihuana Prohibition in the United States* (Charlottsville: University Press of Virginia, 1974), p. 230.
54. National Commission on Marihuana and Drug Abuse, *Marihuana: A Signal of Misunderstanding* (Washington, DC: GPO, 1972), p. 106.
55. National Commission on Marihuana and Drug Abuse, *Marihuana: A Signal of Misunderstanding* (Washington, DC: GPO, 1972).
56. National Commission on Marihuana and Drug Abuse, *Marihuana: A Signal of Misunderstanding* (Washington, DC: GPO, 1972), p. 107
57. A. Rosenfeld, "Marijuana: Millions of Turned-On Users," *Life,* 7 July 1967, p. 17.
58. A. Rosenfeld, "Marijuana: Millions of Turned-On Users," *Life,* 7 July 1967, p. 17.
59. Memorandum, J.P. Hendrick for the Secretary [of the Treasury], 28 July 1967, folder: "Government, Treasury Dept. Bureau of Narcotics," Box 161, Personal Papers/Fowler, L.B.J. Library.
60. Wire, 8 November [1967], folder: "Drugs," Box 7, McPherson files, WHCF, L.B.J. Library.
61. Comments on marijuana, 31 October 1967, folder: "Drugs," McPherson files, WHCF, L.B.J. Library.
62. Memorandum, Harry C. McPherson for the President, 7 November 1967, folder: "Drugs," Box 7, McPherson files, Box 7, L.B.J. Library.
63. D.F. Musto, "Whatever Happened to 'Community Mental Health'?" *Public Interest,* no. 39 (Spring 1975).
64. Health Program Analysis: Five-Year Program Plan for the Prevention and Treatment of Narcotic and Drug Abuse, August 1967, folder: "LEN-12-8," Box 49, PACEO files, Nixon Presidential Materials Staff, National Archives, p. I-1.

65. Health Program Analysis: Five-Year Program Plan for the Prevention and Treatment of Narcotic and Drug Abuse, August 1967, folder: "LEN-12-8," Box 49, PACEO files, WHCF, Nixon Presidential Materials Staff, National Archives, p. I-3.
66. Health Program Analysis: Five-Year Program Plan for the Prevention and Treatment of Narcotic and Drug Abuse, August 1967, folder: "LEN-12-8," Box 49, PACEO files, WHCF, Nixon Presidential Materials Staff, National Archives, p. I-3.
67. Report excerpt, Health Task Force, Section IX, Controlling Drug Abuse . . . , 30 October 1967, folder: "Health 1968 (2)," Box 33, Califano files, L.B.J. Library, p. IX-7.
68. Report of the Health Task Force, 30 October 1967, folder: "Health 1968 (2)," Box 33, Califano files, L.B.J. Library, p. IX-2.
69. Report of the Health Task Force, 30 October 1967, folder: "Health 1968 (2)," Box 33, Califano files, L.B.J. Library, p. IX-21.
70. Memorandum, Henry H. Fowler for Joseph A. Califano, 13 November 1967, folder: "Gov. Treasury Dept., Bureau of: Narcotics," Box 161, Personal Papers/Fowler, L.B.J. Library.
71. Memorandum, Henry H. Fowler for Joseph A. Califano, 13 November 1967, folder: "Gov. Treasury, Dept. of: Narcotics," Box 161, Personal Papers/Fowler, L.B.J. Library.
72. Interview with Henry L. Giordano, 27 May 1993.
73. Memorandum, Henry H. Fowler for Joseph A. Califano, 13 November 1967, folder: "Gov. Treasury, Dept. of: Narcotics," Box 161, Personal Papers/Fowler, L.B.J. Library.
74. Memorandum, Phillip S. Hughes for Mr. Califano, 21 December 1967, folder: "Bureau of Narcotics and Dangerous Drugs [1]," Box 194, Ex. and Gen. FG 135-13, L.B.J. Library.
75. See, for example, D.F. Musto, *The American Disease: Origins of Narcotic Control,* third ed. (New York: Oxford University Press, 1999), pp. 167–175, for an account of Treasury's investigation of Dr. Butler's Shreveport Narcotics Clinic in the early 1920s.
76. Memorandum with cover note, D.F. Markham for Lee White, 1 April 1964, folder: "FG 727, 3/1/64–6/30/64," Box 401, WHCF, L.B.J. Library.
77. Memorandum, J. Califano for L.B. Johnson, 29 January 1968, folder: "Bureau of Narcotics and Dangerous Drugs [1]," Box 194, Ex. and Gen. FG 135-13, L.B.J. Library.
78. Interview with Vernon D. Acree, 28 May 1993.
79. Memorandum with cover note, Matt Nimetz for DeVier Pierson, 2 February 1968, folder: "Bureau of Narcotics and Dangerous Drugs [1]," Box 194, Ex. and Gen. FG 135-13, L.B.J. Library.
80. Memorandum, J.P. Hendrick for the Secretary, 25 January 1968, folder: "Government Treasury, Department of Narcotics," Box 161, Personal Papers/Fowler, L.B.J. Library.
81. Memorandum, J. Califano for the President, 29 January 1968, folder: "Bureau of Narcotics and Dangerous Drugs [1]," Box 194, Ex. and Gen. FG 135-13, L.B.J. Library.
82. Memorandum, Thomas D. Finney, Jr., for Mr. Pierson, 15 February 1968, folder: "Bureau of Narcotics and Dangerous Drugs [1]," Box 194, Ex. and Gen. FG 135-13, L.B.J. Library.
83. Letter, E. McK. Dirkson for John Macy, 24 June 1968, folder: "Bureau of Narcotics and Dangerous Drugs [1]," Box 194, Ex. and Gen. FG 135-13, L.B.J. Library; Letter, H.B. Gonzalez for L.B. Johnson, 10 July 1968, folder: "Bureau of Narcotics and Dangerous Drugs [1]," Box 194, Ex. and Gen. FG 135-13, L.B.J. Library; and Interview with H. Giordano, 27 May 1993.

84. Interview with H. Giordano, 27 May 1993.
85. J.W. Spain, "The United States, Turkey and the Poppy," *Middle East Journal* 29, no. 3 (1975): 296.

CHAPTER 2. THE FIRST NIXON ADMINISTRATION: EARLY APPROACHES TO DRUG POLICY

1. National Commission on Marijuana and Drug Abuse, *Drug Use in America: Problem in Perspective—Second Report of the National Commission on Marijuana and Drug Abuse,* (Washington, DC: GPO, 1973), p. 83.
2. J.S. Marr, C.E. Cherubin, and J. Sapira, "Medical Indices of Narcotics Addiction: Rise and Fall in New York City, 1963–1977," *New York State Journal of Medicine,* April 1979, p. 728.
3. I. Cisin, J.D. Miller, and A.V. Harrell, *Highlights from the National Survey on Drug Abuse: 1977* (Rockville, MD: National Institute on Drug Abuse, 1977), p. 17.
4. National Commission on Marijuana and Drug Abuse, *Drug Use in America: Problem in Perspective—Second Report of the National Commission on Marijuana and Drug Abuse* (Washington, DC: GPO, 1973), pp. 82–83.
5. See, for example, White House Conference on Narcotic and Drug Abuse, *Proceedings,* Washington, DC, 27 and 28 September 1962, pp. 132, 133, 141, 142, 290; and President's Advisory Commission on Narcotic and Drug Abuse, *Final Report,* November 1963 (also known as the Prettyman Report), p. 4; and A.R. Lindesmith, *The Addict and the Law* (New York: Random House, 1965), chapter 4.
6. U.S. Treasury Department, *Traffic in Opium and Other Dangerous Drugs,* Report, 31 December 1966, p. 26.
7. M.D. Brodsky, *History of Heroin Prevalence Estimation Techniques,* National Institute of Drug Abuse Research Monographs, ser. 1985, 57: 98.
8. L.G. Hunt and C.D. Chambers, *The Heroin Epidemics: A Study of Heroin Use in the United States, 1965–75* (New York: Spectrum Publications, 1976), p. 113.
9. Loose sheet of opinion poll data, [May 1969], President's Handwriting file, Box 12, White House Special Files, hereafter WHSF, Nixon Presidential Materials Staff, National Archives.
10. Paper, 13 April 1972, folder: "Selling the Domestic Programs, 1972," Box 19, Egil Krogh files, WHSF, Nixon Presidential Materials Staff, National Archives.
11. See later discussions of the Comprehensive Drug Abuse Prevention and Control Act of 1970 and of Operation Intercept.
12. R.C. Allen, "Drug Abuse on Campus: The Role of the University," in *Drugs and Youth: Proceedings of the Rutgers Symposium on Drug Abuse,* ed. J.R. Wittenborn et al. (Springfield, IL: Charles C. Thomas, 1969), p. 363.
13. R.H. Blum, "An Approach to Constructive Drug Policies," in *Drugs and Youth: Proceedings of the Rutgers Symposium on Drug Abuse,* ed. J.R. Wittenborn et al. (Springfield, IL: Charles C. Thomas, 1969), p. 416.
14. According to the Gallup Organization, concern about crime was at its height between November 1968 and February 1969. Citations of campus unrest as the nation's most important problem reached their peak with the Kent State tragedy in May of 1970 and con-

tinued to occupy second place behind Vietnam throughout that year. Concern about drugs increased fairly steadily throughout Nixon's first term, reaching a high of 12 percent in May of 1972.

15. Memorandum, Daniel P. Moynihan for Henry Kissinger, 6 November 1969, papers of Daniel Patrick Moynihan, Library of Congress.

16. Papers of the Nixon White House, 1969–1974, Part III: John Ehrlichman: Notes of Meetings with the President, 1969–1973, Microfiche (Frederick, MD: University Publications of America, 1987–1991), 3-34-A09, 9 June 1971. Ehrlichman records part of conversation with the president as follows (emphasis in original):

> 10. Pick out 3 issues to concentrate on
> A sharp image
> eg. Tax reduction
> People back to work—
>
> Don't worry about *doing* it
> eg. JFK's phony issues
> Country moving
> Missile Gap
>
> How create them?
> Controversy
> Enemies
>
> Drugs & Law Enforcement
> *Not* unemployment
> or
> inflation

H.R. Haldeman (*The Haldeman Diaries,* Compact Disk, Sony Electronic Publishing, 1994) recorded this conversation in his diary as follows. "He also told E to sit down and pick out the three main issues that really matter. He commented that revenue sharing only matters if it is tied to tax reduction, and welfare reform only if it related to getting people off of welfare. He emphasized that we shouldn't be concerned if it is something we will actually accomplish and pointed out that JFK was doing all of his progress building on phony issues. Rather, we should look in terms of how we create issues. We need an enemy. We need controversy. We need to do something that will build those things. Drugs and law enforcement may be one, especially since we are so weak in our standing in the polls on those." This conversation took place on 9 June 1971, after Nixon had been in office for more than two years but during the period in which major drug initiatives were undertaken—and just one day before SAODAP was launched. How much weight should be given to this glimpse into Nixonian political thought is a difficult question. It is likely that it is indicative of at least some of the thinking that went into such policies as the Turkish moratorium and the establishment of the Cabinet Committee on International Narcotics Control, SAODAP, and ODALE.

17. Statement by Richard M. Nixon, Republican Presidential Nominee, Anaheim, California, 16 September 1968, folder: "LEN-13-3," Box 29, President's Advisory Council on

Executive Organization, WHCF, Nixon Presidential Materials Staff, National Archives.

18. Memorandum, John Ehrlichman for the Secretary of State, 7 April 1969, folder: "450-OA #2890 [Narcotics/Drugs/Law Enforcement]," Box 59, Egil Krogh files, WHSF, Nixon Presidential Materials Staff, National Archives.
19. The Comprehensive Drug Abuse and Control Act was being drafted at this time.
20. Memorandum, D.P. Moynihan for the Attorney General, 11 February 1969, folder: "450-OA #2890 [Narcotics/Drugs/Law Enforcement]," Box 59, Egil Krogh files, WHSF, Nixon Presidential Materials Staff, National Archives.
21. Letter with attachment, E.L. Richardson for John Ehrlichmann, 24 June 1969, folder: "OA 2776/Part I," Box 59, Egil Krogh files, WHSF, Nixon Presidential Materials Staff, National Archives.
22. Memorandum, Richard M. Nixon for John Ehrlichman, John Mitchell, Henry Kissinger, and Elliot Richardson (in Secretary Rogers's absence), 22 September 1969, folder: "Heroin/Turkey—1969," Box 30, Egil Krogh files, WHSF, Nixon Presidential Materials Staff, National Archives.
23. F. Belair, Jr., "U.S. Presses Pacts with 3 Countries in Fight on Heroin," *New York Times,* 7 January 1970.
24. Note forwarded to Dr. Moynihan by Jack W. Carlson of the Bureau of the Budget, 12 January 1970, folder: "OA#3280/Heroin/Confidential," Box 69, Egil Krogh files, WHSF, Nixon Presidential Materials Staff, National Archives. The note makes the following points (emphasis in original):

    1. A reasonable estimate of the number of U.S. heroin addicts is 100,000. Each addict uses, as a maximum, one pound of heroin *per year.*
    2. One acre of opium poppies can produce enough raw opium to make 250 lbs. of heroin. Total U.S. requirements could thus be met by cultivation of 400 acres—less than two-thirds of one square mile. (This is a maximum. Some analysts believe that the average addict uses only one ounce per year. Under this assumption, U.S. demand could be met with only 25 acres.)
    3. The value at the source is very low compared with final retail value. The price increases by a factor of perhaps 10 with every step along the processing pipeline. This makes it unlikely that the U.S. retail price is going to be sensitive even to large changes in the price of raw opium.
    4. While 80 percent of the U.S. heroin comes from Turkish opium, the poppy is also grown in India, Southeast Asia, China and Mexico. Presumably, part of Africa and South America would also have a suitable climate.

    The advisability of spending any large amount on eradicating present sources of opium seems very doubtful. This is especially true if such payments were to be continuing charges for not growing the crop. The likely result would be disruption for a time, and then a resumed flow from other sources. If the price is right, someone is always going to be able to find one square mile of earth on which to grow opium.

25. Undated handwritten notes bearing title "Heroin w/Drug Co. reps," folder: "OA#3280 Heroin/Confidential," Box 69, Egil Krogh files, WHSF, Nixon Presidential Materials

Staff, National Archives. Participants seem to have included Krogh, Daniel Patrick Moynihan, John Ingersoll, and drug company executives Reed, Hormeyer, and Roehm(?). Hormeyer estimated that Turkey produced one quarter to one third of the "free world supply" of opium. Ingersoll said that India produced 1,212 tons while Turkey produced 76 tons. Moynihan is quoted in the notes as saying, "Can we rpt to the Pres. that 3 Co's will undertake buy all opium made available through Turk mkng oper w/understanding that if [this] causes problem for you, & you be judge this, US gov. will in turn buy from you." Hormeyer replied, "Yes, agreed principle couple wks ago." See also Memorandum, Egil Krogh for the President's File, 26 July 1971, p. 4, papers of Jerome H. Jaffe.

26. Memorandum, Henry Kissinger to John Ehrlichman, 26 April 1971, folder: "Meeting with President, Top Civilian and Military Leaders, Thursday, June 3, 1971," Box 32, Egil Krogh files, WHSF, Nixon Presidential Materials Staff, National Archives.
27. Memorandum, Jeffrey Donfeld to the President, 29 June 1971, Box 12, President's Office files, President's Handwriting file, WHSF, Nixon Presidential Materials Staff, National Archives.
28. J. Herbers, "Nixon Says Turks Agree to Ban the Opium Poppy," *New York Times,* 1 July 1971, p. 1.
29. F. Belair, Jr., "Laird Says Agreement Is Near with Turkey to Curb Drug Flow," *New York Times,* 23 June 1971.
30. D.A. Schmidt, "Poppy-Ban Cost to U.S. Disclosed," *New York Times,* 21 November 1971.
31. J.L. Hess, "The Faltering War on Narcotics," *New York Times,* 22 November 1971.
32. H. Kamm, "Turkish Ban on Poppy: Delayed Impact Seen," *New York Times,* 10 October 1972.
33. Heroin Shortage Situation Report, 24 October 1972, folder: "Heroin Shortage Report—BNDD," Box 2, Geoffrey Shepard files, WHSF, Nixon Presidential Materials Staff, National Archives.
34. J.M. Markham, "Curb on Poppies Held Unrealistic," *New York Times,* 24 February 1972, p. 14.
35. U.S. Congress, Senate, Committee on Government Operations, *Report No. 93-469* (Washington, DC: GPO, 1973), p. 11.
36. H. Kamm, "Turkish Ban on Poppy: Delayed Impact Seen," *New York Times,* 10 October 1972.
37. Letter, J.H. Jaffe and M.J. Ambrose to the editor, "Administration's Drive Against Drugs," *New York Times,* 7 October 1972.
38. The letter from Jaffe and Ambrose was countered by another from presidential candidate George McGovern (*New York Times,* 14 October 1972), who took issue with the administration on the existence of a heroin shortage, on the meaning of the increase in heroin prices, and on the amount of heroin entering the country. He charged that President Nixon was unwilling to take effective action against heroin supplies from Southeast Asia because of the necessity of supporting corrupt regimes in the region in order to prosecute the war there.

39. Sibyl Cline, *Turkish Opium in Perspective* (Washington, DC: Drug Abuse Council, 1974), [pages not numbered].
40. Presentation, Department of Defense, [1970], folder: "Len-12-7," Box 48, PACEO files, WHCF, Nixon Presidential Materials Staff, National Archives.
41. Presentation, Department of Defense, [1970], folder: "Len-12-7," Box 48, PACEO files, WHCF, Nixon Presidential Materials Staff, National Archives.
42. U.S. Congress, Senate, Committee on the Judiciary, Subcommittee to Investigate Juvenile Delinquency, *Hearings on Drug Abuse in the Armed Forces,* Part 21 (Washington, DC: GPO, 1971), testimony of Dr. Joel H. Kaplan, 24 March 1970, p. 6278; and testimony of Charles West, 24 March 1970, pp. 6294–6295.
43. U.S. Congress, Senate, Committee on the Judiciary, Subcommittee to Investigate Juvenile Delinquency, *Hearings on Drug Abuse in the Armed Forces,* Part 21 (Washington, DC: GPO, 1971), testimony of Dr. Joel H. Kaplan, p. 6262.
44. U.S. Congress, Senate, Committee on the Judiciary, Subcommittee to Investigate Juvenile Delinquency, *Hearings on Drug Abuse in the Armed Forces,* Part 21 (Washington, DC: GPO, 1971), testimony of Jon Michael Steinberg, 30 October 1970, pp. 6762–6763; and *New York Times,* 31 October 1970, p. 3.
45. Memorandum, Egil Krogh for John Lehman, Jeffrey Donfeld, 6 January 1971, folder: "Cron File/1971," Box 4, Egil Krogh files, WHSF, Nixon Presidential Materials Staff, National Archives.
46. U.S. Congress, House of Representatives, Committee on Foreign Affairs, *The World Heroin Problem: Report of Special Study Mission Composed of Morgan F. Murphy, Illinois, Chairman; Robert H. Steele, Connecticut* . . . , House Report 92-298, (Washington, DC: GPO, 1971).
47. This incident is reported by John Finlator in his book *The Drugged Nation: A "Narc's" Story* (New York: Simon and Schuster, 1973), pp. 99–100, and is corroborated in the authors' conversation with Jeffrey Donfeld of 3 June 1994, although he recalled the congressmen as being from New York and the figure they used as 50,000 addicts among servicemen in South Vietnam. Jerome Jaffe, subsequently named head of the Special Action Office for Drug Abuse Prevention (SAODAP), reported to the president in July of 1971 that the percentage of opiate users among U.S. personnel in South Vietnam was in the neighborhood of 4.5 percent. Memorandum, Jerome H. Jaffe for the President's file, 17 July 1971, folder: "Beginning July 11, 1971," Box 85, President's Office files, President's Meeting files, WHSF, Nixon Presidential Materials Staff, National Archives.
48. Papers of the Nixon White House, 1969–1974, Part III: John Ehrlichman: Notes of Meetings with the President 1969–1973, Microfiche (Frederick, MD: University Publications of America, 1987–1991), 10 June 1971, 3-34-A13.
49. Memorandum, Jerome H. Jaffe for the President's file, 17 July 1971, folder: "Beginning July 11, 1971," Box 85, President's Office files, President's Meeting files, WHSF, Nixon Presidential Materials Staff, National Archives,
50. Telephone interview with Jeffrey Donfeld, 3 June 1994.
51. Undated memorandum, Richard M. Nixon for Melvin R. Laird, Secretary of Defense, folder: "Meeting with President, Top Civilian and Military Leaders, Thursday, June 3,

1971," Box 32, Egil Krogh files, WHSF, Nixon Presidential Materials Staff, National Archives.

52. F. Belair, Jr., "C.I.A. Identifies 21 Opium Refineries," *New York Times*, 6 June 1971.
53. F. Belair, Jr., "C.I.A. Identifies 21 Opium Refineries," *New York Times*, 6 June 1971.
54. A.W. McCoy, *The Politics of Heroin: CIA Complicity in the Global Drug Trade* (Brooklyn, NY: Lawrence Hill Books, 1991), p. 385.
55. "Use of heroin by U.S. servicemen in Vietnam has allegedly reached crisis proportions and threatens to disrupt the Administration's Vietnamization policy." Undated memorandum bearing title "Drugs," folder: "[FY19]73 Initiatives [1971]," Box 32, Egil Krogh files, WHSF, Nixon Presidential Materials Staff, National Archives. "[President:] Maybe the war hypo's narcotics—may find answers earlier—A by-product of war. Must have an answer—will kill us re foreign policy." Papers of the Nixon White House, 1969–1974, Part III: John Erlichman: Notes of Meetings with the President 1969–1973, Microfiche (Frederick, MD: University Publications of America, 10 June 1971, 3-32-E10.
56. J. Ingersoll, Testimony, Narcotics Research, Rehabilitation and Treatment, Hearings, U.S. Congress, House of Representatives, Select Committe on Crime, 92nd Congress, 1st Session, 2, 3, 4, and 23 June 1971, pp. 345–389.
57. This imperative is recorded in John Ehrlichman's meeting notes from 27 May 1971 (Papers of the Nixon White House, 1969–1974, Part III: John Ehrlichman: Notes of Meetings with the President, 1969–1973, Microfiche [Frederick, MD: University Publications of America, 1987–1991], 3-32-E10), 28 May (3-32-F13), and 10 June (3-34-A13) and was publicly expressed by the president in a news conference reported in the *New York Times* on 2 June. The 10 June notes also indicate that the president expressed the opinion that a higher percentage of students at Ivy League schools used drugs than did soldiers in Vietnam. Egil Krogh observed that the drugs of choice in the two situations were not the same.
58. See, for example, Ehrlichman meeting notes dated 10 June 1971 in which John Ingersoll, director of BNDD, is referred to as "pedestrian," which is followed by the remark "Maybe he has to go" and the comment "No confidence in HEW." Papers of the Nixon White House, 1969–1974, Part III: John Erlichman: Notes of Meetings with the President, 1969–1973, Microfiche (Frederick, MD: University Publications of America, 1987–1991), 10 June 1971, 3-34-A13.
59. Memorandum, from Egil Krogh to the president through John Ehrlichman, 27 May 1971, folder: "Meeting with President, Top Civilian and Military Leaders, Thursday, June 3, 1971," Box 32, Egil Krogh files, WHSF, Nixon Presidential Materials Staff, National Archives.
60. Telephone conversation with Walter Minnick, June 1994.
61. Telephone conversation with Walter Minnick, June 1994.
62. Briefing by Nelson Gross cited in Task Force on Federal Heroin Addiction Programs, *Federal Drug Abuse Programs* (Washington, DC: Drug Abuse Council, 1972), p. 26.
63. Letter, Egil Krogh for Robert G. Neumann, 19 January 1972, "Chron Files 1972–73," Box 5, Egil Krogh files, WHSF, Nixon Presidential Materials Staff, National Archives.
64. B. Welles, "House Member Charges Narcotics Smuggling Inquiry Touches 'Highest Levels' of Panama Government," *New York Times*, 16 March 1972.

65. B. Welles, "House Member Charges Narcotics Smuggling Inquiry Touches 'Highest Levels' of Panama Government," *New York Times,* 16 March 1972.
66. Memorandum, Richard M. Nixon for John Ehrlichman, John Mitchell, Henry Kissinger, and Elliot Richardson (in Secretary Rogers's absence), 22 September 1969, folder: "Heroin/Turkey—1969," Box 30, Egil Krogh files, WHSF, Nixon Presidential Materials Staff, National Archives.
67. Memorandum, Will Wilson to the Attorney General, 13 March 1969, folder: "Administration Drug Bill [4 of 5]," Box 27, John W. Dean III files, WHSF, Nixon Presidential Materials Staff, National Archives.
68. Memorandum, Will Wilson for the Attorney General, 13 March 1969, folder: "Administration Drug Bill [4 of 5]," Box 27, John W. Dean III files, WHSF, Nixon Presidential Materials Staff, National Archives.
69. Summary of HEW Staff Views on Justice Draft Bill, "Controlled Dangerous Substances Act of 1969," folder: "Administration Drug Bill [3 of 5]," Box 27, John W. Dean III files, WHSF, Nixon Presidential Materials Staff, National Archives.
70. Memorandum, M.R. Sonnenreich for John W. Dean III, 7 May 1969, folder: "Administration Drug Bill [4 of 5]," Box 27, John W. Dean III files, WHSF, Nixon Presidential Materials Staff, National Archives. Emphasis in original.
71. Letter, Richard H. Poff for John N. Mitchell, 21 May 1969, folder: "Administration Drug Bill [3 of 5]," Box 27, John W. Dean III files, WHSF, Nixon Presidential Materials Staff, National Archives.
72. Memorandum, Michael R. Sonnenreich to John W. Dean III, 9 June 1969, file: "Administration Drug Bill [3 of 5]," Box 27, John W. Dean III files, WHSF, Nixon Presidential Materials Staff, National Archives.
73. Memorandum, John W. Dean III for the Attorney General, 2 July 1969, folder: "Administration Drug Bill [4 of 5]," Box 27, John W. Dean III files, WHSF, Presidential Materials Staff, National Archives.
74. Memorandum, Patrick J. Buchanan for the President, 8 July 1969, folder: "Beginning July 6th," Box 78, President's Office files, President's Meeting files, WHSF, Nixon Presidential Materials Staff, National Archives.
75. Gallup Organization, National Adult Survey, 27 May 1969.
76. Loose sheet of opinion poll data, Box 12, President's Handwriting file, President's Office file, WHSF, Nixon Presidential Materials Staff, National Archives.
77. Memorandum, M. Sonnenreich for J.W. Dean, 22 April 1969, folder: "Administration Drug Bill [3 of 5]," Box 27, John W. Dean III files, WHSF, Nixon Presidential Materials Staff, National Archives.
78. "Text of Nixon's Message to Congress Proposing 10 Steps in Fight on Narcotics," *New York Times,* 15 July 1969, p. 18.
79. *Congressional Quarterly Almanac* (Washington, DC: Congressional Quarterly News Features, 1969), p. 707.
80. Michael R. Sonnenreich, "The Controlled Dangerous Substances Act of 1969, *Status Quo Ante* or Beyond?" in *Communication and Drug Abuse: Proceedings of the Second Rutgers Symposium on Drug Abuse,* ed. J.R. Wittenborn et al. (Springfield, IL: Charles C. Thomas, 1969), p. 497.

81. *Congressional Quarterly Almanac* (Washington, DC: Congressional Quarterly News Features, 1969), p. 708.
82. U.S. Congress, Senate, 91st Congress, 1st Session, Report No. 91-613, Controlled Dangerous Substances Act of 1969 (Washington, DC: GPO, 1969), esp. p. 1 and p. 8.
83. Memorandum, John Ehrlichman for Bud Krogh, 20 October 1969, folder: "Oversized Attachments OA2776—Part I," Box 59, Egil Krogh files, WHSF, Nixon Presidential Materials Staff, National Archives.
84. *Public Papers of the Presidents of the United States: Richard Nixon* (Washington, DC: Federal Register Division, National Archives and Records Service, 1974), p. 834.
85. Task Force Report: Narcotics, Marijuana and Dangerous Drugs—Findings and Recommendations, 6 June 1969, folder: "Ex FG 221-28 Narcotics, Marijuana and Dangerous Drugs [1969–70]," Box 5, FG221 Task Forces, WHCF, Nixon Presidential Materials Staff, National Archives.
86. Letter, David M. Kennedy and John N. Mitchell for the President, 6 June 1969, folder: "Ex FG 221-28 Narcotics, Marijuana and Dangerous Drugs [1969–70]," Box 5, FG 221 Task Forces, WHCF, Nixon Presidential Materials Staff, National Archives.
87. In May of 1969, 15 percent of those polled by Gallup cited this as the nation's most important problem, up from 3 percent in January and 11 percent in February.
88. Special Presidential Task Force Relating to Narcotics, Marijuana and Dangerous Drugs, *Task Force Report: Narcotics, Marijuana and Dangerous Drugs—Findings and Recommendations,* 6 June 1969, p. 7, folder: "Ex FG 221-28 Narcotics, Marijuana and Dangerous Drugs [1969–70]," Box 5, FG 221 "Task Forces," WHCF, Nixon Presidential Materials Staff, National Archives.
89. Special Presidential Task Force Relating to Narcotics, Marijuana and Dangerous Drugs, *Task Force Report: Narcotics, Marijuana and Dangerous Drugs—Findings and Recommendations,* 6 June 1969, p. 7, folder: "Ex FG 221-28 Narcotics, Marijuana and Dangerous Drugs [1969–70]," Box 5, FG 221 "Task Forces," WHCF, Nixon Presidential Materials Staff, National Archives, p. 12.
90. Special Presidential Task Force Relating to Narcotics, Marijuana and Dangerous Drugs, *Task Force Report: Narcotics, Marijuana and Dangerous Drugs—Findings and Recommendations,* 6 June 1969, p. 7, folder: "Ex FG 221-28 Narcotics, Marijuana and Dangerous Drugs [1969–70]," Box 5, FG 221 "Task Forces," WHCF, Nixon Presidential Materials Staff, National Archives, p. 15.
91. Memorandum, Richard Nixon for various cabinet officers, 27 June 1969, folder: "Ex FG 221-28 Narcotics, Marijuana and Dangerous Drugs [1969–70]," Box 5, FG 221 "Task Forces," WHCF, Nixon Presidential Materials Staff, National Archives.
92. *Time,* 29 August 1969, p. 32.
93. F. Belair, "Mexico Is Asked to Help Combat Drug Smuggling." *New York Times,* 9 September 1969, p. 1; Special Presidential Task Force Relating to Narcotics, Marihuana and Dangerous Drugs, *Task Force Report: Narcotics, Marijuana and Dangerous Drugs—Findings and Recommendations,* 6 June 1969, folder: "Ex FG 221-28 Narcotics, Marijuana and Dangerous Drugs [1969–70], Box 5, FG 221 "Task Forces," WHCF, Nixon Presidential Materials Staff, National Archives.
94. Memorandum, Herbert G. Klein for the president, 13 September 1969, folder: "[Ex]

HE5-1 7/1/69–12/31/69," Box 17, Subject Files, HE (Health), WHCF, Nixon Presidential Materials Staff, National Archives.

95. Memorandum, Herbert G. Klein for the president, 13 September 1969, folder: "[Ex] HE5-1 7/1/69–12/31/69," Box 17, Subject Files, HE (Health), WHCF, Nixon Presidential Materials Staff, National Archives.
96. Transcript, The Streets of Laredo, Radio Station KVOZ, 1 October 1969, folder: "[Ex] HE 5-1 7/1/69–12/31/69," Box 17, Subject Files, HE (Health), WHCF, Nixon Presidential Materials Staff, National Archives.
97. Memorandum with attachment, Tom Whitehead for Egil Krogh, 29 September 1969, folder: "Anti-Smuggling Supplem. Appropriats. [1969]," Box 30, Egil Krogh files, WHSF, Nixon Presidential Materials Staff, National Archives.
98. Report, Myles J. Ambrose for Mr. Richard G. Kleindienst, Deputy Attorney General, Mr. Eugene T. Rossides, Assistant Secretary of the Treasury, Co-Chairmen, The President's Task Force on Narcotics, Marihuana and Dangerous Drugs, 6 October 1969, folder: "Report to the President on Operation Intercept," Box 53, Egil Krogh files, WHSF, Nixon Presidential Materials Staff, National Archives.
99. Report, Myles J. Ambrose for Mr. Richard G. Kleindienst, Deputy Attorney General, Mr. Eugene T. Rossides, Assistant Secretary of the Treasury, Co-Chairmen, The President's Task Force on Narcotics, Marihuana and Dangerous Drugs, 6 October 1969, folder: "Report to the President on Operation Intercept," Box 53, Egil Krogh files, WHSF, Nixon Presidential Materials Staff, National Archives, p. 11.
100. Report, Myles J. Ambrose for Mr. Richard G. Kleindienst, Deputy Attorney General, Mr. Eugene T. Rossides, Assistant Secretary of the Treasury, Co-Chairmen, The President's Task Force on Narcotics, Marihuana and Dangerous Drugs, 6 October 1969, folder: "Report to the President on Operation Intercept," Box 53, Egil Krogh files, WHSF, Nixon Presidential Materials Staff, National Archives, p. 12.
101. Memorandum, Egil Krogh for John Ehrlichman and Kenneth Cole, 28 July 1969, folder: "Oversized Attachments OA 2776—Part I," Box 59, Egil Krogh files, WHSF, Nixon Presidential Materials Staff, National Archives.
102. A number of authors have discussed Nixon's abandonment of his cabinet beginning toward the end of 1969. See especially Shirley Ann Warshaw, "The Implementation of Cabinet Government During the Nixon Administration," in *Richard M. Nixon: Politician, President, Administrator*, ed. L. Friedman and W.E. Levantrosser (New York: Greenwood Press, 1991), pp. 331–350; Tom Wicker, *One of Us: Richard Nixon and the American Dream* (New York: Random House, 1991); and Michael Genovese, *The Nixon Presidency: Power and Politics in Turbulent Times* (New York: Greenwood Press, 1990), pp. 24, 29, 30, 32, 73.
103. U.S. Congress, Senate, 91st Congress, 1st Session, Report No. 91-613, Controlled Dangerous Substances Act of 1969 (Washington, DC: GPO, 1969), p. 1.
104. Memorandum, M.R. Sonnenreich for John W. Dean III, 28 April 1970, folder: "Administration Drug Bill [4 of 5]," Box 27, John W. Dean III files, WHSF, Nixon Presidential Materials Staff, National Archives.
105. "200 HEW Scientists Urge Defeat of Drug-Control Bill," *Hospital Tribune*, 1 June 1970.

106. Memorandum, M.R. Sonnenreich to Egil Krogh, 2 February 1970, folder: "(Controlled Dangerous Substances Act?)," Box 39, Egil Krogh files, WHSF, Nixon Presidential Materials Staff, National Archives.
107. Handwritten notes, [May 1970], folder: "Administration Drug Bill [5 of 5]," Box 28, John W. Dean III files, WHSF, Nixon Presidential Materials Staff, National Archives.
108. *Food Drug and Cosmetics Report,* 11 May 1970, folder: "Administration Drug Bill [4 of 5]," Box 27, John W. Dean III files, WHSF, Nixon Presidential Materials Staff, National Archives. See also Memorandum, President's Advisory Council on Executive Organization, 27 January 1970, folder: "LEN 1-2-2," Box 42, PACEO files, WHCF, Nixon Presidential Materials Staff, National Archives: "Underlying the opposition to the 1968 reorganization was the desire of the Treasury appropriations committees in Congress to retain supervision of narcotics matters and the belief, particularly among Republicans, that the Justice Department under Attorney General Ramsey Clark was soft on crime. The vote on the reorganization followed party lines. 166 Republicans opposed the reorganization and only 8 supported it. 192 Democrats supported the reorganization and 24 opposed it. It was approved 200 to 190."
109. Memorandum, Stanley Ebner for Wallace H. Johnson, 30 September 1970, folder: "Administration Drug Bill [2 of 5]," Box 2, John W. Dean III files, WHSF, Nixon Presidential Materials Staff, National Archives.
110. Memorandum, John Dean for the Attorney General, 10 September 1970, folder: "Administration Drug Bill [2 of 5]," Box 2, John W. Dean III files, WHSF, Nixon Presidential Materials Staff, National Archives.

CHAPTER 3. THE FIRST NIXON ADMINISTRATION: TREATMENT AND REHABILITATION

1. It is also true that in late 1969 the administration needed to justify its retreat from the harsh penalty structure it had originally included in the Comprehensive Drug Abuse Prevention and Control Act.
2. P. Grose, "Governors See Simulated 'Trip' at Nixon Presentation on Drugs," *New York Times,* 4 December 1969.
3. Memorandum, John G. Veneman, Acting Secretary of HEW for the President, 13 November, 1969, folder: "Oversized Attachments OA 2776, Part I," Box 59, Egil Krogh files, WHSF, Nixon Presidential Materials Staff, National Archives.
4. Memorandum, Egil Krogh for John Ehrlichman, 4 December 1969, folder: "Oversized Attachments OA 2776—Part I," Box 59, Egil Krogh files, WHSF, Nixon Presidential Materials Staff, National Archives.
5. Of the six issues cited as the most important problem facing the United States at the time by respondents to the Gallup survey, drugs moved from fifth place in January 1970 to third place in December. The Vietnam War remained in first place throughout the year. The cost of living declined from second to fourth place. The civil rights movement and crime began the year in third and fourth place respectively and ended the period tied for fifth. Student unrest occupied sixth place in January and second place in December.
6. Memorandum, Egil Krogh for John Ehrlichman and Kenneth Cole, 28 July 1969, folder:

"Oversized Attachments OA 2776—Part I," Box 59, Egil Krogh files, WHSF, Nixon Presidential Materials Staff, National Archives.

7. Memorandum, Bud Wilkinson for Egil Krogh, 26 February 1970, folder: "LEN 6-4 [1 of 2]," Box 44, PACEO files, WHCF, Nixon Presidential Materials Staff, National Archives.
8. Memorandum for the record, 26 March 1970, "Drug Abuse Study Interview, Mr. Jim Atwater, Special Assistant to the President, Interviewer: Mr. John J. Cohressen," folder: "LEN 6-4 [1 of 2]," Box 44, PACEO files, WHCF, Nixon Presidential Materials Staff, National Archives: "Mr. Atwater related that HEW's funds had been frozen as part of the cut down on federal spending, and that subsequently, BoB or someone decided that the funds could be unfrozen. Bud Wilkinson, and apparently Bud Krogh, had withheld permission to release funds for the programs because they found that the NIMH and OE [Office of Education] programs were not formulated within the Administration's thinking. NIMH had not clarified exactly what they had wanted to do; their thinking appeared to change easily; and each new idea was dependent on unclear variables. OE had a plan to set up six intensive drug education programs in communities with significant drug abuse problems as an experiment to decide what in fact was the best approach to preventive education. Here political considerations entered into having a campaign which would go into many more communities across the Country."
9. Memorandum, Charles Wilkinson to Egil Krogh, 26 February 1970, folder: "LEN 12-3," Box 45, PACEO files, WHCF, Nixon Presidential Materials Staff, National Archives.
10. Memorandum for the record, from the Drug Abuse Study Group of PACEO, 13 April 1970, folder: "LEN 6-4 [1 of 2]," Box 44, PACEO files, WHCF, Nixon Presidential Materials Staff, National Archives.
11. Memorandum, Drug Abuse Study Group for the President's Advisory Council on Executive Organization, 20 May 1970, folder: "LEN 13-3 [1 of 3]," Box 49, PACEO files, WHCF, Nixon Presidential Materials Staff, National Archives.
12. Memorandum, Drug Abuse Study Group for the President's Advisory Council on Executive Organization, 20 May 1970, folder: "LEN 13-3 [1 of 3]," Box 49, PACEO files, WHCF, Nixon Presidential Materials Staff, National Archives.
13. Memorandum, Drug Abuse Study Group for the President's Advisory Council on Executive Organization, 20 May 1970, folder: "LEN 13-3 [1 of 3]," Box 49, PACEO files, WHCF, Nixon Presidential Materials Staff, National Archives.
14. Memorandum, Drug Abuse Study Group for the President's Advisory Council on Executive Organization, 20 May 1970, folder: "LEN 13-3 [1 of 3]," Box 49, PACEO files, WHCF, Nixon Presidential Materials Staff, National Archives.
15. Memorandum for the record, 6 April 1970, folder: "LEN 6-4 [2 of 2]," Box 44, PACEO files, WHCF, Nixon Presidential Materials Staff, National Archives.
16. Health Program Analysis: Five-Year Program Plan for the Prevention and Treatment of Narcotic and Drug Abuse, August 1967, folder: "Len 12-8," Box 49, PACEO files, WHCF, Nixon Presidential Materials Staff, National Archives.
17. R.D. Lyons, "U.S. Health Aide Is Out in Dispute," *New York Times,* 3 June 1970, p. 1.
18. R.D. Lyons, "U.S. Health Aide Is Out in Dispute," *New York Times,* 3 June 1970, p. 1.

19. Memorandum, Jeffrey Donfeld for Egil Krogh, 19 June 1970, papers of Jerome H. Jaffe.
20. D. Courtwright et al., *Addicts Who Survived: An Oral History of Narcotic Use in America, 1923–1965* (Knoxville: University of Tennessee Press, 1989), p. 339.
21. Memorandum, Jeffrey Donfeld for Egil Krogh, 19 June 1970, papers of Jerome H. Jaffe.
22. Memorandum, Jeffrey Donfeld for Egil Krogh, 19 June 1970, papers of Jerome H. Jaffe.
23. Memorandum, President's Advisory Council on Executive Organization for the President, folder: "Ash Council Study—Drug Abuse [1970]," Box 29, Egil Krogh files, WHSF, Nixon Presidential Material Staff, National Archives.
24. Memorandum, Bud Krogh for Jeff Donfeld, 6 July 1970, folder: "Ash Council Study—Drug Abuse [1970]," Alpha Subject—Drugs, Box 29, Egil Krogh files, WHSF, Nixon Presidential Materials Staff, National Archives.
25. Memorandum, Egil Krogh for Jeffrey Donfeld, 6 July 1970, folder: "Ash Council Study—Drug Abuse [1970]," Box 29, Egil Krogh files, WHSF, Nixon Presidential Materials Staff, National Archives. For good discussions of Nixon's relations with his cabinet officers, see Shirley Ann Warshaw, "The Implementation of Cabinet Government During the Nixon Administration," in *Richard M. Nixon: Politician, President, Administrator,* ed. Friedman and Levantrosser (New York: Greenwood Press, 1991), pp. 331–350; Tom Wicker, *One of Us: Richard Nixon and the American Dream* (New York: Random House, 1991); and Michael Genovese, *The Nixon Presidency: Power and Politics in Turbulent Times* (Westport, CT: Greenwood Press. 1990), pp. 24, 29, 30, 32, 73.
26. Memorandum, Egil Krogh for John Ehrlichman, 27 April 1971, papers of Jerome H. Jaffe.
27. Nevertheless, the legislation that finally codified the Nixon treatment and rehabilitation initiatives included the basis for eventual transfer of public health measures to control substance abuse to a new institute within HEW the goals of which would closely resemble those outlined by NIMH in 1967.
28. See, for example, Memorandum, Egil Krogh for Bertram S. Brown, 23 October 1970, folder: "National Drug Rehabilitation Program [1970–71]," Box 32, Egil Krogh files, WHSF, Nixon Presidential Materials Staff, National Archives: "Though the use of and trafficking in illicit drugs is in itself a crime, some forms of drug dependency inexorably lead to the commission of crimes against persons and property in order to sustain expensive drug habits."
29. Letter, Vincent P. Dole for Joseph D. Tydings, 12 June 1970, folder: "[EX] HE5-1 7/1/70–8/31/70," Box 18, Subject files, HE (Health), WHCF, Nixon Presidential Materials Staff, National Archives.
30. Memorandum, Egil Krogh for the Domestic Council Staff, 17 July 1970, folder: "[Ex] HE5-1 7/1/70–8/31/70," Box 18, Subject files, HE (Health), WHCF, Nixon Presidential Materials Staff, National Archives.
31. Memorandum, Kenneth R. Cole, Jr., for the Domestic Council, 19 October, 1970, folder: "White House Domestic Council [1970–71]," Box 5, Edward A. David files, WHCF, Nixon Presidential Materials Staff, National Archives.
32. Memorandum, Egil Krogh for Kenneth Cole, 23 October 1970, folder: "National Drug Rehabilitation Program [1970–71]," Box 32, Egil Krogh files, WHSF, Nixon Presidential Materials Staff, National Archives.

33. Telephone interview with Jeffrey Donfeld, 3 June 1994.
34. Telephone interview with Jeffrey Donfeld, 3 June 1994. The first sentence of this quotation appears almost verbatim on pages 37–38 and 41 in the *First Federal Strategy for Drug Abuse and Drug Traffic Prevention* (June 1973), authored by the Strategy Council pursuant to the Drug Abuse Office and Treatment Act of 1972.
35. Interview with Jerome H. Jaffe, 6 October 1994.
36. Interview with Jerome H. Jaffe, 6 October 1994.
37. Memorandum, marked at top "From Donfeld," undated (probably late autumn 1970), papers of Jerome H. Jaffe.
38. Report of an Ad Hoc White House Committee on the Treatment and Prevention of Drug Addiction and Drug Abuse, 23 December 1970, papers of Jerome H. Jaffe, p. 31.
39. Report of an Ad Hoc White House Committee on the Treatment and Prevention of Drug Addiction and Drug Abuse, 23 December 1970, papers of Jerome H. Jaffe, pp. 17–21.
40. Report of an Ad Hoc White House Committee on the Treatment and Prevention of Drug Addiction and Drug Abuse, 23 December 1970, papers of Jerome H. Jaffe, p. 74.
41. Report of an Ad Hoc White House Committee on the Treatment and Prevention of Drug Addiction and Drug Abuse, 23 December 1970, papers of Jerome H. Jaffe, pp. 5, 12.
42. Report of an Ad Hoc White House Committee on the Treatment and Prevention of Drug Addiction and Drug Abuse, 23 December 1970, papers of Jerome H. Jaffe, pp. 29, 101, 102.
43. Report of an Ad Hoc White House Committee on the Treatment and Prevention of Drug Addiction and Drug Abuse, 23 December 1970, papers of Jerome H. Jaffe, pp. 58–62.
44. Report of an Ad Hoc White House Committee on the Treatment and Prevention of Drug Addiction and Drug Abuse, 23 December 1970, papers of Jerome H. Jaffe, p. 85.
45. Domestic Council Staff Report on National Drug Programs, January 1971, papers of Jerome H. Jaffe, p. 1.
46. Report, Approaches to a National Policy and Program on Narcotics and Drug Abuse, Ad Hoc Inter-Agency Committee—Narcotics and Drug Abuse, 23 December 1970, papers of Jerome H. Jaffe, p. 4.
47. Report, Approaches to a National Policy and Program on Narcotics and Drug Abuse, Ad Hoc Inter-Agency Committee—Narcotics and Drug Abuse, 23 December 1970, papers of Jerome H. Jaffe, p. 83.
48. Report, Approaches to a National Policy and Program on Narcotics and Drug Abuse, Ad Hoc Inter-Agency Committee—Narcotics and Drug Abuse, 23 December 1970, papers of Jerome H. Jaffe, p. 78.
49. Report, Approaches to a National Policy and Program on Narcotics and Drug Abuse, Ad Hoc Inter-Agency Committee—Narcotics and Drug Abuse, 23 December 1970, papers of Jerome H. Jaffe, p. 83.
50. Interview with Jerome H. Jaffe, 6 October 1994.
51. Department of Justice Critique of "Towards a National Policy and Program on Narcotics and Drug Abuse: A Staff Report of an Ad Hoc Interagency Committee," no date, included with cited report, papers of Jerome H. Jaffe.

52. Memorandum, [Egil Krogh for John Ehrlichmann—No cover], undated, folder: "Mtng—Sec. Richardson 5/25/71," cover folder: "Meeting with President, Top Civilian and Military Leaders, Thursday June 3, 1971," Box 31, Egil Krogh files, WHSF, Nixon Presidential Materials Staff, National Archives.
53. *Domestic Council Staff Report on National Drug Programs,* January 1971, papers of Jerome H. Jaffe, pp. 6–7.
54. *Domestic Council Staff Report on National Drug Programs,* January 1971, papers of Jerome H. Jaffe, p. 10.
55. *Domestic Council Staff Report on National Drug Programs,* January 1971, papers of Jerome H. Jaffe, p. 10.
56. *Domestic Council Staff Report on National Drug Programs,* January 1971, papers of Jerome H. Jaffe, p. 61.
57. *Domestic Council Summary Option Paper on a National Drug Program,* papers of Jerome H. Jaffe, pp. 26–27.
58. Memorandum, the Attorney General for John Ehrlichman, 30 March 1971, papers of Jerome H. Jaffe; Memorandum, Eliott L. Richardson for the President, 19 March 1971, papers of Jerome H. Jaffe. The responses of HEW and Justice here discussed are attached to the following document: Memorandum, Egil Krogh for John Ehrlichman, 27 April 1971, papers of Jerome H. Jaffe.
59. Memorandum, Egil Krogh for John Ehrlichman, 14 May 1971, papers of Jerome H. Jaffe.
60. Memorandum, Egil Krogh for John Ehrlichman, 14 May 1971, papers of Jerome H. Jaffe.
61. Papers of the Nixon White House, 1969–1974, Part III: John Ehrlichman: Notes of Meetings with the President, 1969–1973, Microfiche (Frederick, MD: University Publications of America, 1987–1991), 3-32-D13; H.R. Haldeman, *The Haldeman Diaries* (New York: G.P. Putnam's Sons, 1994), p. 291.
62. Memorandum, Egil Krogh for John D. Ehrlichman, 27 May 1971, folder: "Meeting with President, Top Civilian and Military Leaders, Thursday June 3, 1971," Box 32, Egil Krogh files, WHSF, Nixon Presidential Materials Staff, National Archives.
63. Memorandum, no heading or date, folder: "Mtng—Sec. Richardson 5/25/71," cover folder: "Meeting with President, Top Civilian and Military Leaders, Thursday June 3, 1971," Box 32, Egil Krogh files, WHSF, Nixon Presidential Materials Staff, National Archives. This document is attached to the 27 May memorandum cited in the previous note.
64. Papers of the Nixon White House, 1969–1974, Part III: John Ehrlichman: Notes of Meetings with the President, 1969–1973, Microfiche (Frederick, MD: University Publications of America, 1987–1991), 3-32-E10.
65. Robert B. Semple, Jr., "President Gives 'Highest Priority' to Drug Problem," *New York Times,* 2 June 1971, p. 1.
66. Papers of the Nixon White House, 1969–1974, Part III: John Ehrlichman: Notes of Meetings with the President, 1969–1973, Microfiche (Frederick, MD: University Publications of America, 1987–1991), 10 June 1971, 3-34-A13; Memorandum, Jeffrey Donfeld for the President's File, 2 July 1971, papers of Jerome H. Jaffe.
67. Papers of the Nixon White House, 1969–1974, Part III: John Ehrlichman: Notes of Meetings with the President, 1969–1973, Microfiche (Frederick, MD: University Publications of America, 1987–1991), 28 May 1971 3-32-F13.

2. *Drugs*
handle so we get Jaffe for Narc *generally*
not *vets*—
  or
the war— [Emphasis in original.]

68. Interview with Jerome H. Jaffe, 6 October 1994.
69. This later proved to be substantially true. See L.N. Robins, D.H. Davis, and D.W. Goodwin, "Drug Use by U.S. Army Enlisted Men in Vietnam: A Follow-Up on Their Return Home," *American Journal of Epidemiology* 99, no. 4 (April 1974): 235–249.
70. Richard Nixon, *Public Papers of the Presidents of the United States: Richard Nixon* (Washington, DC: Federal Register Division, National Archives and Records Service, 1974) p. 741.
71. U.S. Congress, Senate, 92nd Congress 1st Session, Senate Bill 2217, 30 June 1971, Part D, Sec. 431.
72. Memorandum, John Ehrlichman for the President, 17 August 1971, folder: "Congressional Strategy—SAO," Box 29, Egil Krogh files, WHSF, Nixon Presidential Materials Staff, National Archives.
73. Memorandum on issues concerning alternative bill provisions, 2 September 1971, folder: "Congressional Strategy—SAO," Box 29, Egil Krogh files, WHSF, Nixon Presidential Materials Staff, National Archives.
74. Memorandum, John Meagher for Egil Krogh, 3 September 1971, folder: "Congressional Strategy—SAO," Box 29, Egil Krogh files, WHSF, Nixon Presidential Materials Staff, National Archives.
75. Memorandum, John Meagher for Egil Krogh, 23 September 1971, folder: "Congressional Strategy—SAO," Box 29, Egil Krogh files, WHSF, Nixon Presidential Materials Staff, National Archives.
76. Memorandum, John Meagher for Egil Krogh, 23 September 1971, folder: "Congressional Strategy—SAO," Box 29, Egil Krogh files, WHSF, Nixon Presidential Materials Staff, National Archives.
77. Memorandum, Paul L. Perito for Egil Krogh and Frank Carlucci, 28 September 1971, folder: "Congressional Strategy—SAO," Box 29, Egil Krogh files, WHSF, Nixon Presidential Materials Staff, National Archives.
78. Memorandum, Egil Krogh for John Ehrlichman, 1 October 1971, folder: "Congressional Strategy—SAO," Box 29, Egil Krogh files, WHSF, Nixon Presidential Materials Staff, National Archives.
79. Memorandum, John Meagher for Egil Krogh, 6 October 1971, folder: "Congressional Strategy—SAO," Box 29, Egil Krogh files, WHSF, Nixon Presidential Materials Staff, National Archives.
80. Memorandum, Jerome Jaffe for Egil Krogh, 22 October 1971, folder: "Congressional Strategy—SAO," Box 29, Egil Krogh files, WHSF, Nixon Presidential Materials Staff, National Archives.
81. Memorandum, John Meagher for Egil Krogh, 29 October 1971, folder: "Congressional Strategy—SAO," Box 29, Egil Krogh files, Nixon Presidential Materials Staff, National Archives.

82. Memorandum, John Meager for Egil Krogh, 28 October 1971, "Senate Staff Action on S. 2097," folder: "Congressional Strategy—SAO," Box 29, Egil Krogh files, WHSF, Nixon Presidential Materials Staff, National Archives.
83. D.A. Schmidt, "White House and Senators Deadlocked over Scope of Office on Drug Abuse," *New York Times,* 1 November 1971.
84. U.S. Senate, Committee on Government Operations, *Drug Abuse Office and Treatment Act of 1971: Report of the Committee on Government Operations, United States Senate, Made by Its Subcommittees on Executive Reorganization and Government Research and Intergovernmental Relations to Accompany S. 2097* (Washington, DC: GPO, 1971).
85. D.A. Schmidt, "Panel Backs Bill on Drug Control," *New York Times,* 18 November 1971.
86. D.A. Schmidt, "Senate, 92–0, Votes $1.5 Billion for a Drive Against Drug Abuse," *New York Times,* 3 December 1971.
87. Memorandum, Jerome H. Jaffe for Caspar W. Weinberger, 23 December 1971, folder: "Congressional Strategy—SAO," Box 29, Egil Krogh files, WHSF, Nixon Presidential Materials Staff, National Archives.
88. D.A. Schmidt, "Vietnam Methods of Heroin Control Urged for U.S," *New York Times,* 12 April 1972.
89. Interview with Jeffrey Donfeld, 3 June 1994.
90. Interview with Jerome H. Jaffe, 6 October 1994.
91. Interview with Egil Krogh, Jr., 6 June 1994.
92. Memorandum, The White House for Melvin R. Laird, no date, cover folder: "Meeting with President, Top Civilian and Military Leaders, Thursday June 3, 1971," folder: "Drug Abuse," Box 32, Egil Krogh files, WHSF, Nixon Presidential Materials Project, National Archives.
93. Memorandum, Richard Nixon for the Secretary of Defense, 11 June 1971, folder: "[Ex] HE 5-1 6/1/71–6/15/71," Box 18, Subject files, HE (Health), WHCF, Nixon Presidential Materials Staff, National Archives.
94. Memorandum, Jerome H. Jaffe for the President's file, 17 July 1971, folder: "Beginning July 11, 1971," Box 85, President's Office file, President's Meeting file, WHSF, Nixon Presidential Materials Staff, National Archives.
95. Memorandum, Jerome H. Jaffe for the President's file, 17 July 1971, folder: "Beginning July 11, 1971," Box 85, President's Office file, President's Meeting file, WHSF, Nixon Presidential Materials Staff, National Archives.
96. It should be pointed out that publication of the Pentagon Papers had begun on June 13, and that issue was undoubtedly more pressing to the president than was the drug problem. At the same time that he and Jaffe were examining the problem of addiction among Vietnam servicemen, Egil Krogh was charged with making sure there were no more leaks that might damage administration policies. He recruited Gordon Liddy and Howard Hunt to form the Plumbers' unit at this time.
97. Iver Peterson, "Many G.I. Addicts in Vietnam Discharged Despite U.S. Pledge," *New York Times,* 19 December 1971.
98. L.N. Robins, D.H. Davis, and D.W. Goodwin, "Drug Use by U.S. Army Enlisted Men in Vietnam: A Follow-Up on Their Return Home," *American Journal of Epidemiology* 99, no. 4, (1974): 235.

99. L.N. Robins, *A Follow-Up of Vietnam Drug Users; Interim Final Report,* Special Action Office Monograph, Series A, No. 1, April 1973.
100. L.N. Robins, *A Follow-Up of Vietnam Drug Users; Interim Final Report,* Special Action Office Monograph, Series A, No. 1, April 1973, p. 6.
101. L.N. Robins, D.H. Davis, and D.W. Goodwin, "Drug Use by U.S. Army Enlisted Men in Vietnam: A Follow-Up on Their Return Home," *American Journal of Epidemiology* 99, no. 4 (1974): 248.
102. Public Law 92-255, 21 March 1972, Title III, paragraph 303.
103. The 1968 statistical report of the FBN cited in R.L. Bogomolny, "The Responsibility of an Informed Public," in *Communication and Drug Abuse: Proceedings of the Second Rutgers Symposium on Drug Abuse,* ed., J.R. Wittenborn, Jean Paul Smith, and S.A. Wittenborn (Springfield, IL: Charles C. Thomas, 1969), p. 421.
104. Letter, John E. Ingersoll for Murray Comarow, 5 January 1970, folder: "LEN-14," Box 49, PACEO files, WHCF, Nixon Presidential Materials Staff, National Archives.
105. Memorandum, Egil Krogh for the President's file, 17 June 1971, folder: "Beginning June 13, 1971," Box 85, President's Meeting file, President's Office file, WHSF, Nixon Presidential Materials Staff, National Archives.
106. Attachment to memorandum, Richard Harkness for various department officials, 16 May 1972, folder: "Harkness, Richard," Box 7, Egil Krogh files, WHSF, Nixon Presidential Materials Staff, National Archives. Emphasis added. See also Max Singer, "The Vitality of Mythical Numbers," *Public Interest,* no. 23 (Spring 1971): 3–9.
107. Paper, undated, folder: "Testimony before DALE grand jury, LA 7/6/72," Box 20, Egil Krogh files, WHSF, Nixon Presidential Materials Staff, National Archives. Emphasis added.
108. J.M. Markham, "The Heroin Addict Numbers Game," *New York Times,* 4 June 1972.
109. U.S. Congress, House of Representatives, 92nd Congress, 2nd Session, Committee on the Judiciary, *Treatment and Rehabilitation of Narcotics Addicts: Hearings Before Subcommittee No. 4,* 5 October 1972, pp. 931, 932, and 948.
110. Memorandum, Egil Krogh for Ron Ziegler, 27 July 1972, folder: "Chronological File 1972–73," Box 5, Egil Krogh files, WHSF, Nixon Presidential Materials Staff, National Archives. There is also a good discussion of this in a letter drafted by Jaffe in response to a letter from Senator McGovern to the *Washington Post* but never mailed. Letter, Jerome H. Jaffe to George S. McGovern, 2 October 1972, folder: "Jaffe-McGovern," Box 2, Geoffrey Shepard files, WHSF, Nixon Presidential Materials Staff, National Archives.
111. Memorandum, Richard Harkness for Egil Krogh, 25 September 1972, folder: "Harkness, Richard," Box 7, Egil Krogh files, WHSF, Nixon Presidential Materials Staff, National Archives.
112. "Number of Heroin Addicts Rises 12-Fold in Decade," *New York Times,* 14 December 1972.
113. Strategy Council on Drug Abuse, *Federal Strategy for Drug Abuse and Drug Traffic Prevention, 1973* (Washington, DC: GPO, 1973), p. 12.
114. U.S. Congress, House of Representatives, Subcommittee on Public Health and Environment of the Committee on Interstate and Foreign Commerce, *Hearing on Over-*

sight over Programs Authorized by Present Drug Abuse Control Legislation, 19 October 1973 (Washington, DC: 1974), p. 45.

115. U.S. Congress, House of Representatives, Subcommittee on Public Health and Environment of the Committee on Interstate and Foreign Commerce, *Hearing on Heroin Trafficking and Addiction and Related Drug Abuse Problems,* October 7, 1974 (Washington, DC: GPO, 1974), p. 3. Emphasis added.
116. *Congressional Record,* Senate, 11 July 1974, p. 22908.
117. *Congressional Record,* Senate, 11 July 1974, p. 22908.
118. *New York Times,* 13 July 1974.
119. A report from the RAND Corporation points out that "at best, the federal drug budget provides a descriptive level of effort. And even as a historical description, the numbers may misrepresent the total level of expenditures as well as their distribution across programs to control both supply and demand." Patrick Murphy, "Keeping Score: The Frailties of the Federal Drug Budget," RAND 1994, p. 1. With this in mind, it appears that in 1973 and 1974, 32 percent of federal drug budget obligations were assigned to law enforcement activities. Sibyl Cline, *Governmental Response to Drugs: Fiscal and Organizational* (Washington, DC: Drug Abuse Council, 1974), p. 2. This figure rose to 40 percent in FY 1975. Ibid. From 1976 through 1980 the proportions devoted to treatment and prevention versus law enforcement were roughly equal. Joseph B. Treaster, "20 Years of War on Drugs, and No Victory Yet," *New York Times,* 14 June 1992. Murphy reports that the "proportion of resources devoted to supply-side [law enforcement] efforts rose from 59% in 1981 to a peak of 71% in FY 1986. Since then the share of resources devoted to law enforcement activities has remained fairly constant, representing just over two-thirds of the total." Murphy, "Keeping Score," p. 3.

CHAPTER 4. THE SECOND NIXON ADMINISTRATION: DRUG ABUSE CONTROL

1. See, for example, Edward Jay Epstein, *Agency of Fear: Opiates and Political Power in America* (New York: G.P. Putnam's Sons, 1977); and Henrik Kruger, *The Great Heroin Coup* (Boston: South End Press, 1980), originally published in Danish in 1976.
2. Interview with Myles Ambrose, 27 May 1993.
3. Memorandum, Daniel Patrick Moynihan for the Attorney General, 11 February 1969, folder: "Oversized Attachments OA2776," Box 59, Egil Krogh files, WHSF, Nixon Presidential Materials Staff, National Archives.
4. Note with attachments, Mike [Sonnenreich] for Bud [Krogh], [4 January 1971], folder: "M. Sonnenreich, 1971–72," Box 6, Egil Krogh files, WHSF, Nixon Presidential Materials Staff, National Archives.
5. Memorandum, Ed Harper for Egil Krogh, 4 January 1971, folder: "M. Sonnenreich 1971–72," Box 6, Egil Krogh files, WHSF, Nixon Presidential Materials Staff, National Archives.
6. Memorandum, Donald E. Santarelli for John Mitchell, 18 May 1971, Papers of the Nixon White House, 1969–1974, Part IV, Microfiche (Frederick, MD: University Publications of America, 1989–1991), 4-70-69; and John Ehrlichman, *Witness to Power: The Nixon Years* (New York: Simon and Schuster, 1982), p. 84.

7. John Ehrlichman, *Witness to Power: The Nixon Years* (New York: Simon and Schuster, 1982), p. 84.
8. Edward Jay Epstein (*Agency of Fear: Opiates and Political Power in America* [New York: G.P. Putnam's Sons, 1977], pp. 201–202) implies that this memo was a "much modified" version of a plan that Liddy had begun to develop late in the summer. This is probable given Liddy's penchant for presenting complicated cloak-and-dagger operations to his superiors (the infamous Gemstone project, which was the basis for the Watergate activities, is the prime example). See, for example, Michael Genovese, *The Nixon Presidency: Power and Politics in Turbulent Times* (New York: Greenwood Press, 1990). It is also probable that Krogh collaborated with Liddy in order to produce a practical version of the plan. At least by 1 December Geoffrey Shepard and Walter C. Minnick also knew about the plan. Memorandum, Gordon Liddy for Geoff Shepard, 1 December 1971, Papers of the Nixon White House, 1969–1974, Part IV, Microfiche, (Frederick, MD: University Publications of America, 1989–1991), 4-147-19; Memorandum, Walter C. Minnick for Geoff Shepard, 1 December 1971, Papers of the Nixon White House, 1969–1974, Part IV, Microfiche (Frederick, MD: University Publications of America, 1989–1991) 4-147-16.
9. Liddy quoted the Harris poll as follows: "Where the American people want to get tough on the subject of drugs is with the pushers and the foreign countries who generate hard drugs used in this country. Steps by the Administration in these directions, coupled with extensive rehabilitation programs, would fit the general desires of the public on this highly tense and emotional but not politically-oriented issue." Louis Harris and Associates, Inc., *A Study of the Issues of Concern to the American People,* Study #2132 (October 1971), p. 25.
10. Memorandum, Gordon Liddy for John Ehrlichman, 10 November 1971, folder: "Administration Drug Bill [1 of 5]," Box 27, John W. Dean III files, WHSF, Nixon Presidential Materials Staff, National Archives.
11. Liddy thought that the term "blue ribbon" grand jury implied that the composition of the panel would be too elite to have an accurate perspective on inner-city social problems. "Consider the effect upon the heroin peddler," he said, "as he sits in the witness chair under the implacable gaze of the relatives and neighbors of his victims—a sea of black faces relieved only by a sprinkling of ethnics and chicanos—the 'black ribbon' grand jury." Memorandum, Gordon Liddy for John Erlichman, 10 November 1971, folder: "Administration Drug Bill [1 of 5]," Box 27, John W. Dean III files, WHSF, Nixon Presidential Materials Staff, National Archives.
12. Memorandum, Gordon Liddy for John Ehrlichman, 10 November 1971, folder: "Administration Drug Bill [1 of 5]," Box 27, John W. Dean III files, WHSF, Nixon Presidential Materials Staff, National Archives. The reference to cocaine is interesting here because cocaine was not generally perceived as a problem at this time. Liddy wrote a memo to Krogh (1 October 1971, Papers of the Nixon White House, 1969–1974, Part IV, Microfiche (Frederick, MD: University Publications of America, 1989–1991), 4-70-49) that contained the following: "I have for some time been giving thought to a mission to Latin America in connection with the very serious cocaine problem. I suggest that we take advantage of (a) my knowledge and experience in the field of drug abuse in general and

drug smuggling in particular, and (b) Howard Hunt's language ability, singular familiarity with the Latin American underworld in general and his unique contacts and relationships with the Cubans. As you know, the cocaine trade is dominated by pre-Castro Cubans. It is this element with which Hunt is so intimately familiar."

13. John Ehrlichman: Notes of Meetings with the President, 1969–1973, Papers of the Nixon White House, 1969–1974, Part III, Microfiche (Frederick, MD: University Publications of America, 1989–1991), 3-41-B10.
14. Memorandum, Bud Krogh for the President's file, 6 December 1971, folder: "Beginning December 5, 1971," Box 86, President's Office file, WHSF, Nixon Presidential Materials Staff, National Archives.
15. Edward Jay Epstein, *Agency of Fear: Opiates and Political Power in America* (New York: G.P. Putnam's Sons, 1977), p. 210.
16. John Ingersoll, personal communication, June 1993.
17. For example, on 6 October 1971, Ingersoll wrote to Ambrose complaining of what he described as flagrant interference by Customs agents in BNDD operations. He was particularly upset by a case in which Customs agents had arrested a French suspect whom BNDD had planned to stake out in the hope of catching his associates. Ingersoll stated, "I am, therefore, taking over immediate and complete control of the . . . case." Letter, John Ingersoll to Myles Ambrose, 6 October 1971, folder: "Drug Reorganization," Box 4, Geoffrey Shepard files, Gerald R. Ford Library. Ambrose wrote back on 12 October refuting Ingersoll's allegations and claiming that Customs agents had been asked by BNDD personnel to participate in the cases cited by Ingersoll. He closed by saying, "I have been directed by the Treasury Department to reject your assumption of control over the case." Letter with attachment, Myles Ambrose to John Ingersoll, 12 October 1971, folder: "Drug Reorganization," Box 4, Geoffrey Shepard files, Gerald R. Ford Library.
18. Memorandum, Messrs. Petersen, Leonard, Pellerzi, Ingersoll, Johnson, and Lindenbaum for the Attorney General, [7 January 1972], folder: "Drug Prosecution Program," Box 1, Geoffrey Shepard files, WHSF, Nixon Presidential Materials Staff, National Archives.
19. See Tom Wicker, *One of Us: Richard Nixon and the American Dream* (New York: Random House, 1991), p. 415, for observations on the appeal that this sort of personal style had for Nixon.
20. Memorandum, John Ehrlichman for Secretary Connally, 8 February 1972, folder: "Ehrlichman to Connally memo," Box 1, Geoffrey Shepard files, WHSF, Nixon Presidential Materials Staff, National Archives.
21. Memorandum, Bud Krogh for John Ehrlichman, 10 March 1972, folder: "Chron file 1972–73," Box 5, Egil Krogh files, WHSF, Nixon Presidential Materials Staff, National Archives.
22. Memorandum, Bud Krogh for John Ehrlichman, 10 March 1972, folder: "Chron file 1972–73," Box 5, Egil Krogh files, WHSF, Nixon Presidential Materials Staff, National Archives.
23. Memorandum, Bud Krogh for John Ehrlichman, 10 March 1972, folder: "Chron file

1972–73," Box 5, Egil Krogh files, WHSF, Nixon Presidential Materials Staff, National Archives.

24. National Commission on Marihuana and Drug Abuse, *Marihuana: A Signal of Misunderstanding,* (Washington, DC: GPO, 1973), p. 8.
25. *New York Times,* 23 March 1972, p. 19.
26. *The Gallup Poll: Public Opinion, 1972–1977,* Volume 1: *1972–1975* (Wilmington, DE: Scholarly Resources, Inc.), p. 23.
27. Paper, 13 April 1972, folder: "Selling the Domestic Programs 1972," Box 19, Egil Krogh files, WHSF, Nixon Presidential Materials Staff, National Archives.
28. *New York Times,* 25 March 1972, p. 12.
29. Richard Halloran, "Heroin Hot Line Set Up for Nation," *New York Times,* 8 April 1972, p. 1; and "New 'Heroin Hot Line' Reports Many Calls but Little Results," *New York Times,* 16 April 1972.
30. Memorandum, Robert H. Feldcamp for Myles J. Ambrose, 1 September 1972, folder: "Chron file 1972–73," Box 5, Egil Krogh files, WHSF, Nixon Presidential Materials Staff, National Archives.
31. "U.S. 'Heroin Hotline' Called Ineffective," *New York Times,* 26 September 1972.
32. Memorandum, Richard Harkness for Egil Krogh, 15 August 1972, folder: "Harkness, Richard," Box 7, Egil Krogh files, WHSF, Nixon Presidential Materials Staff, National Archives.
33. Memorandum with attachments, Egil Krogh for the President's file, 24 July 1972, folder: "Beginning July 23 [1972]," Box 89, President's Office file, WHSF, Nixon Presidential Materials Staff, National Archives.
34. Memorandum with attachments, Egil Krogh for the President's file, 24 July 1972, folder: "Beginning July 23 [1972]," Box 89, President's Office file, WHSF, Nixon Presidential Materials Staff, National Archives.
35. Memorandum with attachments, Egil Krogh for the President's file, 24 July 1972, folder: "Beginning July 23 [1972]," Box 89, President's Office file, WHSF, Nixon Presidential Materials Staff, National Archives.
36. Memorandum, Bud Krogh for Ron Ziegler, 27 July 1972, folder: "Chron file 1972–73," Box 5, Egil Krogh files, WHSF, Nixon Presidential Materials Staff, National Archives. In keeping with the dual strategy of a balanced attack on both supply of and demand for illicit drugs, the supplemental request was to cover increased treatment and research, new Customs agents, money for the IRS program, and creation of a new entity in the Justice Department to be called the Office of National Narcotics Intelligence.
37. Cabinet Committee on International Narcotics Control, *World Opium Survey, 1972,* (Washington, DC: U.S. Department of State, 1972), p. 13.
38. Alfred W. McCoy, *The Politics of Heroin in Southeast Asia* (New York: Harper and Row, 1972).
39. See, for example, News Release, Bureau of Public Affairs, Department of State Office of Media Services, 1 September 1972, papers of D.F. Musto; and Jerome H. Jaffe and Myles J. Ambrose, "Administration's Drive Against Drugs" (letter to the editor), *New York Times,* 7 October 1972.

40. Interview with Eugene Rossides, 8 June 1994.
41. George W. McGovern, "McGovern on 'Total War' on Drug Addiction" (letter to the editor), *New York Times,* 14 October 1972; and Robert B. Semple, Jr., "Nixon Defends His Record in Combating Drug Trade," *New York Times,* 19 September 1972.
42. Memorandum, Jeffrey Donfeld for Jerome H. Jaffe and Paul Perito, 5 July 1972, Donfeld chronological file, papers of Jerome H. Jaffe.
43. Memorandum, Jeffrey Donfeld for Jerome H. Jaffe, 21 July 1972, Donfeld chronological file, papers of Jerome H. Jaffe.
44. Memorandum, Paul Burke for Jeffrey Donfeld, 3 July 1972, Donfeld chronological file, papers of Jerome H. Jaffe.
45. Memorandum with attachment, Jeffrey Donfeld for Kathleen B. Ross, 21 August 1972, Donfeld chronological file, papers of Jerome H. Jaffe.
46. Edward Jay Epstein goes into some detail on this and is probably correct on most points. See *Agency of Fear: Opiates and Political Power in America* (New York: G.P. Putnam's Sons, 1977), pp. 225–228 and 306.
47. Memorandum, Jeff Donfeld for Walt Minick, 11 July 1972, Donfeld chronological file, papers of Jerome H. Jaffe.
48. *New York Times,* 16 January 1974, p. 1.
49. Memorandum with attachment, Jeffrey Donfeld for Kathleen B. Ross, 21 August 1972, Donfeld chronological file, papers of Jerome H. Jaffe. This memo reports that only two grants had been made at that date but does not specify which cities had received them. Since the Wilmington and Philadelphia grants are well documented elsewhere, they are most likely the ones to which this memo refers. There is some chance that Donfeld considered the demonstration grants outside the normal program and that two others had in fact been granted.
50. Strategy Council on Drug Abuse, *Federal Strategy for Drug Abuse and Drug Traffic Prevention, 1973* (Washington, DC: GPO, 1973), p. 99.
51. Special Action Office for Drug Abuse Prevention, *First Annual Report, 1973* (Washington, DC: GPO, 1973), p. 20.
52. Special Action Office for Drug Abuse Prevention, *First Annual Report, 1973* (Washington, DC: GPO, 1973), p. 65.
53. Special Action Office for Drug Abuse Prevention, *First Annual Report, 1973* (Washington, DC: GPO, 1973), pp. 14–15.
54. David Courtwright, *Addicts Who Survived: An Oral History of Narcotic Use in America, 1923–1965* (Knoxville: University of Tennessee Press, 1989), p. 341.
55. Strategy Council on Drug Abuse, *Federal Strategy for Drug Abuse and Drug Traffic Prevention, 1973* (Washington, DC: GPO, 1973), p. 25.
56. *New York Times,* 13 March 1972.
57. *New York Times,* 6 September 1972, p. 44.
58. Peter Goldberg, "The Federal Government's Response to Illicit Drugs, 1969–1978," in Drug Abuse Council, *The Facts About Drug Abuse* (New York: Free Press/Macmillan Publishing Co., 1980), p. 42. Nixon's statement is also recorded in the *New York Times,* 12 September 1973, p. 20.
59. Peter Goldberg, "The Federal Government's response to Illicit Drugs, 1969–1978," in

Drug Abuse Council, *The Facts About Drug Abuse* (New York: Free Press/Macmillan Publishing Co., 1980), p. 43.

60. The Gallup poll for May 1972 showed that concern about drugs was as high as it had been at the same time the previous year. However, it declined sharply in June, recovered a bit in July and September, and dropped again in October. Concern about the two other related issues, crime and campus unrest, behaved in much the same way, whereas references to the cost of living as the country's most important problem soared.
61. Memorandum, Roy L. Ash for the President, 16 January 1970, folder: "LEN 1-2," Box 42, PACEO files, WHCF, Nixon Presidential Materials Staff, National Archives.
62. Memorandum, John D. Ehrlichman for Bud Krogh, 28 February 1970, folder: "Ash Council Study Drug Abuse [1970]," Box 29, Alpha Subject Drugs, Egil Krogh files, WHSF, Nixon Presidential Materials Staff, National Archives.
63. Memorandum, Ed Harper for Egil Krogh, 4 January 1971, folder: "M. Sonnenreich 1971–72," Box 6, Egil Krogh files, WHSF, Nixon Presidential Materials Staff, National Archives.
64. John D. Ehrlichman, *Witness to Power: The Nixon Years* (New York: Simon and Schuster, 1982), p. 89.
65. Memorandum for the record, 18 May 1970, folder: "LEN 6-4 [1 of 2], Box 44, PACEO files, WHCF, Nixon Presidential Materials Staff, National Archives.
66. Patricia Rachel, *Federal Narcotics Enforcement: Reorganization and Reform* (Boston: Arbor House, 1982).
67. Memorandum, Walter Minnick for Bud Krogh, 25 October 1972, folder: "Drug Reorganization (2)," Box 4, Geoffrey Shepard files, Gerald R. Ford Library.
68. Patricia Rachel, *Federal Narcotics Enforcement: Reorganization and Reform* (Boston: Arbor House, 1982), p. 74
69. Telephone interview with Walter Minnick, 28 May 1994; Memorandum, Geoff Shepard for Ken Cole, 15 January 1973, folder: "[EX] HE 5-1 Narcotics 1/1/73–2/28/73," Box 20, Subject files, HE (Health), WHCF, Nixon Presidential Materials Staff, National Archives (at the time of this writing, Walter Minnick's papers included among the Nixon Presidential Materials had not been processed for research); Memorandum, Walter Minnick through Fred Malek for Roy Ash, 16 May 1973, folder: "Drug Reorganization Plan #2," Box 4, Geoffrey Shepard files, Gerald R. Ford Library.
70. Memorandum, Geoff Shepard to Ken Cole, 15 January 1973, folder: "[EX] HE 5-1 Narcotics 1/1/73–2/28/73," Box 20, Subject files, HE (Health), WHCF, Nixon Presidential Materials Staff, National Archives.
71. Memorandum, L. Patrick Gray III for Mark Alger, 27 January 1973, folder: "Drug Reorganization," Box 4, Geoffrey Shepard files, Gerald R. Ford Library.
72. Memorandum, Mark Alger for Roy Ash, 29 January 1973, folder: "Drug Reorganization," Box 4, Geoffrey Shepard files, Gerald R. Ford Library.
73. Memorandum, Geoff Shepard for Roy Ash, 7 February 1973, folder: "Drug Reorganization," Box 4, Geoffrey Shepard files, Gerald R. Ford Library.
74. H.R. Haldeman, *The Haldeman Diaries* (New York: G.P. Putnam's Sons, 1994), entry for Friday, 9 March 1973, p. 586.
75. Peter Goldberg, "The Federal Government's Response to Illicit Drugs, 1969–1978, in

Drug Abuse Council, *The Facts About Drug Abuse* (New York: Free Press/Macmillan Publishing Co., 1980).

76. H.R. Haldeman, *The Haldeman Diaries* (New York: G.P. Putnam's Sons, 1994), entry for Sunday, 25 March 1973, pp. 601, 602.
77. Memorandum, the President for John Ehrlichman and Bud Krogh, 2 June 1971, papers of Jerome H. Jaffe.
78. Richard Nixon, State of the Union, 14 March 1973, in *1973 CQ Almanac* (Washington, DC: Congressional Quarterly), p. 34A.
79. National Commission on Marihuana and Drug Abuse, *Drug Use in America: Problem in Perspective* (Washington, DC: GPO, 1973), p. 8 and p. 25.
80. Patricia Rachel, *Federal Narcotics Enforcement: Reorganization and Reform* (Boston: Arbor House, 1982), p. 81.
81. A memorandum from Walter Minnick for Roy Ash begins, "The Drug Reorganization is in serious trouble," and goes on to detail various responses to the lobbying "blitz" launched by organized labor. He also notes that "Myles Ambrose chaired the most recent in a series of meeting with union leadership yesterday in an attempt to resolve substantive differences. Largely because Myles was too abrasive, our latest proposed compromises were never seriously discussed and the meeting deteriorated into a shouting match." Memorandum from Walter Minnick through Fred Malek for Roy Ash, 16 May 1973, folder: "Drug Reorganization Plan #2," Box 4, Geoffrey Shepard files, Gerald R. Ford Library. With respect to the ability of the administration to impose discipline on its appointees at this point, it should be kept in mind that H.R. Haldeman and John Ehrlichman, the two most powerful members of the Nixon team, had been forced to resign on 30 April and that the Senate Watergate hearings would begin on 17 May.
82. Letter, Roy L. Ash to Peter W. Rodino, Jr., 6 June 1973, folder: "[EX] HE 54," Box 20, Subject files, HE (Health), WHCF, Nixon Presidential Materials Staff, National Archives.
83. Patricia Rachel, *Federal Narcotics Enforcement: Reorganization and Reform* (Boston: Arbor House, 1982), p. 117.
84. Interview with Vernon Acree, 4 June 1993.
85. Interview with Myles Ambrose, 23 May 1993.
86. These incidents provided critics of the administration with an irresistible and most inopportune chance to say "I told you so," and paved the way for the eventual abrogation of the "no-knock" legislation.
87. In 1974, Bartels engaged in a number of questionable activities involving ill-advised social relationships and attempts to protect himself and his friends from internal DEA investigations (see Chapter 5).
88. Rachel is particularly informative on this point. She quotes a former Customs official as saying, "We wanted to slam DEA so bad that we would even fool with or manipulate their statistics, keeping some back, making up others, fouling up their data; it was almost criminal. And we were obsessed with it" (pp. 123–124).
89. "Nixon Optimistic on Drug Abuses," *New York Times,* 12 September 1973, p. 20.
90. "Nixon Optimistic on Drug Abuses," *New York Times,* 12 September 1973, p. 20.
91. U.S. Congress, House of Representatives, Committee on Interstate and Foreign Com-

merce, Subcommittee on Public Health and Environment, *Oversight—Drug Abuse Prevention Legislation,* Hearing, 19 October 1973 (Washington, DC: GPO, 1973), p. 45.

92. Robert L. DuPont and Mark H. Greene, "The Dynamics of a Heroin Addiction Epidemic," *Science,* 24 August 1973, pp. 716–722; John S. Marr, Charles E. Cherubin, and Joseph Sapira, "Medical Indices of Narcotics Addiction," *New York State Journal of Medicine,* April 1979, pp. 727–730.
93. Leon Gibson Hunt, *Recent Spread of Heroin Use in the United States: Unanswered Questions* (Washington, DC: Drug Abuse Council, 1974), p. 1.
94. Lana D. Harrison, "Trends in Illicit Drug Use in the United States: Conflicting Results from National Surveys," *International Journal of the Addictions* 27, no. 7 (1992): 817–847.
95. Memorandum, Geoffrey Shepard for Mel Laird, 12 November 1973, folder: "[Ex] HE 5-1 11/1/73–12/31/73," Box 2, Subject files, HE (Health), WHCF, Nixon Presidential Materials Staff, National Archives.
96. Memorandum, Frederic V. Malek for the President, 26 November 1973, folder: "[EX] HE 5-1 11/1/73–12/31/73," Box 2, Subject files, HE (Health), WHCF, Nixon Presidential Materials Staff, National Archives.
97. Memorandum, Geoffrey Shepard for the President's file, 27 November 1973, folder: "Beginning November 25 [1973]," Box 93, President's Office file, WHSF, Nixon Presidential Materials Staff, National Archives.
98. Memorandum, Frederic V. Malek for the President, 26 November 1973, folder: "[Ex] HE 5-1 11/1/73–12/31/73," Box 2, Subject files, HE (Health), WHCF, Nixon Presidential Materials Staff, National Archives.
99. *New York Times,* 5 December 1973.
100. Report, 1 June 1974, folder: "Drug Abuse—General (1)," Box 3, F. Lynn May files, Gerald R. Ford Library.
101. Report, 5 June 1974, folder: "Drug Abuse—General (1)," Box 3, F. Lynn May files, Gerald R. Ford Library.
102. Memorandum, Richard Bucher for Geoffrey Shepard, 24 July 1974, folder: "Dept. of Defense Urinalysis Suspension," Box 3, F. Lynn May files, Gerald R. Ford Library. The U.S. Court of Military Appeals, in a decision on 5 July 1974 (*U.S. v. Ruiz,* No. 27,249, SPCM 8294), held that the army could not separate a person from the service with penalty (i.e., other than an honorable discharge) based upon evidence gathered through mandatory urinalysis. The court held this would be in violation of Article 31 of the Uniform Code of Military Justice, which prohibits self-incrimination. The program was reinstated in early 1975 after the Department of Defense issued new guidelines that called for honorable discharge for drug-addicted armed services personnel, thus avoiding the difficulty of self-incrimination raised by the Ruiz decision.

CHAPTER 5. THE FORD ADMINISTRATION: THE WHITE PAPER ON DRUG ABUSE

1. Draft memorandum, Robert L. DuPont for the President, [July 1974], folder: "Conference—Drug Abuse Prevention," Box 3, F. Lynn May files, Gerald R. Ford Library.
2. Typescript, Drug Abuse, [17 August 1974], folder: "Questions and Answers (1)," Box 7, Geoffrey Shepard files, Gerald R. Ford Library.

3. DEA wanted to add a "slam at Turkey," and Customs wanted revisions meant to overturn Reorganization Plan 2. Memorandum with attachments, Ed Johnson for Geoff Shepard, 16 October 1974, folder: "Administration Initiatives," Box 3, F. Lynn May files, Gerald R. Ford Library.
4. Letter, William B. Saxbe for the President, 17 October 1974, folder: "Internal Revenue Service Traffickers Program," Box 5, Geoffrey Shepard files, Gerald R. Ford Library.
5. The program was reinstated in early 1975 after the Department of Defense issued new guidelines that called for honorable discharge (rather than dishonorable) for drug-addicted armed services personnel, thus avoiding the difficulty of self-incrimination raised by the Ruiz decision.
6. Memorandum with attachments and cover note, Ed Johnson for Dale McOmber, 9 August 1974, folder: "Administration Initiatives," Box 3, F. Lynn May files, Gerald R. Ford Library.
7. Memorandum, Ed Johnson for John Bartels, Sheldon Vance, Bob DuPont, Geoff Shepard, 20 August 1974, folder: "Drug Abuse General (1)," Box 3, F. Lynn May files, Gerald R. Ford Library.
8. Memorandum with attachments, Ed Johnson for Geoff Shepard, 16 October 1974, folder, "Administration Initiatives," Box 3, F. Lynn May files, Gerald R. Ford Library, p. 7.
9. Opinion poll summaries with attachment, n/d, folder: "Special Action Office (2)," Box 4, F. Lynn May files, Gerald R. Ford Library.
10. Gallup Organization, Gallup Poll AIPO for dates shown in Table 5-1.
11. U.S. Congress, Senate, Committee on Government Operations, Report No. 94-1039, Federal Narcotics Enforcement, 19 July 1976, 94th Congress, 2nd Session, p. 47.
12. Memorandum, Robert F. Gaber for Commissioner of Customs, [April 1975], folder: "Drug Abuse—Drug Enforcement Administration, Exhibit A (1)," Box 4, Geoffrey Shepard files, Gerald R. Ford Library.
13. U.S. Congress, Senate, Committee on Government Operations, Report No. 94-1039, Federal Narcotics Enforcement, 19 July 1976, 94th Congress, 2nd Session, p. 88.
14. U.S. Congress, Senate, Committee on Government Operations, Report No. 94-1039, Federal Narcotics Enforcement, 19 July 1976, 94th Congress, 2nd Session, p. 88.
15. U.S. Congress, Senate, Committee on Government Operations, Report No. 94-1039, Federal Narcotics Enforcement, 19 July 1976, 94th Congress, 2nd Session, pp. 87 and 97.
16. U.S. Congress, Senate, Committee on Government Operations, Report No. 94-1039, Federal Narcotics Enforcement, 19 July 1976, 94th Congress, 2nd Session, p. 87.
17. U.S. Congress, Senate, Committee on Government Operations, Report No. 94-1039, Federal Narcotics Enforcement, 19 July 1976, 94th Congress, 2nd Session, p. 97.
18. U.S. Congress, Senate, Committee on Government Operations, Report No. 94-1039, Federal Narcotics Enforcement, 19 July 1976, 94th Congress, 2nd Session, p. 124.
19. U.S. Congress, Senate, Committee on Government Operations, Report No. 94-1039, Federal Narcotics Enforcement, 19 July 1976, 94th Congress, 2nd Session, p. 134.
20. U.S. Congress, Senate, Committee on Government Operations, Report No. 94-1039, Federal Narcotics Enforcement, 19 July 1976, 94th Congress, 2nd Session, p. 133.
21. Memorandum, John R. Bartels for Richard Parsons, 27 May 1975, folder: "Drug

Abuse—Drug Enforcement Administration, Exhibit A (1)," Box 4, Geoffrey Shepard files, Gerald R. Ford Library.

22. U.S. Congress, Senate, Committee on Government Operations, Report No. 94-1039, Federal Narcotics Enforcement, 19 July 1976, 94th Congress, 2nd Session, pp. 81–82.
23. Memorandum, James B. Clawson for Kenneth R. Cole, Jr., "Drug Enforcement Strategy," 21 February 1974, folder: "Memorandum of Understanding—Drug Enforcement Administration, Customs Service and Internal Revenue Service, Feb. 1974–Nov. 1975," Box 21, Richard D. Parsons files, Gerald R. Ford Library.
24. Record of telephone conversation, 19 December 1974, folder: "Memorandum of Understanding—Drug Enforcement Administration, Customs Service, and Internal Revenue Service, Feb. 1974–Nov. 1975," Box 21, Richard D. Parsons files, Gerald R. Ford Library.
25. Memorandum, M.P. Crinigen and Bill Larkin for Dick Parsons et al., [13 June 1975], folder: "Drug Enf. Admin—General, Apr.–July 1975," Box 19, Richard D. Parsons files, Gerald R. Ford Library.
26. See especially Letter with attachment, David R. Macdonald for Richard D. Parsons, 18 September 1975, folder: "Drug Review Task Force—General, Sept. 1975," Box 20, Richard D. Parsons files, Gerald R. Ford Library: "We are going nuts over the attached article, which I was shown yesterday. I must say that I do not think Customs had anything to do with it, unless some disgruntled Customs agent did it in an effort to 'get Acree.' Acree thinks it is possible that a DEA agent had this brilliant idea. I am at present just mad enough to think that this suggestion cannot be rejected out of hand. In any event, we are all totally dismayed at the inability to keep the task force activities within the task force."
27. Memorandum, Joe Linnemann for Dick Parsons, 24 July 1975, folder: "Southwest Border Steering Group," Box 23, Richard D. Parsons files, Gerald R. Ford Library.
28. Draft memorandum with attachment, Dick Parsons for Jim Cannon, 12 November 1975, folder: "Office of Drug Abuse Policy," Box 23, Richard D. Parsons files, Gerald R. Ford Library.
29. Draft memorandum, James M. Cannon for the President, 30 October [1975], folder: "International Narcotics Control, May 1975–Feb. 1976," Box 21, Richard D. Parsons files, Gerald R. Ford Library.
30. Interview with Vernon D. Acree, 4 June 1993.
31. Memorandum of Understanding, 11 December 1975, folder: "Memoranda of Understanding—Drug Enforcement Administration, Customs Service and Internal Revenue Service, Dec. 1975–Aug. 1976," Box 22, Richard D. Parsons files, Gerald R. Ford Library.
32. Interview with Karst Besteman, 17 March 1994.
33. Memorandum with attachments, Robert L. DuPont for the President, 17 December 1974, folder: "Miscellaneous Mar.–Apr. 1975," Box 22, Richard D. Parsons files, Gerald R. Ford Library.
34. Attachment to memorandum, Paul H. O'Neill for Don Rumsfeld, 30 December 1974, folder: "Drug Abuse—Special Action Office Extension," Box 4, Geoffrey Shepard files, Gerald R. Ford Library.
35. Memorandum, Ken Cole for Donald Rumsfeld, 7 January 1975, folder: "Special Action

Office for Drug Abuse Prevention (1)," Box 15, Presidential Handwriting file, Gerald R. Ford Library.

36. Memorandum with attachment, Robert L. DuPont for James M. Cannon and Paul H. O'Neill, 10 March 1975, folder: "Miscellaneous Mar.–Apr. 1975," Box 22, Richard D. Parsons files, Gerald R. Ford Library.
37. Memorandum and attached draft, Robert L. DuPont for James M. Cannon and Paul H. O'Neill, 10 March 1975, folder: "Drug Review Task Force—General, Feb.–Mar, 1975," Box 20, Richard D. Parsons files, Gerald R. Ford Library.
38. Memorandum, Dick Parsons for James Cannon, 17 March 1975, folder: "Drug Review Task Force—General, Feb.–Mar. 1975," Box 20, Richard D. Parsons files, Gerald R. Ford Library.
39. Letter, Robert L. DuPont for Richard Parsons, 12 March 1975, folder: "Miscellaneous Mar.–Apr. 1975," Box 22, Richard D. Parsons files, Gerald R. Ford Library.
40. See Chapter 4.
41. James Q. Wilson, "The Return of Heroin," *Commentary* April 1975, pp. 46–50.
42. Memorandum, Geoff Shepard for the President, 4 February 1975, folder: "Drug Abuse—General," Box 4, Geoffrey Shepard files, Gerald R. Ford Library.
43. Memorandum, Jim Cannon for the President, [22 April 1976], folder: "Chron file Jan.–Apr.," Box 3, Richard D. Parsons files, Gerald R. Ford Library: "The Strategy Council on Drug Abuse was established by statute in 1972 to annually provide an assessment of the drug abuse problem in the United States, a plan for comprehensive Federal response and an analysis of the effectiveness of major Federal drug programs. The membership of the Strategy Council included the Director of the Special Action Office for Drug Abuse Prevention (SAODAP) as Chairman, the Secretaries of State, Defense, and Health, Education, and Welfare, the Attorney General and the Administrator of the Veterans Administration. When the legislative authority for SAODAP expired in June of 1975, the Council was left without a chairman or supporting staff and it simply ceased functioning." After the November 1976 *Strategy* no similar document was published until after President Carter revitalized the Strategy Council in August 1977 and included several nongovernmental or "public" members. This body produced a Federal Strategy in May of 1979, and the Reagan administration brought one out in 1982. The enterprise was again abandoned until September 1989, when President Bush's Office of National Drug Control Policy under William Bennett produced a "National" Strategy.
44. Memorandum, Dick Williams for Ed Johnson, 12 March 1975, folder: "Drug Review Task Force—General, Feb.–Mar. 1975," Box 20, Richard D. Parsons files, Gerald R. Ford Library.
45. Talking Points, 13 March 1975, folder: "Drug Review Task Force—General, Feb.–Mar. 1975," Box 20, Richard D. Parsons files, Gerald R. Ford Library.
46. Talking Points for Phone Conversation with Bob DuPont, 13 March 1975, folder: "Drug Review Task Force—General, Feb.–Mar. 1975, Box 20, Richard D. Parsons files, Gerald R. Ford Library.
47. U.S. Congress, Senate, Subcommittee on Alcoholism and Narcotics of the Committee on Labor and Public Welfare, *Hearing on Examination into the Justification for the Con-*

tinuance of Federal Programs for Drug Abuse Prevention and Treatment, March 24 and 25, 1975, 94th Congress, 1st Session (Washington, DC: GPO, 1975), p. 58.

48. U.S. Congress, Senate, Subcommittee on Alcoholism and Narcotics of the Committee on Labor and Public Welfare, *Hearing on Examination into the Justification for the Continuance of Federal Programs for Drug Abuse Prevention and Treatment, March 24 and 25, 1975, 94th Congress, 1st Session* (Washington, DC: GPO, 1975), p. 62.
49. Memorandum, Jim Cannon for the President, 21 April 1975, folder: "Chron file Feb.–July 1975," Box 3, Richard D. Parsons files, Gerald R. Ford Library.
50. Richard Tropp is identified in a handwritten note on an organization chart for the Drug Review Task Force as "Rick Trope," under the heading, "HEW detailee." Organization chart, [May 1975], folder: "Drug Review Task Force—Work Groups," Richard D. Parsons files, Gerald R. Ford Library.
51. Memorandum, Richard Tropp for Richard Parsons, Edward Johnson, and Richard Williams, 15 May 1975, folder: "Drug Review Task Force—General, May 1975," Box 20, Richard D. Parsons files, Gerald R. Ford Library.
52. Federal Drug Abuse Program Briefing Outline, Dick Parsons and Ed Johnson, 28 May 1975, folder: "Drug Review Task Force—General, May 1975," Box 20, Richard D. Parsons files, Gerald R. Ford Library.
53. Gerald R. Ford, Special Message to the Congress on Crime, June 19, 1975, *Public Papers of the Presidents of the United States, 1975* (in two books), Book I: *January 1 to July 17, 1975* (Washington, DC: GPO, 1977), p. 840.
54. Gerald R. Ford, Special Message to the Congress on Crime, 19 June 1975, *Public Papers of the Presidents of the United States, 1975* (in two books), Book 1: *January 1 to July 17, 1975* (Washington, DC: GPO, 1977), p. 849.
55. Gerald R. Ford, Special Message to the Congress on Crime, 19 June 1975, *Public Papers of the Presidents of the United States, 1975* (in two books), Book 1: *January 1 to July 17, 1975* (Washington, DC: GPO, 1977), pp. 849–850.
56. Strategy Council on Drug Abuse, *Federal Strategy for Drug Abuse and Drug Traffic Prevention, 1974* (Washington, DC: GPO, 1974), p. 7.
57. Strategy Council on Drug Abuse, *Federal Strategy for Drug Abuse and Drug Traffic Prevention, 1974* (Washington, DC: GPO, 1974), p. 7.
58. Strategy Council on Drug Abuse, *Federal Strategy for Drug Abuse and Drug Traffic Prevention, 1974* (Washington, DC: GPO, 1974), p. 59.
59. Strategy Council on Drug Abuse, *Federal Strategy for Drug Abuse and Drug Traffic Prevention, 1975* (Washington, DC: GPO, 1975), p. 50.
60. Strategy Council on Drug Abuse, *Federal Strategy for Drug Abuse and Drug Traffic Prevention, 1975* (Washington, DC: GPO, 1975), p. 65.
61. Memorandum, Richard D. Parsons for the file, 23 July 1975, folder: "Drug Review Task Force—General, July 17–Aug. 31, 1975," Box 20, Richard D. Parsons files, Gerald R. Ford Library.
62. Memorandum, Richard D. Parsons for Members of the Drug Review Task Force, 23 July 1975, folder: "Drug Review Task Force—General, July 17–Aug. 31, 1975," Box 20, Richard D. Parsons files, Gerald R. Ford Library.

63. Memorandum, Dick Parsons for Jim Cannon, 29 August 1975, folder: "Chron file Aug.–Dec. 1975," Box 3, Richard D. Parsons files, Gerald R. Ford Library.
64. Memorandum, Stephen S. Gardner for James M. Cannon, 15 December 1975, folder: "White Paper on Drug Abuse—Agency Comments on Final Report," Box 24, Richard D. Parsons files, Gerald R. Ford Library, p. 5.
65. Memorandum, Stephen S. Gardner for James M. Cannon, 15 December 1975, folder: "White Paper on Drug Abuse—Agency Comments on Final Report," Box 24, Richard D. Parsons files, Gerald R. Ford Library, p. 5.
66. Memorandum, David R. Macdonald for Richard D. Parsons, 15 September 1975, folder: "White Paper on Drug Abuse—Agency Comments on Drafts," Box 24, Richard D. Parsons files, Gerald R. Ford Library.
67. William F. Mooney and William Clements, "Feud Flares in Heroin War, Customs Is Given Minor Role," *Chicago Daily News,* 15 September 1975, p. 3.
68. Memorandum, David R. Macdonald for Richard D. Parsons, 15 September 1975, folder: "White Paper on Drug Abuse—Agency Comments on Drafts," Box 24, Richard D. Parsons files, Gerald R. Ford Library.
69. Memorandum, David R. Macdonald for Richard D. Parsons, 15 September 1975, folder: "White Paper on Drug Abuse—Agency Comments on Drafts," Box 24, Richard D. Parsons files, Gerald R. Ford Library.
70. Memorandum, Henry S. Dogin for Richard D. Parsons, 24 September 1975, folder: "White Paper on Drug Abuse—Agency Comments on Drafts," Box 24, Richard D. Parsons files, Gerald R. Ford Library.
71. National Commission on Marihuana and Drug Abuse, *Drug Use in America: Problem in Perspective* (Washington, DC: GPO, 1973), pp. 236–237.
72. Memorandum with attachments, Robert L. DuPont for the President, 17 December 1974, folder: "Miscellaneous Mar.–Apr. 1975," Box 22, Richard D. Parsons files, Gerald R. Ford Library.
73. Memorandum with attachment, Jim Cannon for the President, 9 October 1975, folder: "Health-Drug Abuse," Box 23, Presidential handwriting file, Gerald R. Ford Library.
74. Memorandum, James M. Cannon for Cabinet Secretaries et al., 16 October 1975, folder: "White Paper on Drug Abuse—Agency Comments on Final Report," Box 24, Richard D. Parsons files, Gerald R. Ford Library.
75. Memorandum, Ed Johnson for Paul O'Neill, 28 November 1975, folder: "White Paper on Drug Abuse—Follow Up," Box 24, Richard D. Parsons files, Gerald R. Ford Library.
76. Editorial, "Drugs and Public Policy," *Washington Post,* 5 December 1975.
77. Memorandum, Dick Parsons for Jim Cannon, 5 December 1975, folder: "White Paper on Drug Abuse—Follow Up," Box 24, Richard D. Parsons files, Gerald R. Ford Library.
78. Report to the Secretary on the White Paper on Drug Abuse, Theodore Cooper for the Secretary of Health, Education and Welfare, 15 December 1975, folder: "White Paper on Drug Abuse—Agency Comments on Final Report," Box 24, Richard D. Parsons files, Gerald R. Ford Library, p. 1.
79. Press release with cover memorandum, 1 October 1975, folder: "Drug Review Task Force—General, Oct. 1–5, 1975," Richard D. Parsons files, Gerald R. Ford Library.

80. Press release with cover memorandum, 1 October 1975, folder: "Drug Review Task Force—General, Oct. 1–5, 1975," Richard D. Parsons files, Gerald R. Ford Library.
81. Memorandum, Ira Cisin for Dr. Richards, 22 September 1975, folder: "Drug Review Task Force—General, Oct. 1–5, 1975," Box 20, Richard D. Parsons files, Gerald R. Ford Library, p. 4.
82. Summary of Findings, Drug Use Among Young Men in the United States, [Autumn 1975], folder: "Drug Review Task Force—General, Oct. 1–5, 1975," Box 20, Richard D. Parsons files, Gerald R. Ford Library, p. [x].
83. Statement to the press, Lloyd Johnston and Jerald Bachman, 1 October 1975, folder: "Drug Review Task Force General, Oct. 1–5, 1975," Box 20, Richard D. Parsons files, Gerald R. Ford Library, p. 4.
84. Information from the Gallup Organization indicated that 78 percent of the public was against decriminalization of marijuana in 1973. The weakest opposition on record is 66 percent in 1977.
85. Press release with cover memorandum, 1 October 1975, folder: "Drug Review Task Force—General, Oct. 1–5, 1975," Richard D. Parsons files, Gerald R. Ford Library.
86. Memorandum, Dick Parsons for the Vice President, 29 October 1975, folder: "Chron file Aug.–Dec. 1975," Box 3, Richard D. Parsons files, Gerald R. Ford Library.
87. Letter, Charles Rangel for Gerald R. Ford, 29 October 1975, folder: "Congressional Correspondence," Box 19, Richard D. Parsons files, Gerald R. Ford Library.
88. Letter [transcript], Charles H. Percy for Henry A. Kissinger, 14 November 1975, folder: "Congressional Correspondence," Box 19, Richard D. Parsons files, Gerald R. Ford Library.
89. Letter, Members of Congress for Gerald R. Ford, 18 November 1975, folder: "Congressional Correspondence," Box 19, Richard D. Parsons files, Gerald R. Ford Library.
90. Memorandum for the file, Subject: Drug Abuse Meeting with the President, [22 December 1975], folder: "President—Meetings," Box 23, Richard Parsons file, Gerald R. Ford Library.
91. *New York Times,* 27 December 1975, p 37.
92. Letter, Henry S. Dogin for Charles B. Rangel, 2 January 1976, folder: "Congressional Correspondence," Box 19, Richard Parsons files, Gerald R. Ford Library.
93. "Four Nations Vow Antidrug Effort," *Facts on File World News Digest,* 31 January 1976.
94. Typescript, International Narcotics Control, 23 February 1976, folder: "International Narcotics Control," Box 21, Richard D. Parsons files, Gerald R. Ford Library.
95. Gerald R. Ford, State of the Union speech, January 1976, in *Public Papers of the Presidents of the United States: Gerald R. Ford* (Washington, DC: Federal Register Division, National Archives and Records Service, 1977).
96. Summary [for the press?], International Narcotics Situation, [February 1976], folder: "International Narcotics Control," Box 21, Richard D. Parsons files, Gerald R. Ford Library.
97. Memorandum, Jim Cannon for the President, 12 February 1976, folder: "Chron file, Jan.–Apr. 1976," Box 3, Richard D. Parsons files, Gerald R. Ford Library.
98. Draft memorandum with attachment, Dick Parsons for Jim Cannon, 12 November 1975,

folder: "Office of Drug Abuse Policy," Box 23, Richard D. Parsons files, Gerald R. Ford Library.

99. Typescript, Office of Drug Abuse Prevention Policy Cannon-O'Neill Talking Points, 24 June 1975, folder: "Drug Review Task Force—General, June 1975," Box 20, Richard D. Parsons files, Gerald R. Ford Library.
100. Memorandum with attachment, Dick Parsons for Jim Cannon, 26 September 1975, folder: "Chron file Aug.–Dec. 1975," Box 3, Richard D. Parsons files, Gerald R. Ford Library.
101. Letter, Charles H. Percy for James M. Cannon, 30 October 1975, folder: "Office of Drug Abuse Policy," Box 23, Richard D. Parsons files, Gerald R. Ford Library.
102. Memorandum, Ed Johnson for Paul O'Neill and Dick Parsons, 26 February 1976, folder: "Office of Drug Abuse Policy," Box 23, Richard D. Parsons files, Gerald R. Ford Library.
103. Memorandum, Jim Cannon for the President, [17 March 1976], folder: "Chron file Jan.–Apr. '76," Box 3, Richard D. Parsons files, Gerald R. Ford Library.
104. Memorandum, Jim Cannon for the President, [17 March 1976], folder: "Chron file Jan.–Apr. '76," Box 3, Richard D. Parsons files, Gerald R. Ford Library.
105. Draft, Statement of approval, [19 March 1976], folder: "Office of Drug Abuse Policy," Box 23, Richard D. Parsons files, Gerald R. Ford Library.
106. Press release, Remarks of the President at the Federal Bar Association Dinner, 14 February 1976, folder: "International Narcotics Control," Box 21, Richard D. Parsons files, Gerald R. Ford Library.
107. Press release, Statement by the President, 23 February 1976, folder: "International Narcotics Control," Box 21, Richard D. Parsons files, Gerald R. Ford Library.
108. Script for presidential briefing on drug abuse, [prepared and delivered by Jim Cannon], 7 April 1976, folder: "President and Senior Administration Officials Briefing," Box 23, Richard D. Parsons files, Gerald R. Ford Library.
109. Script for presidential briefing on drug abuse, [prepared and delivered by Jim Cannon], 7 April 1976, folder: "President and Senior Administration Officials Briefing," Box 23, Richard D. Parsons files, Gerald R. Ford Library.
110. Memorandum for the file, Drug Briefing for the President, April 7, 1976, [written] 25 May 1976, folder: "President and Senior Administration Officials Briefing," Box 23, Richard D. Parsons files, Gerald R. Ford Library.
111. Memorandum for the file, Drug Briefing for the President April 7, 1976, 25 May 1976, folder: "President and Senior Administration Officials Briefing," Box 23, Richard D. Parsons files, Gerald R. Ford Library.
112. Memorandum with attachment, Jim Cannon for the President, [22 April 1976], folder: "Chron file Jan.–Apr.," Box 3, Richard D. Parsons files, Gerald R. Ford Library.
113. Memorandum with attachment, Jim Cannon for the President, 22 April 1976, folder: "Chron file Jan.–Apr.," Box 3, Richard D. Parsons files, Gerald R. Ford Library.
114. Memorandum, Ed Johnson for Paul O'Neill and Dick Parsons, 14 May 1976, folder: "Office of Drug Abuse Policy," Box 23, Richard D. Parsons files, Gerald R. Ford Library: "On Wednesday, the Senate passed HR 13172, the Second Supplemental Appropriations Act, 1976, with an amendment providing $250,000 to fund the Office of Drug Abuse

Policy through the transition quarter. In floor debate, Senator Montoya advised that he intended to direct OMB to revise its FY 1977 budget estimate to include ODAP, and Senator Hathaway expressed his intent to seek funding if OMB did not request it."

115. Memorandum, Ed Johnson through Paul O'Neill for Jim Lynn, 17 May 1976, folder: "Office of Drug Abuse Policy," Box 23, Richard D. Parsons files, Gerald R. Ford Library.
116. Memorandum, Ed Johnson for Paul O'Neill, 24 May 1976, folder: "Office of Drug Abuse Policy," Box 23, Richard D. Parsons files, Gerald R. Ford Library.
117. Memorandum, Dick Parsons for Jim Cannon, 8 June 1976, folder: "Office of Drug Abuse Policy," Box 23, Richard D. Parsons files, Gerald R. Ford Library.
118. Memorandum, Paul H. O'Neill for the President, 7 June 1976, folder: "Health—Drug Abuse," Box 23, President's Handwriting file, Gerald R. Ford Library.
119. Gerald R. Ford, "Special Message to Congress on a Proposed Appropriation Rescission for the Office of Drug Abuse Policy," in *Public Papers of the Presidents of the United States: Gerald R. Ford* (Washington, DC: Federal Register Division, National Archives and Records Service, 1979).
120. "Drugs: A $27-Billion-a-Year Habit That U.S. Can't Break," *U.S. News and World Report,* 10 May 1976.
121. Memorandum, Dick Parsons for Jim Cannon, 12 August 1976, folder: "Chron file May–Sept. 1976," Box 3, Richard D. Parsons files, Gerald R. Ford Library.
122. Memorandum, Jim Cannon for the President, 10 December 1976, folder: "Chron file Oct. 1976–Jan. 1977," Box 3, Richard D. Parsons files, Gerald R. Ford Library.
123. Strategy Council on Drug Abuse, *Federal Strategy for Drug Abuse and Drug Traffic Prevention* (Washington, DC: GPO, 1976), p. 22.
124. Strategy Council on Drug Abuse, *Federal Strategy for Drug Abuse and Drug Traffic Prevention* (Washington, DC: GPO, 1976), p. 32.
125. Strategy Council on Drug Abuse, *Federal Strategy for Drug Abuse and Drug Traffic Prevention* (Washington, DC: GPO, 1976), p. 54.

CHAPTER 6. THE CARTER ADMINISTRATION: THE END OF ACCOMMODATION

1. Memorandum, Robert DuPont for Peter Bourne, 8 August 1977, folder: "[Cocaine Policy paper 7/28/77–8/9/77] [OA 6047]," Box 32, Special Assistant to the President for Health Issues—Bourne, Jimmy Carter Library.
2. Lee Dogoloff noted the trend in Montgomery County at the Principals' meeting of 24 October 1978, where he "pointed out that Montgomery County—which has always been very liberal—is becoming more responsive to the problem of marihuana use among adolescents." Meeting notes, Principals Meeting of October 24, 1978, 30 October 1978, papers of David F. Musto. See also D.F. Musto, *The American Disease: Origins of Narcotic Control,* third ed. (New York: Oxford University Press, 1999), p. 265.
3. Memorandum, Peter Bourne for President-elect Jimmy Carter, 2 December 1976, papers of Peter G. Bourne.
4. Memorandum, Peter Bourne for President-elect Jimmy Carter, 5 January 1977, papers of Peter G. Bourne.

5. Memorandum, Peter Bourne for Thomas B. Lance, 28 January 1977, folder: "ODAP [Office of Drug Abuse Policy] 1/13/77–6/21/77 [OA 6044]," Box 28, Special Assistant to the President—Bourne, Jimmy Carter Library.
6. Memorandum, Jimmy Carter for various Cabinet officers, 14 March 1977, folder: "ODAP [Office of Drug Abuse Policy] 1/13/77–6/21/77 [OA 6044]," Box 28, Special Assistant to the President—Bourne, Jimmy Carter Library.
7. Attachment to memorandum, Peter Bourne for Various Cabinet Members, 21 March 1977, folder: "ODAP [Office of Drug Abuse Policy] 1/13/77–6/21/77 [OA 6044]," Box 28, Special Assistant to the President—Bourne, Jimmy Carter Library.
8. Memorandum with attachments, Peter Bourne for Rich Hutcheson, 14 May 1977, folder: "ODAP [Office of Drug Abuse Policy] 1/13/77–6/21/77 [OA 6044]," Box 28, Special Assistant to the President—Bourne, Jimmy Carter Library.
9. Memorandum, [L. Dogoloff in absence of P. Bourne] for Bert Lance, 15 June 1977, papers of Peter G. Bourne.
10. Undated document with title, "Office of Drug Abuse Policy," papers of Peter G. Bourne.
11. Memorandum, Peter Bourne for the President, 29 July 1977, folder: "ODAP—Drug Policy Message O/A 6245 [2]," Stuart Eizenstat files, Jimmy Carter Library.
12. Note with attachment, J.C. for Stu and Peter, 24 July 1977, folder: "Drug Abuse (Narcotics), [CF, O/A/36]," Box 188, Stuart Eizenstat files, Jimmy Carter Library.
13. Memorandum with attachment, Bert Lance for the President, 2 September 1977, folder: "ODAP—Drug Policy Message CF, O/A 36 [1]," Box 247, Stuart Eizenstat files, Jimmy Carter Library.
14. Memorandum, Peter Bourne for the President, 8 September 1977, papers of Peter G. Bourne.
15. U.S. Congress, House of Representatives, Select Committee on Narcotics Abuse and Control, *Annual Report for the Year 1977*, Report No. 95-841 (Washington, DC: GPO, 1977), p. 16.
16. Letter, Various Congressmen for the President, 6 October 1977, folder: "FG 6-8, 1/20/77–1/20/81," Box FG 83, Federal Government Organizations, WHCF, Jimmy Carter Library.
17. Executive Order, 27 March 1978, folder: "FG 6-8, 1/20/77–1/20/81," Box FG 83, Federal Government Organizations, WHCF, Jimmy Carter Library.
18. Office of Drug Abuse Policy, *Annual Report* (Washington, DC: GPO, 1978), p. 27.
19. Letter, Jacob K. Javits, Alan Cranston, and Edward I. Koch for the President, 2 February 1977, folder: "HE 6-1 1/20/77–6/30/77," Box HE 10, Health files, Jimmy Carter Library.
20. Memorandum with attachment, Peter Bourne for the President, 7 April 1977, folder: "ODAP [Office of Drug Abuse Policy] 1/13/77–6/21/77 [OA 6044]," Box 28, Special Assisstant to the President—Bourne, Jimmy Carter Library.
21. U.S. Congress, House of Representatives, Select Committee on Narcotics Abuse and Control, *Considerations For and Against the Reduction of Federal Criminal Penalties for Possession of Small Amounts of Marihuana for Personal Use* (Washington, DC: GPO, 1977), p. 2.

22. U.S. Congress, House of Representatives, Select Committee on Narcotics Abuse and Control, *Considerations For and Against the Reduction of Federal Criminal Penalties for Possession of Small Amounts of Marihuana for Personal Use* (Washington, DC: GPO, 1977) p. 20.
23. U.S. Congress, House of Representatives, Select Committee on Narcotics Abuse and Control, *Considerations For and Against the Reduction of Federal Criminal Penalties for Possession of Small Amounts of Marihuana for Personal Use* (Washington, DC: GPO, 1977), p. 21.
24. U.S. Congress, House of Representatives, Select Committee on Narcotics Abuse and Control, *Considerations For and Against the Reduction of Federal Criminal Penalties for Possession of Small Amounts of Marihuana for Personal Use* (Washington, DC: GPO, 1977), p. 23.
25. Memorandum, Stu Eizenstat for the President, 7 July 1977, folder: "Drug Abuse (Narcotics), [CF, O/A 36], Box 188, Stuart Eizenstat files, Jimmy Carter Library.
26. Patrick Anderson, *High in America: The True Story Behind NORML and the Politics of Marijuana* (New York: Viking Press, 1981), pp. 210–211.
27. Memorandum, Stu Eizenstat for the President, 7 July 1977, folder: "Drug Abuse (Narcotics) [CF, O/A 36], Box 188, Stuart Eizenstat files, Jimmy Carter Library.
28. Note with attachment, J.C. for Stu and Peter, 24 July 1977, folder: "Drug Abuse (Narcotics), [CF, O/A/36]," Box 188, Stuart Eizenstat files, Jimmy Carter Library.
29. Note with attachment, J.C. for Stu and Peter, 24 July 1977, folder: "Drug Abuse (Narcotics), [CF, O/A/36]," Box 188, Stuart Eizenstat files, Jimmy Carter Library.
30. Memorandum, Stu Eizenstat for the President, 7 July 1977, folder: "Drug Abuse (Narcotics) [CF, O/A 36], Box 188, Stuart Eizenstat files, Jimmy Carter Library.
31. Memorandum with attachment, Bernard H. Martin for Legislative Liaison Officer, 7 December 1977, folder: "Drugs [O/A 8111] [1]," Box 16, Domestic Policy Staff—Civil Rights and Justice Cluster, Annie Gutierrez files, Jimmy Carter Library.
32. Memorandum, Peter Bourne for President-elect Jimmy Carter, 14 December 1976, papers of Peter G. Bourne.
33. Memorandum, Peter Bourne for the President, 2 June 1977, folder: "[Colombia Drug Traffic] 6/2/77–2/28/78 [CF, O/A 156], Box 32, Special Assistant to the President for Health Issues—Bourne, Jimmy Carter Library.
34. Memorandum, Peter Bourne for the President, 20 June 1977, folder: "FG 6-8, 1/20/77–1/20/81," Box FG 83, Federal Government Organizations, WHCF, Jimmy Carter Library.
35. Memorandum with attachment, Peter Bourne for Peter Bensinger, Robert DuPont, Robert Dickerson, and Mathea Falco, 29 July 1977, folder: "[Cocaine Policy Paper 7/28/77–8/9/77 [OA 6047]," Box 32, Special Assistant to the President for Health Issues—Bourne, Jimmy Carter Library.
36. Memorandum, Robert L. DuPont for Peter G. Bourne, 8 August 1977, folder: "[Cocaine Policy Paper 7/28/77–8/9/77] [OA 6047]," Box 32, Special Assistant to the President for Health Issues—Bourne, Jimmy Carter Library.
37. Summary with attachment, [17 September 1977], folder: "Cocaine Policy 7/28/77–9/29/77 [CF, O/A 154]," Box 32, Special Assistant to the President for Health Issues—Bourne, Jimmy Carter Library.

38. Memorandum with attachment, Peter Bourne for Peter Bensinger, Robert DuPont, Robert Dickerson, and Mathea Falco, 29 July 1977, folder: "[Cocaine Policy Paper 7/28/77–8/9/77 [OA 6047]," Box 32, Special Assistant to the President for Health Issues—Bourne, Jimmy Carter Library, p. 8.
39. Memorandum with attachment, Peter Bourne for the President, 25 April 1977, folder: "ODAP [Office of Drug Abuse Policy] 1/13/77–6/21/77 [OA 6044]," Box 28, Special Assistant to the President—Bourne, Jimmy Carter Library.
40. Memorandum, Stu Eizenstat for the President, 27 April 1977, folder: "ODAP—Drug Policy Message [CF O/A36] [1]," Box 247, Stuart Eizenstat files, Jimmy Carter Library.
41. Memorandum with attachment, Peter Bourne for Various Cabinet Members, 26 May 1977, folder: "ODAP—Drug Policy Message CF, O/A 36 [1]," Box 247, Stuart Eizenstat files, Jimmy Carter Library.
42. Summary with attachment, [17 September 1977], folder: "Cocaine Policy 7/28/77–9/29/77 [CF, O/A 154]," Box 32, Special Assistant to the President for Health Issues—Bourne, Jimmy Carter Library.
43. Office of Drug Abuse Policy, *1978 Annual Report* (Washington, DC: GPO, 1978), p. 31.
44. Memorandum, Robert L. DuPont for Peter G. Bourne, 8 August 1977, folder: "[Cocaine Policy Paper 7/28/77–8/9/77] [OA 6047]," Box 32, Special Assistant to the President for Health Issues—Bourne, Jimmy Carter Library.
45. Edward Walsh, "Carter Endorses Decriminalization of Marijuana," *Washington Post,* 3 August 1977, p. A1.
46. Thomas Margan, "The Heat Is Off for Marijuana Users: De Facto Decriminalization Result of Change in Public Opinion," *Washington Post,* 8 August 1977, p. A9.
47. Press Release, Jimmy Carter's Address to Congress, 2 August 1977, folder: "Drug Abuse (O/A 8111)," Box 16, Domestic Policy Staff—Civil Rights and Justice Cluster, Annie Gutierrez files, Jimmy Carter Library.
48. *Border Management and Interdiction,* 7 September 1977, folder: "Drug Abuse Policy [O/A 6468] [1]," Box 16, Domestic Policy Staff—Civil Rights and Justice Cluster, Annie Gutierrez files, Jimmy Carter Library.
49. *Border Management and Interdiction,* 7 September 1977, folder: "Drug Abuse Policy [O/A 6468] [1]," Box 16, Domestic Policy Staff—Civil Rights and Justice Cluster, Annie Gutierrez files, Jimmy Carter Library.
50. *Border Management and Interdiction,* 7 September 1977, folder: "Drug Abuse Policy [O/A 6468] [1]," Box 16, Domestic Policy Staff—Civil Rights and Justice Cluster, Annie Gutierrez files, Jimmy Carter Library.
51. *Supply Control: Drug Law Enforcement, an Interagency Review,* 19 December 1977, folder: "Drug programs," Box 16, Domestic Policy Staff—Civil Rights and Justice Cluster, Annie Gutierrez files, Jimmy Carter Library, p. 8.
52. Letter with attachment, Peter G. Bourne for the President, 31 March 1978, folder: "Narcotics [O/A 6245]," Box 239, Stuart Eizenstat files, Jimmy Carter Library.
53. Jesse Kornbluth, "Paraquat and the Marijuana War," *New York Times Magazine,* 13 August 1978, p. 13.
54. Jesse Kornbluth, "Paraquat and the Marijuana War," *New York Times Magazine,* 13 August 1978, pp. 11–30.

55. Jesse Kornbluth, "Paraquat and the Marijuana War," *New York Times Magazine,* 13 August 1978, p. 11; Patrick Anderson, *High in America: The True Story Behind NORML and the Politics of Marijuana* (New York: Viking Press, 1981), pp. 205–206.
56. D.F. Musto, *The American Disease: Origins of Narcotic Control,* third ed. (New York: Oxford University Press, 1999), p. 267.
57. Lynn Darling, "A Tarnish on Acapulco Gold," *Washington Post,* 11 March 1978, p. A3.
58. Memorandum, Peter Bourne for the President, 22 March 1978, folder: "Narcotics [O/A 6245]," Box 239, Stuart Eizenstat files, Jimmy Carter Library.
59. Patrick Anderson, *High in America: The True Story Behind NORML and the Politics of Marijuana* (New York: Viking Press, 1981), pp. 232–235, 249.
60. U.S. Congress, House of Representatives, Select Committee on Narcotics Abuse and Control, *Annual Report for the Year 1977,* Report No. 95-841 (Washington, DC: GPO, 1977), p. 22.
61. U.S. Congress, House of Representatives, Select Committee on Narcotics Abuse and Control, *Problems of Law Enforcement and Its Effort to Reduce the Level of Drug Trafficking in South Florida* (Washington, DC: GPO, 1978), p. 4.
62. U.S. Congress, House of Representatives, Select Committee on Narcotics Abuse and Control, *Problems of Law Enforcement and Its Effort to Reduce the Level of Drug Trafficking in South Florida* (Washington, DC: GPO, 1978), p. 1.
63. U.S. Congress, House of Representatives, Select Committee on Narcotics Abuse and Control, Report, *Problems of Law Enforcement and Its Effort to Reduce the Level of Drug Trafficking in South Florida* (Washington, DC: GPO, 1978), p. 5.
64. U.S. Congress, House of Representatives, Select Committee on Narcotics Abuse and Control, *Problems of Law Enforcement and Its Effort to Reduce the Level of Drug Trafficking in South Florida* (Washington, DC: GPO, 1978), p. 15.
65. Memorandum with attachments, Stuart Eizenstat for the President, 27 October 1978, folder: "ODAP—Drug Policy Message [1] [OA 6245]," Box 247, Stuart Eizenstat files, Jimmy Carter Library.
66. Audio tape of exit interview, Lee Dogoloff with Emily [Soaps], 26 November 1980, Jimmy Carter Library.
67. Jimmy Carter, "The State of the Union, Annual Message to the Congress, 25 January 1979," in *Public Papers of the Presidents of the United States, Jimmy Carter 1979,* Book 1: Jan. 1–June 22, 1979 (Washington, DC: GPO, 1980), p. 135.
68. U.S. Congress, Senate, Subcommittee on Alcoholism and Drug Abuse of the Committee on Labor and Human Resources, *Drug Abuse Prevention, Treatment and Rehabilitation Act of 1979, Hearing, March 2, 1979* (Washington, DC: GPO, 1979), p. 91.
69. U.S. Congress, Senate, Subcommittee on Alcoholism and Drug Abuse of the Committee on Labor and Human Resources, *Drug Abuse Prevention, Treatment and Rehabilitation Act of 1979, Hearing, March 2, 1979* (Washington, DC: GPO, 1979), p. 104.
70. Memorandum, Stu Eizenstat and Lee Dogoloff for the President, 30 March 1979, folder: "FG 288—1/20/77–1/20/81," Box FG 216, Federal Government Organizations, Jimmy Carter Library.
71. Memorandum with attachment, Peter Bourne for the President, 4 November 1977,

folder: "FG 288—1/20/77–1/20/81," Box FG 216, Federal Government Organizations, Jimmy Carter Library:

Public Members of Council
Milton F. Bryant, M.D.: Surgeon, Atlanta
Vernon E. Jordan, Jr.: Exec. Dir. Urban League
Joyce H. Lowinson, M.D.: Psychiatrist, Prof. Einstein College of Med.
David F. Musto, M.D. [psychiatrist and historian, Yale University]
Donald D. Pomerleau: Police Commissioner of Baltimore
Harvey I. Sloane, M.D.: Mayor of Louisville, KY
Charles B. O'Keeffe: Bourne's deputy

The strategy developed by the Council is required by law to contain:

(1) An analysis of the nature, character, and extent of the drug abuse problem in the United States;
(2) A comprehensive Federal plan which shall specify the objectives of the Federal Strategy and how all available resources authorized under relevant Federal law should be used; and,
(3) An analysis and evaluation of the major programs conducted, expenditures made, results achieved, plans developed, and problems encountered in the operation and coordination of the various Federal drug abuse prevention functions and drug traffic prevention functions.

To facilitate the preparation of the strategy, the Council is mandated by law to:

(1) Engage in the planning necessary to achieve the objectives of a comprehensive, coordinated long-term Federal strategy, including examination of the overall Federal investment to combat drug abuse;
(2) At the request of any member, require Departments and agencies engaged in Federal drug abuse prevention functions and drug traffic prevention functions to submit such information and reports and to conduct such studies and surveys as are necessary to carry out the purposes of the National Drug Abuse Strategy; and,
(3) Evaluate the performance and results achieved by Federal drug abuse prevention functions and drug traffic prevention functions and the prospective performance and results that might be achieved by programs and activities in addition to or in lieu of those currently being administered.

72. Memorandum, Stu Eizenstat and Lee Dogoloff for Fran Voorde, 31 January 1979, folder: "FG 288—1/20/77–1/20/81," Box FG 216, Federal Government Organizations, Jimmy Carter Library.
73. Memorandum with attachment, Peter Bourne for the President, 4 November 1977, folder: "FG 288—1/20/77–1/20/81," Box FG 216, Federal Government Organizations, Jimmy Carter Library.
74. Memorandum with attachment, Bert Lance for the President, 2 September 1977, folder: "ODAP—Drug Abuse Policy Message" CF, O/A 36 [1], Box 247, Stuart Eizenstat files, Jimmy Carter Library,
75. U.S. Congress, House of Representatives, Select Committee on Narcotics Abuse and

Control, *Annual Report for the Year 1979,* Report No. 96-731 (Washington, DC: GPO, 1980), p. 28.

76. *Annual Report on the Federal Drug Program* (Washington, DC: The White House, 1980), p. 5.
77. Memorandum, Stu Eizenstat and Lee Dogoloff for Fran Voorde, folder: "FG288—1/20/77–1/20/81," Box FG 216, Federal Government Organizations, Jimmy Carter Library.
78. Letter, Lee I. Dogoloff for the President, 2 April 1979, folder: "FG 288—1/20/77–1/20/81," Box FG 216, Federal Government Organizations, Jimmy Carter Library.
79. Strategy Council on Drug Abuse, *Federal Strategy for Drug Abuse and Drug Traffic Prevention* (Washington, DC: GPO, 1979), p. 1.
80. Office of Drug Abuse Policy, *1978 Annual Report* (Washington, DC: GPO, 1978), p. 32.
81. Strategy Council on Drug Abuse, *Federal Strategy for Drug Abuse and Drug Traffic Prevention, 1979* (Washington, DC: GPO, 1979), p. 57.
82. Office of Drug Abuse Policy, *1978 Annual Report* (Washington, DC: GPO, 1978), p. 32.
83. Strategy Council on Drug Abuse, *Federal Strategy for Drug Abuse and Drug Traffic Prevention, 1979* (Washington, DC: GPO, 1979), p. 58.
84. Public Law 95-384—Sept. 26, 1978.
85. U.S. Congress, House of Representatives, Select Committee on Narcotics Abuse and Control, *Annual Report,* Report No. 96-731 (Washington DC: GPO, 1980).
86. Letter, Joseph A. Califano for Cyrus Vance, 2 August 1979, folder: "Drug Policy [CF, O/A 727] [1]," Box 189, Stuart Eizenstat files, Jimmy Carter Library.
87. Press Release, 3 August 1979, folder: "Drug Policy [CF, O/A 727] [1]," Box 189, Stuart Eizenstat files, Jimmy Carter Library.
88. Letter, Lester L. Wolff to Patricia Roberts Harris, 6 August 1979, folder: "Drug Policy [CF, O/A 727] [1]," Box 189, Stuart Eizenstat files, Jimmy Carter Library.
89. Memorandum with attachment, Stu Eizenstat and Lee Dogoloff for Griffin Bell, 9 August 1979, folder: "Drug Policy [CF, O/A 727] [1]," Box 189, Stuart Eizenstat files, Jimmy Carter Library.
90. Memorandum with attachment, Stu Eizenstat and Lee Dogoloff for Griffin Bell, 9 August 1979, folder: "Drug Policy [CF, O/A 727] [1]," Box 189, Stuart Eizenstat files, Jimmy Carter Library.
91. Memorandum, J. Philip Jordan for files, 10 August 1979, folder: "Drug Policy [CF, O/A 727] [1]," Box 189, Stuart Eizenstat files, Jimmy Carter Library.
92. Memorandum with attachment, Lee Dogoloff for Stu, 21 September 1979, folder: "Mexico: Paraquat 8–9/79 [CF O/A 743], Stuart Eizenstat files, Jimmy Carter Library.
93. Memorandum, Dick Williams for Stu, 25 September 1979, folder: "Drug Policy [CO, O/A 727] [1]," Box 189, Stuart Eizenstat files, Jimmy Carter Library.
94. U.S. Congress, House of Representatives, Select Committee on Narcotics Abuse and Control, *Annual Report,* Report No. 96-731 (Washington DC: GPO, 1980), p. 54.
95. Meeting minutes, 19 March 1980, "Minutes Principals Meeting March 13, 1980," papers of David F. Musto.
96. Meeting minutes, 19 March 1980, "Minutes Principals Meeting March 13, 1980," papers of David F. Musto.

97. Meeting minutes, 1 April 1980, Principals' Meeting, papers of David F. Musto.
98. Memorandum, Lee Dogoloff for the Record, 21 August 1979, folder: "HE 6-1, 7/1/79–9/30/79," Box 12, HE (Health), Jimmy Carter Library.
99. Letter, Joyce Nalepka for President Jimmy Carter, 28 September 1979, folder: "FG 288—1/20/77–1/20/81," Box FG 216, Federal Government Organizations, Jimmy Carter Library.
100. Memorandum, Lee Dogoloff for the record, 28 November 1979, folder: "FG 288—1/20/77–1/20/81," Box FG 216, Federal Government Organizations, Jimmy Carter Library.
101. Memorandum, Lee Dogoloff for the record, 28 November 1979, folder: "FG 288—1/20/77–1/20/81," Box FG 216, Federal Government Organizations, Jimmy Carter Library.
102. U.S. Congress, House of Representatives, Select Committee on Narcotics Abuse and Control, *Drug Paraphernalia, Hearing* (Washington, DC: GPO, 1980), p. 4.
103. U.S. Congress, House of Representatives, Select Committee on Narcotics Abuse and Control, *Drug Paraphernalia, Hearing* (Washington, DC: GPO, 1980), pp. 10–11.
104. U.S. Congress, House of Representatives, Select Committee on Narcotics Abuse and Control, *Drug Paraphernalia, Hearing* (Washington, DC: GPO, 1980), p. 85.
105. U.S. Congress, House of Representatives, Select Committee on Narcotics Abuse and Control, *Drug Paraphernalia* (Washington, DC: 1980), p. 18.
106. U.S. Congress, House of Representatives, Select Committee on Narcotics Abuse and Control, *Answering Questions About Marijuana Use,* Report (Washington, DC: GPO, 1980), p. v.
107. D.F. Musto, *The American Disease: Origins of Narcotic Control,* third ed. (New York: Oxford University Press, 1999), p. 265.
108. See earlier discussion of ODAP.
109. Draft of Five-Year Plan (Drug Abuse), [January 1980], folder: "Drug Policy [CF, O/A 727] [1]," Box 189, Stuart Eizenstat files, Jimmy Carter Library.
110. Memorandum, Benjamin R. Civiletti for the President, 5 February 1980, folder: "Drug Policy [CF, O/A 727] [1]," Box 189, Stuart Eizenstat files, Jimmy Carter Library.
111. Talking Points, 13 February 1980, folder: "Drug Policy [CF, O/A 727] [1]," Box 189, Stuart Eizenstat files, Jimmy Carter Library.
112. Memorandum, Lee for Stu, 13 February 1980, folder: "Drug Policy [CO, O/A 727] [1]," Box 189, Stuart Eizenstat files, Jimmy Carter Library.
113. Memorandum, Lee I. Dogoloff for various agency heads, 16 May 1980, folder: "HE6-1, 5/16/80–1/20/81," Box HE 12, Health files, Jimmy Carter Library.
114. City Visit Summary, Philadelphia, Heroin Strategy Task Force, 11 July 1980, folder: "Drug Policy [CF, O/A 727] [3]," Box 189, Stuart Eizenstat files, Jimmy Carter Library.
115. Progress Report, Domestic Enforcement Group, Southwest Asian Heroin Initiative, folder: "Drug Policy [CF, O/A 727] [3]," Box 189, Stuart Eizenstat files, Jimmy Carter Library.
116. Progress Report, Domestic Monitor Program, Southwest Asian Heroin Initiative, folder: "Drug Policy [CF, O/A 727] [3]," Box 189, Stuart Eizenstat files, Jimmy Carter Library.

117. Progress Report, Public Information Group, Southwest Asian Heroin Initiative, folder: "Drug Policy [CF, O/A 727] [3]," Box 189, Stuart Eizenstat files, Jimmy Carter Library.
118. "A Heroin Wave and No Steersman," *New York Times,* 14 June 1980, p. 22.
119. Annual Report on the Federal Drug Program, 1980, [May 1980], folder: "HE 6-1 5/16/80–1/20/81," Box HE 12, Health files, Jimmy Carter Library.
120. U.S. Congress, House of Representatives, Select Committee on Narcotics Abuse and Control, *Recommendation for Continued House Oversight of Drug Abuse Problems,* Report No. 96-1380, 24 September 1980 (Washington, DC: GPO), pp. 4–5.
121. U.S. Congress, House of Representatives, Select Committee on Narcotics Abuse and Control, *Recommendation for Continued House Oversight of Drug Abuse Problems,* Report No. 96-1380, 24 September 1980 (Washington, DC: GPO), p. 5.
122. U.S. Congress, House of Representatives, Select Committee on Narcotics Abuse and Control, *Recommendation for Continued House Oversight of Drug Abuse Problems,* Report No. 96-1380, 24 September 1980, (Washington, DC: GPO), p. 6. See also D.F. Musto and J.H. Lowinson, "Drug Crisis and Strategy," *New York Times,* 22 May 1980.
123. Memorandum, Lee Dogoloff for Stu Eizenstat, 15 May 1980, folder: "HE 6-1 10/1/79–5/15/80," Box HE 12, Health files, Jimmy Carter Library.
124. Letter, Lee I. Dogoloff for Patricia R. Harris, 26 June 1980, folder: "HE 6-1 5/16/80–1/20/81," Box HE 12, Health files, Jimmy Carter Library.
125. Letter, Lee I. Dogoloff for Joseph Biden, 30 June 1980, folder: "HE 6-1 5/16/80–1/20/81," Box HE 12, Health files, Jimmy Carter Library.
126. Press release, 18 August 1980, folder: "Drug Policy [CF, O/A 727] [3]," Box 189, Stuart Eizenstat files, Jimmy Carter Library.
127. Memorandum, Kathy Collins and Barbara Kivimae for Rodger Schlickeisen and Gil Omenn, 2 October 1980, folder: "HE 6-1 5/16/80–1/20/81," Box HE 12, Health files, Jimmy Carter Library.
128. Memorandum, for Gene from Lee, 10 October 1980, folder: "HE 6-1 5/16/80–1/20/81," Box HE 12, Health files, Jimmy Carter Library.
129. Stuart Eizenstat, personal communication, 5 April 1999.

Index

Page numbers in *italics* refer to illustrations.